Teach Yourself VISUALLY™

iLife® '09

by Mike Wooldridge

Wiley Publishing, Inc.

Teach Yourself VISUALLY™ iLife® '09

Published by
Wiley Publishing, Inc.
10475 Crosspoint Boulevard
Indianapolis, IN 46256

www.wiley.com

Published simultaneously in Canada

Library of Congress Control Number: 2009931456

ISBN: 978-0-470-50839-8

Manufactured in the United States of America

10 9 8 7 6 5 4 3 2 1

Trademark Acknowledgments

Contact Us

For general information on our other products and services please contact our Customer Care Department within the U.S. at 877-762-2974, outside the U.S. at 317-572-3993, or fax 317-572-4002.

For technical support please visit www.wiley.com/techsupport.

Wiley Publishing, Inc.

Sales

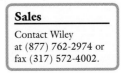

Contact Wiley
at (877) 762-2974 or
fax (317) 572-4002.

Praise for Visual Books

"Like a lot of other people, I understand things best when I see them visually. Your books really make learning easy and life more fun."

John T. Frey (Cadillac, MI)

"I have quite a few of your Visual books and have been very pleased with all of them. I love the way the lessons are presented!"

Mary Jane Newman (Yorba Linda, CA)

"I just purchased my third Visual book (my first two are dog-eared now!), and, once again, your product has surpassed my expectations."

Tracey Moore (Memphis, TN)

"I am an avid fan of your Visual books. If I need to learn anything, I just buy one of your books and learn the topic in no time. Wonders! I have even trained my friends to give me Visual books as gifts."

Illona Bergstrom (Aventura, FL)

"Thank you for making it so clear. I appreciate it. I will buy many more Visual books."

J.P. Sangdong (North York, Ontario, Canada)

"I have several books from the Visual series and have always found them to be valuable resources."

Stephen P. Miller (Ballston Spa, NY)

"Thank you for the wonderful books you produce. It wasn't until I was an adult that I discovered how I learn – visually. Nothing compares to Visual books. I love the simple layout. I can just grab a book and use it at my computer, lesson by lesson. And I understand the material! You really know the way I think and learn. Thanks so much!"

Stacey Han (Avondale, AZ)

"I absolutely admire your company's work. Your books are terrific. The format is perfect, especially for visual learners like me. Keep them coming!"

Frederick A. Taylor, Jr. (New Port Richey, FL)

"I have several of your Visual books and they are the best I have ever used."

Stanley Clark (Crawfordville, FL)

"I bought my first Teach Yourself VISUALLY book last month. Wow. Now I want to learn everything in this easy format!"

Tom Vial (New York, NY)

"Thank you, thank you, thank you...for making it so easy for me to break into this high-tech world. I now own four of your books. I recommend them to anyone who is a beginner like myself."

Gay O'Donnell (Calgary, Alberta, Canada)

"I write to extend my thanks and appreciation for your books. They are clear, easy to follow, and straight to the point. Keep up the good work! I bought several of your books and they are just right! No regrets! I will always buy your books because they are the best."

Seward Kollie (Dakar, Senegal)

"Compliments to the chef!! Your books are extraordinary! Or, simply put, extra-ordinary, meaning way above the rest! THANK YOU THANK YOU THANK YOU! I buy them for friends, family, and colleagues."

Christine J. Manfrin (Castle Rock, CO)

"What fantastic teaching books you have produced! Congratulations to you and your staff. You deserve the Nobel Prize in Education in the Software category. Thanks for helping me understand computers."

Bruno Tonon (Melbourne, Australia)

"Over time, I have bought a number of your 'Read Less - Learn More' books. For me, they are THE way to learn anything easily. I learn easiest using your method of teaching."

José A. Mazón (Cuba, NY)

"I am an avid purchaser and reader of the Visual series, and they are the greatest computer books I've seen. The Visual books are perfect for people like myself who enjoy the computer, but want to know how to use it more efficiently. Your books have definitely given me a greater understanding of my computer, and have taught me to use it more effectively. Thank you very much for the hard work, effort, and dedication that you put into this series."

Alex Diaz (Las Vegas, NV)

Credits

Sr. Acquisitions Editor
Jody Lefevere

Project Editor
Sarah Hellert

Technical Editor
Dennis R. Cohen

Copy Editor
Scott Tullis

Editorial Director
Robyn Siesky

Editorial Manager
Cricket Krengel

Business Manager
Amy Knies

Sr. Marketing Manager
Sandy Smith

Vice President and Executive Group Publisher
Richard Swadley

Vice President and Executive Publisher
Barry Pruett

Project Coordinator
Patrick Redmond

Production Specialists
Carrie A. Cesavice
Jennifer Mayberry

Quality Control Technician
Melissa Cossell

Proofreader
Linda Seifert

Indexer
Potomac Indexing, LLC

Screen Artists
Ana Carrillo
Jill A. Proll

Illustrators
Ronda David-Burroughs
Cheryl Grubbs
Mark Pinto

About the Author

Mike Wooldridge writes books and teaches classes that help people use computers and the Internet creatively. Based in the San Francisco Bay area, he has authored more than 20 books for the Visual series.

Author's Acknowledgments

Mike thanks Sarah Hellert once again for her top-notch project editing, Dennis Cohen for his knowledgeable technical editing, and Scott Tullis for his careful copy editing. He thanks Stephanie and Cody for loaning him technology for use in the examples. This book is dedicated to Mike's wife and son, who provide him with plenty of interesting life moments to record.

Table of Contents

INTRODUCING iLIFE '09

Getting Started with iLife '09

chapter 2

Exploring iLife '09 on the Mac

chapter 3 Importing and Viewing Photos

chapter 4 Organizing Photos

Table of Contents

Editing Photos

Sharing Photos

chapter 7 Importing and Organizing Movies

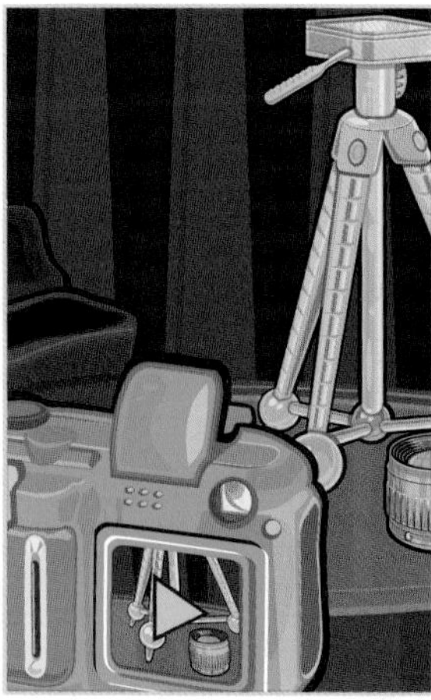

chapter 8 Editing Movies

Table of Contents

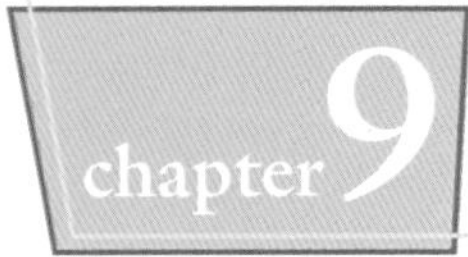

Adding Audio to Movies

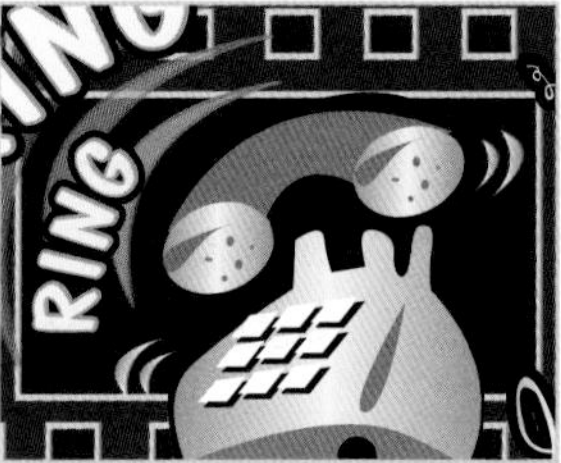

chapter 10

Adding Special Effects to Movies

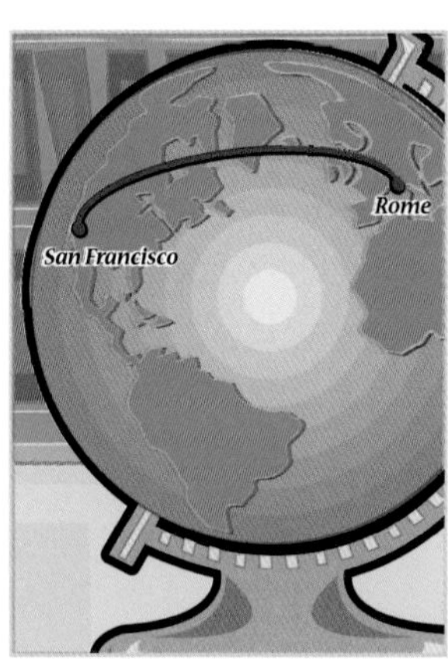

Sharing a Movie

WORKING WITH GARAGEBAND '09

chapter 12 Editing and Mixing Music

Table of Contents

chapter 13 Recording Music

chapter 14 Sharing Music

chapter 15 Learning to Play Music

WORKING WITH iWEB '09

chapter 16 Setting Up a Web Site

chapter 17 Editing Web Site Content

Table of Contents

chapter 18 Adding Custom Features to a Web Site

chapter 19 Publishing a Web Site

WORKING WITH iDVD

chapter 20 Creating a DVD Project

chapter 21 Editing a DVD Project

chapter 22 Sharing a DVD Project

How to use this book

Do you look at the pictures in a book or newspaper before anything else on a page? Would you rather see an image instead of read about how to do something? Search no further. This book is for you. Opening *Teach Yourself VISUALLY iLife '09* allows you to read less and learn more about iLife.

Who Needs This Book

This book is for a reader who has never used this particular technology or application. It is also for more computer literate individuals who want to expand their knowledge of the different features that iLife has to offer.

Book Organization

Teach Yourself VISUALLY iLife '09 has 22 chapters and is divided into 6 parts.

Part I, **Introducing iLife '09**, introduces you to the suite of applications that make up iLife: iPhoto '09, iMovie '09, GarageBand '09, iWeb '09, and iDVD. It teaches you basics about the Mac workspace and how to start an iLife application. It also briefly explains how you import and work with different digital media using the iLife programs.

Part II, **Working with iPhoto '09**, shows you how to organize, optimize, and share digital photos on your Mac using the image editor in iLife '09. You can import photos from your digital camera and organize them by event, location, or the people in the photos. Editing tools let you improve the color and lighting in photos, whereas keepsakes enable you to create photo books, calendars, and more.

Part III, **Working with iMovie '09**, teaches you how to assemble video clips and still photos into professional-looking movies using the video editor in iLife '09. It shows you how to organize your content on the timeline, add background music and sound effects, and fine-tune transitions between scenes. When you are finished with your project, you can share your movie on a DVD, your Web site, or YouTube.

Part IV, **Working with GarageBand '09**, introduces you to the audio editor in iLife '09. GarageBand lets you build songs using hundreds of prerecorded loops or from music recorded from a guitar, a piano, and other instruments. You can save your projects to music CDs, move them to iTunes, or use them in other iLife applications. The Learn to Play feature teaches you guitar or piano with instructional videos.

Part V, **Working with iWeb '09**, covers how to build cutting-edge Web sites that feature photo galleries, blogs, podcasts, and more. A variety of themes let you get the look and feel you want, and page templates mean you do not have to start your pages from scratch. You create your pages by dragging and dropping photos, movies, and music from the different iLife libraries. You can publish your site to your own Web server or Apple's MobileMe service.

Part VI, **Working with iDVD**, shows you how to create DVDs that feature digital media created in the iLife applications. You can showcase movies from iMovie and slideshows of images from iPhoto. iDVD comes with dozens of themes that provide graphics, animations, and buttons for your DVD projects.

Chapter Organization

This book consists of sections, all listed in the book's table of contents. A *section* is a set of steps that show you how to complete a specific computer task.

Each section, usually contained on two facing pages, has an introduction to the task at hand, a set of full-color screen shots and steps that walk you through the task, and a set of tips. This format allows you to quickly look at a topic of interest and learn it instantly.

Chapters group together three or more sections with a common theme. A chapter may also contain pages that give you the background information needed to understand the sections in a chapter.

What You Need to Use This Book

A Mac computer with iLife '09 installed. iLife '09 requires Mac OS X version 10.5.6 or later, 512MB of RAM (1GB recommended), approximately 4GB of available disk space, and an Intel, PowerPC G5, or PowerPC G4 processor (867MHz or faster).

Using the Mouse

This book uses the following conventions to describe the actions you perform when using the mouse:

Click

Press your left mouse button once. You generally click your mouse on something to select something on the screen.

Double-click

Press your left mouse button twice. Double-clicking something on the computer screen generally opens whatever item you have double-clicked.

Right-click

Press your right mouse button. When you right-click anything on the computer screen, the program displays a shortcut menu containing commands specific to the selected item.

Click and Drag, and Release the Mouse

Move your mouse pointer and hover it over an item on the screen. Press and hold down the left mouse button. Now, move the mouse to where you want to place the item and then release the button. You use this method to move an item from one area of the computer screen to another.

The Conventions in This Book

A number of typographic and layout styles have been used throughout *Teach Yourself VISUALLY iLife '09* to distinguish different types of information.

Bold

Bold type represents the names of commands and options that you interact with. Bold type also indicates text and numbers that you must type into a dialog or window.

Italics

Italic words introduce a new term and are followed by a definition.

Numbered Steps

You must perform the instructions in numbered steps in order to successfully complete a section and achieve the final results.

Bulleted Steps

These steps point out various optional features. You do not have to perform these steps; they simply give additional information about a feature.

Indented Text

Indented text tells you what the program does in response to you following a numbered step. For example, if you click a certain menu command, a dialog may appear, or a window may open. Indented text may also tell you what the final result is when you follow a set of numbered steps.

Notes

Notes give additional information. They may describe special conditions that may occur during an operation. They may warn you of a situation that you want to avoid – for example, the loss of data. A note may also cross-reference a related area of the book. A cross reference may guide you to another chapter, or another section within the current chapter.

Icons and Buttons

Icons and buttons are graphical representations within the text. They show you exactly what you need to click to perform a step.

You can easily identify the tips in any section by looking for the TIPS icon. Tips offer additional information, including tips, hints, and tricks. You can use the TIPS information to go beyond what you have learned in the steps.

PART I

Introducing iLife '09

iLife '09 is a powerful suite of applications that lets you create, edit, and share digital media on your Mac. You can edit images in iPhoto, assemble movies in iMovie, create and learn music in GarageBand, build Web sites in iWeb, and produce DVDs in iDVD. This part introduces you to the iLife applications and their capabilities.

Introducing the iLife '09 Applications

iLife '09 is a suite of software programs for organizing, editing, and sharing digital media. The suite is made by Apple for Mac computers and requires the Mac OS X operating system version 10.5.6 or later.

Managing Photos

iLife '09 lets you organize, optimize, customize, and share digital photos using iPhoto '09. The iPhoto application can download photos directly from your digital camera or import images already on your computer. You can organize your photo collection by event, place, or the people in the photos. The program enables you to create slideshows and keepsakes, such as photo books and calendars, from your photos.

Working with Movies

iMovie '09 is the video editor in iLife '09. With it you can construct movie projects from video clips shot with your camcorder or downloaded from the Internet. You can also include still images and music from the other iLife applications. You can choose from dozens of transition effects and color filters to make your productions interesting. You can also share your work on a Web site or through services such as iTunes or YouTube.

Composing Music

With GarageBand '09, the music editing program in iLife '09, you can construct songs and podcasts from prerecorded loops, real instrument recordings, and software instruments. GarageBand includes effects for electric guitars that let you imitate the sound made famous by different bands. GarageBand also has a music lesson feature. You can learn to play piano or guitar with free lessons and also download how-tos from famous artists for a fee.

Designing Web Sites

You can create and manage Web sites with iLife's iWeb '09 program. Page templates and themes make it easy to create professional-looking sites with cutting-edge features such as interactive maps, blogs, and podcasts. You add content to pages by clicking and dragging from libraries of other iLife programs. The visual interface means you do not have to write any HTML or other code.

Burning DVDs

You can create full-featured DVD projects to showcase your digital media in the iDVD program. IDVD comes with a variety of themes to create interactive DVD menus to complement the content on your disc. You can customize the menus with video, still images, and music. You can build DVD projects to feature movies created in iMovie or slideshows made with images from iPhoto.

Sharing Between Applications

One of the powerful features of iLife is the way you can use media created in one iLife program in the projects of another program. For example, you can use images from iPhoto as still frames in your iMovie movies, burn your iMovie projects to disc in iDVD, and create online podcasts in iWeb using music from GarageBand. You can use the iLife media browser feature in the different programs to make content available across the software suite.

Introducing iPhoto '09

With iPhoto, you can organize all the digital photos on your Mac in one place. You can make adjustments to the color and lighting in your photos and then share them as a slideshow, on the Web, and more.

Importing Photos

When you connect a digital camera to your Mac, iPhoto opens and allows you to import your photos into the program. iPhoto organizes the imported photos from your camera by date, placing photos taken on the same day into an iPhoto event. You can also import photos that already reside on your computer, or on a CD-ROM, DVD, or flash drive connected to your computer. You can import a photo from a Web site as well.

Events, Faces, and Places

You can organize pictures in iPhoto by the time they were taken, by the people that appear in them, and by the place where they were taken. iPhoto groups photos taken at the same time into an event. You might create an iPhoto event for a birthday party or a holiday vacation. iPhoto can recognize faces in your photos and tag those faces with names. This allows you to then view photos that feature a particular person. You can also place iPhoto images on a geographic map and then browse your photos by location.

Creating Albums

iPhoto albums allow you to organize your photos in a freeform manner. You can create an album for photos from an event, of particular people, from a specific place, or a mix of criteria. A photo in the iPhoto library can exist in multiple albums. Once you group photos in an album, you can easily use those photos in an iPhoto slideshow or in a keepsake such as a photo book or calendar.

Automatic Organization

Organizing thousands of photos in a personal collection can be a daunting, time-consuming task. iPhoto makes it easier by learning the people in your photos as you tag them using the program's Faces feature. iPhoto can retrieve latitude and longitude information from photos taken with GPS-enabled cameras to map the photos to geographic locations. You can also create smart albums that automatically group photos in your library that share specific criteria such as the same rating or keyword.

Editing and Optimizing

iPhoto includes a number of photo-editing tools that let you improve the appearance of poorly exposed or washed-out photos. You can fine-tune lighting levels, boost or reduce color intensity, or convert photos to black and white. The iPhoto retouching tool enables you to fix small tears and scratches on a scanned image, or smooth the wrinkles in the face of a subject. The red eye tool lets you get rid of the red lighting that can be added to eyes by a camera flash.

Share Photos

Once you have organized and optimized your photos, you can share them by e-mail or by outputting them to a printer. You can create slideshows with customized slide durations and transitions. You can publish hardback and softback photo books with page themes that match the subject of your images. iPhoto also connects to the popular online services Facebook and Flickr and allows you to upload photos in your library to those Web sites.

Introducing iMovie '09

With iMovie, you can take video clips, such as those shot with your camcorder, and edit them into full-featured movies with professional effects. You can apply themes to help set the mood. You can also complement your video clips with still images and background music.

Movie Project Themes

When you start a new project in iMovie, you can choose a theme to add a predefined set of graphics and transitions to the clips that you add. For example, you can apply a vacation theme that adds colorful scenery around your movie or a photo album theme that makes clips look like snapshots mounted in an album. You can always change the theme of a project later on, change the theme transitions to other ones from the iMovie library, or start with no theme at all and add special touches on your own.

Editing Clips

Most of your work in iMovie is done in the project editor, where you arrange the sequence of video clips, still photos, and title graphics that make up your project. You click and drag to position clips where you want them in the flow of your project. You also click and drag to select the best region of each clip so you can ignore the parts that are uninteresting. You can crop a clip to focus tightly on a subject or rotate a clip that was shot in the wrong orientation. You can also open the Precision Editor to zoom in on a transition between clips and fine-tune where exactly the change between scenes occurs.

Special Effects

iMovie comes with a variety of special effects that you can apply to your video clips to enhance the mood. You can overlay specks and scratches to a clip to make it look like it was from a movie reel from the early 1900s. You can also apply effects that intensify or shift the colors to give it a sci-fi feel. You can slow down, speed up, or freeze a clip to call attention to an action scene. You can also add a picture-in-picture effect, where two clips are shown simultaneously, one set within the other.

Movie Audio

Background music can help establish the mood of a movie. iMovie gives you options for adding music from your iTunes and GarageBand libraries. You can also choose from a selection of generic theme music that comes with iMovie. You can add beat markers to background music so that your video content can change to the beat of the song. This is a useful feature when creating a music video. You can also add sound effects to punctuate key moments or voiceover content to explain what is going on in the movie.

Fixing Shaky Footage

Even if you have the steadiest of hands, some movie footage will turn out shaky – for example if you shoot it off-road from a moving vehicle. iMovie offers a stabilization tool that analyzes your video clips and attempts to remove shakiness by constantly panning and zooming the clips to remove jiggles. The result is smoother footage that allows the viewer to focus on the subject matter and not be distracted by the shaking.

Sharing Movies

Once you have created your movie masterpiece, you can save it as a file on your computer. iMovie helps you choose the size and format of the movie based on how you plan to view it, be it on a mobile device, on a computer, or on a DVD. You can publish the movie online to your MobileMe account if you have one, and then publicize the movie to others. iPhoto also connects to the popular video-sharing site, YouTube, and allows you to upload your movie to your account.

Introducing GarageBand '09

With GarageBand, you can create musical arrangements made up of prerecorded instrument loops and music you record yourself. You can also get guitar and piano instruction using the Learn to Play feature.

Music Loops

GarageBand comes with hundreds of predefined music snippets, or *loops*, that you can assemble into a song. You can browse the loops by instrument, musical genre, and other categories. Loops let you create a song without recording any music yourself. You can add a drum loop to give your song a backbeat, add a guitar riff for a melody, and then layer loops of a piano and other instruments. There are also sound effects that let you tailor the mood in your songs.

Recording Music

GarageBand can record three types of tracks. With electric guitar tracks, you plug an electric guitar into your Mac and strum away to create your music. You can modify the sound of your electric guitar with virtual amps and stompboxes, which mimic the guitar amplifiers and special-effects pedals that guitarists use in the real world. By setting up Real Instrument tracks, you can record any instrument whose tune you can capture with a microphone. You can also record software instruments such as a MIDI keyboard.

Editing Music

You assemble and edit your GarageBand project on a timeline, where you place loops or recorded segments in the order in which they should play in a song. You can also arrange music to play simultaneously in different *tracks*, which exist vertically as different levels in the timeline. Usually you place each instrument in your song in a different track. You can control the volume of each track to emphasize or de-emphasize an instrument in your song.

Fine-Tuning the Sound

Once you have your song arranged, you can make changes to get just the sound you want. You can raise all the notes in part or all of a song by changing the pitch. In the Track Info pane, you can add echo, reverb, distortion, and other effects to make your instrument sound like it is being played in a large symphony hall or out of an old guitar amp. With software instrument music, you can adjust any note in a tune up or down, change when it is played, and change the duration.

Sharing Music

You can save GarageBand music to an MP3 or other file type that you and others can then play. You can burn your songs to a CD-ROM for use in any CD player, upload your songs to iTunes, or make ringtones for an iPhone. You can use your GarageBand work in iMovie projects, in iPhoto slideshows, and on podcast pages in iWeb.

Taking Lessons

You can take lessons in GarageBand to learn how to play piano or guitar. GarageBand comes with two beginner lessons installed. You can download more lessons online for free or buy lessons that feature major recording artists teaching famous songs. The lesson workspace includes instructional video, music notation, and instrument graphics to help you understand concepts and learn the instrument.

Introducing iWeb '09

With iWeb, you can create a professional-looking Web site that includes photo galleries, blog pages, and podcasts. You build your pages by dragging images, movies, and other media from your iPhoto, iMovie, iTunes, and GarageBand libraries.

Page Types

iWeb does a lot of the work for you by providing templates for commonly used page types. You can create Welcome or About Me pages where you replace text and images with your own. You can create image galleries that have interactive buttons and slideshow functionality to showcase your photo collection. If you use the blog and podcast templates, iWeb manages your postings to these pages, making them easy to keep up to date online.

Themes

With iWeb, you do not have to be a trained graphic designer to have nice-looking pages. iWeb offers a number of themes that add color schemes and graphics to your pages. You can use a single theme for your entire site, or use different themes for different pages. Some of the iWeb themes are simple, with black and white colors and minimal graphics. You can start with these if you want to add your own custom look and feel. You can also choose from more elaborate themes if you want your pages to be festooned with vacation, birthday, or new-baby decorations.

Adding and Editing Content

When you first create a page, iWeb displays it with generic placeholder content for the text, images, and movies on the page. To make the site your own, you replace placeholder text by typing your own text, add photos from your iPhoto library, and add movies from your iMovie library. You can modify the page layout by adding new text boxes and other content or by resizing existing elements. iWeb keeps track of the pages that you create for your site and displays links between them in the navigation on each page.

Widgets

In addition to displaying text, images, and movies on your pages, iWeb offers interactive modules called *widgets* that you can add to your site. Widgets let you insert Google maps to provide location information and directions on your site, countdown clocks that can keep visitors informed of upcoming events, and RSS feeds that automatically show links to news on another Web sites. You add a widget like you do an image or movie in the program – by dragging it from the browser pane and then applying a few settings.

Blogs and Podcasts

Some of the more popular features on the Web today are blogs and podcasts. A *blog* is an online journal you can write in to keep viewers up to date on your activities or to comment on current events. With the blog template, you can write periodic entries within the iWeb interface. iWeb keeps track of the entries, displaying them in reverse chronological order on your Web site. You can similarly create a *podcast* in iWeb, which is a Web page that offers downloadable audio or video to Web site viewers.

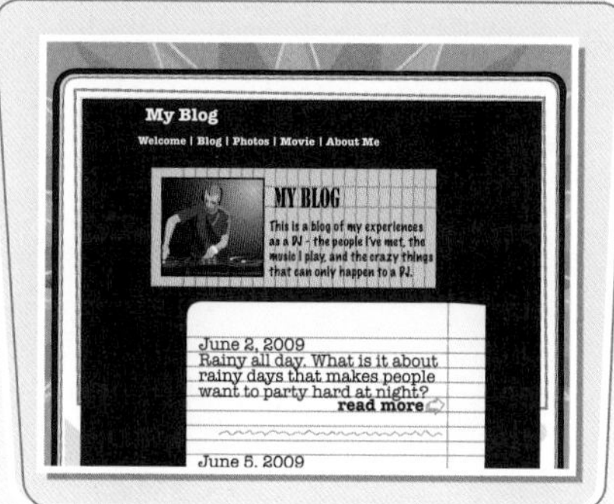

Publishing Site

Once you have created your Web site in iWeb, you need to publish it to allow the world to view it online. iWeb includes an integrated FTP client that lets you connect to a Web host and upload your site files to a Web server so that the pages are publicly accessible. Alternatively, you can publish your site online to your MobileMe account, if you have one. iWeb also can interface with Facebook and automatically post updates to your Facebook account when you have added new content to a site.

Introducing iDVD

With iDVD, you can create high-quality DVD projects that showcase the movies, photos, and music you create in your other iLife applications. Once you organize your content with navigable menus, you can burn the project to disc using the optical drive on your computer.

DVD Projects

You can create a new project in iDVD to organize the movies, photos, and other media that you want to burn to a DVD. You choose a theme to specify the graphics and animations that appear in your DVD menus. Once you add the content and customize the menus to your liking, you can burn the project to a DVD.

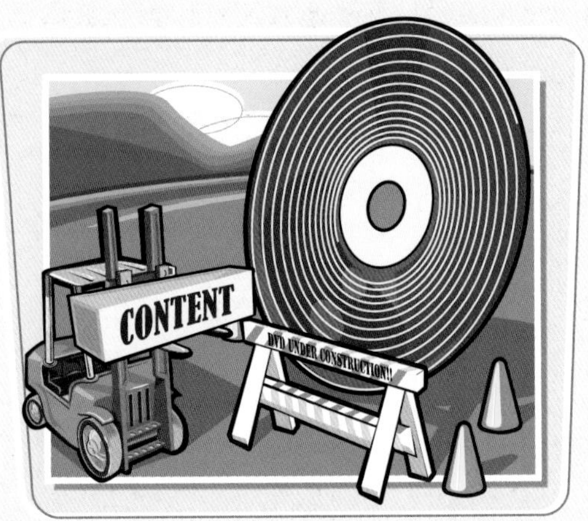

Custom Themes

Themes give you an easy way to create a professional-looking DVD project. You can choose themes for specific events such as travel, weddings, or a new baby. Or you can choose themes for a certain style such as ones with modern shapes or ones with natural decorations. Most themes come with one or more drop zones, which are sections in a menu where you can add previews of the video or slideshows in your project.

Organizing with Menus

A DVD menu is a screen that combines graphics, animations, short previews of DVD content, and clickable buttons. You attach the menu buttons to the videos and slideshows that are featuring in the DVD project. You can also attach buttons to other menus. This lets you nest content on secondary menus in the project. You can open a map view of a project to view the menus and content as connected boxes. This can be useful for complicated projects.

Adding Content

iDVD gives you easy access to the projects that you create in iMovie. You can associate a movie with a menu button by clicking and dragging an iMovie project to the editing window. You can access your images from iPhoto to create slideshows to place on your DVD. iDVD includes slideshow editing tools that let you control slide duration and add transitions. Content can also be added to the drop zones in the iDVD menus, which offer a preview of the disc content.

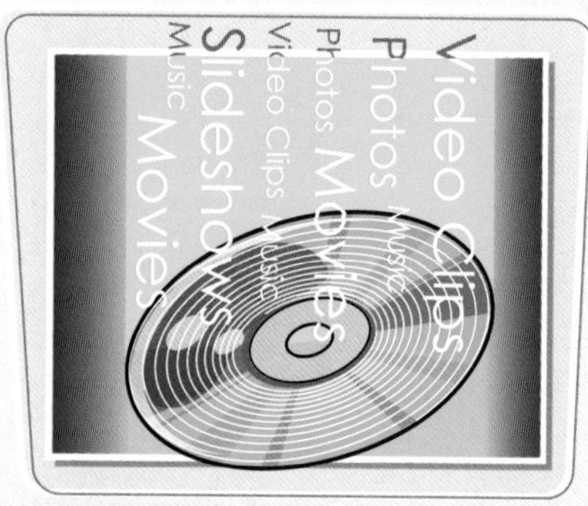

Creating DVDs Quickly

iDVD has a Magic iDVD feature that automates the process of building your DVD. You simply choose a theme, the video clips, and the slideshows that you want on your disc. iDVD organizes the content, creates the menus, and presents a DVD project ready to burn. The Magic iDVD feature is great if you are not picky about the menu and button styles in your DVD project.

Burning a DVD

When you are done with your project, iDVD walks you through the process of burning your content to a DVD. iDVD can burn to most of the major DVD formats, including double-layer discs. If you want to simply copy video content from a camcorder tape to a disc, you can use iDVD's OneStep feature. iDVD copies tape content straight to disc and then ejects a DVD that plays automatically when you insert it into a player.

Explore the Mac Workspace

Before you start using the iLife applications to manage your digital media, you should become familiar with the workspace on your Mac computer.

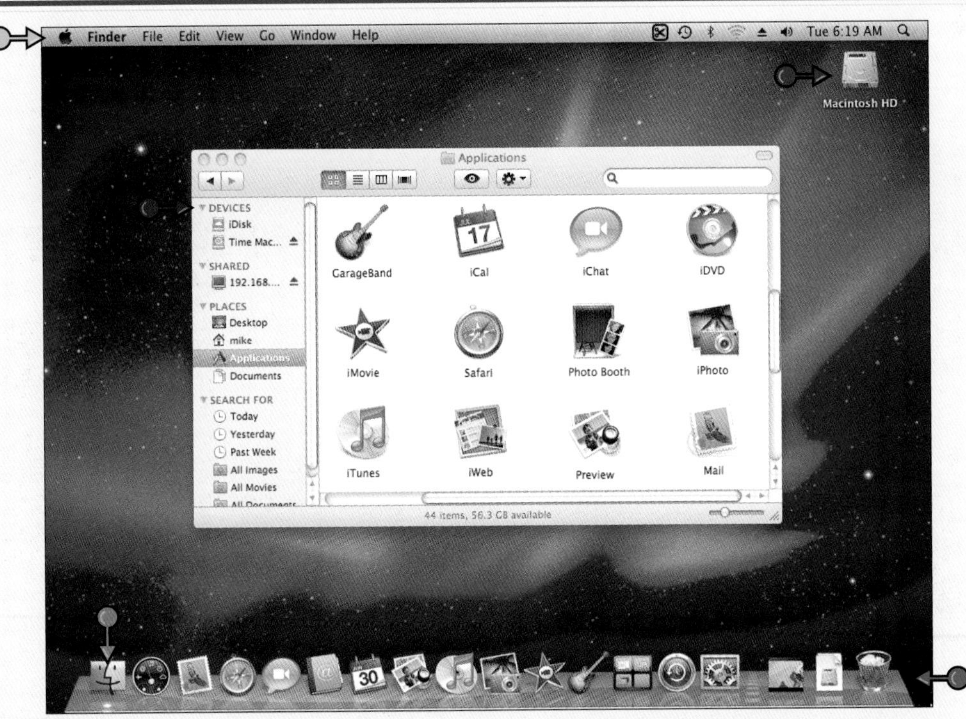

Menu Bar

You can open menus from the top menu bar to access commands for the currently running program. When you first start your Mac, the Finder is running and menus for the Finder are shown.

Desktop

The desktop is the background area of the Mac workspace. When you open a program on your Mac, the program opens over the desktop. The icon for your computer hard drive appears on the desktop as do icons for any files you save to the desktop.

Dock

The Mac Dock gives you convenient access to commonly used applications, files, and folders. To access an item on the Dock, click its icon. For more information, see "Tour the Dock."

Finder Icon

You can click this icon on the Dock to open a Finder window for viewing and accessing the applications, folders, and files on your computer.

Finder Window

The Finder application lets you view and manage the programs, folders, and files on your Mac. You can click the **Applications** icon in the Finder to view and access the programs installed on your Mac, including the iLife programs.

Tour the Dock

The Dock is a row of icons that give you quick access to important programs, folders, and files on your Mac. Below are some of the Dock icons that you may access when using iLife.

iLife adds icons for iPhoto, iMovie, and GarageBand to the Dock by default.

Finder

An always-running program that lets you open applications, files, and folders on your computer.

Mail

A program for sending e-mail over the Internet. Some e-mail features in the iLife applications open new messages in the Mail program.

Safari

A Web browser for accessing Web pages and other content on the Internet. If you publish content from iWeb, you can then use Safari to view the content online. iWeb is covered in Part V.

iTunes

A program for viewing and sharing music, movies, and other digital media. You can add your finished GarageBand songs and iMovie projects to your iTunes library.

iPhoto

A program for viewing, managing, and editing digital photos. iPhoto is covered in Part II of this book.

iMovie

A program that lets you assemble movies using video clips, still images, special effects, and more. iMovie is covered in Part III of this book.

GarageBand

A music-editing program that allows you to assemble songs from prerecorded loops and audio that you record yourself. GarageBand is covered in Part IV of this book.

System Preferences

You can configure various Mac settings using System Preferences. Settings include the monitor resolution, speaker volume, and login settings for your MobileMe account.

Documents

You can access the Documents folder on your Mac here. You can save or export movies, songs, and other projects from iLife to this folder.

Trash

When you delete a media file in iLife, the file typically is sent to the Trash on your Mac. You can view these files or delete them permanently by accessing the Trash.

Open an iLife '09 Application

You can open an iLife application to start organizing and editing the digital content on your computer.

Open an iLife '09 Application

FROM THE DOCK

1. Click an iLife icon on the Mac Dock.

Note: *See "Tour the Dock" for details.*

If the Dock is hidden, you can move your cursor to the bottom of the screen to display the Dock.

- The iLife application for that icon opens.

This example shows opening the iPhoto application.

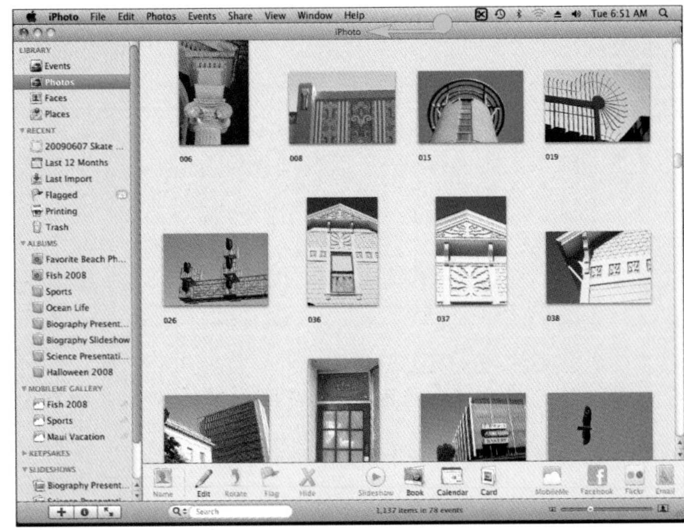

FROM THE FINDER WINDOW

1. Click the Finder icon to open a Finder window.
2. Click **Applications**.

   The Finder displays applications installed on your Mac.
3. Double-click an iLife application icon.

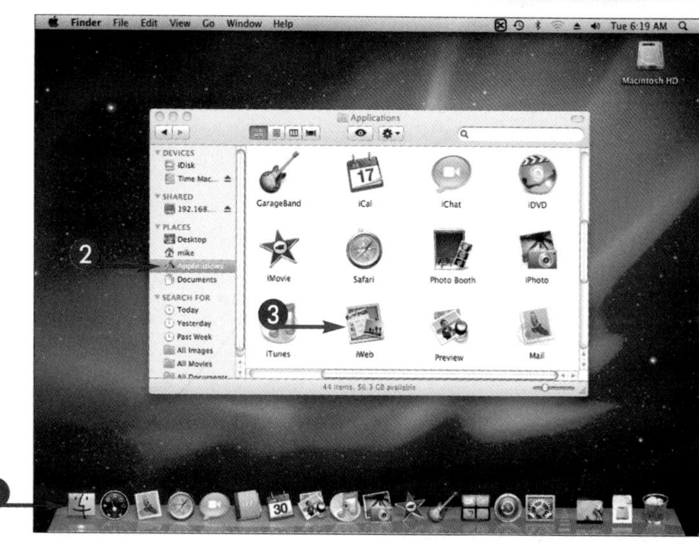

- The iLife application opens.

  This example shows opening the iWeb application.

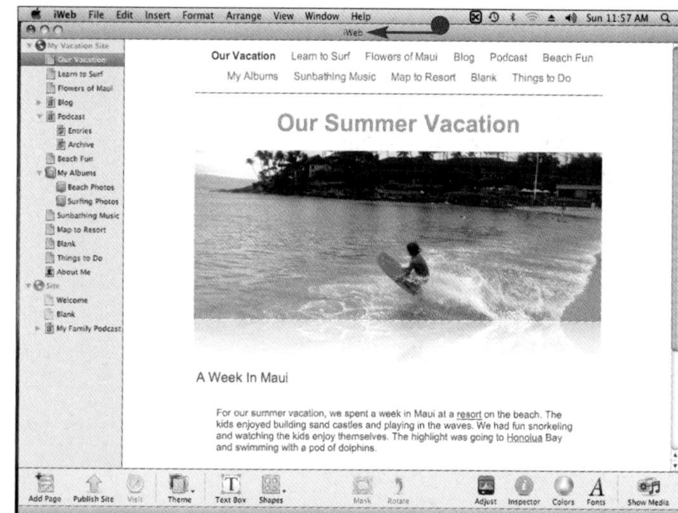

TIPS

How can I quickly open a recently used application or document?

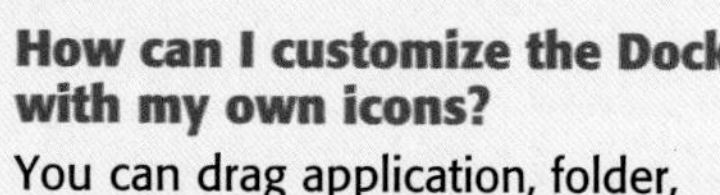

Click the **Apple** menu () and then click **Recent Items**. Your recently accessed applications, documents, and servers are listed. Click the list to access one.

How can I customize the Dock with my own icons?

You can drag application, folder, and document icons to the Dock to make them accessible on the Dock. For example, you can drag the iWeb and iDVD icons to the Dock from the Applications folder in the Finder to make them accessible. You can remove icons from the Dock by clicking and dragging them from the Dock to the desktop.

Importing, Exporting, and Sharing Content

You can import digital media into the iLife programs and then export finished projects to files and share them on Web sites and with discs.

iPhoto

You can open digital images in iPhoto by importing them from a digital camera, the file system on your computer, or the Internet (●). After editing the photos, you can export them to a folder on your computer or upload them to photo-sharing sites such as Flickr and Facebook. You can also export slideshows and keepsakes such as photo books and calendars that you create from your photos.

iMovie

You can import video clips to iMovie from a tape-based or memory-based camcorder, or your computer's file system (●). Once imported, you can play your clips and assemble them into full-featured movies. You can export your finished movie projects to a file, share them to YouTube, and more. You can also burn the final product to a disc using the iDVD application.

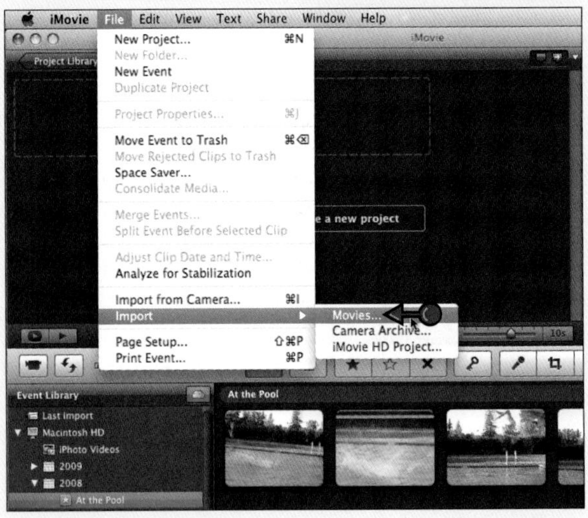

GarageBand

In GarageBand, you can import music from your computer file system or record new music from real or software-based instruments. After you finish editing and mixing you music project, you can export the song in different formats to your computer. You can share it with iTunes, present it as a podcast on a Web site (●), or burn it to a music CD. You can also access your work in other iLife applications to add music to movies, slideshows, and more.

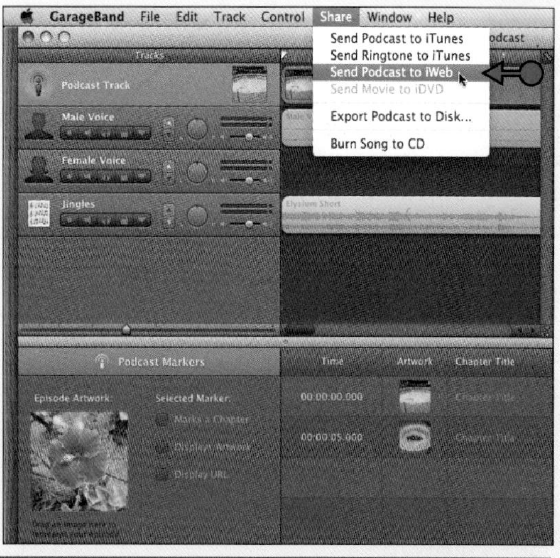

iWeb

You can add digital media to Web pages in iWeb using the Insert command or by dragging the files from the media browser. Different page templates make it easy to present different types of media on your site. For example, with the blog and podcast templates, you can easily feature photos, videos, and music on your pages. You can share your finished pages by uploading them to a server via FTP (●) or publishing to your MobileMe account.

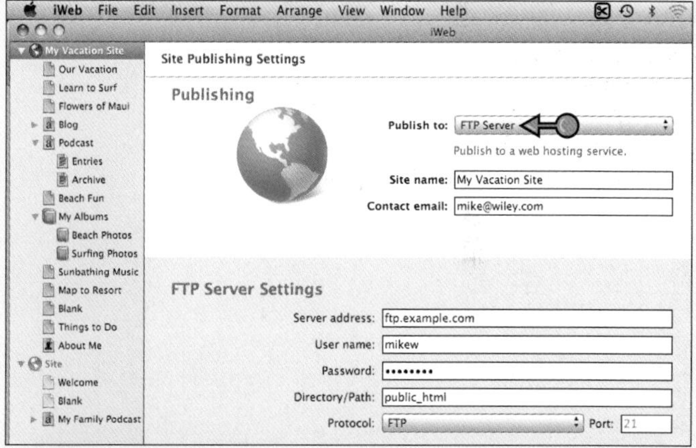

iDVD

iDVD lets you import movies, still images, and music from your computer file system or from the media browser. The media browser gives iDVD access to content created in the other iLife applications. After you assemble your content into a DVD project, you can burn the project to a DVD (●). You can also save it as a disc image for archiving or burning later.

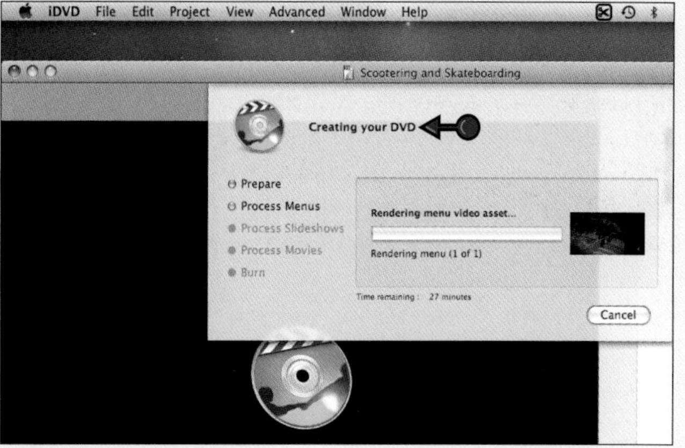

You can search for answers to questions using the search box in the iLife Help menu. You can also use the menu to get help at the Apple Web site.

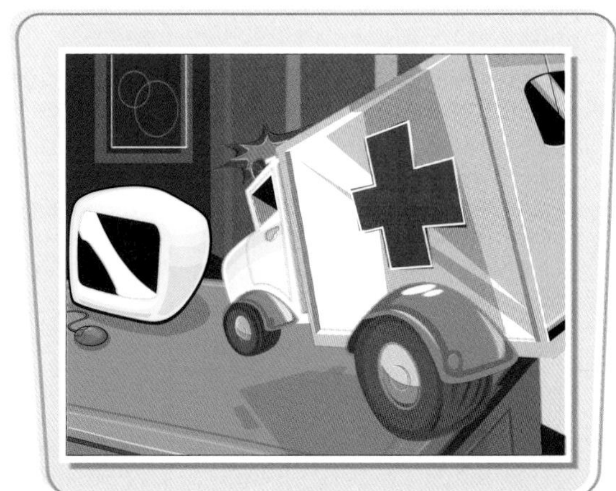

Get Help

1. In an iLife application, click **Help**.

   In this example, help is accessed from the iPhoto application.

   The Help menu opens.

- You can click to access general help topics.

2. Type a keyword in the Search box.

- Results for the keyword appear.

3. Click a result.

- You can click **Show All Results** to view all the results for the keyword.

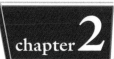

A window opens showing help information.

- A list of related results appears at the bottom. You can click one for more information.
- You can click in the search box to start a new search.

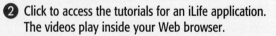

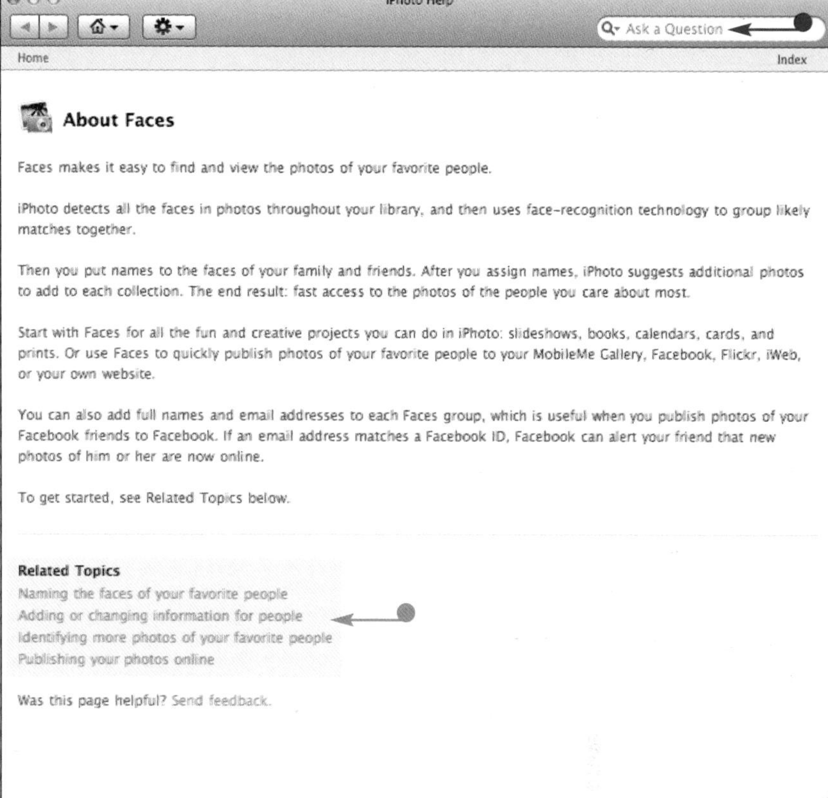

How do I access a video tutorial?

You can access online video tutorials that step you through common tasks in the iLife applications.

1. Click **Help** and then click **Video Tutorials**.

   A Web browser window opens showing the tutorial page for iLife.

2. Click to access the tutorials for an iLife application. The videos play inside your Web browser.

Change Monitor Resolution

You can change the monitor resolution to give you more area for the workspace of your iLife applications.

Change Monitor Resolution

1. Click the **Apple** menu (🍎).
2. Click **System Preferences**.

   The System Preferences window opens.
3. Click **Displays**.

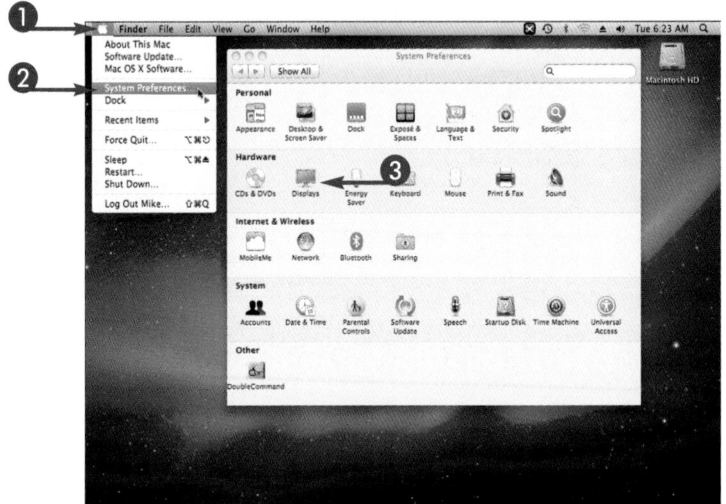

4. Click a new resolution.

   The monitor resolution changes.

   In this example, the monitor resolution is increased to offer more space to application windows.

   For LCD monitors, the maximum resolution listed offers the sharpest picture.
5. Click ● to close the System Preferences window.

   The changes are saved.

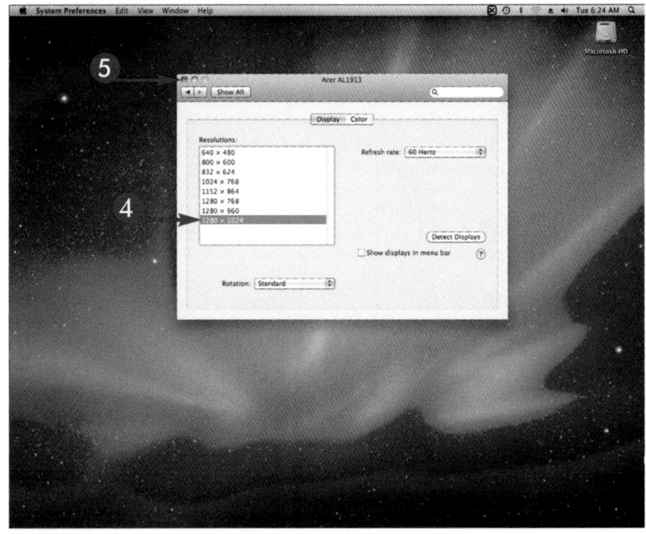

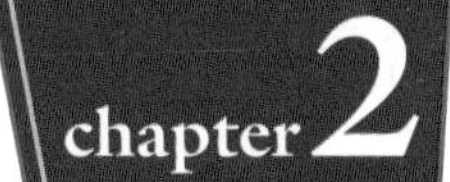

Quit an iLife '09 Application

You can quit an iLife application after you have finished viewing, organizing, and sharing your digital media.

Quit an iLife Application

1. Click the menu named for the iLife application.

   This example shows the GarageBand application, so **GarageBand** is clicked.

2. Click the **Quit** command.

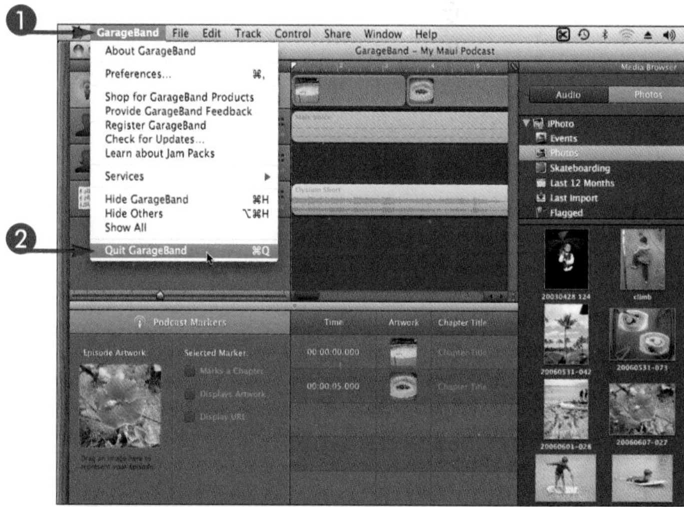

The application quits.

Sign In to MobileMe

Many of the iLife applications can publish media such as photos, movies, and Web pages to MobileMe. MobileMe is a service run by Apple that lets you store content online and share it with friends and family. To use the MobileMe-based features of iLife, you must sign in to your MobileMe account.

Sign In to MobileMe

1. Click the **Apple** menu (🍎).
2. Click **System Preferences**.

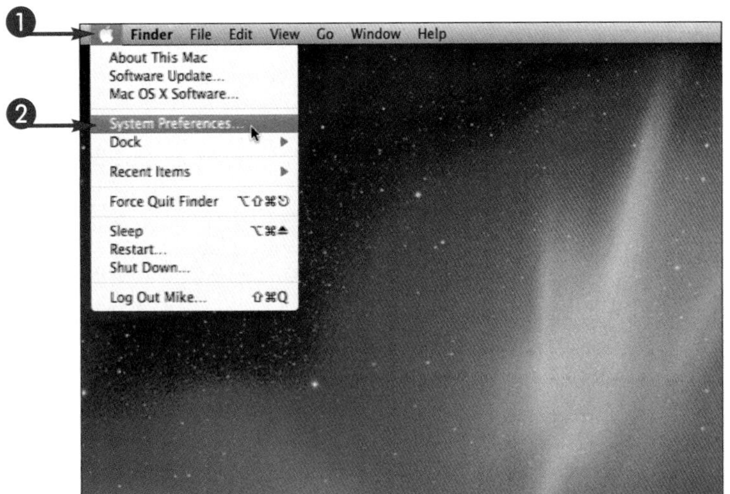

The System Preferences window opens.

3. Click **MobileMe**.

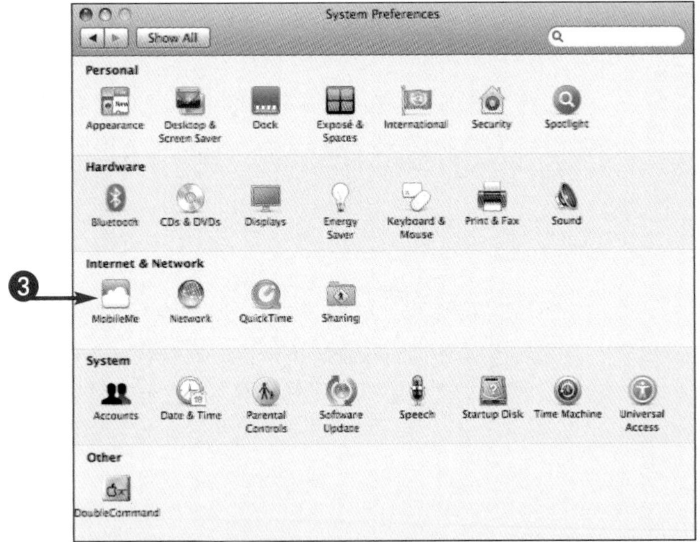

Sign-in fields appear if you are not signed in.

4. Type your member name.
5. Type your password.
6. Click **Sign In**.

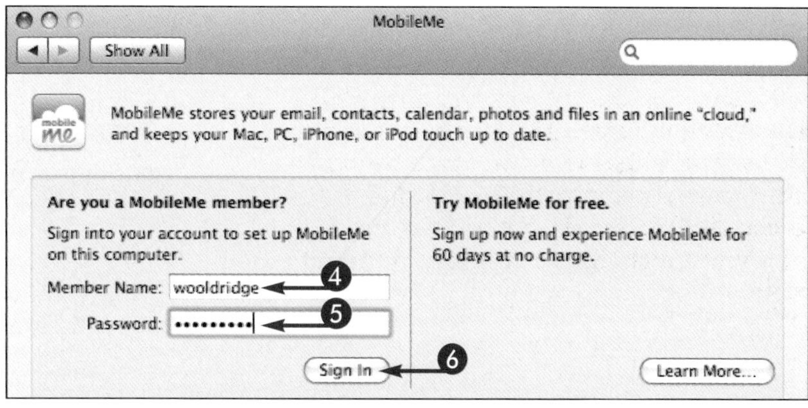

- You are signed in and your account status appears.

Note: *See the other chapters in this book for details about using MobileMe-based features.*

- You can click to sign out.

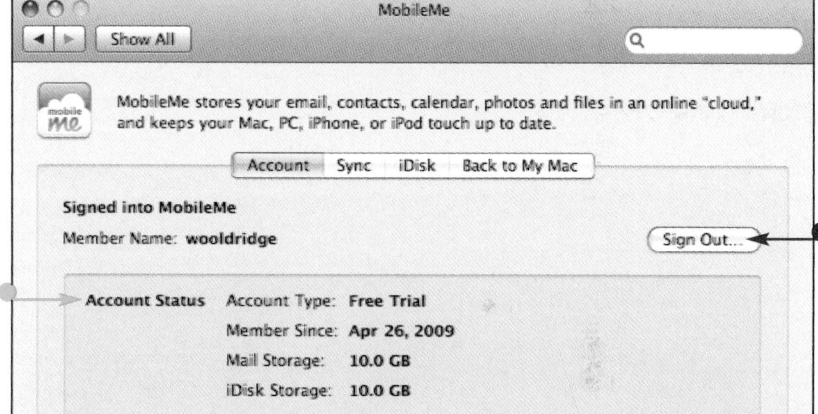

How do I sign up for a MobileMe account and what does it include?

Visit www.me.com to sign up for a MobileMe account. An account costs $99 per year from Apple. You can try the service free for 60 days. You can also purchase MobileMe from online vendors such as Amazon.com, sometimes for a discount. A MobileMe account includes:

- E-mail access with a personalized address at *membername*@me.com.
- Synchronized access to your contact list for all your computers and mobile devices.
- Synchronized access to your calendar for all your computers and mobile devices.
- An online system for sharing photos and videos.
- The iDisk service, which lets you share and back up files from your computers and other devices. You can also access your Web pages published from iWeb in your iDisk files.

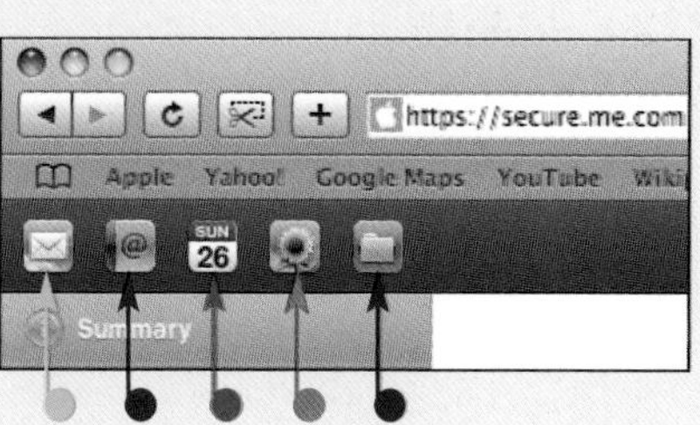

PART II

Working with iPhoto '09

With iPhoto '09, you can easily edit, enhance, and share the images on your Mac. The program helps you download images from a digital camera, optimize color and lighting of the images, and assemble the images into photo books, slideshows, and other projects. This part teaches you to how to make the most of this powerful program.

Understanding the iPhoto Workspace

iPhoto enables you to organize, enhance, and share your collection of digital photos. Take a moment to familiarize yourself with the iPhoto workspace.

Thumbnails

Small versions of your photos, called *thumbnails*, appear here in the photo browser. You can change their size using the slider in the bottom-right corner of the workspace or magnify them by double-clicking. See the tasks in this chapter for more about viewing photos.

Source List

By clicking different buttons in the source list, you can filter and sort your library photos by when or where they were taken, or by the faces that appear in them. See Chapter 4 for more about organizing photos.

Organization

You can organize photos into subject-specific albums or display them as slideshows. With slideshows, you can control the transitions between photos as well as slide durations.

Name Faces

The Name feature allows you to label the faces in your photos with names. iPhoto automatically recognizes faces in your images to help you with the labeling.

Editing Tools

You can edit the color, lighting, and other characteristics of a photo using various tools. This can help you fix poorly exposed or washed-out photos. You can also remove unwanted objects or blemishes with a Retouch tool. See Chapter 5 for more.

Search Box

A search box allows you to search by title or description, date, keyword, or rating.

Play Slideshow

A button at the bottom of the workspace lets you quickly show the currently displayed photos as a slideshow with a theme and background music.

Keepsakes

Keepsakes are photo-related projects such as photo books and calendars that you can create in iPhoto. You can have your finished keepsakes printed professionally. See Chapter 6 for more about keepsakes.

Sharing

You can share your photos by posting them to Web galleries, sending them by e-mail, or transferring them to online services such as Facebook and Flickr. See Chapter 6 for more information.

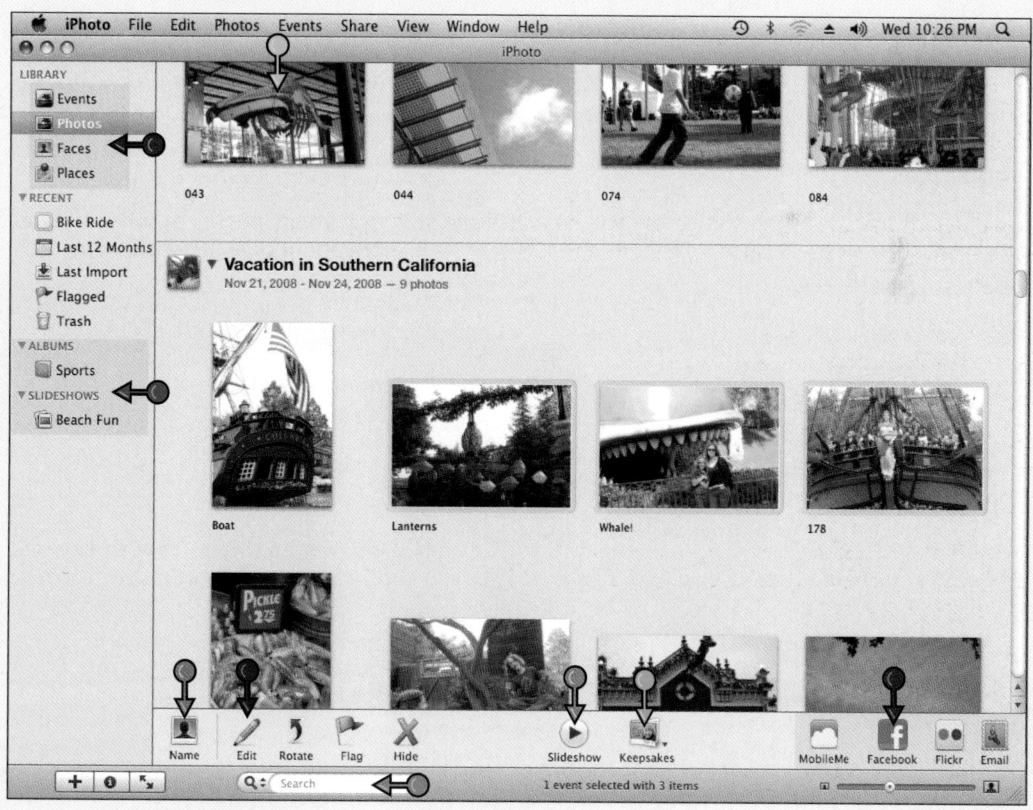

Import Photos from a Camera

You can bring digital images into iPhoto directly from a camera. Most digital cameras connect to a Mac through a USB cable. Mac computers come with multiple USB ports where you can connect cables.

For details about connecting your specific camera, see the documentation that came with the device.

Import Photos from a Camera

1. Connect your camera to your Mac using a USB cable and turn the camera on.

   iPhoto launches and displays the photos on your camera.

   If iPhoto does not launch automatically, click iPhoto in the Dock to launch it.

- The camera name appears here.

2. ⌘-click the photos you want to import.

3. Type an event name to categorize the selected photos.

Note: *For more about how iPhoto organizes photos by event, see Chapter 4.*

4. Type a description of the event.
5. Select **Autosplit events after importing** to automatically group your photos by date (☐ changes to ☑).
6. Click **Import Selected**.

- You can click **Import All** to import all the photos on your camera at once.

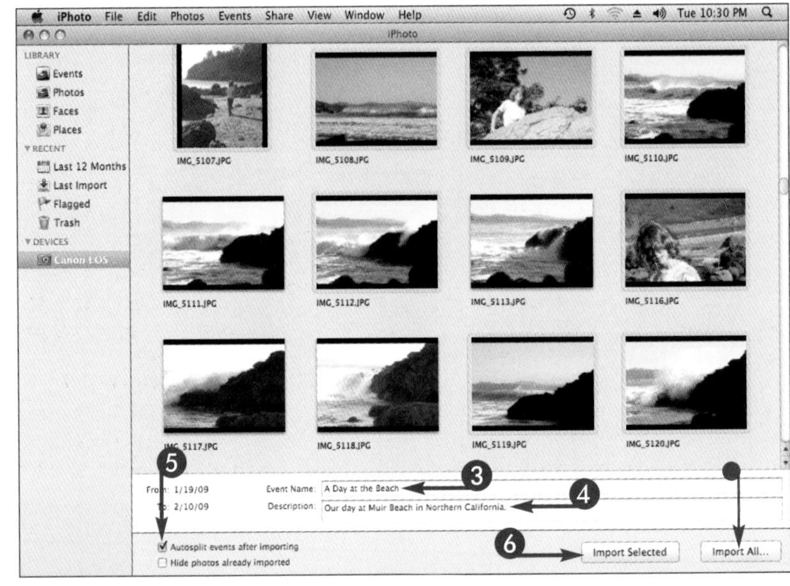

iPhoto downloads the photos from your camera and adds them to the iPhoto library.

iPhoto displays a dialog enabling you to delete the imported photos.

7 Click **Delete Photos** to erase the imported photos from your camera.

iPhoto displays the imported photos in the photo browser.

- The event name appears above the photos.

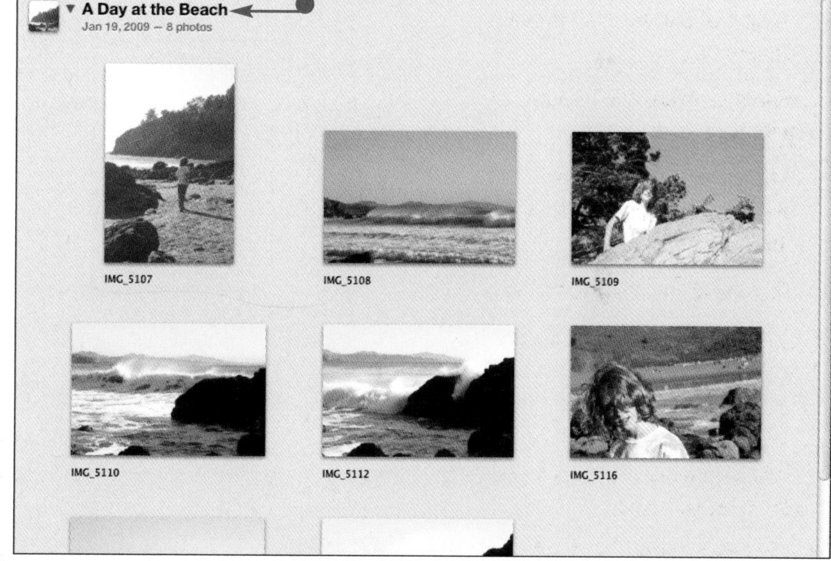

TIPS

What photo file formats does iPhoto support?

iPhoto supports the JPEG, TIFF, and RAW file formats, which are how most digital cameras save their photo files. It can also import Web formats such as GIF and PNG, Photoshop (PSD) files, and many other types.

Can I import and play movies in iPhoto?

You can import movies from a digital camera into iPhoto just like you do still photos. iPhoto can import and play many popular video formats including QuickTime (MOV), MPEG, and AVI. Double-clicking a movie in iPhoto opens the movie in QuickTime Player. If you want to edit movies, see Part III of this book, which covers iMovie.

Import Photos from Your Computer

If you already have photos stored on your computer, you can bring them into iPhoto to organize and edit them. This is useful if you have a collection of scanned photos or art on your Mac. You can also use these steps to bring photos into iPhoto from a CD-ROM, DVD, memory card, or flash drive.

Import Photos from Your Computer

USE THE IMPORT COMMAND

1. Click **File**.
2. Click **Import to Library**.

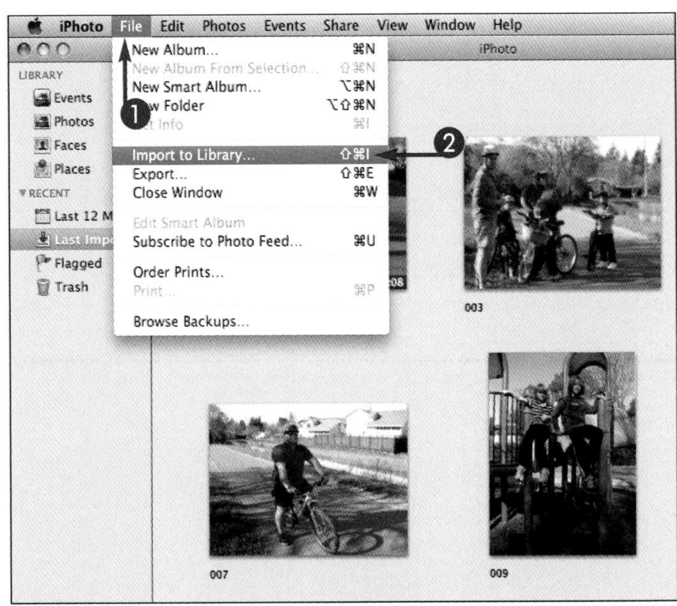

The Import Photos dialog appears.

3. Navigate to the folder on your computer that contains the photos.

***Note:** You can also navigate to a CD-ROM, DVD, memory card, or flash drive to import photos.*

4. ⌘-click to select the photos. You can press ⌘ + A to select all the photos.
5. Click **Import**.

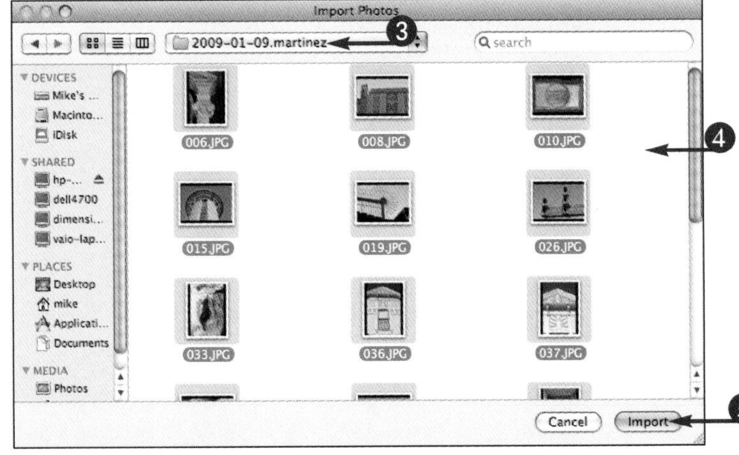

- iPhoto imports the selected photos and displays them in the photo browser.

***Note:** For information about how to organize imported photos, see Chapter 4.*

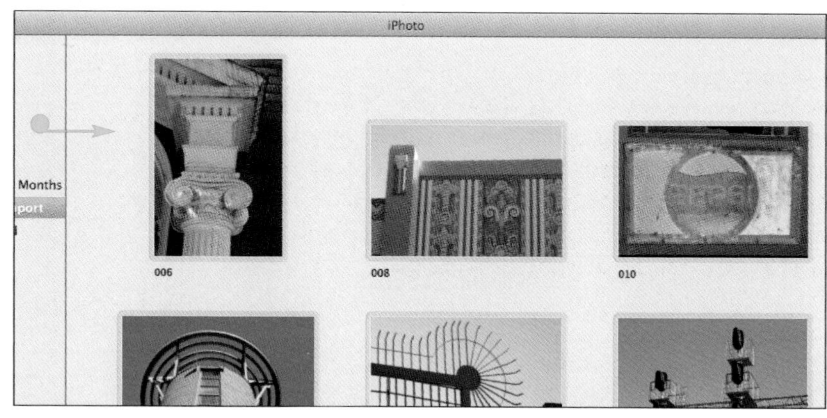

CLICK AND DRAG FROM THE FINDER

1. Open the folder containing the photos to import in the Mac Finder.
2. ⌘-click to select the photos. You can press ⌘ + A to select all the photos.
3. Click and drag the photos from the Finder to iPhoto.

   iPhoto imports the selected photos and displays them in the photo browser.

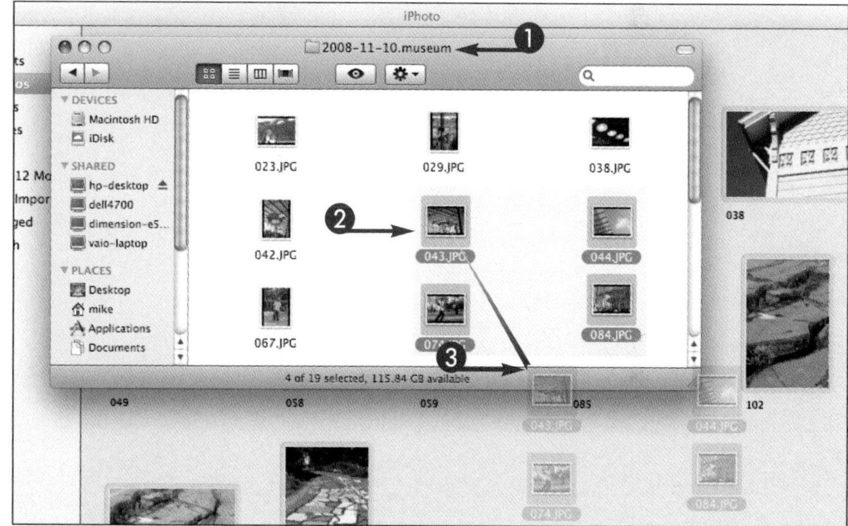

Does iPhoto make copies of my photos when I import them?

By default, iPhoto makes copies of imported photos and puts the copies in the iPhoto library. You can change the preferences to keep iPhoto from making copies. This can help save space on your hard drive.

1. Click **iPhoto** and then **Preferences**.
2. In the Preferences dialog, click **Advanced**.
3. Click **Copy items to the iPhoto Library** (☑ changes to ☐).
4. Click ● to close the Preferences dialog.

   iPhoto saves the changes.

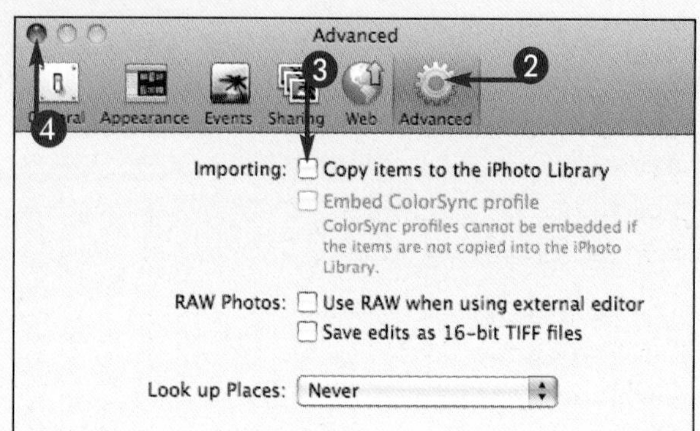

Import Photos from the Web

You can easily import a Web photo into your iPhoto library from your Safari Web browser. This is useful if you store photos on a photo-hosting site and want to use one of the photos in an iPhoto project.

Import Photos from the Web

1. Click **Safari** in the Mac Dock.

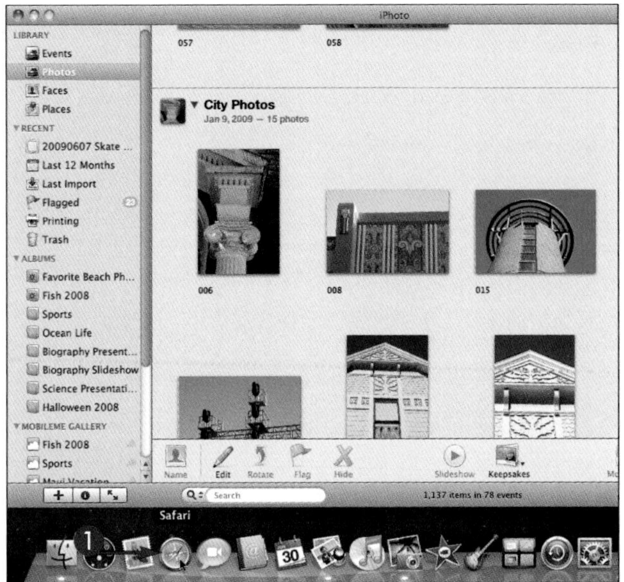

The Safari Web browser opens.

2. View a Web page with the photo you want to import.
3. ⌘-click the image you want to import.
4. From the menu that appears, click **Add Image to iPhoto Library**.

iPhoto imports the photo and titles it with the file name.

5 Click the title.

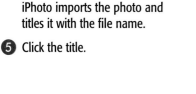

The title becomes editable.

6 Type a new title.

7 Press Enter.

iPhoto saves the title.

TIP

How do I import a photo using a Web browser other than Safari?

Getting your photos into iPhoto from another Web browser takes a few more steps. Here is how to do it in Firefox:

1 In Firefox, open the Web page that contains the image you want to save.

2 ⌘-click the image.

3 Select **Save Image As** from the menu that appears.

4 From the Save Image dialog that appears, type a file name for the image.

5 Click here to select where to save the image.

6 Click **Save**.

The browser saves the image to your computer.

7 See "Import Photos from Your Computer" to bring image into iPhoto.

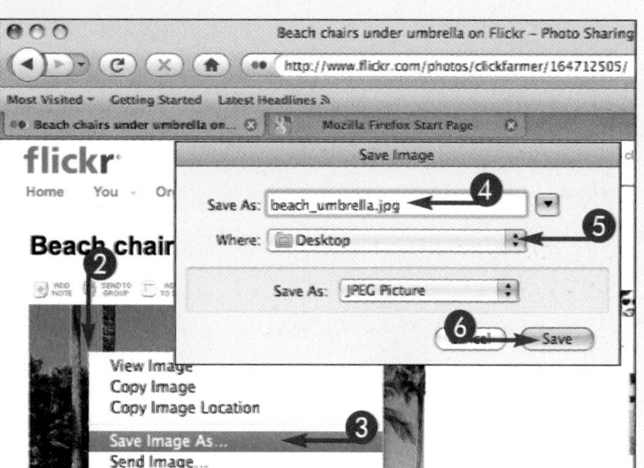

Magnify a Photo

You can view magnified versions of your photos that you have imported by clicking the small versions, also called *thumbnails*, in the iPhoto photo browser. You can also view photos at full-screen size. You can cycle through the photos using the arrow keys.

Magnify a Photo

1. Double-click a thumbnail in the photo browser.

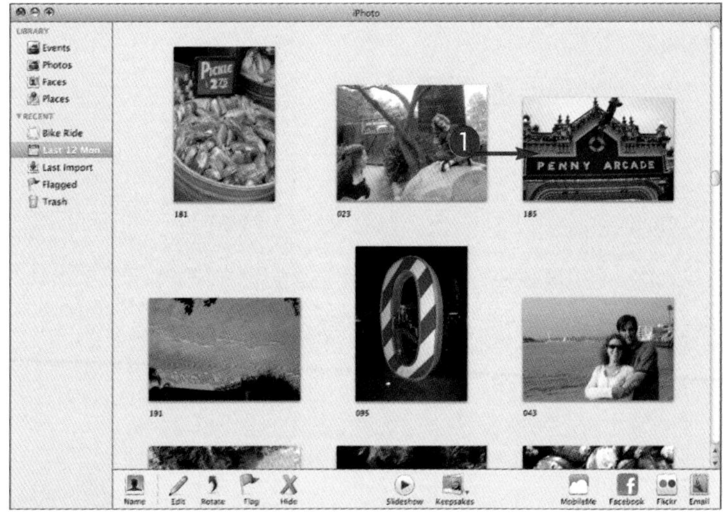

iPhoto magnifies the photo to a larger size.

You can click the enlarged photo once to return to the thumbnail view.

2. Click **Enter full screen** ( ).

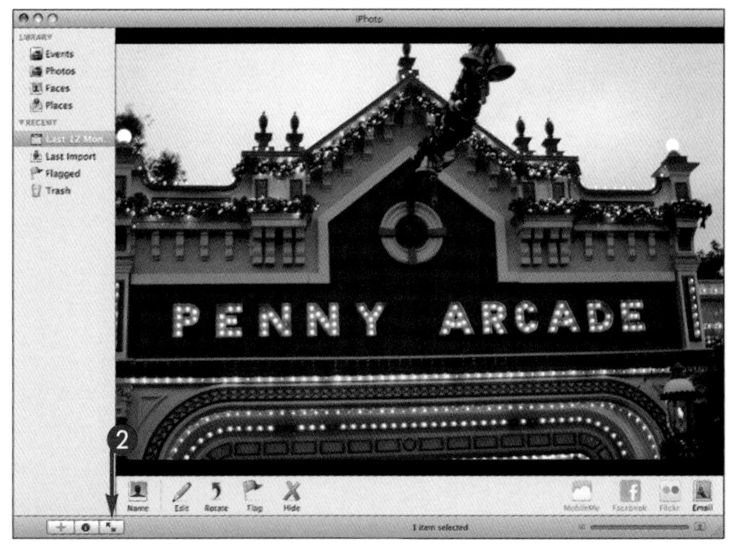

iPhoto expands the photo to full-screen size.

3. Move the cursor to the top of the photo.

- iPhoto shows thumbnails of the other photos in the group you are viewing.
- You can click the thumbnail of a photo to view that photo in full-screen view.

Press ⬅ or ➡ to view the previous or next photo in your library.

4. Move the cursor to the bottom of the photo.

- iPhoto displays editing buttons. For details about editing, see Chapter 5.

5. Press Esc to return to the thumbnail view of the library.

TIP

How do I adjust the size of the thumbnail versions of my photos in the photo browser?

You can use the thumbnail slider:

- Click and drag the slider left to shrink or right to enlarge the thumbnails.
- Click to minimize the thumbnails.
- Click to maximize the thumbnails.

When viewing the photo browser, you can also press number keys (0, 1, 2, or 3) to resize the thumbnails.

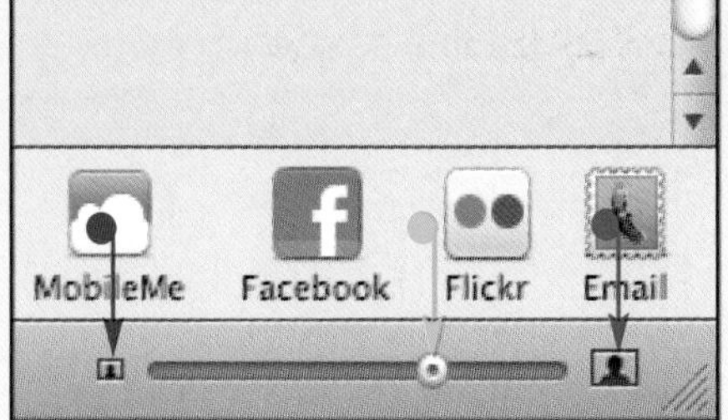

View Photo Information

You can view extra information about a photo, including its description, map location, and camera settings. This can help you categorize a photo.

View Photo Information

1. Click to select a photo in the library.
2. Click ![info] (![info] changes to ![info]).
   - iPhoto displays basic information about the photo, including the dimensions and time taken.
3. Click **Photos**.
4. Click **Show Extended Photo Info**.

- iPhoto displays the extended information, including any existing location information and camera settings.

5. Position your cursor over an image.

   iPhoto displays an information icon (![i]).

6. Click the icon.

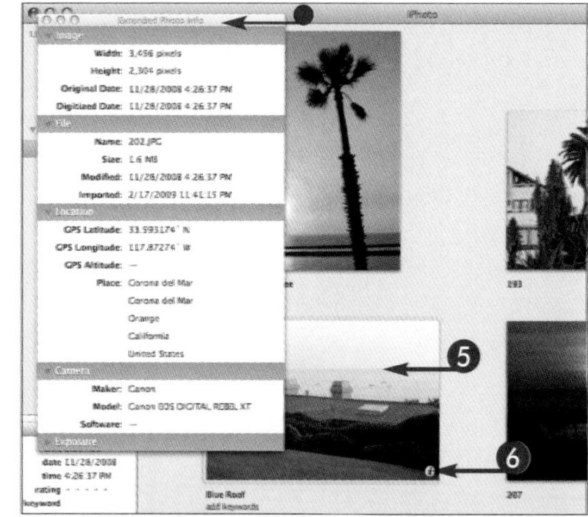

- iPhoto displays map and other information about the photo.

***Note:** To add a photo to the map, see Chapter 4.*

7 Click **Done** to close the information box.

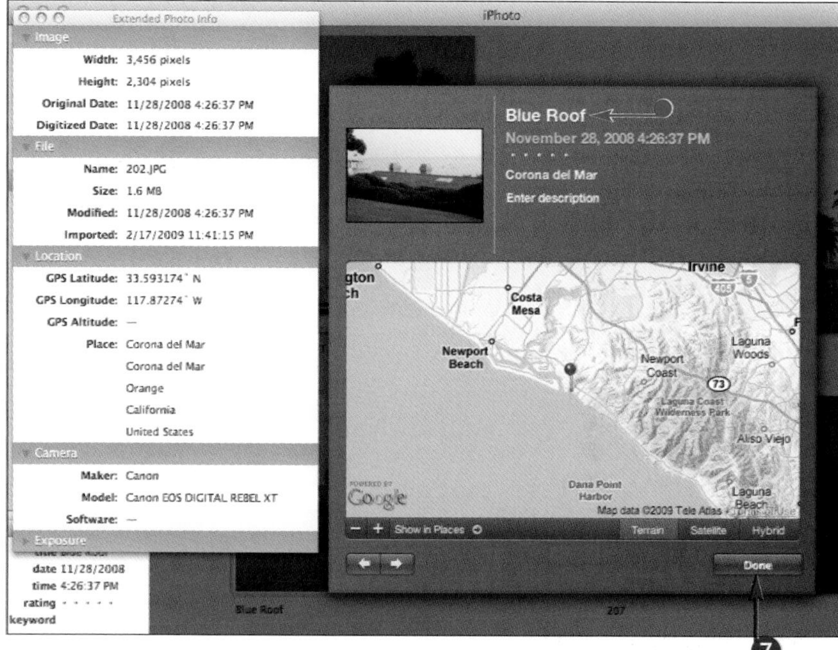

How do I find a photo on the Mac file system?

You can open a Finder window that shows where the photo is stored outside of iPhoto on the Mac file system.

1 ⌘-click the photo thumbnail.

2 In the menu that appears, click **Show File**.

- If the file has been edited, you can click **Show Original File** to view the unedited version.

- A Finder window opens showing the file and its location in the file system.

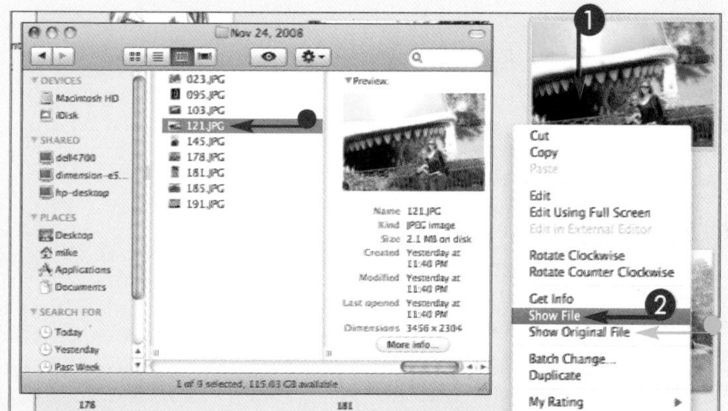

Change the Title and Description of a Photo

You can edit the title and description of a photo to add information about its subject and location. When you import a photo, iPhoto assigns the file name as the title and a blank description.

Change the Title and Description of a Photo

1. Under a photo thumbnail, click the title text.

   The title becomes editable.

2. Type a new name for the photo.
3. Press Enter.

   iPhoto saves the title.

4. Position the cursor over the thumbnail.

   iPhoto displays an information icon (ⓘ).

5. Click the icon.

iPhoto displays map and other information about the photo.

6 Click **Enter description**.

The description becomes editable.

Note: *You must keep the cursor within the edit box to edit the text.*

7 Type a description.

8 Position the cursor outside the edit box.

iPhoto saves the description.

TIPS

How can I include titles and descriptions when I share a photo?

When you share a photo by e-mail in iPhoto, you have the option of automatically adding the title and description to the e-mail message. Click the Titles and Descriptions options (☐ changes to ☑) in the Mail Photo dialog to add them. For more details, see Chapter 6.

How can I search for photos by title or description?

Perform a search using the search box at the bottom of the iPhoto workspace. For more information about searching, see Chapter 4.

Change the Date and Time of a Photo

You can edit the date and time associated with a photo in your iPhoto library. This can be helpful if the time on your camera was incorrect when you took the picture. Because iPhoto organizes photos by time in the photo browser, this can also change where the thumbnail displays when you browse photos.

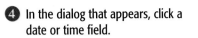

Change the Date and Time of a Photo

1. Click to select a photo thumbnail.

   You can ⌘-click to select multiple photos to adjust their date and time to a single setting.

2. Click **Photos**.
3. Click **Adjust Date and Time**.

4. In the dialog that appears, click a date or time field.
5. Click here to adjust the field.
6. Repeat steps **4** and **5** to adjust the other fields.

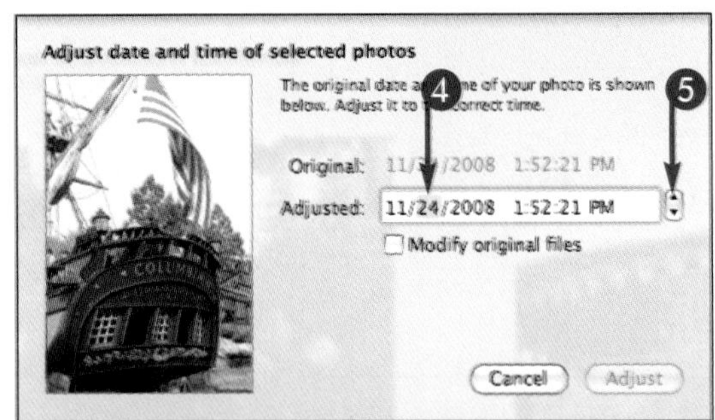

- iPhoto displays a summary of the adjustment.
- If you are changing the settings of an edited photo, you can optionally click to modify the original copy as well (☐ changes to ☑).

7 Click **Adjust**.

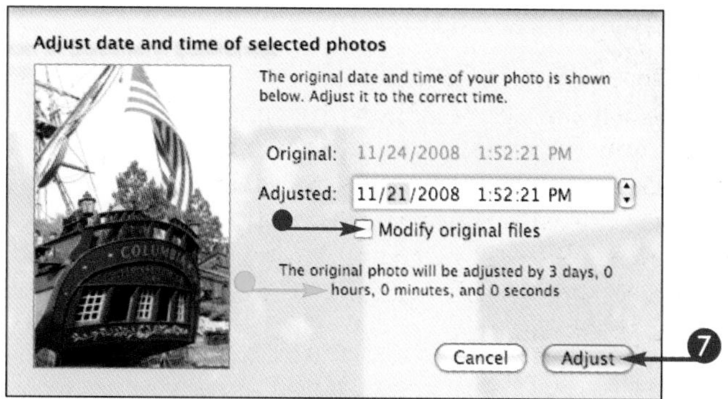

iPhoto adjusts the date and time.

- The date for the associated event changes as well.

***Note:** For more about events, see Chapter 4.*

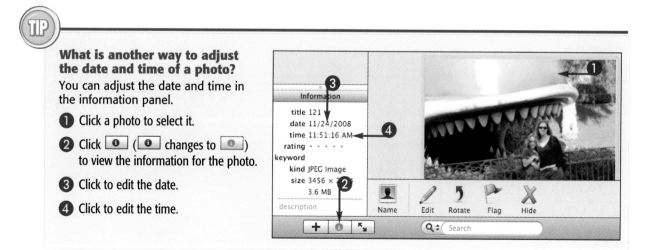

TIP

What is another way to adjust the date and time of a photo?

You can adjust the date and time in the information panel.

1. Click a photo to select it.
2. Click the info button (it changes to the highlighted state) to view the information for the photo.
3. Click to edit the date.
4. Click to edit the time.

Change Settings for a Batch of Photos

You can use the batch feature to change the title, date, or description for multiple photos all at once. This is useful for adding common information to photos from the same event or place, or with the same subjects.

Change Settings for a Batch of Photos

1. ⌘-click to select the photos.
2. Click **Photos**.
3. Click **Batch Change**.

4. Click here and select **Title**.
5. Click here and select a title type.

- You can click to add an incremental number to each photo in the batch (☐ changes to ☑).

6 Click here and select **Date**.

7 Click a date or time field.

8 Click here to adjust the field.

- You can optionally click **Add** to adjust the time applied to each photo in the batch (☐ changes to ☑).

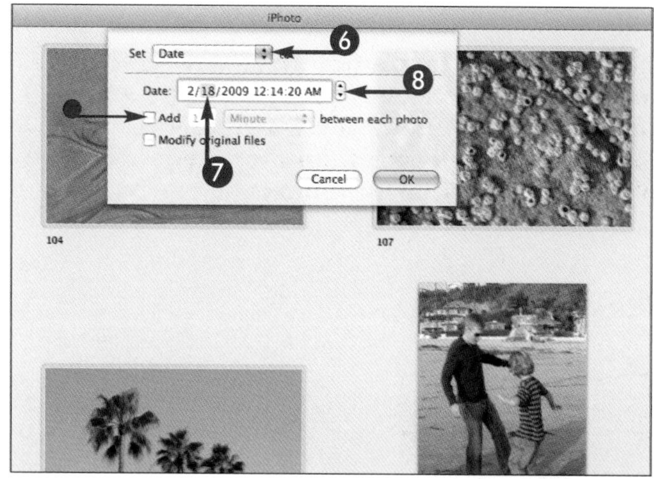

9 Click here and select **Description**.

10 Type a description.

- You can optionally click to keep any existing descriptions (☐ changes to ☑).

11 Click **OK**.

iPhoto applies the changes to the batch.

What are some keyboard shortcuts when browsing the iPhoto library?

Here are some useful shortcuts. For more, see the iPhoto help documentation.

Shortcut	Action
Home	View the first photo in the library
End	View the last photo in the library
⌘ +]	Edit next photo in library
⌘ + [	Edit previous photo in library
M	Magnify the selected photo
Enter	Edit the selected photo
⌘ + Shift + I	Import photos from the computer

Manage Events

iPhoto can group photos into events based on the time the photos were taken. When you import photos, iPhoto automatically organizes photos into events based on the day the photos were taken. You can customize the name of the event to describe the photos in it.

Manage Events

VIEW EVENT PHOTOS

1. Click **Events**.

   iPhoto displays each event as a square thumbnail.

- You can move your cursor horizontally across a thumbnail to preview the event photos, a feature known as *skimming*.

2. Double-click an event.

iPhoto displays the photos in the event.

- You can click **Slideshow** to display the photos as a slideshow.
- You can click **Keepsakes** to create a project out of the event photos.

***Note:** Depending on your monitor resolution, you may see separate buttons for creating books, calendars, and cards. See Chapter 6 for details about creating these projects.*

3. Click **All Events** to return to the event thumbnails.

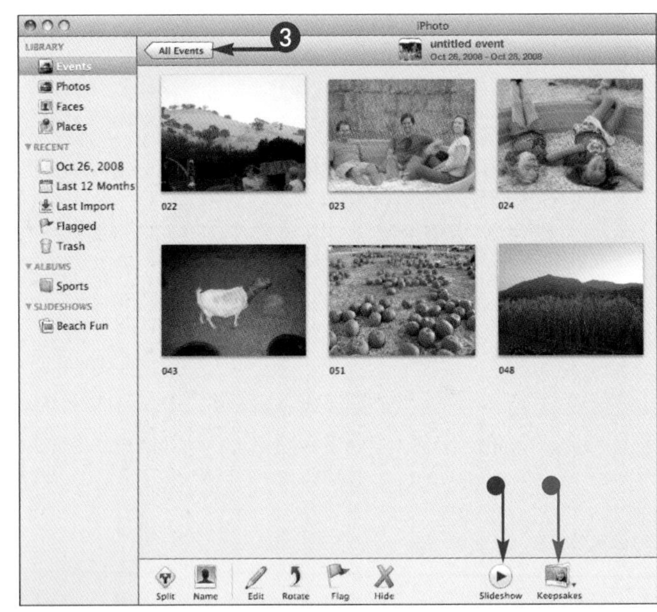

NAME AN EVENT

1. Click **Events**.

   In the Events view, untitled events are titled with their date.

2. Click a title.

   The title becomes editable.

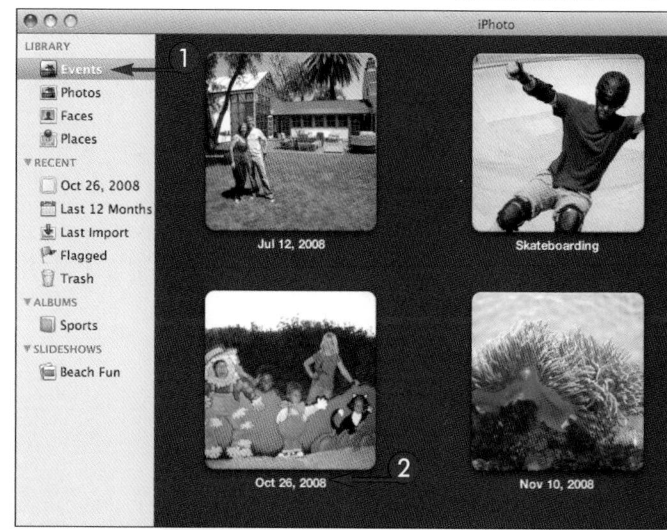

3. Type a new title.
4. Press Enter.

   iPhoto saves the new title.

How do I determine what photo iPhoto uses for the event thumbnail?

By default, iPhoto uses the first photo as the thumbnail. You can change it using the following steps:

1. View the photos for the event.
2. ⌘-click a photo.
3. Click **Make Key Photo**.

   iPhoto uses that photo for the event thumbnail.

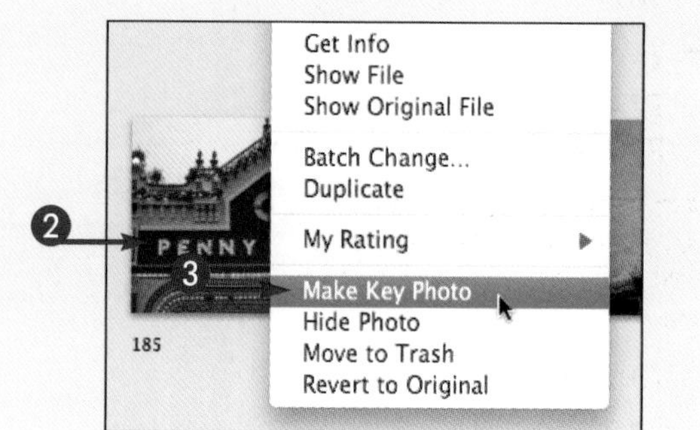

Create a New Event

You can create a new event to group together photos that occur at the same time. You might group photos from a birthday party into one event and photos taken during a holiday vacation into another event.

You can group photos that were taken at different times as an album. See "Create an Album" for details.

Create a New Event

1. Click **Photos**.

   iPhoto displays the photos in your library with event labels as headings.

2. ⌘-click to select photos to add to your new event.
3. Click **Events**.
4. Click **Create Event**.

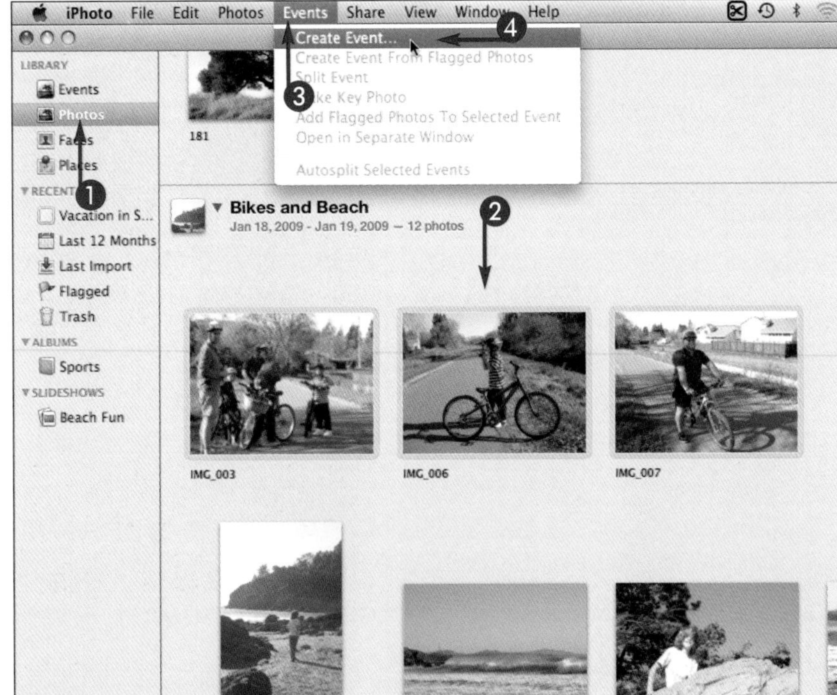

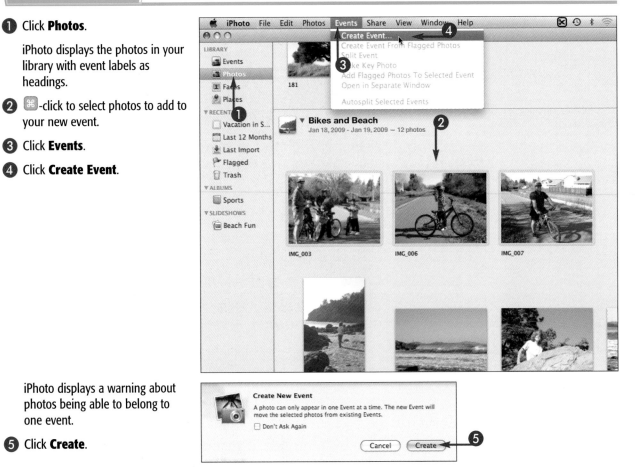

iPhoto displays a warning about photos being able to belong to one event.

5. Click **Create**.

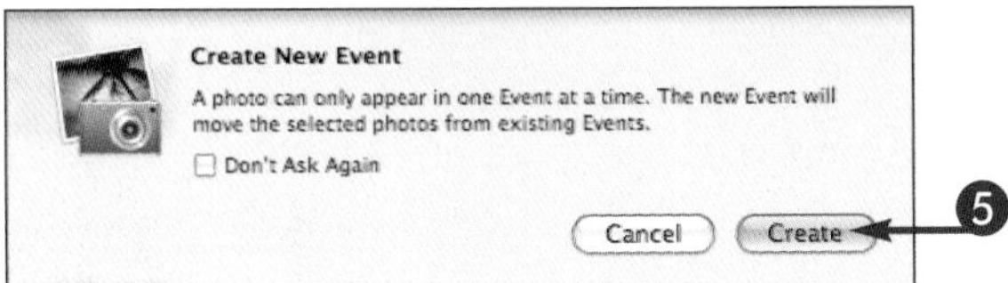

iPhoto creates a new event for the photos.

- You can click the event title to edit it.

6 Click **Events**.

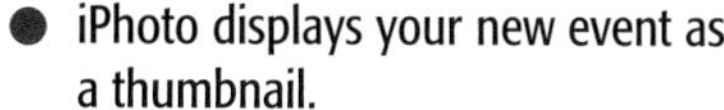

- iPhoto displays your new event as a thumbnail.

Note: For more about viewing events, see "Manage Events."

TIP

How do I merge the photos in several events into one event?

Follow these steps:

1. Click **Events**.
2. ⌘-click the events you want to merge.
3. Click **Events**.
4. Click **Merge Events**.

iPhoto merges the events.

Name a Face

iPhoto can automatically recognize faces in your photos based on shape and coloring. After it recognizes the faces, you can add names to them. Over time, iPhoto can start to match names to faces itself by recognizing specific faces.

Name a Face

1. View a photo that includes faces.
2. Click **Name**.

   iPhoto attempts to recognize the faces in the photo.
3. Click a face label.

   The label becomes editable.
4. Type a name for the face.
5. Press Enter.

iPhoto assigns the name to the face.

6. Repeat steps **3** to **5** to name other faces in the photo.
7. Click **Faces**.

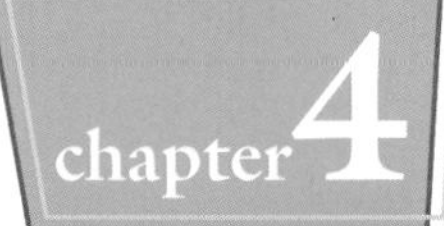

iPhoto groups your photos based on named faces.

- You can double-click a face photo to view the named photos.

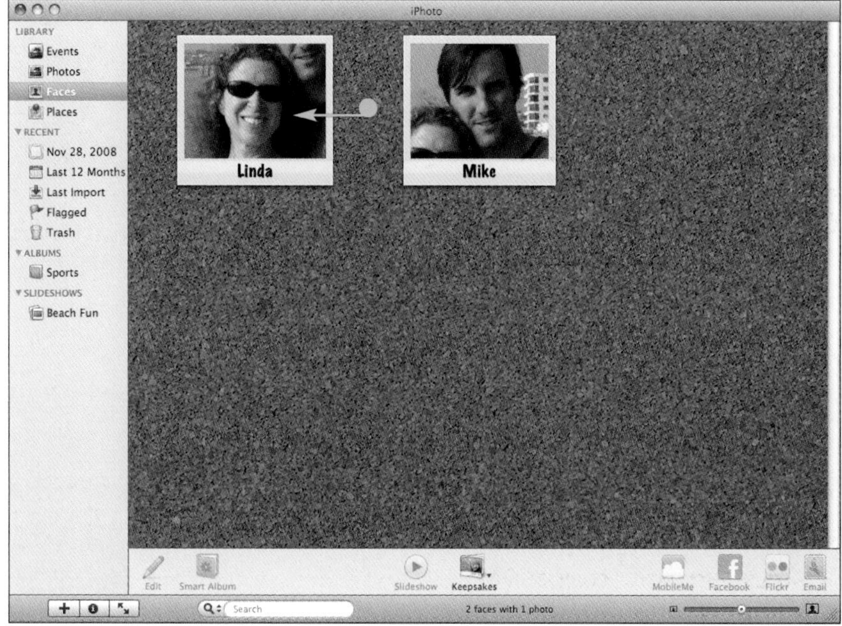

How do I name a face that iPhoto does not recognize?

Sometimes iPhoto cannot recognize a face because the face is at an angle or is obscured. Follow these steps to name it:

1. Open the photo and click **Name** to open the labeling view.
2. Click **Add Missing Face**.

   iPhoto displays an editable box and label.
3. Click and drag the box corners to surround the face.
4. Click here to name the face.
5. Click **Done**.

   iPhoto labels the face with the name.

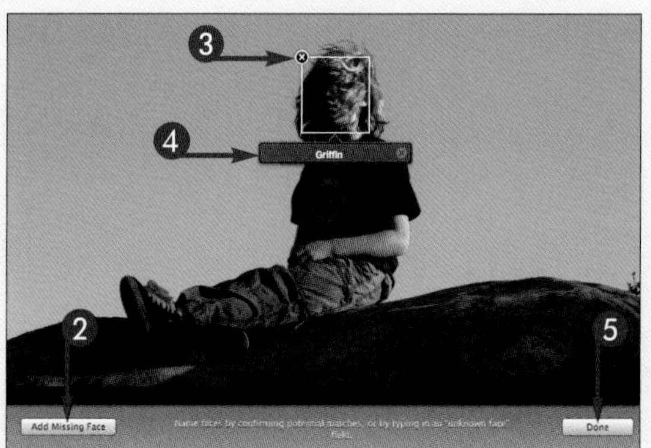

Manage Faces

As you name faces in your photos, iPhoto examines other photos in your library and attempts to name them for you. You can view iPhoto's face suggestions to confirm them. To label faces with names yourself, see "Name a Face."

Manage Faces

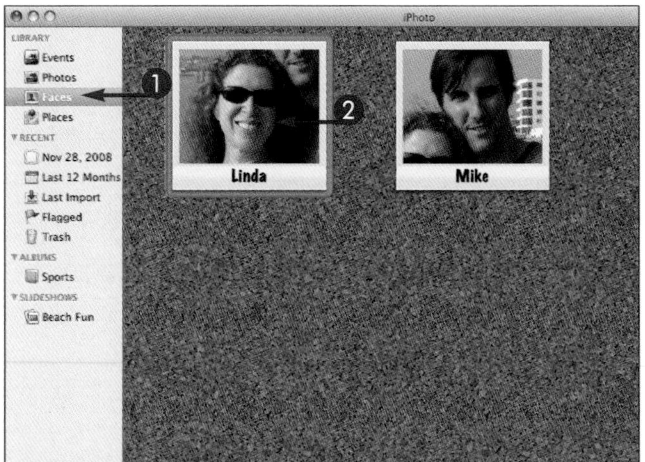

1. Click **Faces**.

   iPhoto displays the faces you have labeled.

2. Double-click a face.

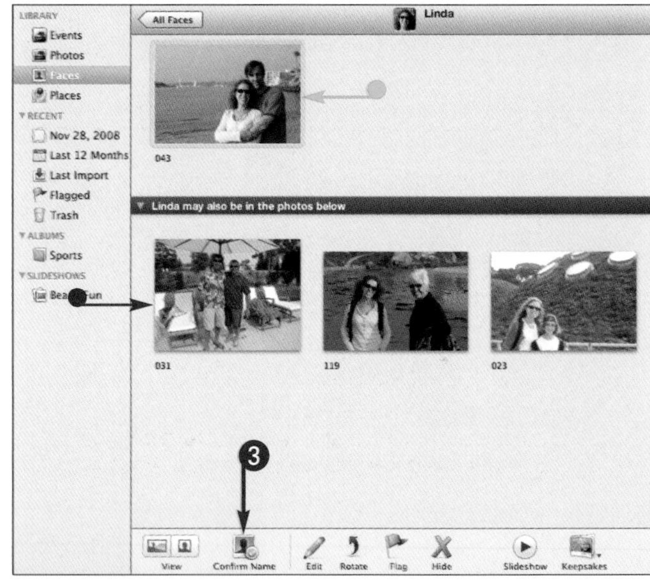

- iPhoto displays the photos you have named here.
- Photos with name suggestions appear here.

3. Click **Confirm Name**.

- iPhoto displays the unconfirmed faces here.

4. Click a face once to confirm it.

- iPhoto marks a confirmed face with a green label.

5. Click a face twice to reject it.

- iPhoto marks a rejected face with a red label.

6. Click **Done**.

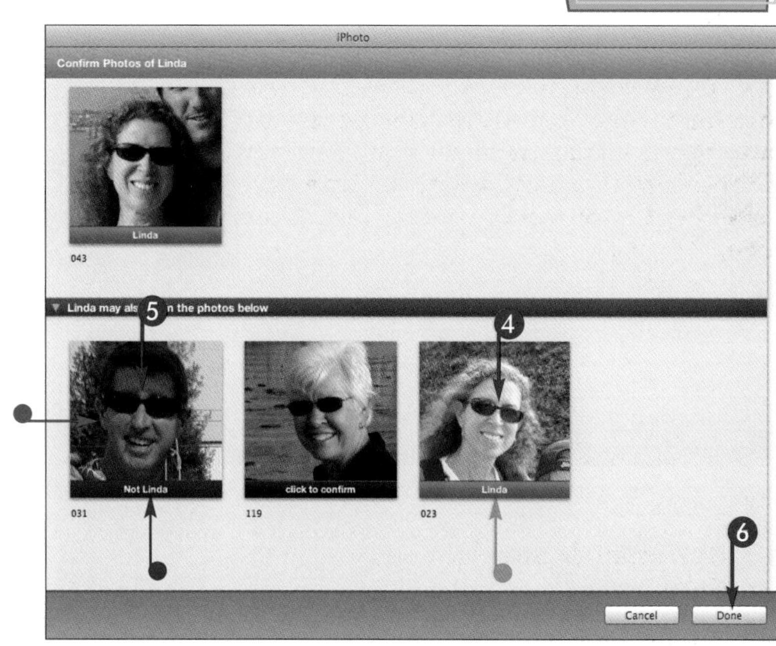

iPhoto updates the photos for that face.

TIPS

What happens if two faces have the same name?

If two faces in your photo library are labeled with the same name, iPhoto sees them as the same person and merges their photos in the Faces view. You can add a last name or initial to distinguish such faces and keep them separate in iPhoto.

How can I add additional information to faces?

In the Faces view, position your cursor over a face, then click the info icon (i) that appears in the lower-right corner. A box appears that enables you to add a full name and an e-mail address.

Map Photos to a Place

You can associate images in iPhoto with the places where they were taken. By zooming in on the map in iPhoto, you can pinpoint the exact street corner or landmark where you shot the photos.

To make mapping photos easier, you can turn on place lookups in the iPhoto preferences.

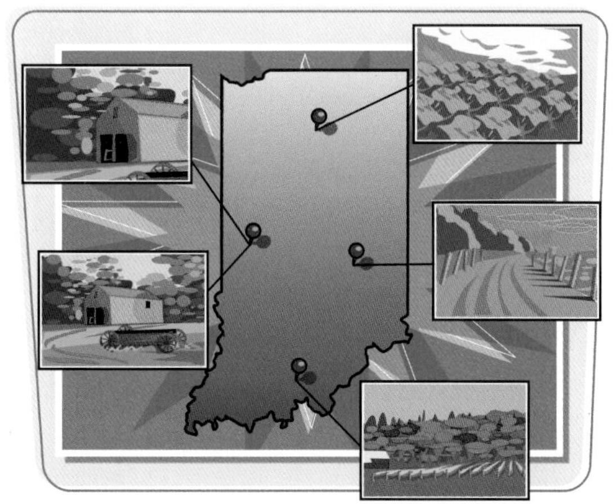

Map Photos to a Place

TURN ON PLACE LOOKUPS

❶ Click **iPhoto**.

❷ Click **Preferences**.

❸ In the dialog that appears, click **Advanced**.

❹ Click here and select **Automatically**.

❺ Click to close the dialog.

MAP A PHOTO

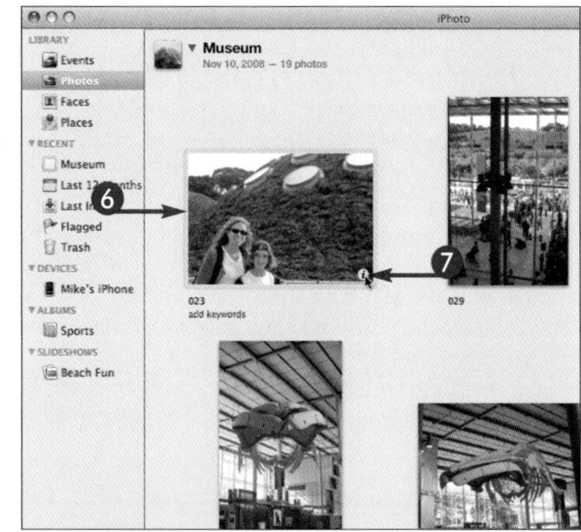

❻ Position the cursor over a photo thumbnail.

A icon appears.

❼ Click .

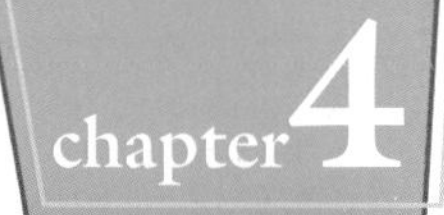

The location information for the photo appears.

8. Type the location of the photo.

   iPhoto looks up the location and offers suggestions.

9. Click the location of the photo from the list.

- If the location is not listed, you can click **New place** to perform a search.

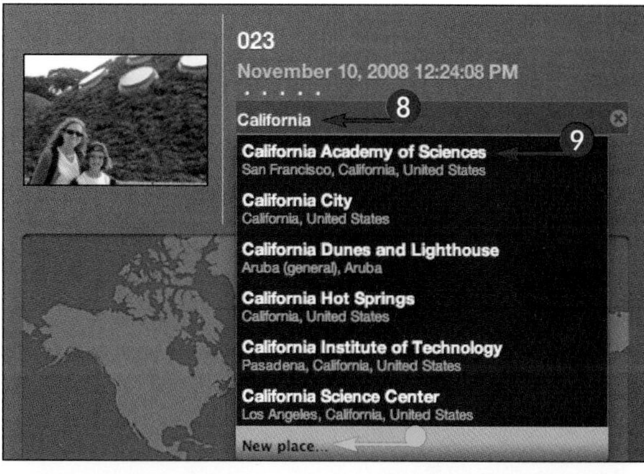

10. iPhoto adds a pin to the map at the location.

11. Click **Done** to return to the photo library.

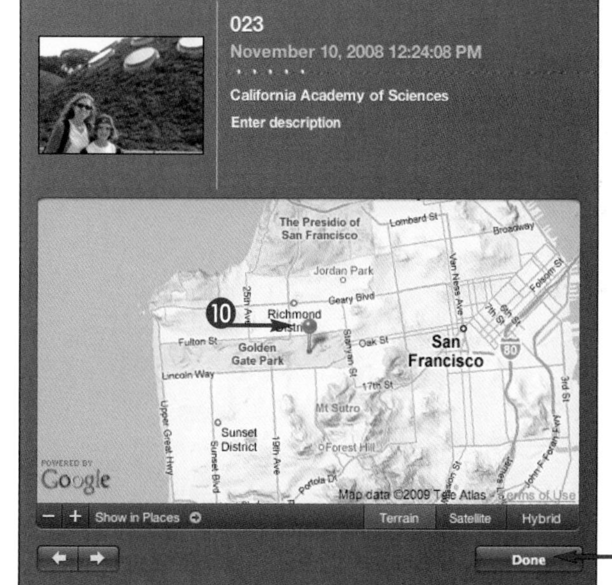

Can iPhoto automatically assign photos to a location?

If your camera has global positioning system (GPS) capability and you have place lookups turned on in iPhoto, your imported photos can be automatically added to the map. Newer versions of the iPhone include GPS capability. To view GPS data for a photo, do the following:

1. Click a photo.
2. Click **Photos** and then click **Show Extended Photo Info**.

- The Extended Photo Info pane appears, showing the GPS data.

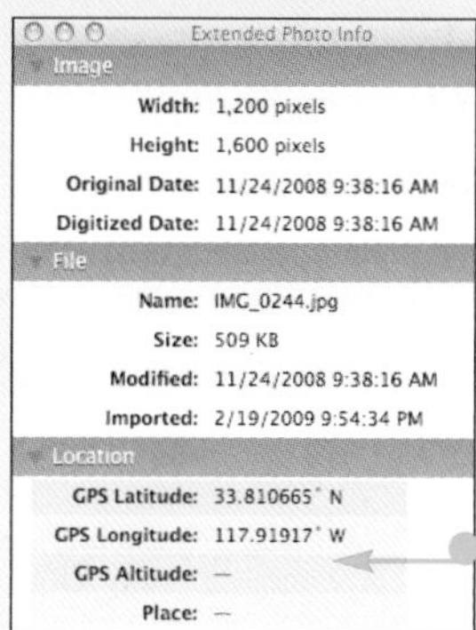

View Photo Places

You can view a map that shows the places where you have located photos. You can click a place on the map to see the photos that were taken there. You can also browse locations by geographic name.

View Photo Places

USE A MAP

1. Click **Places**.

   iPhoto displays a map showing pins where you have located photos.

- You can click and drag the slider to zoom the map.
- You can click **Show Photos** to show all the photos from the locations shown on the map.

2. Position the cursor over a pin.

   A location label appears.

3. Click the arrow (⊙).

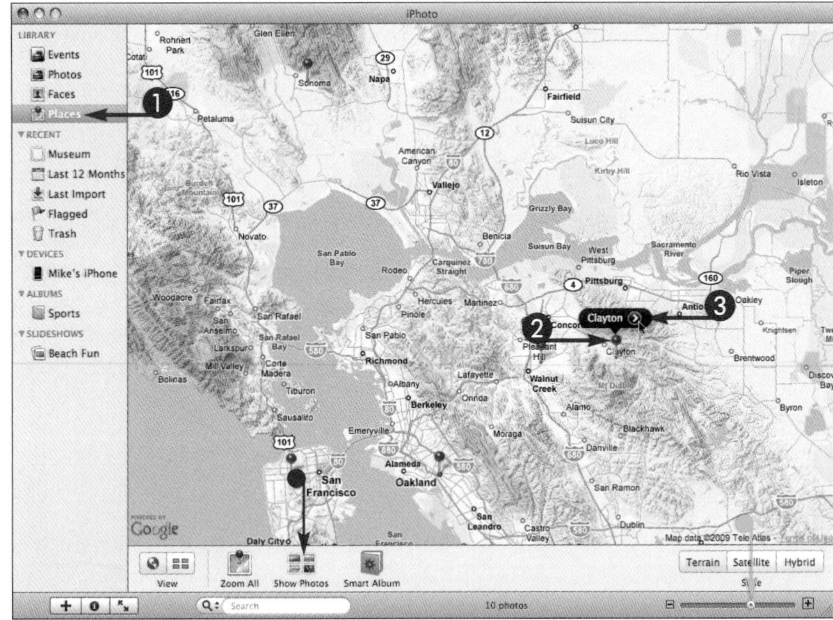

   iPhoto displays photos from the location.

4. Click **Map** to return to the map view.

BROWSE LOCATIONS

1. Click to display your locations in list view.

- iPhoto displays your locations hierarchically with all photos shown.

2. Click a location in a list.

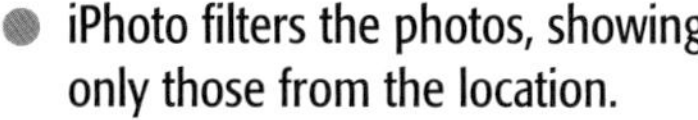

- iPhoto filters the photos, showing only those from the location.

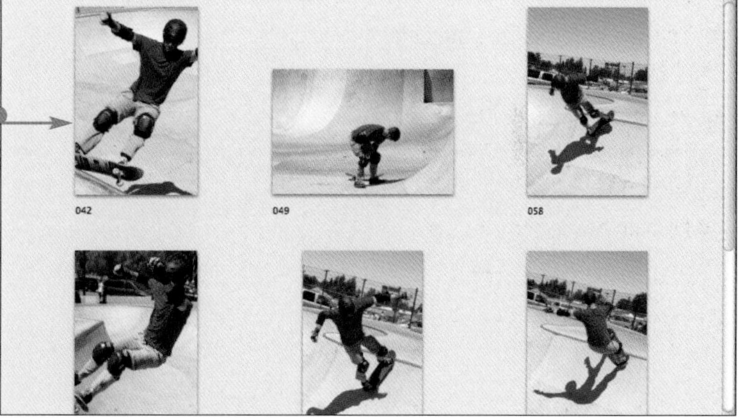

TIP

What are the style options in the lower-right corner of the map view?

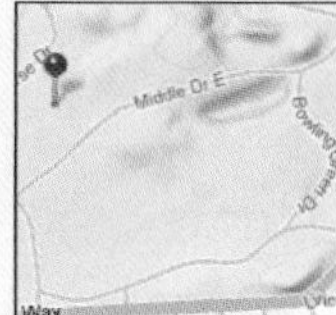

Terrain displays a graphical map.

Satellite displays satellite photos.

Hybrid is a combination of satellite photos and graphics.

Create an Album

You can organize photos into subject-specific albums. Creating an album makes it easy to turn those photos into slideshows, photo books, Web galleries, and other projects.

For more about creating projects in iPhoto, see Chapter 6.

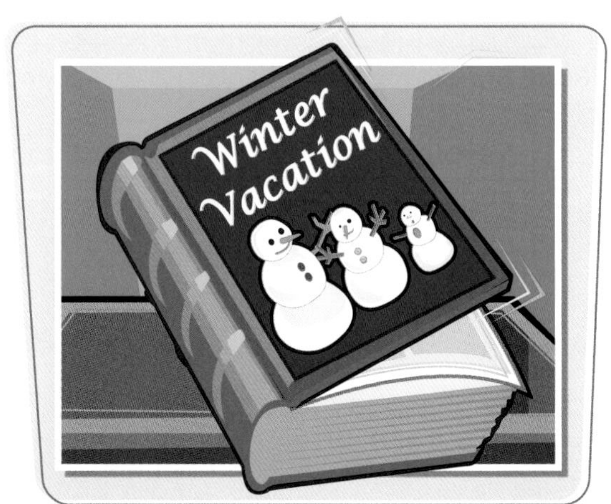

Create an Album

1. ⌘-click to select photos to add to the album.
2. Click the **Create** button (+).

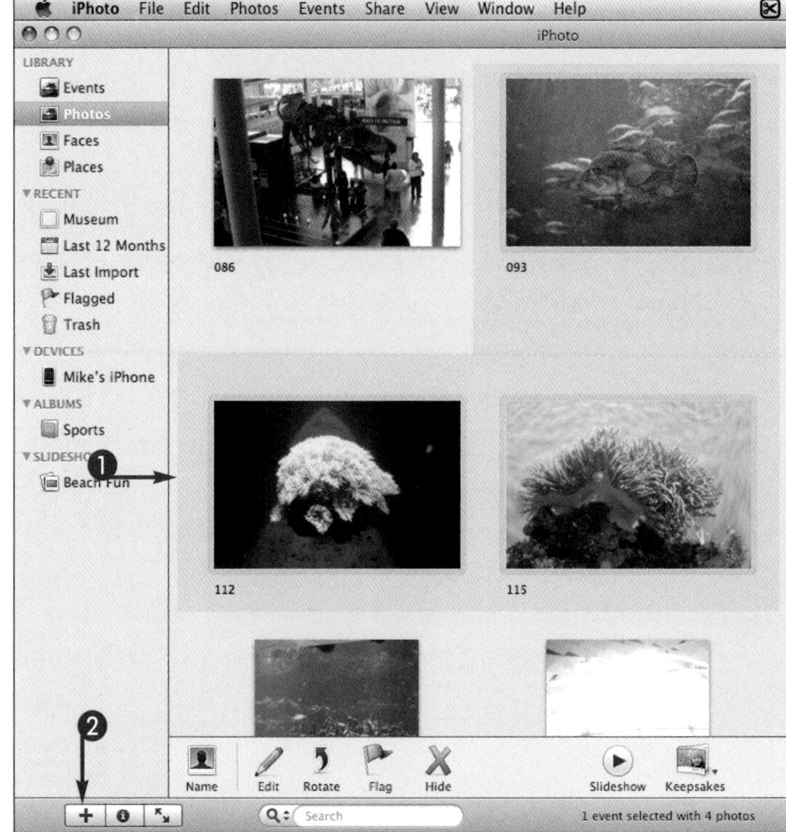

3. Make sure Album is selected.

- You can click to create an empty album (☑ changes to ☐).

4. Type a name for the album.
5. Click **Create**.

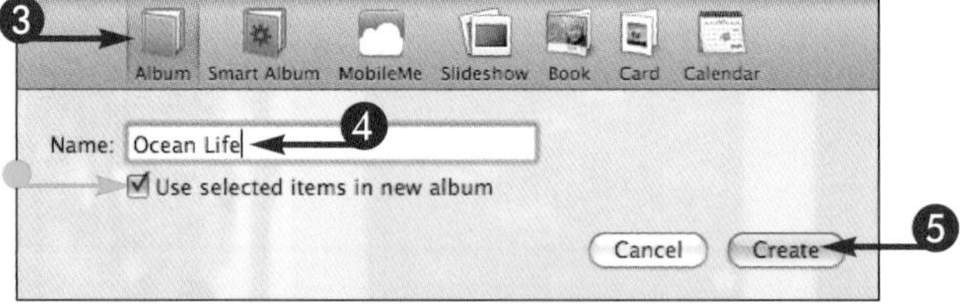

iPhoto creates the album and displays its contents.

- The album name is displayed in the source list.

6 Click **Photos**.

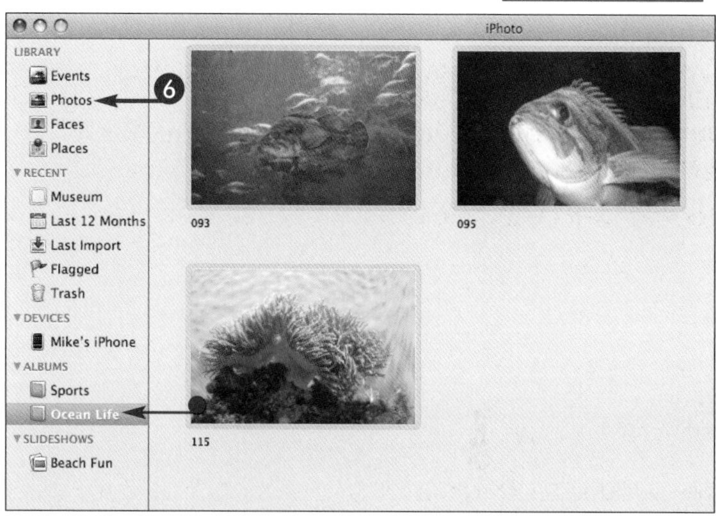

7 Click and drag a photo to the album.

iPhoto adds the photo to the album.

How are albums different from events?

A photo in your library can be associated with multiple albums but only one event. For example, a photo might be associated with a "December 25, 2008" event but also "Christmas," "Winter Vacation," and "Family" albums.

How can I quickly create an album?

You can ⌘-click to select a group of photos in your library and then click and drag the photos to the source list. You can also select a group of photos and click **File** and then **New Album from Selection**. iPhoto creates an untitled album for the photos.

Create a Smart Album

You can create a smart album by setting one or more criteria based on date, keywords, rating, and other photo characteristics. Photos that meet the criteria are automatically added to the album and iPhoto updates the album as the library changes.

Create a Smart Album

1. Click +.
2. In the dialog that appears, click **Smart Album**.
3. Type a name for the smart album.

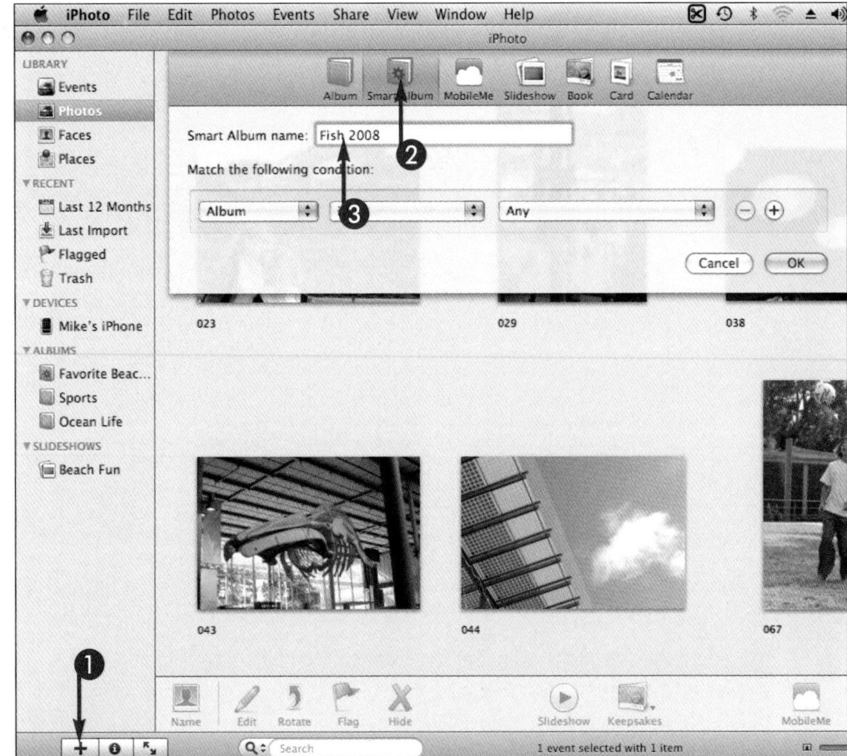

4. Click here to specify the first type of criteria.
5. Set the conditions.

   In this example, the term "fish" must be present in any of the text fields associated with the photo.

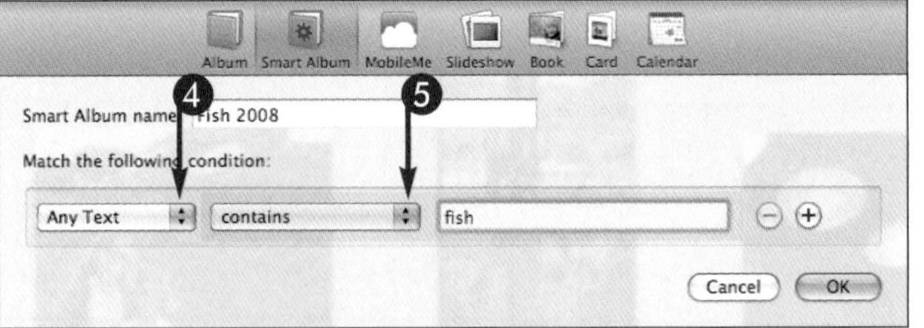

6 Click ⊕.

A second criterion is added.

7 Set the conditions.

In this example, the date must be in the year 2008.

You can click ⊕ to set additional criteria.

8 Click **OK**.

iPhoto creates the smart album.

- The album name is displayed in the source list.
- Photos that meet the album criteria are displayed.

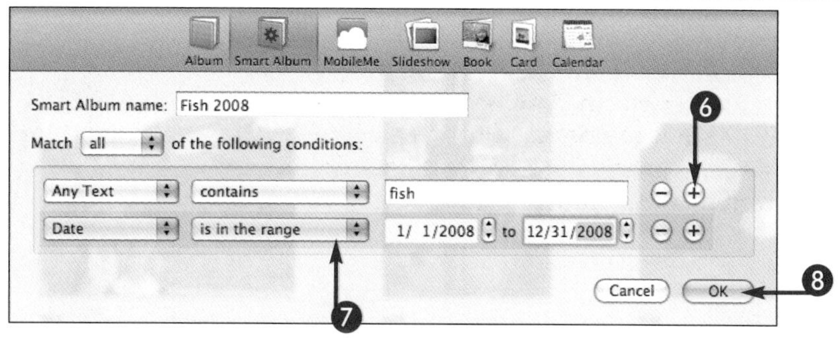

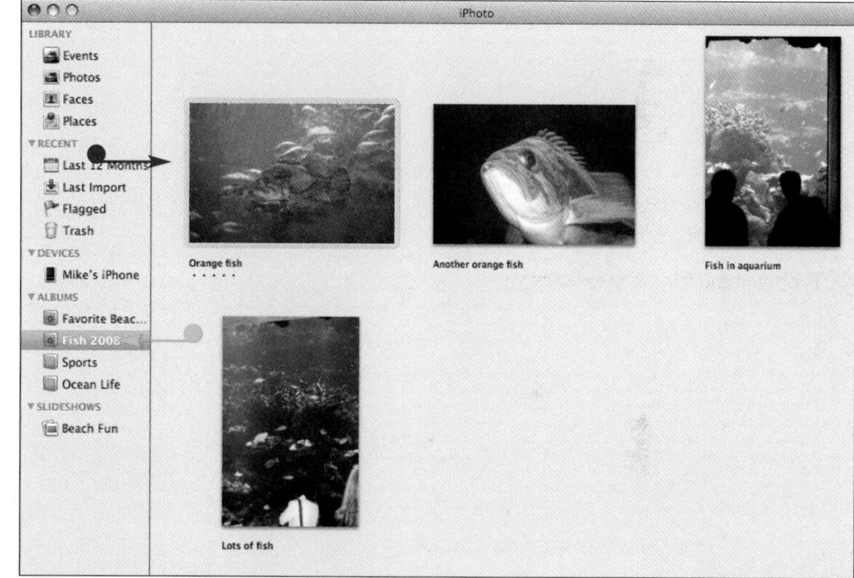

TIP

How can I create a smart album based on places?

You can use the map to define geographic criteria for your smart album.

1 Click **Places.**

2 Zoom the map to display the locations that you want to include in your smart album.

- Alternatively, to include a single location, you can select a pin by clicking it. The pin turns blue.

3 Click **Smart Album.**

iPhoto creates a new location-based smart album.

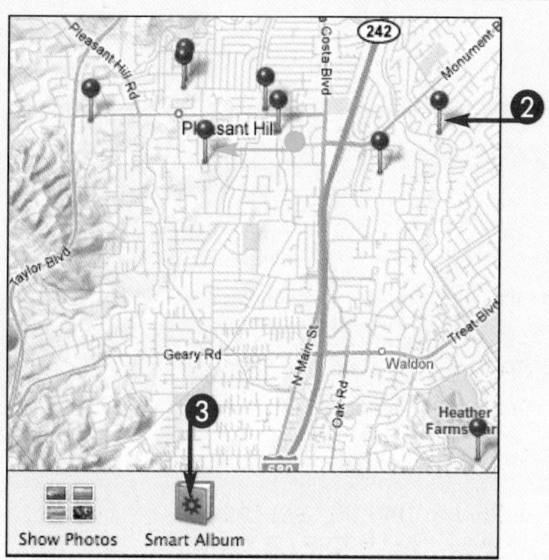

Add a Keyword to a Photo

You can add a keyword to a photo to associate the photo with a subject. You might add keywords that describe objects in the photo or the event at which the photo was taken.

See "Find Photos" to learn how to use keywords to find specific photos.

Add a Keyword to a Photo

USE THE KEYWORD DIALOG

❶ ⌘-click to select the photos to label.

❷ Click **Window**.

❸ Click **Show Keywords**.

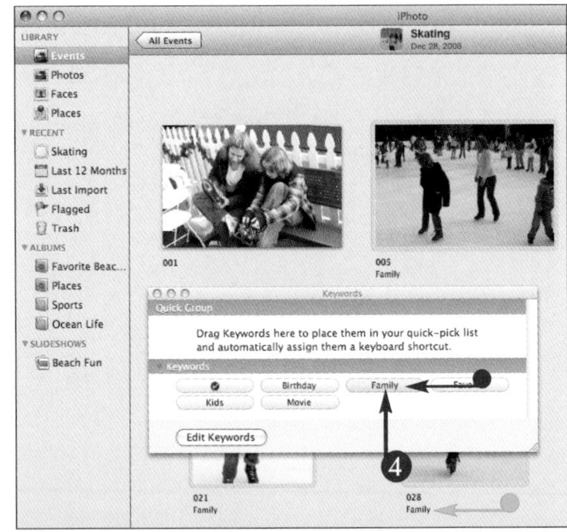

The Keywords dialog opens.

❹ Click a keyword.

- iPhoto adds the keywords to the photo.
- You can click the keyword again to remove it from the photos.

TYPE KEYWORDS

1. Position the cursor over the photo to label.
2. Click **add keywords** below the photo.

   If a photo already has keywords listed below it, click the keywords.

An edit box appears.

3. Type a keyword.
4. Press Enter.

   iPhoto adds the keyword to the photo.

   iPhoto also adds the keyword to the list in the Keywords dialog.

5. Press Enter again to close the edit box.

***Note:** To use keywords to filter photos, see "Find Photos."*

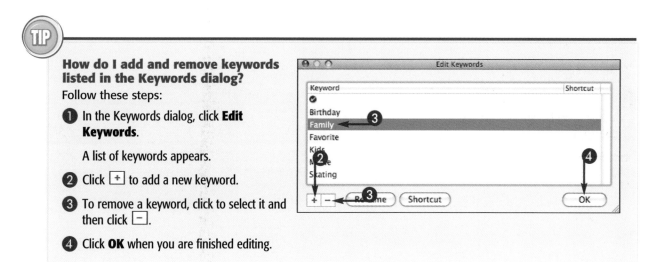

TIP

How do I add and remove keywords listed in the Keywords dialog?

Follow these steps:

1. In the Keywords dialog, click **Edit Keywords**.

   A list of keywords appears.

2. Click + to add a new keyword.
3. To remove a keyword, click to select it and then click −.
4. Click **OK** when you are finished editing.

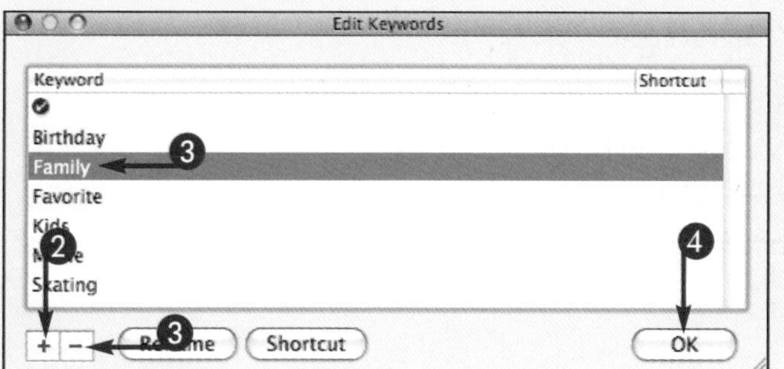

Rate a Photo

You can rate a photo to label the photo with one to five stars. This can help you pinpoint which photos in your library are worth adding to slideshows, Web galleries, and other projects.

See "Find Photos" to learn how to use ratings to find specific photos.

Rate a Photo

1. Click **View**.
2. Click **Rating**.

iPhoto displays ratings for photos that have them.

3. Click to select the photo to rate.
4. Click **Photos**.
5. Click **My Rating**.
6. Click a rating.

- iPhoto assigns the rating to the photo.

7 You can also assign or edit a rating by clicking a star or dot.

- iPhoto assigns the rating to the photo.

TIP

How do I easily create an album made up of my five-star photos?

You can create a smart album with a five-star rating as the album's criterion.

1 Create a new smart album.

Note: *For details, see "Create a Smart Album."*

2 Type a name for the album.

3 Select **My Rating**.

4 Select **is**.

5 Select five stars.

6 Click **OK** (not shown).

iPhoto creates the album and automatically adds photos that have five-star ratings.

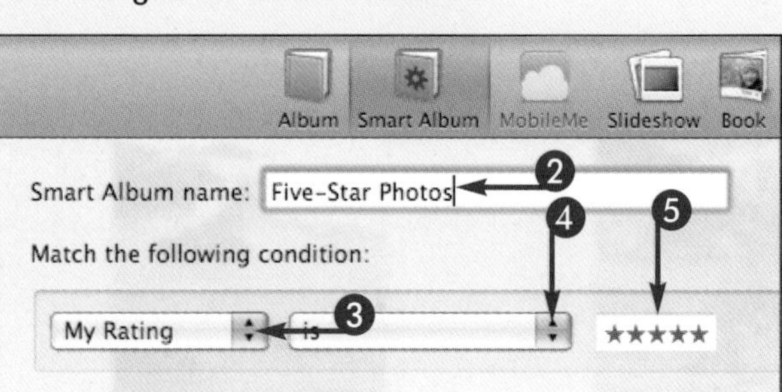

Flag a Photo

You can flag a photo to mark it for editing or adding to an event or album. iPhoto adds a flag icon to flagged photos.

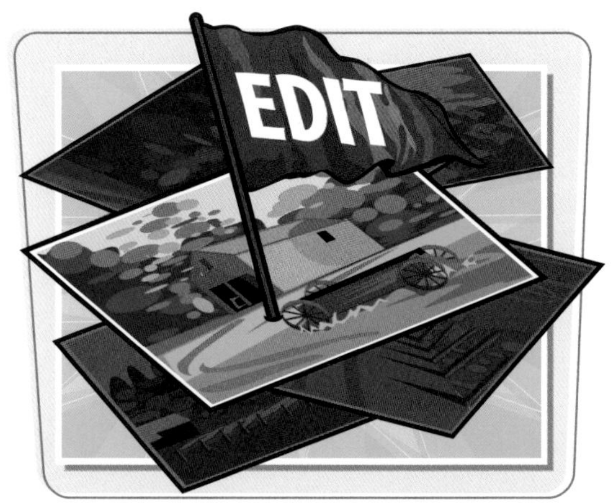

Flag a Photo

❶ Click to select the photo to flag.

❷ Click **Flag**.

iPhoto flags the photo.

- An icon is added to the photo thumbnail.
- You can click **Unflag** to remove the flag.

❸ Click **Flagged**.

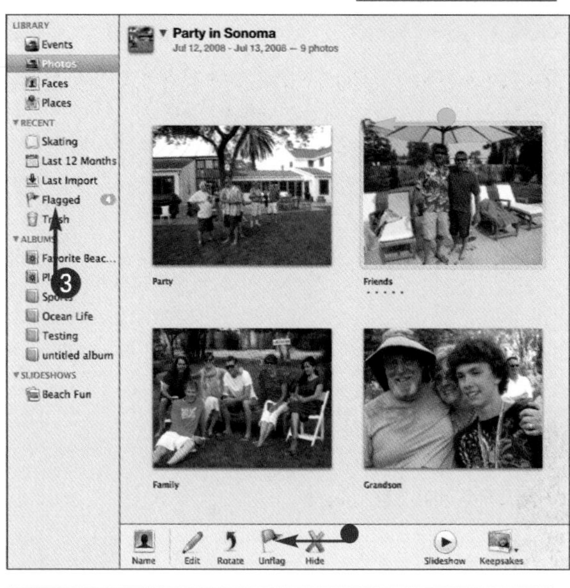

iPhoto displays your flagged photos.

TIP

How do I create an event out of flagged photos?

Follow these steps:

❶ Flag the photos you want to add to the event.

❷ Click **Events**.

❸ Click **Create Event From Flagged Photos**.

iPhoto creates a new event and adds the photos to it.

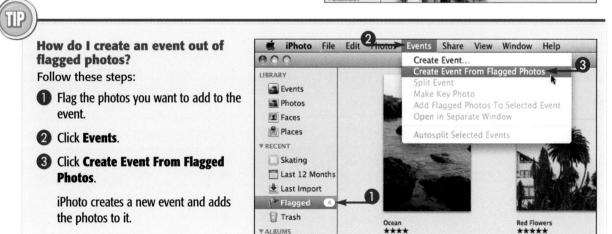

Find Photos

As the number of photos in your library grows, being able to find photos quickly can become challenging. The search tool in iPhoto allows you to search for photos by text, date, rating, and more.

Find Photos

SEARCH BY TEXT

1. Type one or more terms into the search box.

   iPhoto searches for photos as you type.

- iPhoto displays the photos whose title or description contains the search terms.

2. Click here to open the search menu.

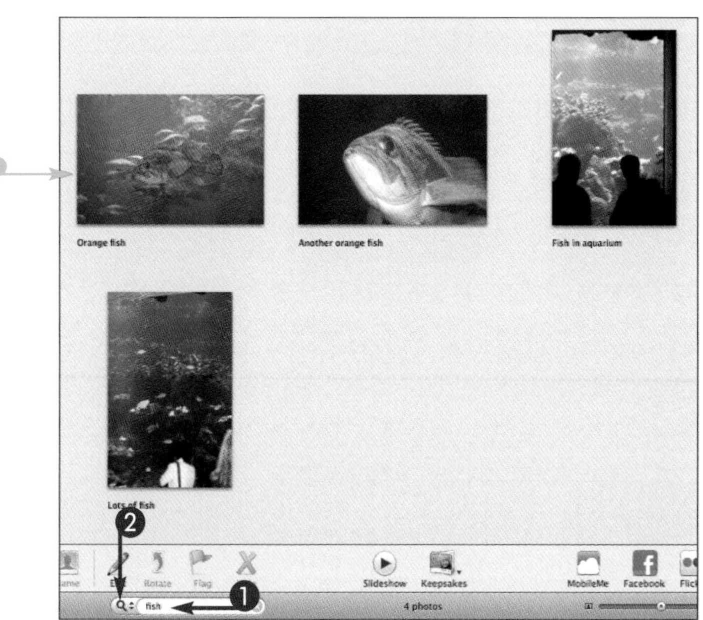

SEARCH BY KEYWORD

3. Click **Keyword**.

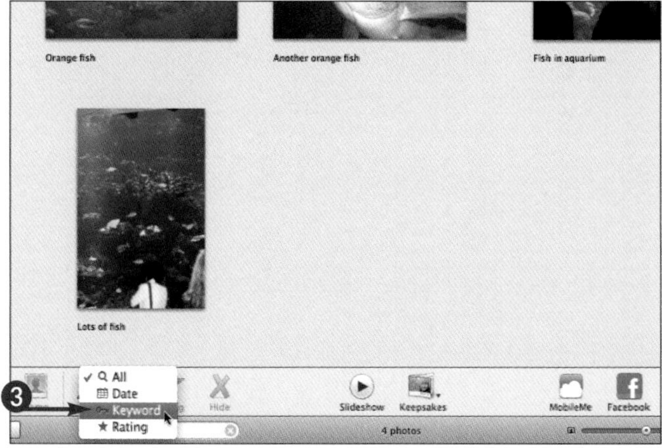

iPhoto displays a keyword panel.

4 Click one or more keywords.

- iPhoto displays photos with the keywords.

Note: *To add keywords to a photo, see "Add a Keyword to a Photo."*

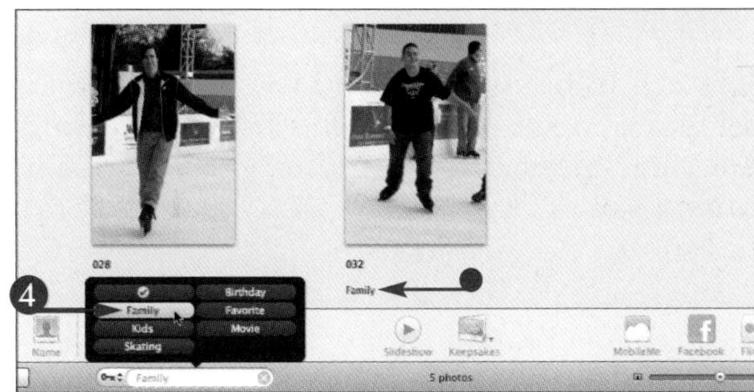

5 Click [clear button] to clear your search.

- iPhoto displays all the photos in the library.
- You can also click here and select **Date** to search by a time range.

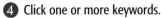

TIP

How do I search by rating?

Follow these steps:

1 Click here and select **Rating**.

iPhoto displays five dots.

2 Click a dot.

- The corresponding dots change to stars.

iPhoto searches for photos with that star rating.

- The matching photos are displayed.

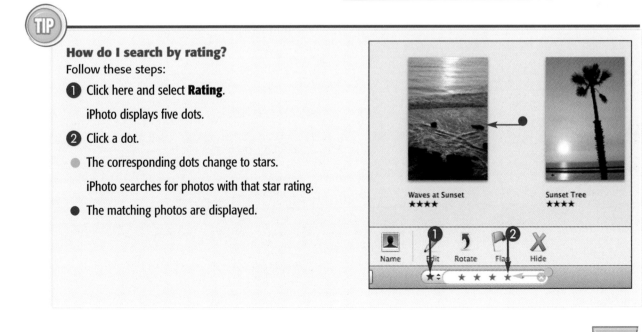

Hide and Unhide Photos

You can hide a photo so that it does not appear in your photo library. This is helpful if you do not want to use the photo but are unsure about deleting it.

Hide and Unhide Photos

HIDE A PHOTO

1. Click to select a photo to hide.
2. Click **Hide**.

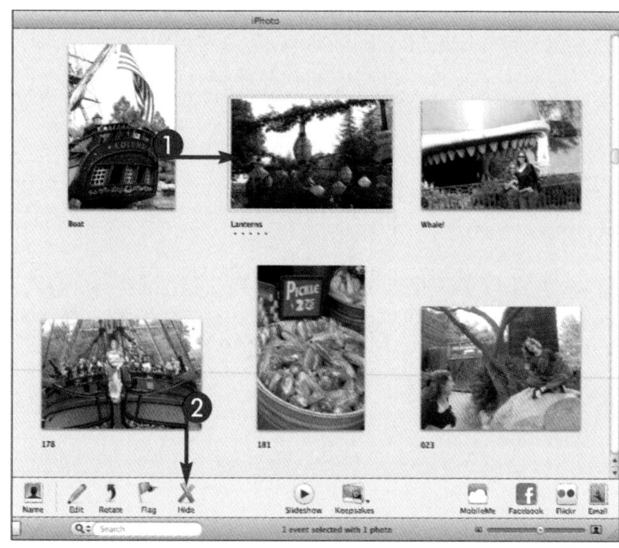

iPhoto hides the photo.

3. Click the **Show** text.

iPhoto displays the hidden photos.

- Hidden photos are marked with an icon.

UNHIDE A PHOTO

4. Click to select the hidden photo.
5. Click **Unhide**.

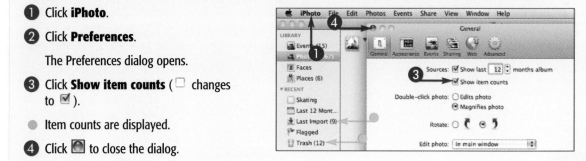

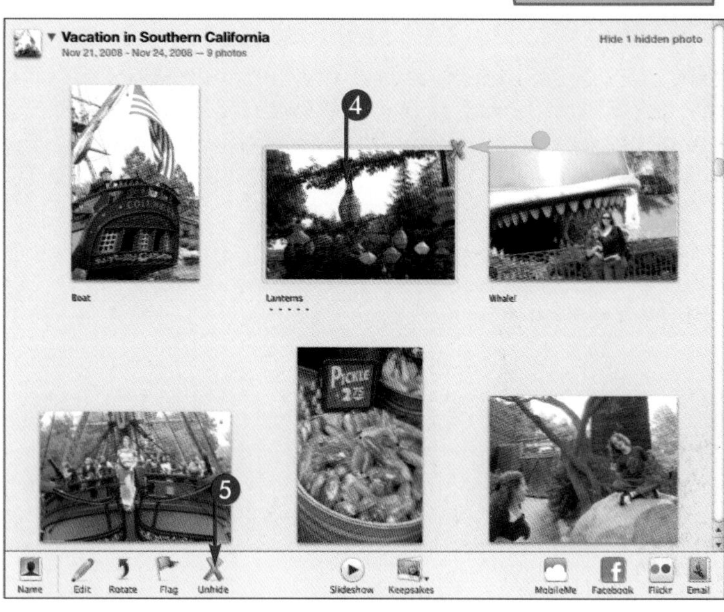

iPhoto unhides the photo.

How do I display photo counts in the source list?

You can make iPhoto display counts next to the items in the source list in the preferences. This helps you keep track of where the most photos are organized in your library, even if the photos are hidden.

1. Click **iPhoto**.
2. Click **Preferences**.

   The Preferences dialog opens.

3. Click **Show item counts** (☐ changes to ☑).

- Item counts are displayed.

4. Click to close the dialog.

Delete a Photo

You can delete a photo when you are sure you do not need it. Deleting is done in two steps. First the photo is moved to the iPhoto trash, where it can be recovered. Then the trash is emptied, which removes the photo from the library.

If you originally imported a photo from another location on your computer, deleting the photo from iPhoto does not delete the photo from its other location.

Delete a Photo

MOVE A PHOTO TO THE TRASH

1. Click to select the photo to delete.
2. Press Delete.

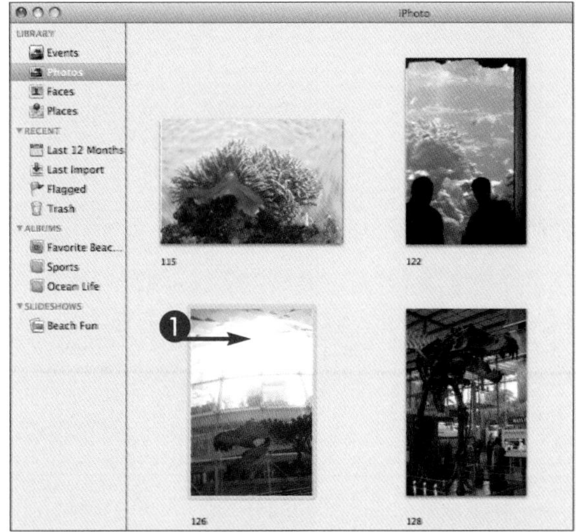

iPhoto moves the photo to the trash.

3. Click **Trash** to view photos in the trash.

- To recover a photo, select it, click **Photos**, and then click **Restore to Photo Library**.

EMPTY THE TRASH

4. Click **iPhoto**.
5. Click **Empty iPhoto Trash**.

iPhoto prompts you to confirm the deletion.

6. Click **OK** to delete the photos in the trash.

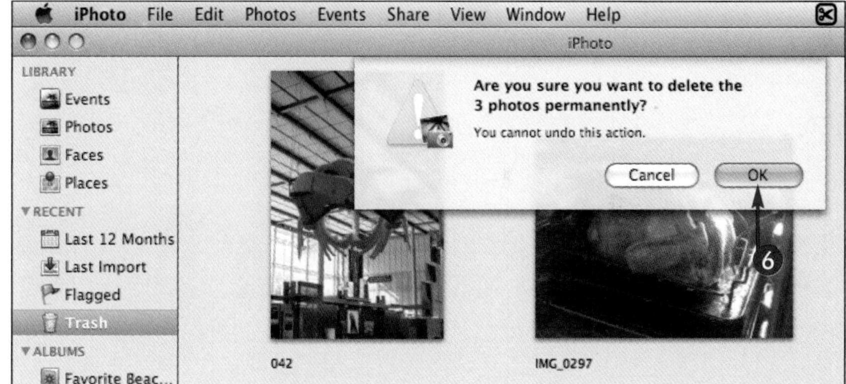

TIPS

How do I delete an album, book, calendar, card, or slideshow?

You can delete albums and keepsake projects listed in the source list by selecting them and then pressing Delete. iPhoto displays a dialog letting you confirm the deletion. Once these items are deleted they cannot be retrieved.

How do I delete an event?

Click **Events** to display the event thumbnails and then select an event. Select **Photos** and then **Move to Trash**. iPhoto deletes the event and moves the photos to the trash.

Use the Edit View

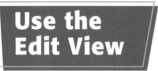

Edit view allows you to apply various commands to change the orientation, lighting, and coloring of your photos. You can crop and rotate photos, improve photos that are over- or underexposed, and brighten the colors in photos that look washed out.

Use the Edit View

1. Click a photo thumbnail.
2. Click **Edit**.

iPhoto opens the edit view.

- Click a thumbnail to edit other photos in your library. Which thumbnails appear depend on the source list selection when you entered edit view.
- You can click ↘ to enter the edit view in full screen.

3. Click and drag the slider to zoom in or out on the photo.

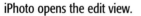

iPhoto zooms the photo and the Navigation window appears.

- You can click and drag to view a different part of the photo.

4. Click ⊠ to close the window.
5. Click an edit command.

iPhoto applies the command.

In this example, the photo is rotated.

***Note:** To undo the command, click **Edit** and then **Undo**.*

6. Click **Done** to exit edit view.

How do I undo all the commands that I have applied in the edit view?

You can revert your photo to its state when it first entered the edit view.

1. Click **Photos**.
2. Click **Revert to Previous**.

iPhoto reverts the photo.

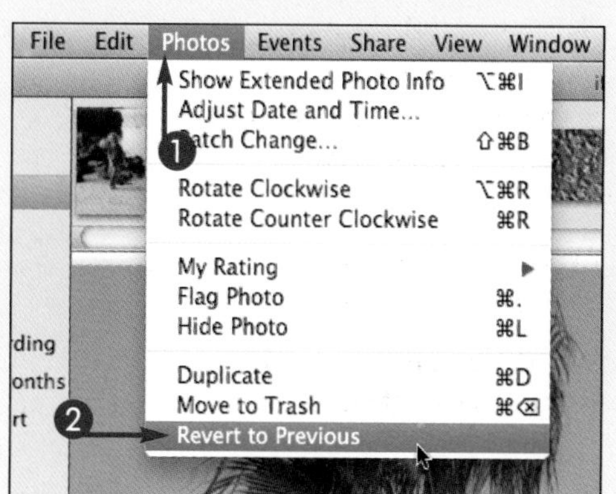

Rotate a Photo

You can rotate a photo to change its orientation. A landscape-oriented photo can be changed to portrait, and vice versa.

A landscape photo has the longest side oriented horizontally, whereas a portrait photo has the longest side oriented vertically.

Rotate a Photo

USING THE ROTATE BUTTON

1. Click a photo thumbnail.
2. Click **Rotate**.

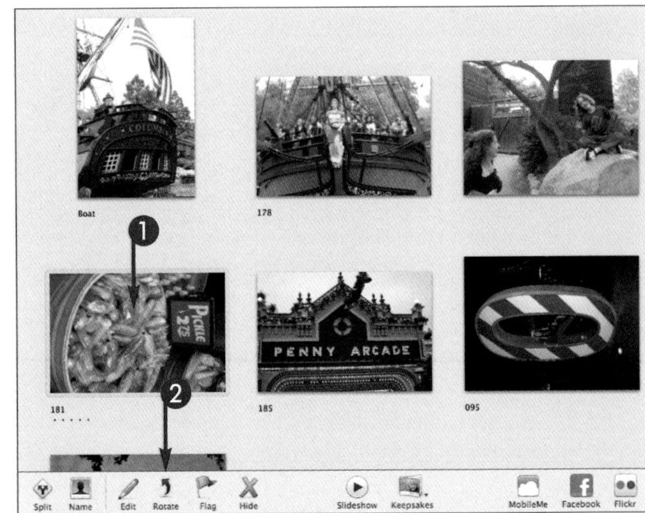

- iPhoto rotates the photo 90 degrees counterclockwise.

  You can click **Rotate** again to turn the photo another 90 degrees.

- To undo the rotation, click **Edit** and then **Undo**.

***Note:** You can also rotate a photo using the same button in the edit view. See "Use the Edit View" for details.*

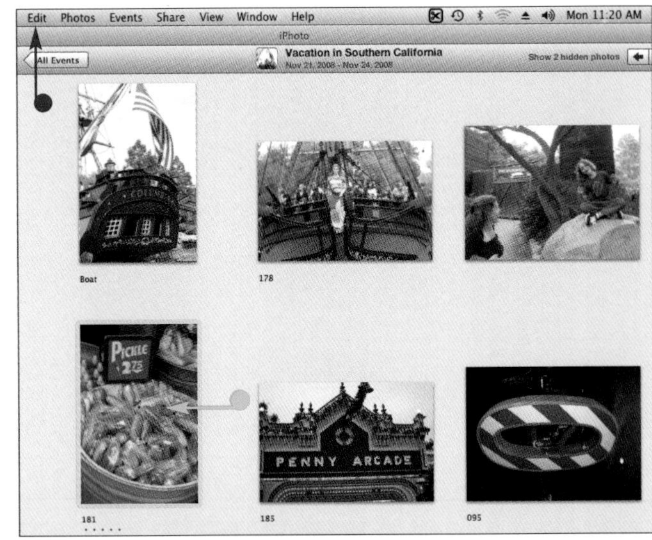

USING THE MENU COMMAND

1. Click a photo thumbnail.
2. Click **Photos**.
3. Click **Rotate Clockwise** or **Rotate Counter Clockwise**.

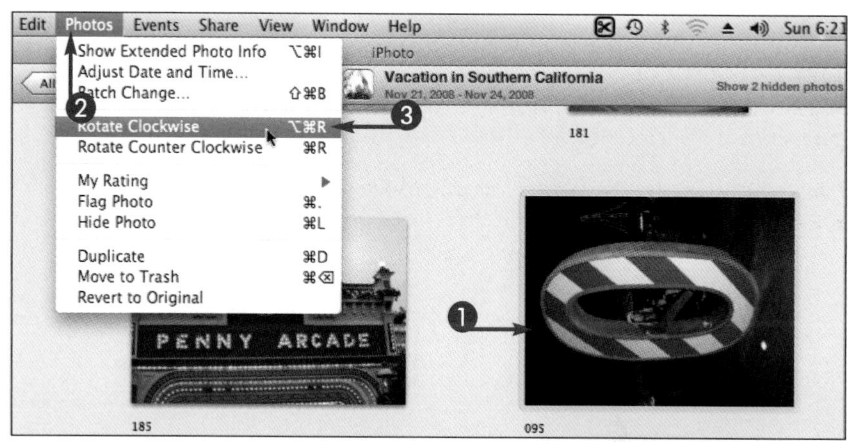

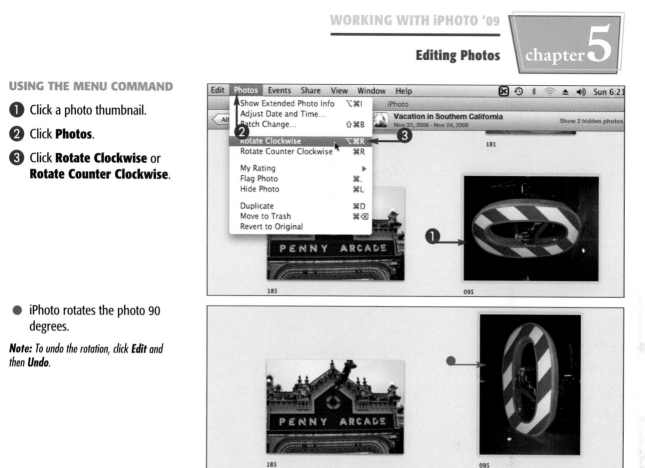

- iPhoto rotates the photo 90 degrees.

*Note: To undo the rotation, click **Edit** and then **Undo**.*

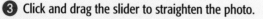

How do I straighten a photo?

You can fix a tilted photo by rotating it up to 10 degrees to either side. This can be helpful for fixing scanned content.

1. Enter the edit view. See "Use the Edit View" for details.
2. Click **Straighten**.

   The straighten guidelines appear.

3. Click and drag the slider to straighten the photo.
4. Click **Done** to exit the edit view.

Crop a Photo

You can crop a photo to remove unneeded space on the sides. By cropping, you can remove unwanted background elements or reposition the subject in the photo.

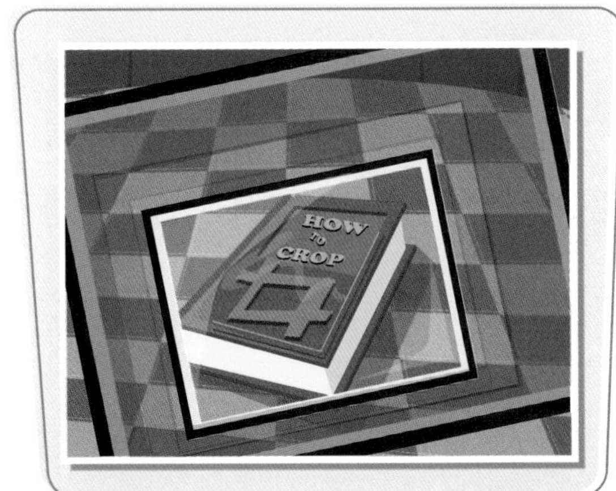

Crop a Photo

1. Select a photo and open the edit view.

Note: See "Use the Edit View" for details.

2. Click **Crop**.

   iPhoto displays the Crop tool.

3. Click and drag a side to adjust the vertical or horizontal dimension.

4. Click and drag a corner to adjust both dimensions at once.

   iPhoto adjusts the crop box.

5. Click **Apply** to perform the crop.

- You can click **Cancel** to close the tool without cropping.

iPhoto crops the photo.

6 Click **Done** to exit the edit view.

How do I constrain my cropping to fixed dimensions?

You can select the Constrain option to crop your photo to a fixed height and width ratio. You might want to do this if you are printing the photo to fit a certain-sized frame.

1. In the Crop tool, click **Constrain** (☐ changes to ☑).
2. Click the **Constrain** and select the dimensions.
3. Repeat the steps in this task to crop your photo.

- iPhoto adjusts the dimensions of the Crop tool and keeps the height and width the same relative sizes if you adjust either of them.

Enhance a Photo

You can quickly improve a photo that is too dark or too light with the Enhance tool. You click the tool and iPhoto makes automatic adjustments to the photo.

To make more controlled adjustments, see "Adjust Lighting in a Photo" or "Adjust Colors in a Photo."

Enhance a Photo

1. Select a photo and open the edit view.

***Note:** See "Use the Edit View" for details.*

2. Click **Enhance**.

iPhoto applies the enhancement.

- To undo the enhancement, click **Edit** and then **Undo**.

3. Click **Done** to exit edit view.

Remove Red Eye

You can use the red eye tool to remove the red eye color that a camera flash can cause. Red eye is a common problem in snapshots taken in dim light, where the light from the camera flash reflects off the back of the subject's eyes.

Remove Red Eye

1. Select a photo and open the edit view.

Note: *See "Use the Edit View" for details.*

2. Click **Red-Eye**.

   The red eye tool appears.

- You can click **Auto** to apply the tool automatically throughout the photo.

3. Click and drag the slider to set the tool to the same size as the subject's eyes.
4. Click an eye.

- iPhoto darkens the eye and removes the red color.

5. Click ⊗ to close the tool.
6. Click **Done** to exit edit view.

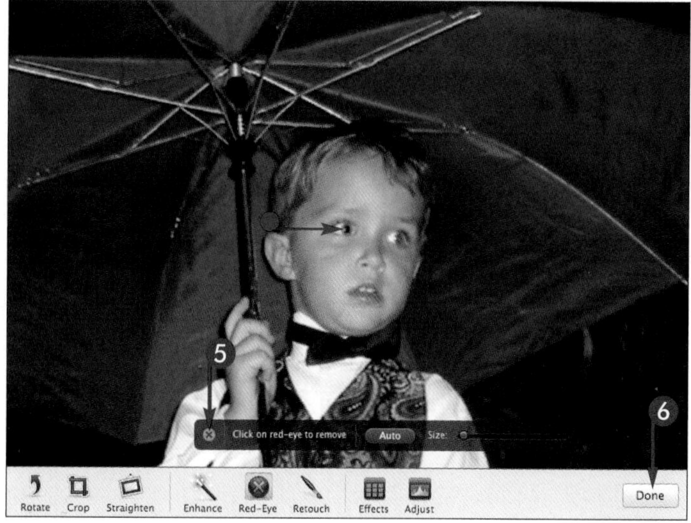

Retouch a Photo

You can clean up flaws or erase elements in your photo with the Retouch tool. Clicking an object in a photo erases the object by covering it with the surrounding color and texture. The tool works best when an object is on an even-textured background.

Retouch a Photo

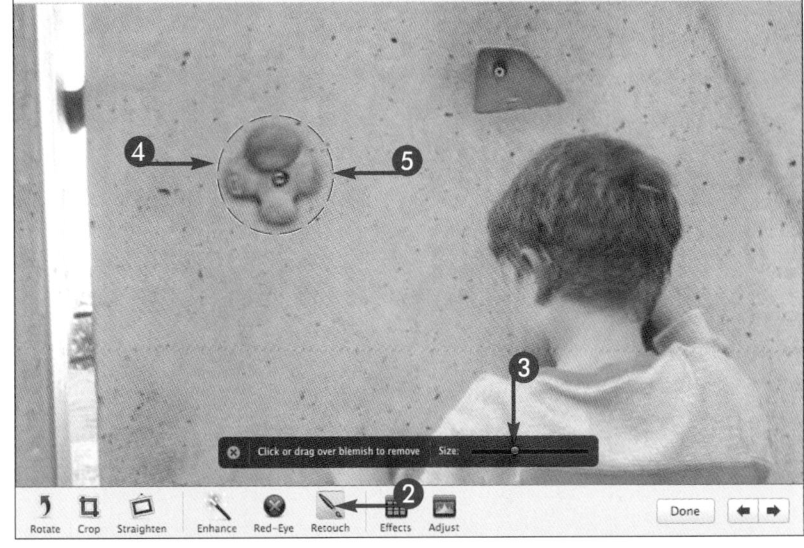

1. Select a photo and open the edit view.

Note: *See "Use the Edit View" for details.*

2. Click **Retouch**.

   The Retouch tool appears.

3. Click and drag the slider to set the tool to the same size as the object you want to retouch.
4. Center the tool over the object.
5. Click the object.

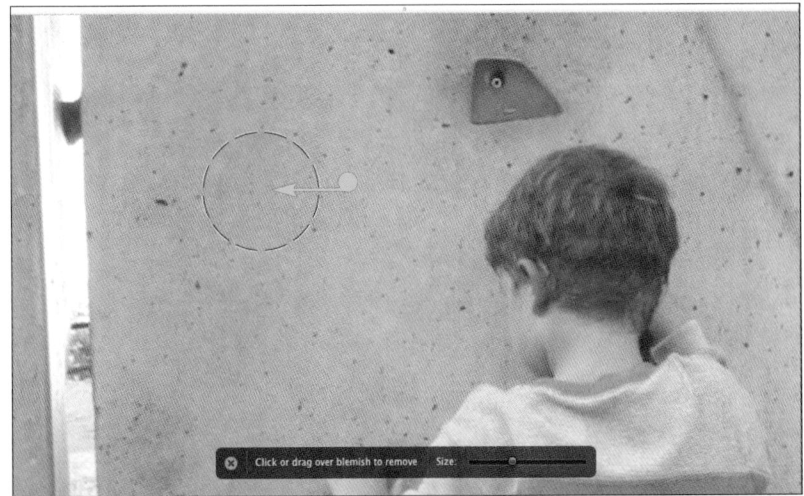

- iPhoto removes the object by covering it with the surrounding color and texture.

6. Press and hold Shift.

- iPhoto displays the previous version of the photo with the object visible again.

  You can press and release Shift to compare the before and after versions.

7. Click ⊠ to close the tool.
8. Click **Done** to exit edit view.

TIP

How do I retouch wrinkles on a face?

You can set your Retouch tool to a small size and then click and drag along the wrinkles to remove them.

1. Open the Retouch tool.
2. Click and drag the slider to the left to shrink the tool size.
3. Click and drag along a wrinkle.

   iPhoto retouches the wrinkle.

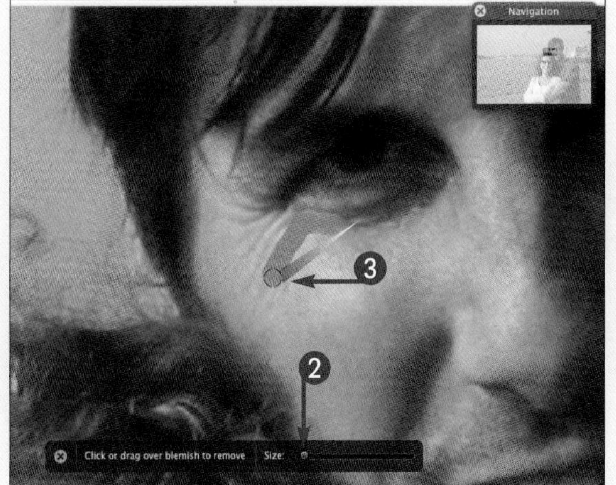

Apply Effects to a Photo

You can apply one of several effects to your photo to boost or fade color, change the photo to black and white, add a matte, and more. You can combine effects to get just the look you want.

Apply Effects to a Photo

1. Select a photo and open the edit view.

Note: See "Use the Edit View" for details.

2. Click **Effects**.

The Effects tool appears.

3. Click an effect.

iPhoto applies the effect.

4 Click another effect.

iPhoto applies the effect, combining it with the first.

- With effects such as Vignette you can click multiple times to increase the intensity. iPhoto increments the number overlaying the effect each time you click.
- You can click **Original** to remove the effects and start over.

5 Click ⊠ to close the tool.

6 Click **Done** to exit edit view.

TIP

How do I keep an unaffected copy of a photo?

You can duplicate the photo before you apply the effect to keep an original copy in your library.

1 Click **Photos**.

2 Click **Duplicate**.

- iPhoto creates a copy of the photo in your library.

Adjust Lighting in a Photo

You can use the Adjust tool in iPhoto to change the exposure and contrast of a photo. This can improve an overly light or dark photo. You can also fine-tune colors using the tool. See "Adjust Colors in a Photo" for details.

Adjust Lighting in a Photo

1. Select a photo and open the edit view.

Note: *See "Use the Edit View" for details.*

2. Click **Adjust**.

The Adjust tool appears.

- iPhoto displays a *histogram* that shows the distribution of the colors in the photo. Darker colors are on the left and light colors are on the right.

3. Click and drag the **Exposure** slider to adjust the overall lighting.

4. Click and drag the **Contrast** slider to the right or left to increase or decrease the contrast.

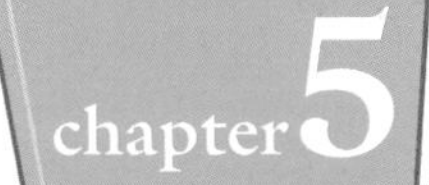

iPhoto adjusts the photo.

You can adjust dark and light tones in the photo more precisely with the Levels sliders.

5 Click and drag the left slider to boost the darker tones.

6 Click and drag the right slider to boost the lighter tones.

7 Click and drag the middle slider to adjust the midtones.

iPhoto adjusts the photo.

You can press and release Shift to compare the photo before and after the adjustments.

- You can click **Reset** to reset the tool.

8 Click [x] to close the Adjust tool.

9 Click **Done** to exit edit view.

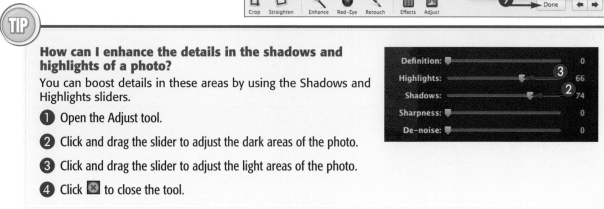

How can I enhance the details in the shadows and highlights of a photo?

You can boost details in these areas by using the Shadows and Highlights sliders.

1 Open the Adjust tool.

2 Click and drag the slider to adjust the dark areas of the photo.

3 Click and drag the slider to adjust the light areas of the photo.

4 Click [x] to close the tool.

Adjust Colors in a Photo

You can use the Adjust tool in iPhoto to boost or lessen the colors in a photo. This can enhance a photo that appears washed-out or remove color to convert a photo into black and white.

You can also adjust color using the Effects tool. See "Apply Effects to a Photo" for details.

Adjust Colors in a Photo

1. Select a photo and open the edit view.

Note: *See "Use the Edit View" for details.*

2. Click **Adjust**.

The Adjust tool appears.

3. Click and drag the **Saturation** slider to change the intensity of the colors.

iPhoto adjusts the photo.

4. Click and drag the **Temperature** slider to the left to make the colors in the photo cooler, by boosting the blue component, or to the right to make them warmer, by boosting the yellow component.
5. Click and drag the **Tint** slider to shift the colors in the photo.

iPhoto adjusts the photo.

You can press and release Shift to compare the photo before and after the adjustments.

- You can click **Reset** to reset the tool.

6. Click ⊗ to close the tool.
7. Click **Done** to exit edit view.

How do I convert a color photo to black and white?

You can convert a photo to black and white in the Adjust tool by moving the Saturation slider all the way to the left. You can also convert it using the B & W option in the Effects tool. For more about the Effects tool, see "Apply Effects to a Photo."

How can I correct an unwanted color cast in a photo?

You can use the eyedropper ( ) located in the Adjust tool to correct a color cast. Sometimes sunlight can cause a bluish cast, whereas incandescent light can cause a yellowish cast. Click the and then click a part of the photo that should be white or gray. iPhoto adjusts the colors to remove the cast. This is also called a *white point adjustment*.

Compare Multiple Photos

You can compare two or more photos by opening them simultaneously in the edit view. This allows you to easily pick the best photo out of several similar ones. You can also edit the photos side by side to match their lighting and coloring.

Compare Multiple Photos

OPEN MULTIPLE PHOTOS

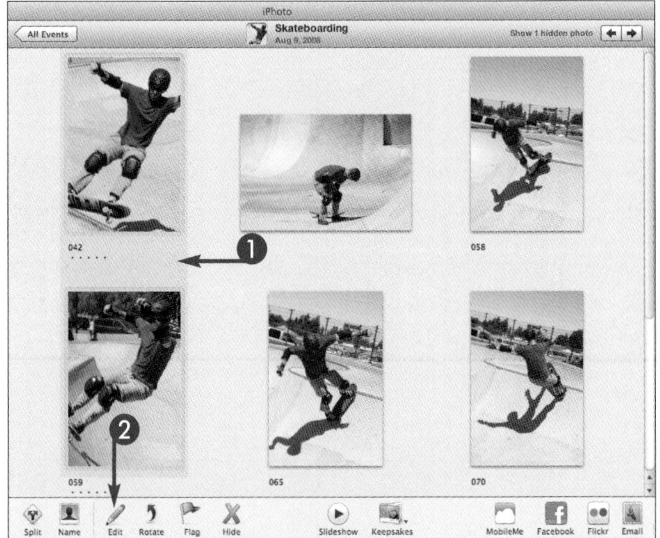

1. ⌘-click to select two or more photos in the photo browser.
2. Click **Edit**.

iPhoto opens the photos in the edit view together.

- Editing commands are applied to the outlined photo. You can click a different photo to move the outlining.
- Thumbnails for the open photos are highlighted.

3. ⌘-click another photo thumbnail.

iPhoto opens the photo with the others.

CLOSE A PHOTO

4 Click ⊗.

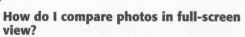

iPhoto closes the photo.

5 Click **Done** to close all the photos.

TIP

How do I compare photos in full-screen view?

You can open multiple photos side by side in full-screen view. Other elements of the iPhoto workspace are hidden. Follow these steps:

1 ⌘-click to select the photos to compare.

2 Click ⤢.

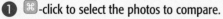

iPhoto opens the photos together in full-screen view

Print a Photo

You can print your iPhoto photos to create hard copies of your work. You can then add the photos to a physical photo album or scrapbook.

Print a Photo

1. ⌘-click to select what to print in the photo browser.
2. Click **File** and then **Print**.

   The print settings appear.
3. Click a theme.
4. Select your printer settings.
   - You can select a common print size or create a custom size here.
   - You can click **Print** to print the photo as shown.
5. Click **Customize**.

   iPhoto opens the customize settings.
6. Click here to change the theme, background, and border.

   These features enable you to add matting, colored backgrounds, and borders around photos.
7. Click **Layout** to adjust the orientation of the photo.

   This enables you to crop a photo in a portrait or landscape orientation.
8. Click a photo.

The adjustment tools appear.

9 Click and drag the slider to zoom the photo in or out.

10 Click [hand icon] and then click and drag to specify how a zoomed photo is cropped.

11 Some layouts include caption text. Click the text to edit it.

The caption text becomes editable.

12 Type a caption.

- You can click **Settings** to change the font style and size.

13 Click **Print**.

The photo prints.

TIPS

How do I print multiple copies of the same photo on a page?

In the print settings, choose a print size that displays multiple copies on a page such as **3 x 5** on a US Letter page. In the customize settings, click **Settings**. Then in the Photos Per Page menu, select **Multiple of the same photo per page**. Your photo is arranged as multiple copies on the page, which you can then print.

How do I adjust the color and lighting of a photo when printing?

In the customize settings, click a photo and then click **Adjust**. A tool appears enabling you to make color and lighting adjustments before you print. For more about adjusting color and lighting, see Chapter 5.

Share by E-mail

You can embed your images in an e-mail message and send them to others. This feature requires you to already have an e-mail program such as Mail configured on your Mac. See the documentation for your e-mail program for details.

Share by E-mail

1. Click a photo to share by e-mail.
2. Click **Share**.
3. Click **Email**.

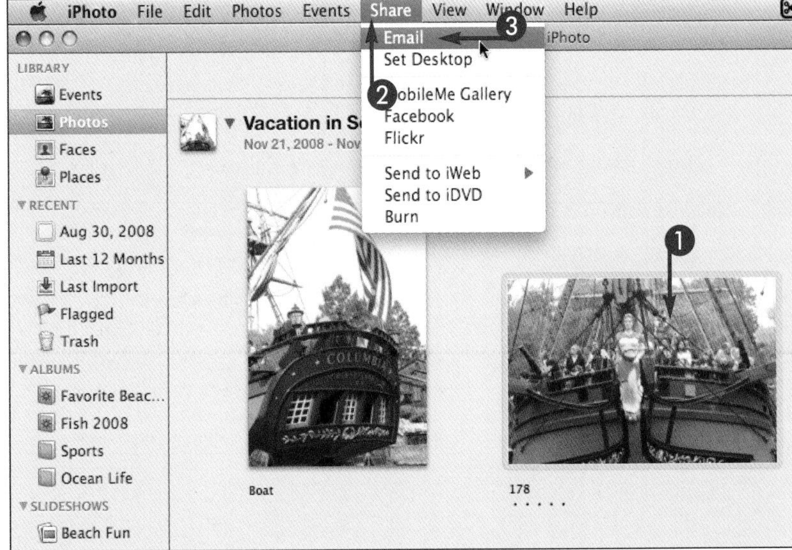

A Mail Photo dialog appears.

4. Select a photo size to send in the e-mail.

Note: Selecting a smaller size makes delivery faster.

5. Click to select photo information to include in the e-mail (☐ changes to ☑).
6. Click **Compose Message**.

An e-mail message window opens with the photo added.

7 Type the e-mail address of the recipient.

8 Type a subject.

9 Click **Send** ( ).

Note: *The commands may differ depending on the e-mail program.*

The e-mail message and photo are sent.

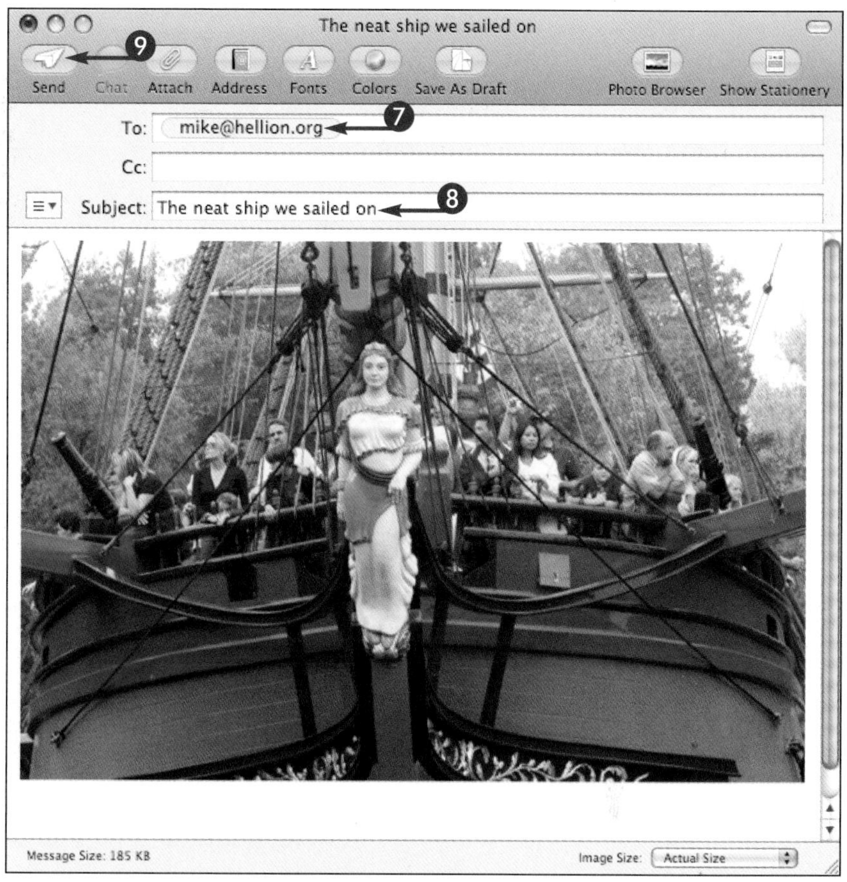

TIP

How do I select the e-mail program to use with iPhoto?

You can select the e-mail program in the iPhoto preferences.

1 Click **iPhoto.**

2 Click **Preferences.**

3 In the Preferences window, click **General.**

4 Click here and select an e-mail program.

5 Click to close and save your preferences.

Create a MobileMe Gallery

You can publish your photos to your MobileMe gallery. You can then send your friends and family a Web address where they can access the photos on MobileMe.

To use this feature, you must have a MobileMe account. See Chapter 2 for details.

Create a MobileMe Gallery

1. Sign in to your MobileMe account.
2. ⌘-click the photos to publish.
   - You can also click an album to publish.
3. Click **Share**.
4. Click **MobileMe Gallery**.

5. Select a privacy setting.
6. Click to select your album settings (☐ changes to ☑).
7. Click **Show Advanced**.

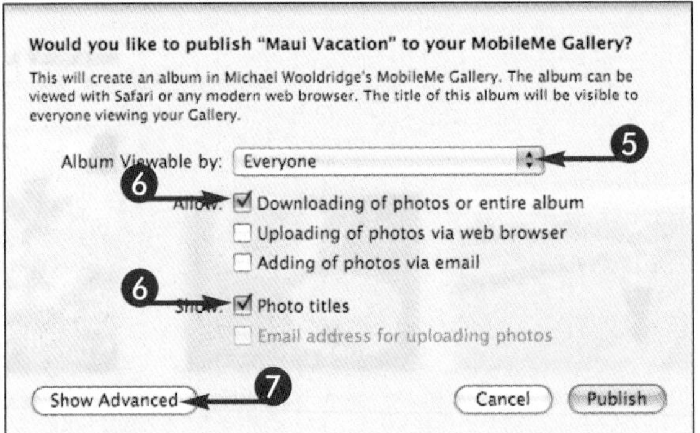

The advanced settings appear.

- You can hide the gallery on your main MobileMe gallery page (☐ changes to ☑).
- If you allow downloading, you can select a quality.

8 Click **Publish**.

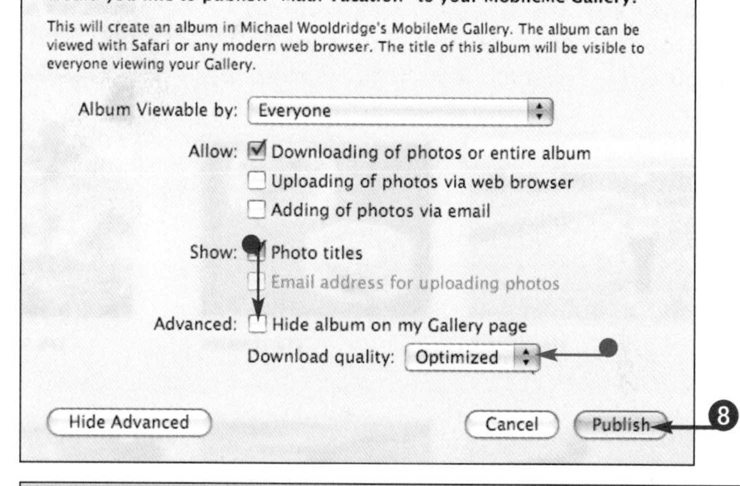

iPhoto uploads the photos.

9 Click the Web address of the gallery to view it online.

What features can viewers access in a MobileMe gallery?

When you create a MobileMe gallery in iPhoto, you can enable various features. Viewers can access the features by clicking links on the gallery Web page:

- Download gallery photos as a ZIP file.
- Subscribe to the RSS feed of the gallery to keep track of new photos.
- Upload photos to the gallery.
- Add to the gallery via e-mail.
- Send invitations to others about the gallery.

Share with Facebook

You can upload your iPhoto images directly to your account on Facebook, the popular social network site. People connected to you on Facebook can then view and comment on the photos.

To use this feature, you must have an active Internet connection and a Facebook account.

Share with Facebook

1. ⌘-click to select the photos to share.
2. Click **Facebook**.
   - The first time you share on Facebook, you are prompted to set up access.
3. Click **Set Up**.

A login screen appears.

4. Type the e-mail address associated with your Facebook account.

Note: *To set up a Facebook account, visit www.facebook.com.*

5. Type your password.
6. Click **Login**.

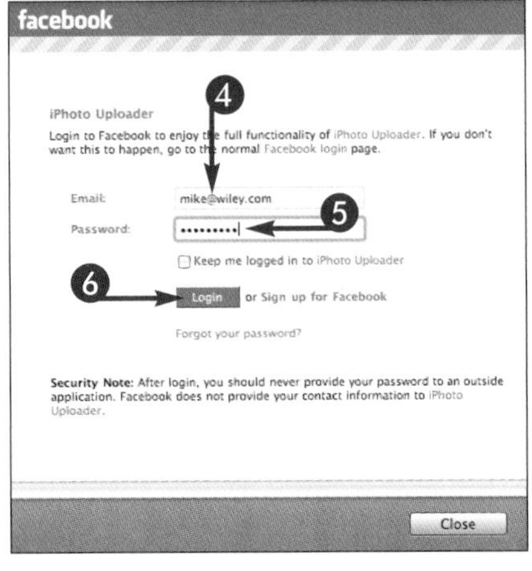

An Allow Access dialog appears.

For iPhoto and other applications to interact with Facebook, you must allow them access to your account information.

7. Click **Allow**.
8. In the confirmation dialog that follows, click **Close**.

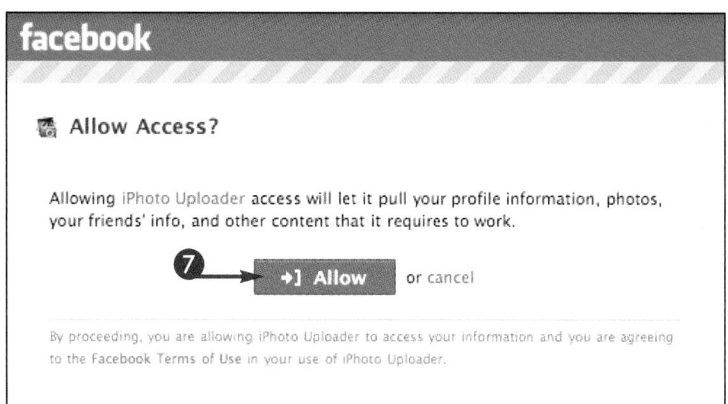

facebook
Beach Fun
Pumpkin Patch
http://www.facebook.com/album.php?aid=91510&id=538654008
Allow Access?
Allowing iPhoto Uploader access will let it pull your profile information, photos, your friends' info, and other content that it requires to work.
7
Allow
or cancel
By proceeding, you are allowing iPhoto Uploader to access your information and you are agreeing to the Facebook Terms of Use in your use of iPhoto Uploader.

9. Select who can see your photos.

   To access the photos, users also need to have Facebook accounts.

10. Click **Publish**.

    iPhoto uploads the photos to your Facebook account.

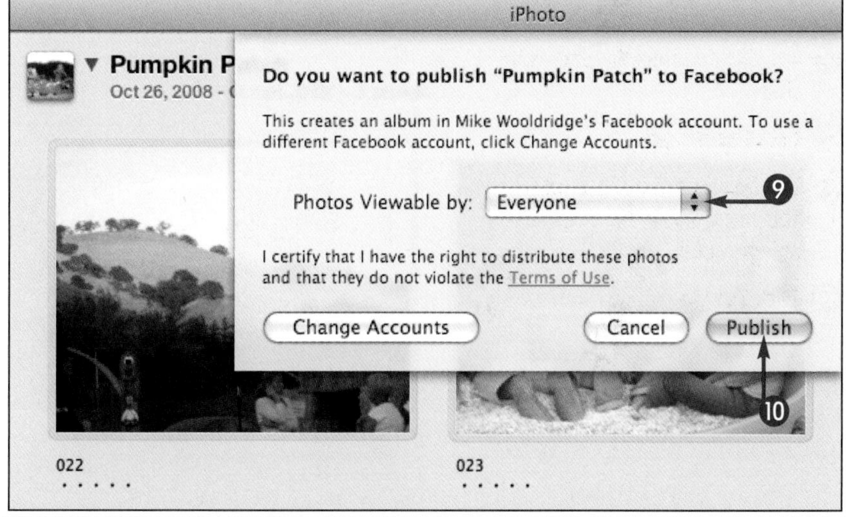

Pumpkin P
Oct 26, 2008 -
Do you want to publish "Pumpkin Patch" to Facebook?
This creates an album in Mike Wooldridge's Facebook account. To use a different Facebook account, click Change Accounts.
Photos Viewable by:

I certify that I have the right to distribute these photos and that they do not violate the Terms of Use.
Change Accounts

TIP

How do I view my shared Facebook photos from iPhoto?

When you upload photos to Facebook, iPhoto creates a new Facebook photo album in the source list. Follow these steps to view the photos online:

1. In the source list, click the name of the Facebook album.

   The album photos appear.

2. Click the Facebook Web address button for the album.

   A Web browser opens to display the photos.

Share with Flickr

You can upload your iPhoto images directly to your account on Flickr, the popular photo hosting site. Others can visit Flickr to view and comment on the photos.

To use this feature, you must have an active Internet connection and a Flickr account.

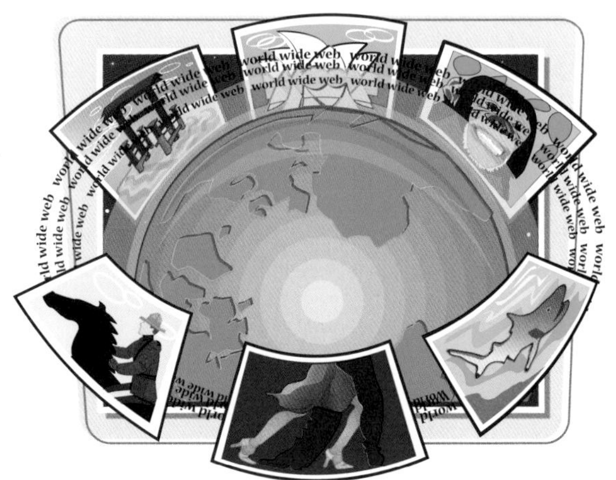

Share with Flickr

1. ⌘-click to select the photos to share.
2. Click **Flickr**.
   - The first time you share on Flickr, you are prompted to set up access.
3. Click **Set Up**.

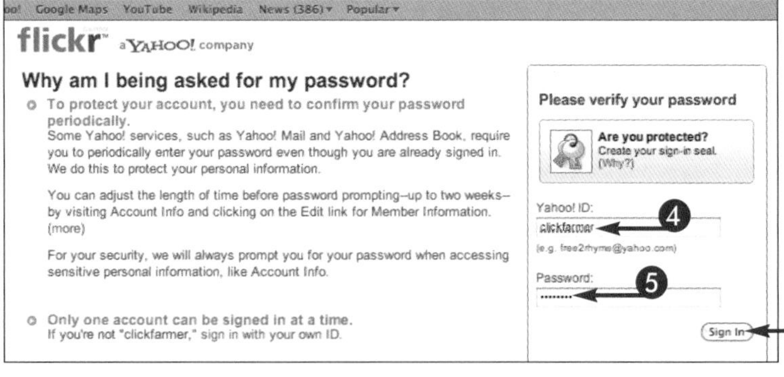

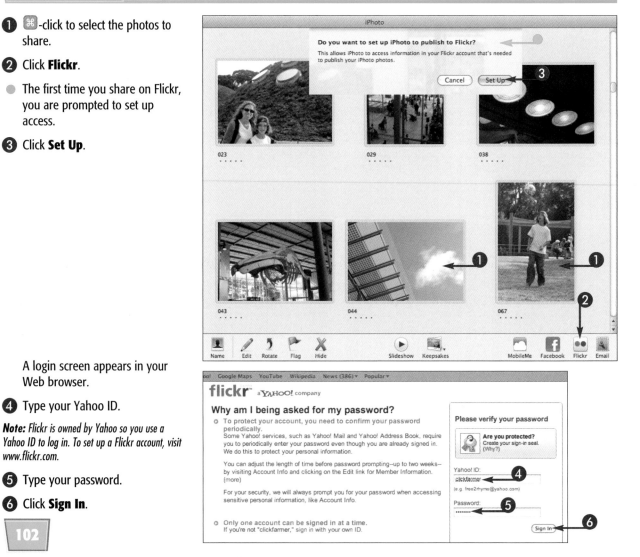

A login screen appears in your Web browser.

4. Type your Yahoo ID.

***Note:** Flickr is owned by Yahoo so you use a Yahoo ID to log in. To set up a Flickr account, visit www.flickr.com.*

5. Type your password.
6. Click **Sign In**.

An access page appears.

For iPhoto and other applications to interact with Flickr, you must allow them access to your account.

7 Click **OK, I'll Allow It**.

A confirmation page appears.

8 Return to iPhoto from the Web browser. You can click **iPhoto** on the Dock.

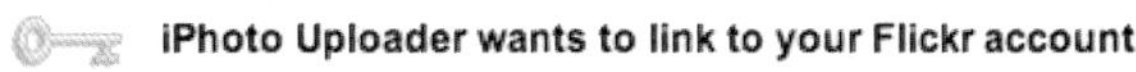

9 Select who can view your photos.

You can select Anyone to make the photos public.

10 Select a photo size to upload.

11 Click **Publish**.

iPhoto uploads the photos to your Flickr account.

TIP

How do I view my shared Flickr photos from iPhoto?

When you upload photos to Flickr, iPhoto creates a new Flickr photo album in the source list. Follow these steps to view the photos online:

1 In the source list, click the name of the Flickr album.

The album photos appear.

2 Click the Flickr Web address button for the album.

A Web browser opens to display the photos.

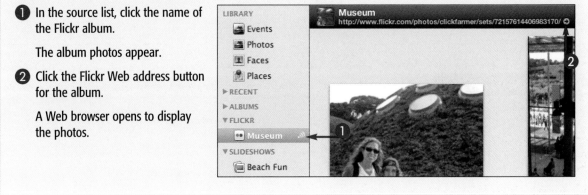

Create an Instant Slideshow

You can quickly create a slideshow in iPhoto with a custom theme, music, and transitions. You can then display the slideshow in full-screen mode to automatically cycle through the photos.

To have more control of your slideshow options, see "Create a Slideshow Project."

Create an Instant Slideshow

1. ⌘-click to select the photos for the slideshow.

- You can also select an Event, Places or Faces group, or album.

2. Click **Slideshow**.

The first time you create an instant slideshow, the slideshow dialog appears.

3. Click **Themes**.
4. Click to select a presentation style.

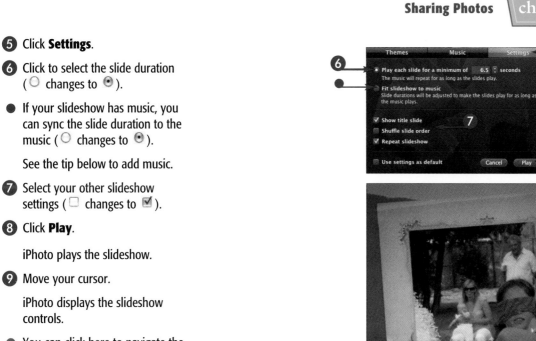

5 Click **Settings**.

6 Click to select the slide duration (○ changes to ◉).

- If your slideshow has music, you can sync the slide duration to the music (○ changes to ◉).

  See the tip below to add music.

7 Select your other slideshow settings (☐ changes to ☑).

8 Click **Play**.

  iPhoto plays the slideshow.

9 Move your cursor.

  iPhoto displays the slideshow controls.

- You can click here to navigate the slideshow.
- You can click here to open the slideshow Themes, Music, and Settings options.
- You can click here to exit the slideshow.

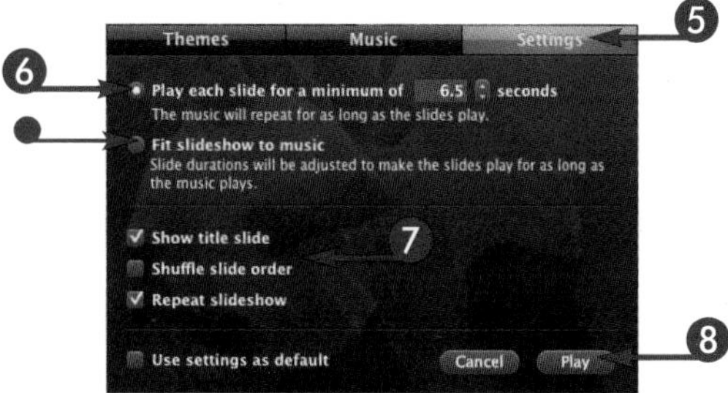

How can I add background music to a slideshow?

1 In the slideshow dialog, click **Music**.

2 You can click the **Source** menu to choose music from sample music, iTunes, GarageBand, and other sources on your Mac.

3 Click to select a background song.

- You can click ▶ to play the song.

4 Click **Play**.

  iPhoto plays the slideshow with background music.

Create a Slideshow Project

You can create a custom slideshow project that allows you to add a theme, transitions, and music and also order your slides. You can export the project as a separate movie file when you are finished. A slideshow project appears in the source list so you can play or edit it later.

Create a Slideshow Project

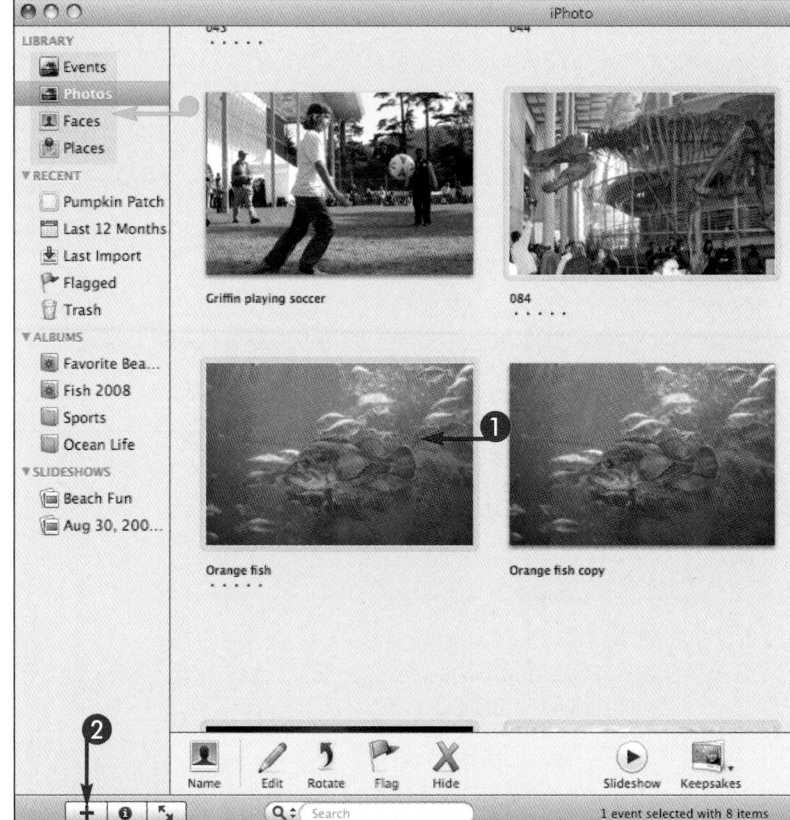

1. ⌘-click to select the photos for the slideshow.
   - You can also select an Event, Places or Faces group, or album.
2. Click +.

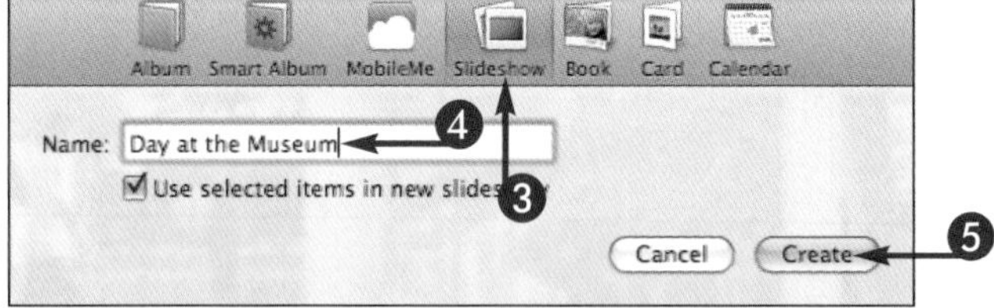

3. Click **Slideshow**.
4. Type a name for the slideshow.
5. Click **Create**.

- iPhoto adds the slideshow to the source list.

6 Click and drag the thumbnails to rearrange the slide order.

- The first slide shows the slideshow name. You can double-click the name to edit it.

7 Click here to select the theme, music, and other settings. For more details, see "Create an Instant Slideshow."

- You can click **Preview** to preview the slideshow in the project window.

8 Click **Play**.

iPhoto plays the slideshow at full screen.

How do I export slideshow?

You can export your slideshow project to a QuickTime movie file that you can use on an iPod, Apple TV, and other devices.

1 Click **Export**.

The Export Your Slideshow dialog opens.

2 Click one or more sizes based on how you want to use the movie (☐ changes to ☑).

- You can click **Custom Export** to select the QuickTime format, specify frame rate and compression, and other advanced settings.

3 Click **Export** to create your movie.

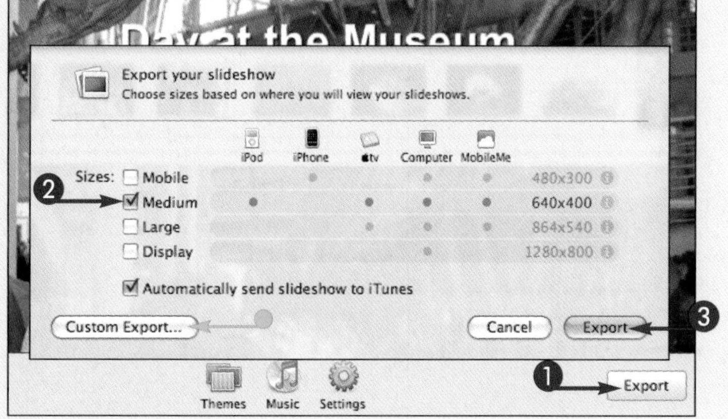

Create a Book

You can create a photo book that showcases the images from a vacation, party, or other event. You can customize the book with a number of colorful themes and page layouts. iPhoto can even create a map page to display where photos were taken. See "Create a Travel Map in a Book" for details.

You can purchase a printed version of the book through Apple's printing services.

Create a Book

1. ⌘-click to select the photos for the book.
   - You can also select an Event, Places or Faces group, or album.
2. Click +.
3. Click **Book** in the dialog that appears.
4. Type a name for the book.

5. Select a hardcover, softcover, or wire-bound format.
6. Click a theme to choose the colors and layout for your book.
   - Example pages appear here.
7. Click **Choose**.
8. If a dialog about adding photos appears, click **OK**.

- The book name appears in the source list.
- Thumbnails of the selected photos appear here.
- Book pages appear here.

9. Click and drag a thumbnail to add a photo to a page.

- You can click Autoflow to add all the photos in order automatically.

10. Click the arrows to view other pages in the book, to which you can then add photos.

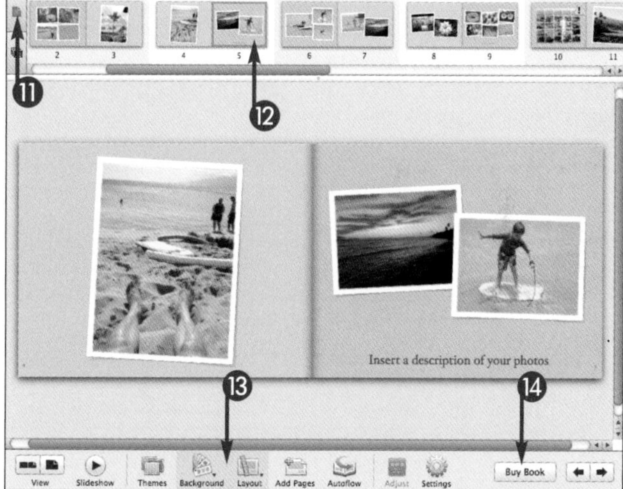

11. Click the **Page View** button (■) to view the pages as thumbnails.
12. Click a page that you want to redesign.
13. Click here to change the page background or layout.
14. When you are finished customizing the pages, click **Buy Book**.

    iPhoto prompts you for your Apple account information for purchasing the book.

How do I edit text on a page?

Most book themes, such as Picture Book and Travel Book, include title and caption text. You can edit the text and change the font to suit your liking.

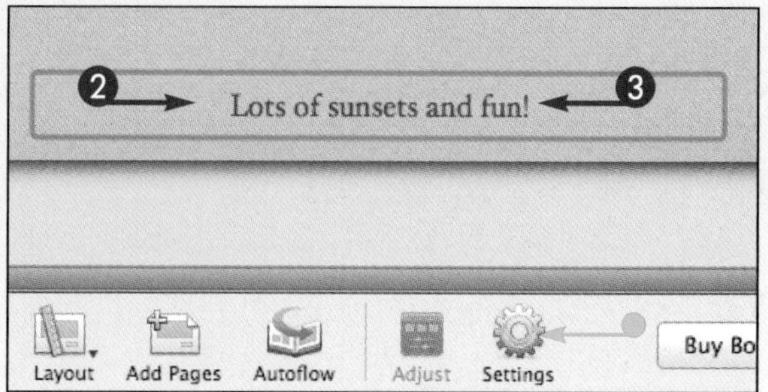

1. View a page with text.
2. Click the text.

   The text becomes editable.

3. Type your title or caption.

- You can click **Settings** to change the style and size of the text.

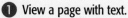

Create a Travel Map in a Book

You can create a map page in an iPhoto book that illustrates the locations of your book photos. You can edit the places on the map and even connect them to show a journey.

For more about associating your photos with places, see Chapter 4.

Create a Travel Map in a Book

❶ Create a photo book.

Note: *See "Create a Book" for details.*

❷ Click to select the page to which you want to add a map.

❸ Click **Layout**.

❹ In the menu that appears, click **Map** and then the map icon.

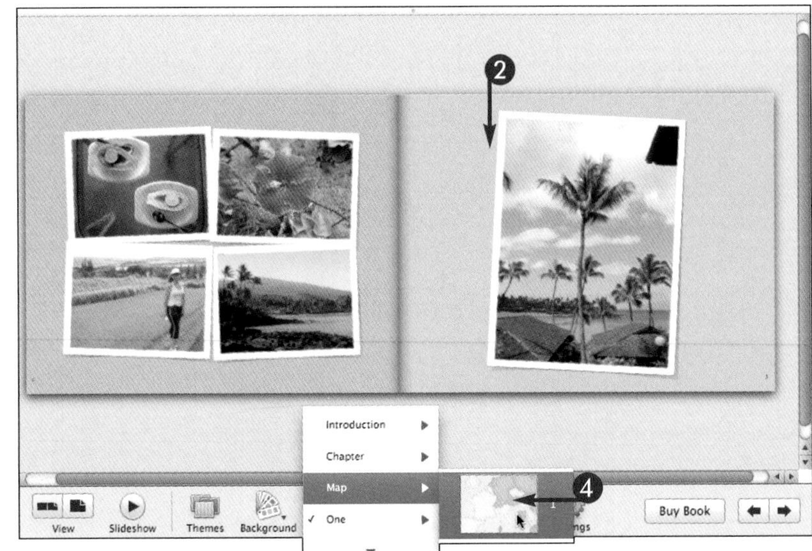

iPhoto adds a map to the page.

- If your book photos include place information, iPhoto automatically adds the places.

❺ Click the map to edit it.

An edit dialog appears.

❻ Type a title for the map.

- You can click plus to add a place.
- You can select a place and then click minus to remove it.

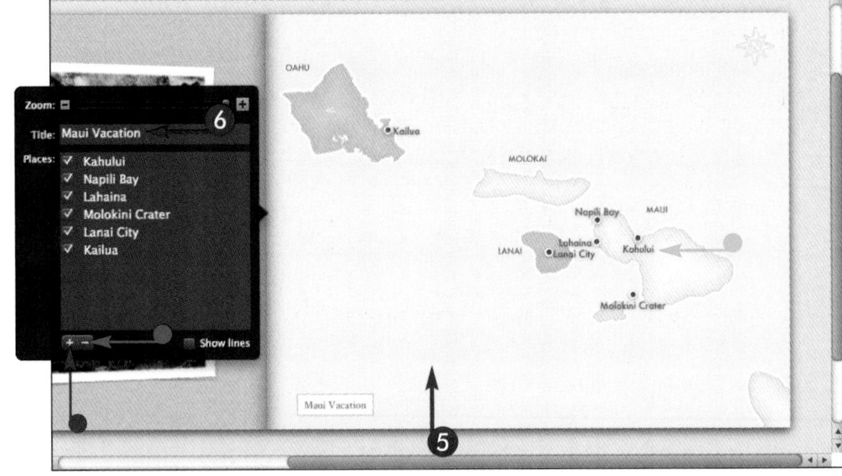

7. To connect the places in the order they are listed, click **Show lines** (☐ changes to ☑).

- iPhoto connects the places.
- You can click and drag the places in the list to reorder them.

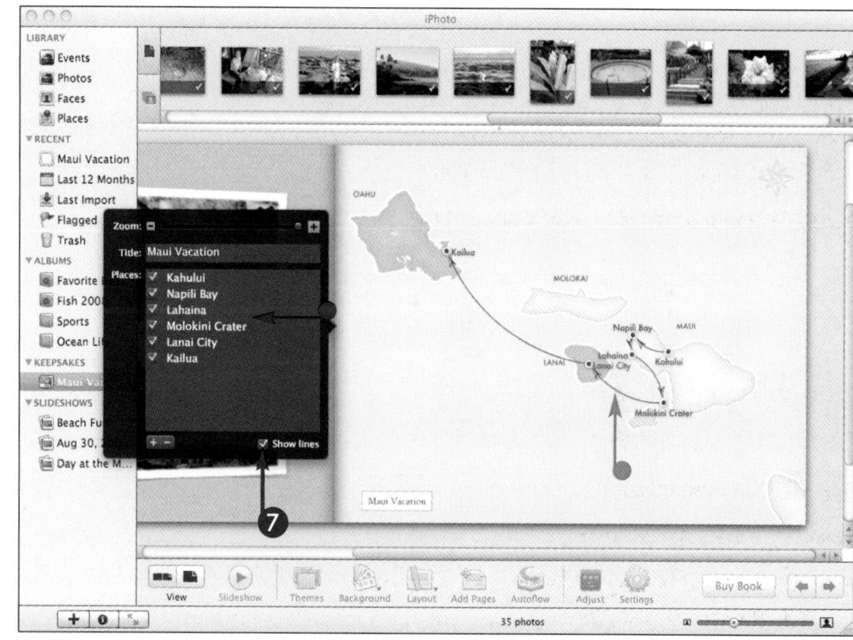

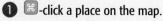

TIP

How do I edit the places on my map?

Follow these steps:

1. ⌘-click a place on the map.

   A menu appears.

- Click to delete the place.
- Click to move the label. This is helpful if labels on the map overlap.
- You can click other commands to change other aspects of the map.
- You can ⌘-click a line to make changes to it.

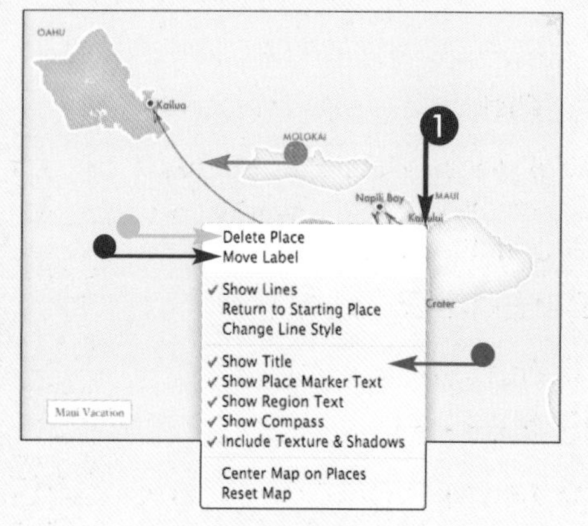

Create a Calendar

You can create a calendar that features photos from your iPhoto library. You can customize the pages with a colorful theme and add one or more photos to each month. iPhoto can also automatically add national holidays or information from your iCal calendar to the dates.

You can purchase a printed version of the calendar through Apple's printing services.

Create a Calendar

1. ⌘-click to select the photos for the calendar.
   - You can also select an Event, Places, or Faces group, or album.
2. Click [+].
3. Click **Calendar** in the dialog that appears.
4. Type a name for the calendar.
5. Click to select a theme.
6. Click **Choose**.
7. If a dialog about adding photos appears, click **OK**.

8. Select when to start the calendar.
9. Select the number of months in the calendar.
10. Select a country to display national holidays or **None** to display none.
11. If you use iCal, you can import iCal data into your calendar.
12. Click **OK**.

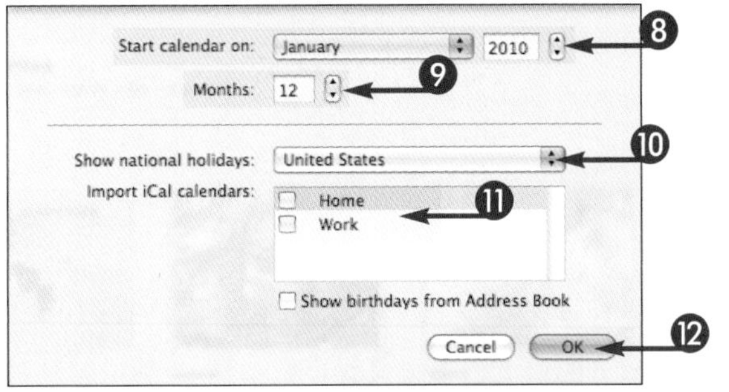

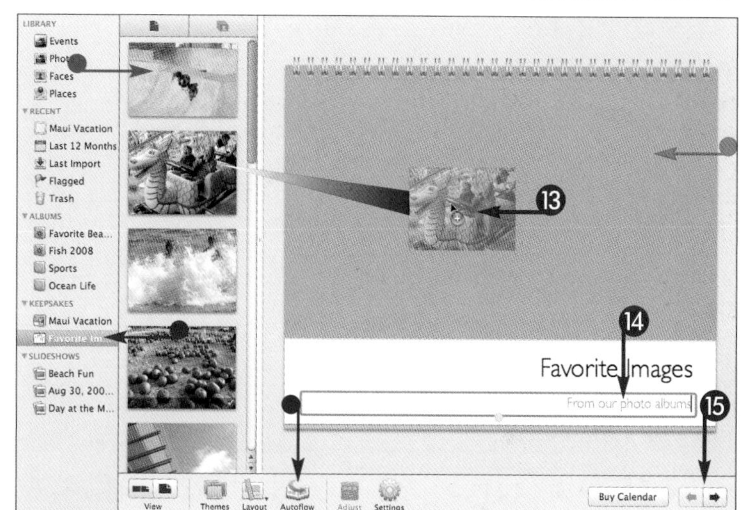

- The calendar name appears in the source list.
- Thumbnails of the selected photos appear here.
- Calendar pages appear here.

13 Click and drag a thumbnail to add a photo to a page.

- You can click **Autoflow** to add all the photos in order automatically.

14 Click can click placeholder text on the pages to add text to your calendar.

15 Click the arrows to view other pages in the calendar, to which you can then add photos.

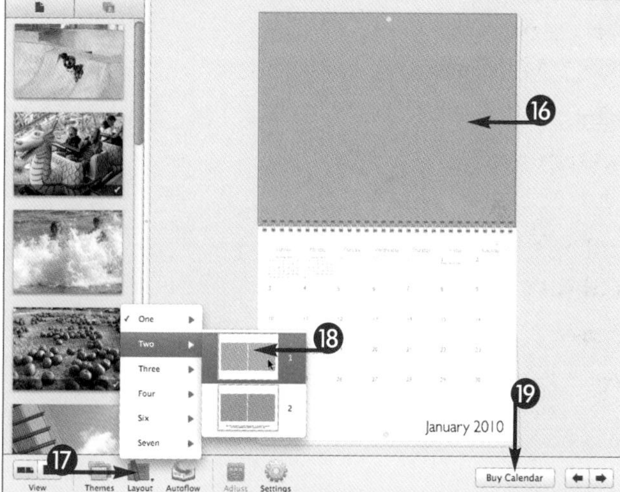

16 Click to select a calendar page whose layout you want to edit.

17 Click **Layout**.

18 In the menus that appear, click a layout.

iPhoto applies the layout to the page.

19 When you are finished customizing the pages, click **Buy Calendar**.

iPhoto prompts you for your Apple account information for purchasing the book.

TIP

How do I edit a date in a calendar?

You can edit a date to add or change the text of a birthday, holiday, or other event.

1 Double-click a date in the calendar.

The date opens in a separate dialog.

2 Type to add or edit the date text.

3 Click ☒ to save the changes and close the dialog.

Export Photos

You can save photos from iPhoto to separate files so you can open them in another application or on a non-Mac computer. You can control the file format, image size, and file names used for the export.

Export Photos

1. Select the photos, Event, Places or Faces group, or album you want to export.
2. Click **File**.
3. Click **Export**.

The Export Photos dialog appears.

4. Select a file type.

   iPhoto allows you to export to three common formats: JPEG, TIFF, or PNG. You can also export photos as they were originally imported or as their current file type in iPhoto.

5. If you are exporting to JPEG, select a quality.
6. If you are exporting to JPEG or TIFF, you can click to include descriptive information in the files (☐ changes to ☑).

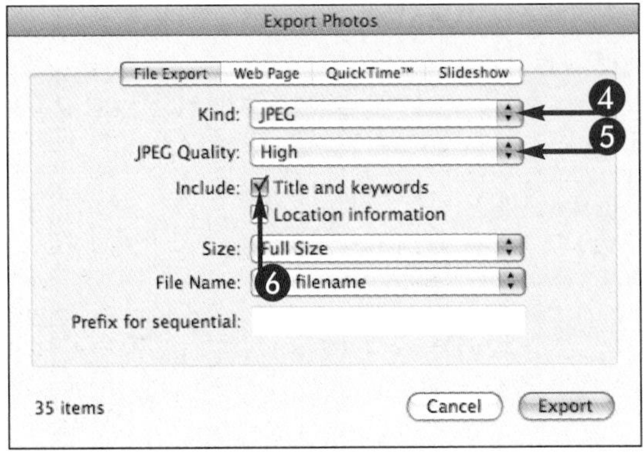

7 Click a size.

You can select a setting other than Full Size to decrease file size. Choosing this also decreases the image quality.

8 Click a file name.

- If you select **Sequential**, you can specify a prefix to be placed before the number.

9 Click **Export**.

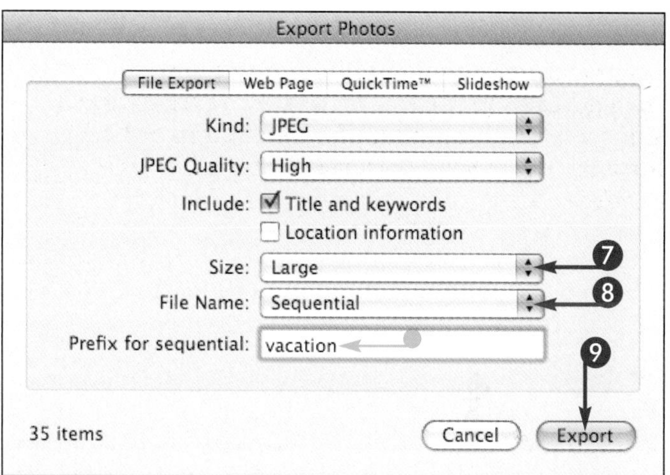

10 Select where to save the files.

11 Click **OK**.

iPhoto saves the files.

After the export is complete, you can view the files in the Finder.

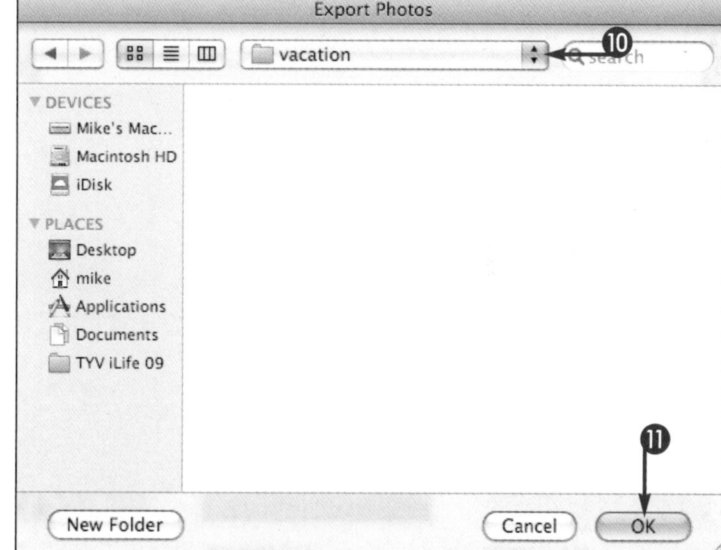

TIPS

How do I send photos to iWeb for use on a Web page?

Select photos, an Event, Places or Faces group, or an album. Click **Share** and then **iWeb**. From the submenu that appears, select **Photo Page** to place the photos on a photo page template or **Blog** to place the photos on a blog template. iWeb opens and the photos are added to the template. See Part V of this book for more about iWeb.

How do I send photos to iDVD for use in a DVD project?

Select photos, an Event, a Places or Faces group, or an album. Click **Share** and then **iDVD**. iDVD opens and the photos are added to a new project. If iDVD is already open, the photos are added to the current project. See Part VI of this book for more about iDVD.

Burn to a Disc

You can write your image files from iPhoto to a CD or DVD for archiving or to give to a friend. This process creates a disc that can be viewed only in iPhoto.

Burn to a Disc

1. Select the photos, Event, Places or Faces group, or album you want to burn to a disc.
2. Click **Share**.
3. Click **Burn**.

iPhoto prompts you to insert a disc.

4. Insert a blank, recordable CD or DVD into your disc drive.
5. Click **OK**.

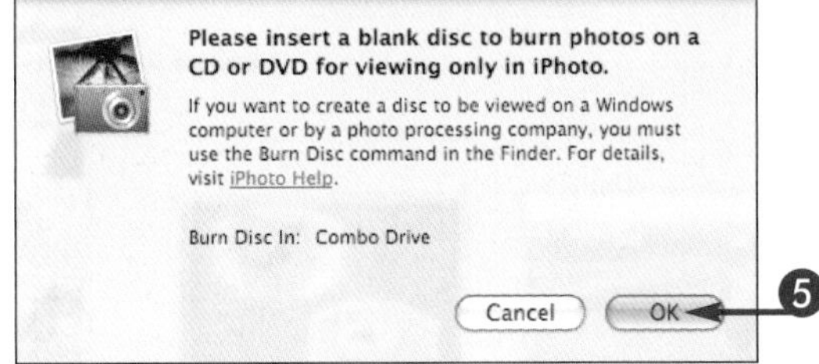

- iPhoto reads the disc and displays summary information.

6. Type a title for the disc.
7. Click **Burn**.

iPhoto displays a Burn Disc dialog.

8. Click **Burn**.

iPhoto writes the selected photos to the disc.

- You can click **Eject** to eject the disc without burning the photos.
- You can click **Cancel** to close the dialog without burning the photos.

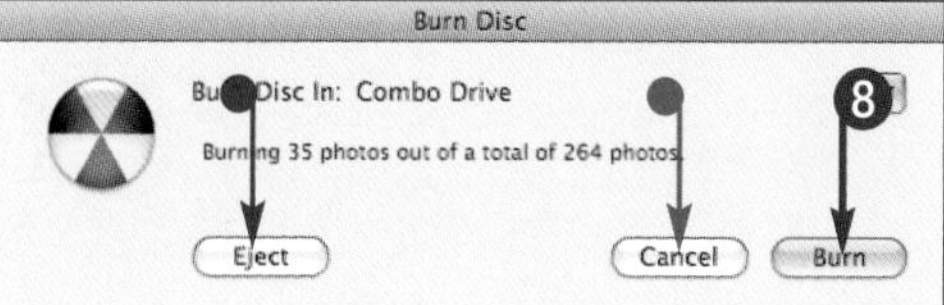

How do I burn a disc to be used in applications other than iPhoto or on a Windows PC?

First export your photos from iPhoto. See "Export Photos" for details. Then switch from iPhoto to the Finder. In the Finder, insert a blank, recordable CD or DVD into your Mac and drag the folder containing your exported files to the icon for the disc.

How do I set a photo as the desktop picture on my Mac?

Select the photo to use in the photo library. Click **Share** and then **Set Desktop**. iPhoto sets the photo as the desktop picture on your Mac. You can reset the desktop picture by clicking the Apple menu, **System Preferences**, and then **Desktop & Screen Saver**.

PART

III

Working with iMovie '09

This part of the book covers the iMovie '09 video editor, which lets you author professional-looking movies on your Mac. You can assemble clips shot with your tape-based or memory-based camcorder and combine them with still photos, transitions, special effects, and more. When you are finished, you can share your work by burning it to disc in iDVD or uploading it online.

Understanding the iMovie Workspace

iMovie enables you to import and organize video clips taken with a camcorder, digital camera, or other device. You can then assemble the clips into professional-looking movies that have transitions, background music, special effects, and more. Take a moment to familiarize yourself with the iMovie workspace.

Event Browser

iMovie organizes video clips into events based on the time they were created. You can select an event in the event library to display the associated clips. See "Import Video from Your Computer" for more information.

Project Browser

You build a movie by selecting clips in the event browser and then adding them to your project, which is built using the project browser. Here, you can rearrange the clips, add special effects, preview your movie, and more. See Chapter 8 for more about creating a project.

Viewer

When you play a clip from the event browser or project browser, the clip appears in the viewer. You can also view clips in full-screen mode. See "View a Clip at Full Screen" for details.

Content Browsers

You can click here to open panes for adding music, still photos, text overlays, and more to your project. Chapter 10 goes into detail about these features.

Play Project

You can click here to view the clips in your project plus any special effects you have added.

Play Event Clips

You can click here to play a video clip from your event library to help decide how to use it in your project.

Evaluate Clips

You can click buttons to mark clips in your library as favorites if you want to use them later, or reject clips to unclutter your workspace. See the tasks in this chapter to find out more.

Adjust Thumbnails

You can click and drag sliders to display more or fewer thumbnails in the event and project browsers.

Get Video to Use in iMovie

In order to edit your video clips into an award-winning movie, you must first acquire them.

Taped-based Camcorder

iMovie can import video content captured on videotape from miniDV and Digital-8 camcorders. You can connect your camcorder to your Mac using a FireWire cable. You can operate the camera while it is connected using the iMovie controls and then capture the content as the camera plays it. If you have an older camcorder that does not include a FireWire connection, you may have to purchase extra hardware to capture your recordings.

Memory-based Camcorder

Newer camcorders capture video content on miniDVDs or flash-based or miniature hard drives instead of on traditional tape. iMovie can import video from those as well. These memory-based cameras are advantageous in that you can preview clips quickly because the camera can access the clips directly like a computer accesses files, instead of having to scan through a tape from start to finish. Memory-based camcorders connect using a USB cable.

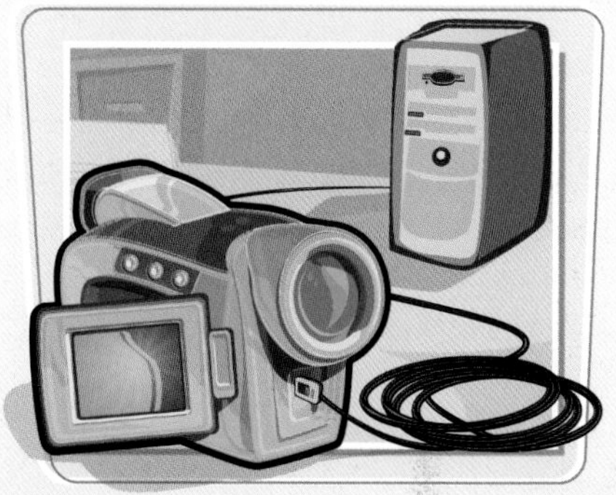

Digital Still Camera

Nowadays, many digital cameras that take still photos can also record video. You can download both still photos and video clips from such cameras into iPhoto. iMovie can access those iPhoto video clips in the event library. See "Import Video from Your Computer" for details. For more about iPhoto, see Part II of this book.

Web Cam

If your Mac has an iSight camera, or you have a FireWire-based Web camera connected to your Mac, you can capture video to use in iMovie. Click **Open Camera Import Window** (▪) to select the camera and then use the **Capture** and **Stop** commands to record video clips.

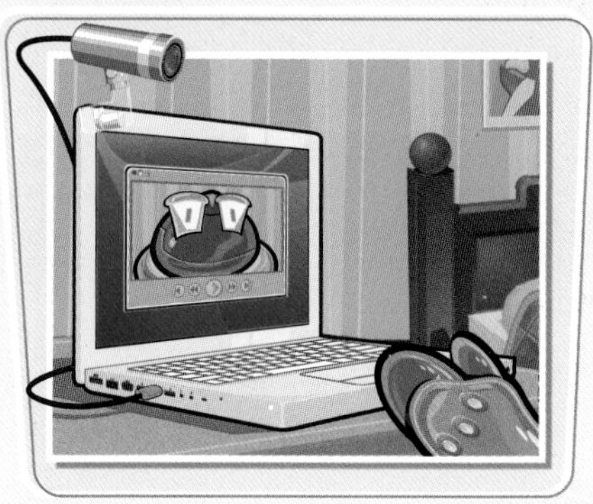

Import Video from a Tape-based Camcorder

You can connect a tape-based camcorder to your Mac and import video into iMovie as the camcorder plays. iMovie saves the video clips as digital files that you can then assemble into professional-looking movies.

For details about connecting your specific camcorder, see the documentation that came with the device.

Import Video from a Tape-based Camcorder

1. Turn your tape-based camcorder on and connect it to your Mac.

   Connect the camera using a FireWire cable.

Note: *Make sure your camcorder is switched to VTR, VCR, or Play mode. The terminology may vary depending on the model of your camcorder.*

   The import window opens.

- If the import window does not open, click **File** and then **Import from Camera** to open it.
- To import all the video on the camcorder, select **Automatic** and then click **Import**.

2. If Manual is not selected, click to select it.
3. Use the controls to play the movie to where you want to begin recording.

- You can click ◀◀ to rewind.
- You can click ▶▶ to fast-forward.
- You can click ■ to stop.
- You can click ▶ to play.

4. Click **Import**.

5 In the dialog that appears, select a save location.

iMovie organizes imported content as events. The default is to save imported clips taken on the same day to separate events.

6 Type the event name.

- You can optionally save to an existing event (○ changes to ◉).
- You can click to keep all clips in one event instead of dividing clips by day (☑ changes to ☐).

7 Click **Import**.

iMovie imports the video.

- You can click **Stop** to stop the video before the end of the tape.

8 When the importing is complete, click **Done** to close the import window.

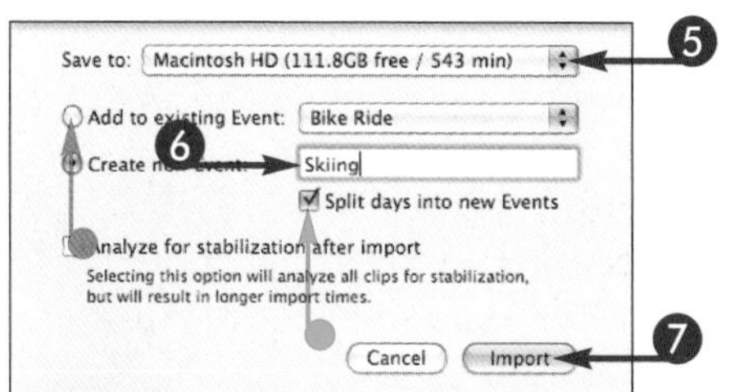

TIP

How do I add stabilization to clips as I import them?

iMovie can analyze clips to help smooth out motion caused by a shaky camera. Follow these steps:

1 In the import dialog, click **Analyze for stabilization after import** (☐ changes to ☑).

iMovie automatically performs stabilization analysis after the video clips finish importing.

Note: *For more about stabilization, see Chapter 10.*

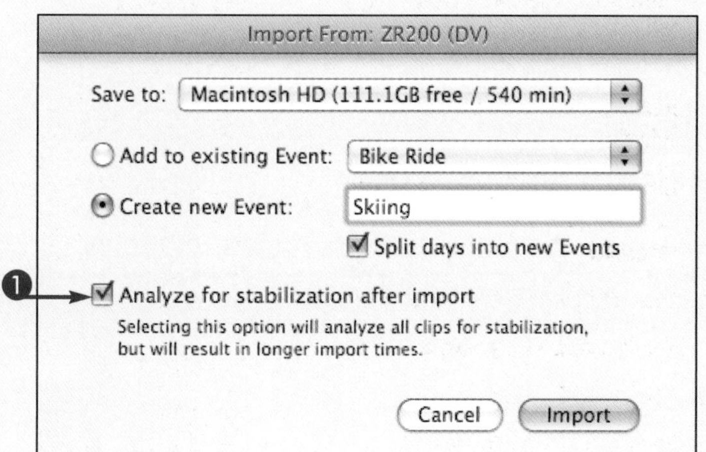

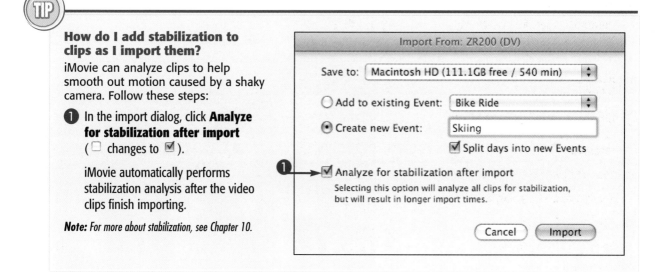

Import Video from a Memory-based Camcorder

You can connect a memory-based camcorder to your Mac and import video into iMovie. You can import all the clips from the camcorder or just selected ones. iMovie saves the video clips as digital files that you can then assemble into professional-looking movies.

For details about connecting your specific camcorder, see the documentation that came with the device.

Import Video from a Memory-based Camcorder

1. Turn your memory-based camcorder on and connect it to your Mac.

   Connect the camera using a USB cable.

Note: *Make sure your camcorder is switched to PC Connect mode. The terminology may vary depending on the model of your camcorder.*

- The import window opens and displays the video clips on the camcorder.
- If the import window does not open, click **File** and then **Import from Camera** to open it.
- To import all the video on the camcorder, select **Automatic** and then click **Import All**.

2. If Manual is not selected, click to select it.
3. Select the check boxes for the clips you want to import. All the clips are selected initially by default.
4. Click **Import Checked**.

5 In the dialog that appears, select a save location.

iMovie organizes imported content as events. The default is to save imported clips taken on the same day to the same event.

6 Type the event name.

- You can optionally save to an existing event (○ changes to ⦿).
- You can click to keep all clips in one event instead of dividing clips by day (☑ changes to ☐).

7 Click **Import**.

iMovie imports the video clips and marks them.

8 Click **OK**.

9 Click **Done** to close the import window.

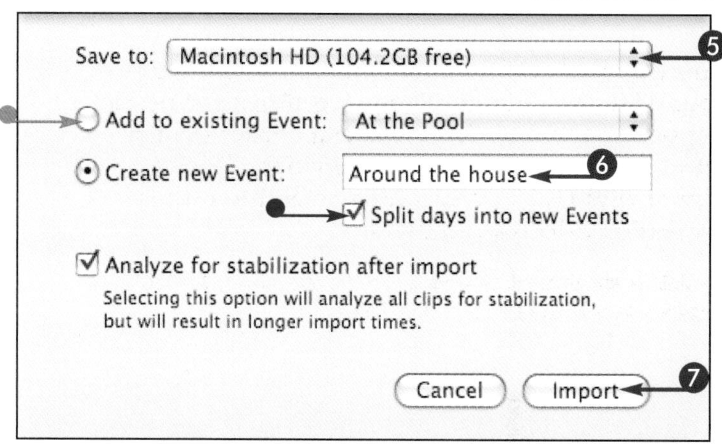

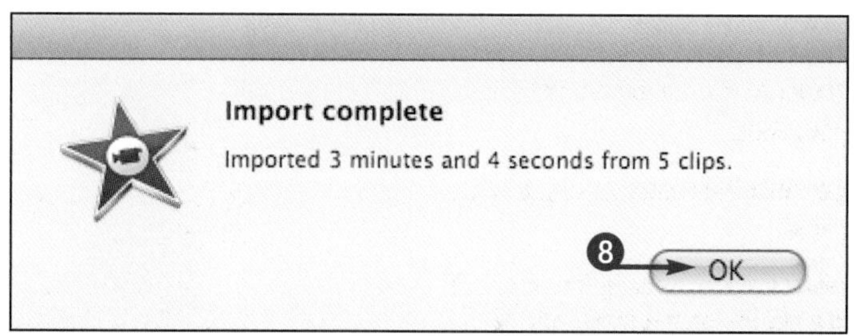

How can I quickly back up the video clips on my memory-based camcorder?

In iMovie, you can archive the video clips on your camcorder by backing them up to a folder on your computer.

1 Turn your memory-based camcorder on and connect it to your Mac.

- The import window opens and displays the video clips on the camcorder.

2 Click **Archive All**.

3 In the dialog that appears, select where to save the video clips.

4 Click **Create**.

iMovie backs up the camcorder video.

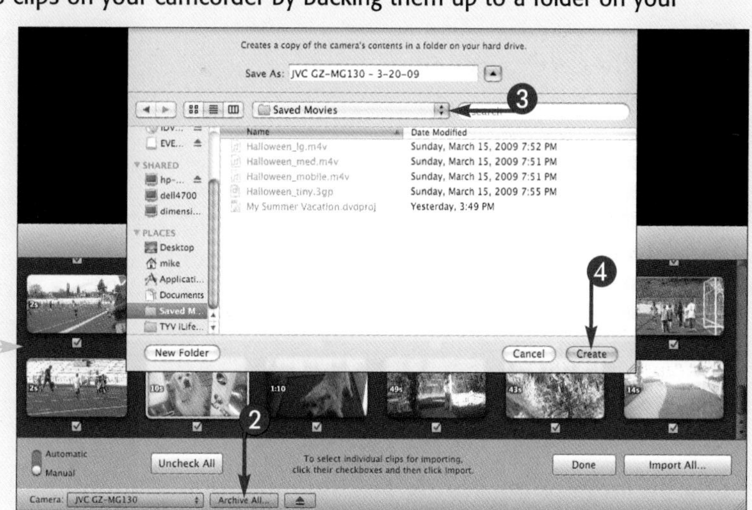

Import Video from Your Computer

You can import video clips that already exist on your Mac. When you import the clips, iMovie creates thumbnails and performs other analysis required to work with the clips.

iMovie supports the import of most MPEG, AVI, DV, and MOV video files. Some variants of these file formats are not supported or require plugins.

Import Video from Your Computer

1. Click **File**.
2. Click **Import**.
3. Click **Movies**.

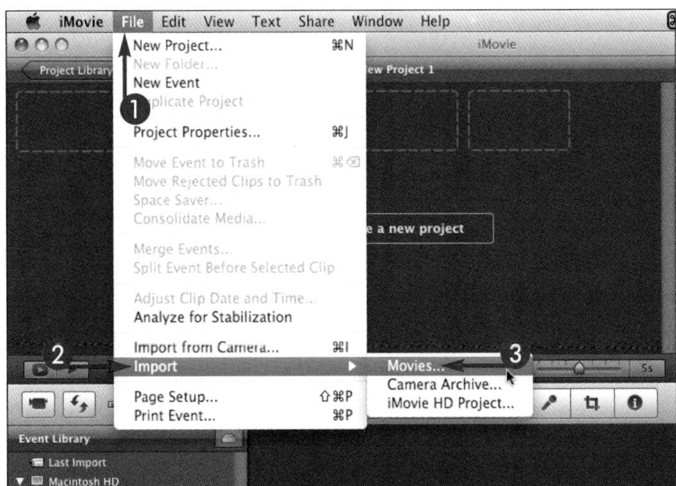

4. Select the location of the video files.
5. ⌘-click to select the files to import.
6. Select a save location.

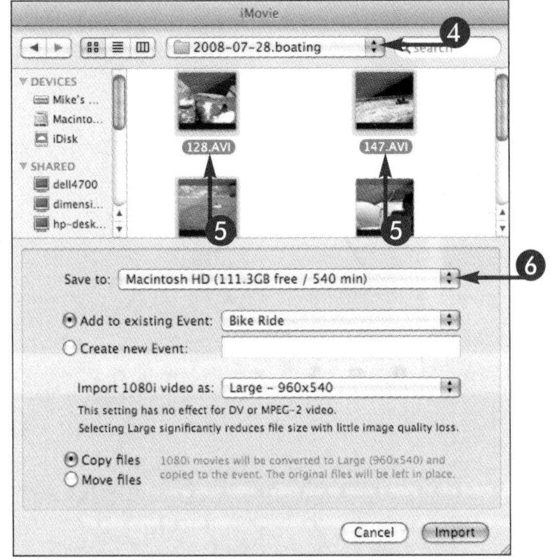

iMovie organizes imported content as events.

7. Click to create a new event (○ changes to ◉).
8. Type a name for the event.

   By default, iMovie makes copies of the imported files.

   - You can click to move the files instead and save space (○ changes to ◉).

9. Click **Import**.

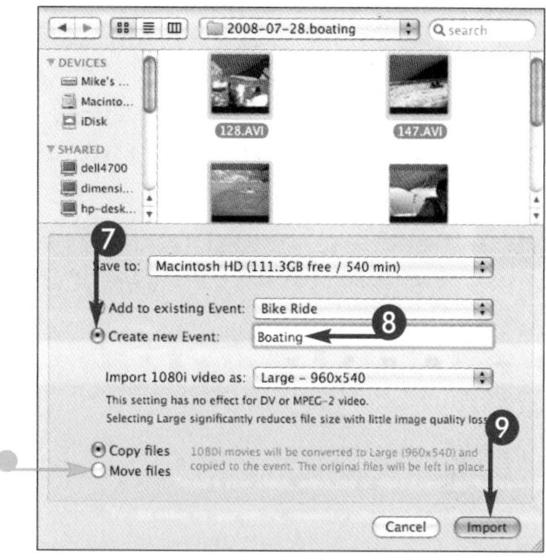

iMovie imports the files.

- When the process is complete, the imported clips appear.
- A new event is created in the event library.

TIP

How do I access videos imported into iPhoto?

iPhoto can import both still photos and video clips from digital cameras. To access the iPhoto video clips from iMovie, follow these steps.

1. If the event library is not open, click [icon] to open it.
2. Click **iPhoto Videos**.

   - The video clips from iPhoto appear.

Note: *See Part II for more about iPhoto.*

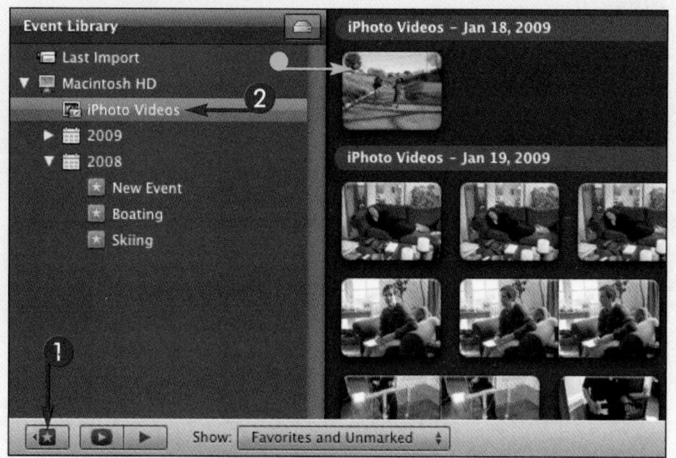

View a Clip

You can play the video content that you have imported into your iMovie library to determine what you want to use in your project. You can play all the clips in an event in sequence or just a small selection of a single clip.

View a Clip

VIEW ALL THE CLIPS IN AN EVENT

iMovie organizes clips taken at the same time into events.

1. If the event library is not open, click [button] to open it.
2. Select an event.
3. Click [▶].

- iMovie plays the clips in the event, starting from the first clip.
- You can click [▶] again or press Spacebar to pause.
- Similarly, you can click [▶] to play a project from the beginning.

PLAY FROM A SPECIFIC POINT

4. Position the cursor over a point in a clip.
5. Press Spacebar.

- iMovie plays the clip, beginning at that point.

  You can press Spacebar again to pause.

- Similarly, you can position your cursor over a clip in your project and press Spacebar to play.

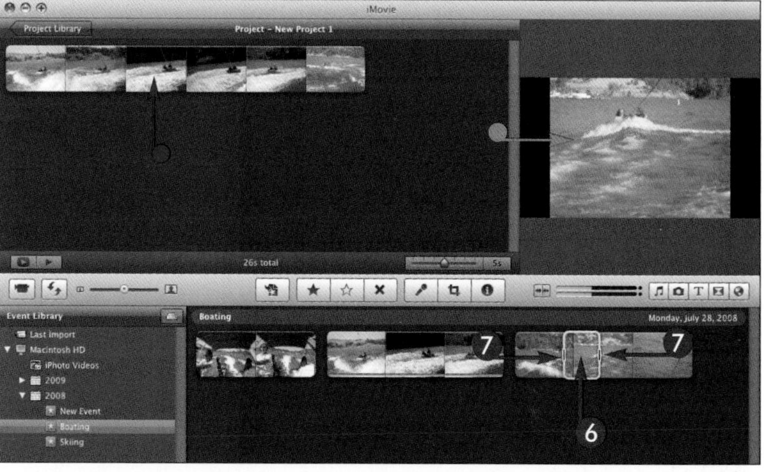

PLAY A SELECTION

6 Click inside a clip in the event browser.

iMovie selects four seconds of video, surrounding it with a yellow box. You can adjust this default time length in the iMovie preferences.

7 Click and drag the box edges to adjust the selection duration.

8 ⌘-click inside the selection.

9 In the menu that appears, click **Play Selection**.

iMovie plays the selection.

TIP

How can I preview edits?

You can quickly preview the few seconds of video footage near where you made an edit.

1 Position your cursor over the location of the edit.

- You can press] to play two seconds of video, starting one second before and ending one second after the selected location.
- You can press [to play six seconds of video, starting three seconds before and ending three seconds after the selected location.

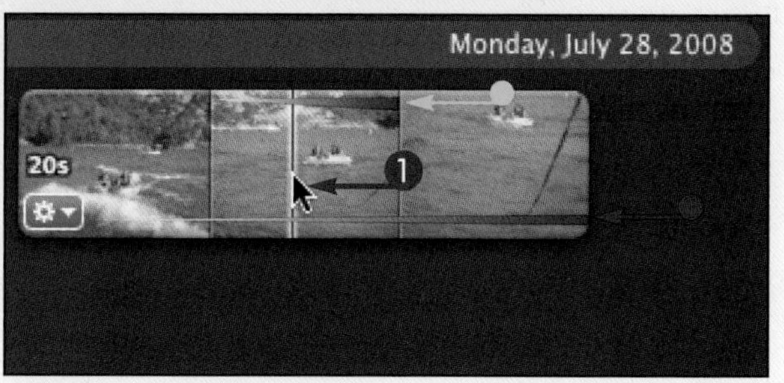

View a Clip at Full Screen

You can preview imported video clips or your project in full screen to get a clear view of how your work looks. While in full screen, you can scan through parts of your clip or switch to other clips in the iMovie project library.

View a Clip at Full Screen

1. Select a video clip in the event browser.
2. Click .
   - You can click to play a project at full screen.

The clip opens and plays at full screen.

3. Move your cursor.

   iMovie displays a thumbstrip view of the clip.

   - A playhead shows the part of the video being played.
4. Click to switch to coverflow view.

- iMovie displays the coverflow view with thumbnails showing other clips in the event library.
- You can click to switch between showing events and projects.

5 Click or press Spacebar.

iMovie pauses the clip.

- You can drag the cursor across the thumbnail to skim through the video.

6 Click a different thumbnail.

iMovie switches to a new video clip.

7 Click or press Spacebar to play the new clip.

8 Click or press Esc to exit full-screen view.

How do I choose different full-screen sizes?

You can select different sizes for full-screen mode in the iMovie preferences.

1 Click **iMovie** and then **Preferences**.

2 Click **General**.

3 Select a full-screen size option.

4 Click .

iMovie saves the option.

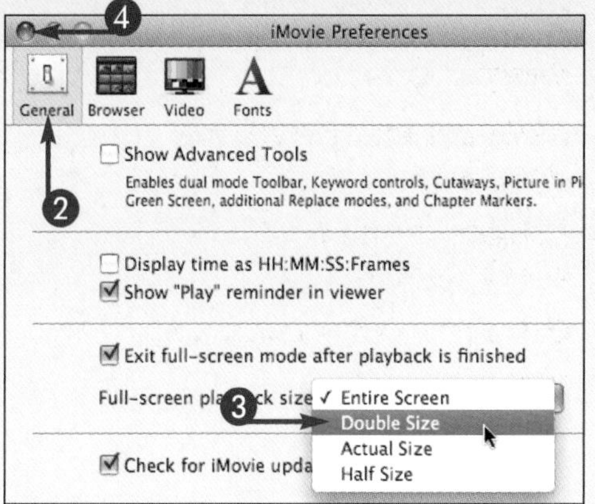

Mark a Clip as a Favorite

You can mark as a favorite a clip or a portion of a clip that you want to use later. Favorite clips are highlighted with a green line. You can choose to display only favorite clips in the workspace. See "Show Different Types of Clips" for details.

Mark a Clip as a Favorite

1. Click a clip.

   iMovie displays a selection box.

2. Click and drag the box edges to select the range that you want to mark.

   To choose the whole clip, you can ⌘-click the selection and then click **Select Entire Clip**.

3. Click ★ or press F.

- iMovie marks the selection as a favorite, highlighting it with a green line.
- You can click ☆ or press U to unmark a selected clip as a favorite.

Reject a Clip

You can reject a clip that you do not want to use in your project. Rejected clips are removed from view in the iMovie workspace but still remain the library. You can view rejected clips using a show setting. See "Show Different Types of Clips" for details.

Reject a Clip

1. Click a clip.

   iMovie displays a selection box.

2. Click and drag the box edges to select the range that you want to reject.

   To choose the whole clip, you can ⌘-click it and select **Select Entire Clip**.

3. Click ✕ or press R.

iMovie removes the selection from view.

- In this example, the parts of the clip that were not rejected remain.
- You can click **Edit** and then **Undo** to undo the rejection.

Show Different Types of Clips

You can set your iMovie library to show just the clips you have marked as favorites and want to use in your project. You can also view your rejected clips in case you want to revert a rejection.

Show Different Types of Clips

1. Click here to select a show setting.

- You can select **Favorites Only** to display only your good clips.
- You can select **Rejected Only** to view the clips you have rejected, which are usually hidden.

- iMovie shows the selected type of clips.
- To revert a rejection, you can select a rejected clip and then click ☆ or press U.

You can delete a clip from your library when you are sure you have no need for it. iMovie moves the clip to the Trash on your Mac. If you think you may still have a need for the clip and want to keep it accessible, you can reject it. See "Reject a Clip" for details.

Delete a Clip

1. Click to select the clip you want to delete.

Note: *iMovie selects a four-second portion by default. However, these steps delete the entire clip.*

2. Click **File**.
3. Click **Move Entire Clip to Trash**.

   You can also select a clip and press Delete to move it to the Trash.

- You can click **Move Rejected Clips to Trash** to move everything marked as rejected.

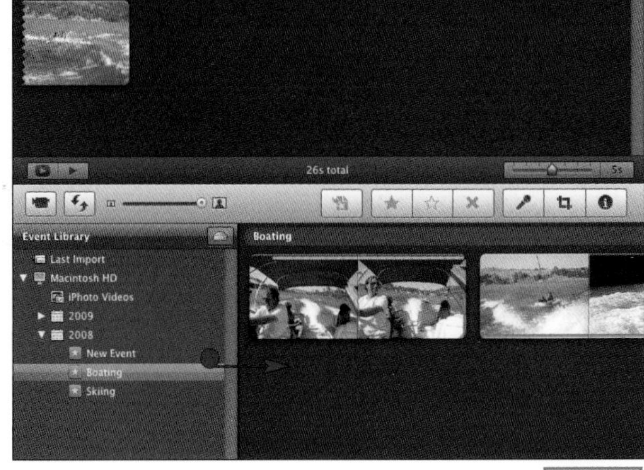

- The clip disappears from the library and is moved to the Mac Trash.

  To delete the clip entirely from your computer, empty the Trash in the Mac Finder.

Create a Project

An iMovie project is a collection of video clips and special effects combined and edited to create a movie. Your iMovie projects can be accessed from the project library. To learn about exporting and sharing finished projects as movies, see Chapter 11.

Create a Project

1. Click **Project Library**.

iMovie displays a list of your projects.

- Project names, lengths, and dates are displayed.
- Thumbnail images of frames for each project are displayed.

You can double-click a project's thumbnails to open it.

2. Click +.

3. Type a name for the project.
4. Select an aspect ratio based on the type of device on which the finished movie will be played.
5. Select a theme to add special titles and transitions to your project. You can always change the theme later.
6. Click **Create**.

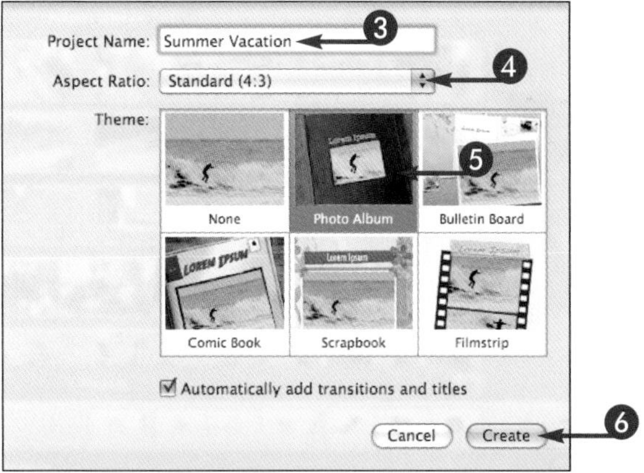

iMovie creates a new project that opens in the project browser.

- You can drag video clips from the event browser to the project browser to create a movie.

***Note:** For details, see "Add a Clip to a Project."*

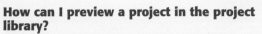

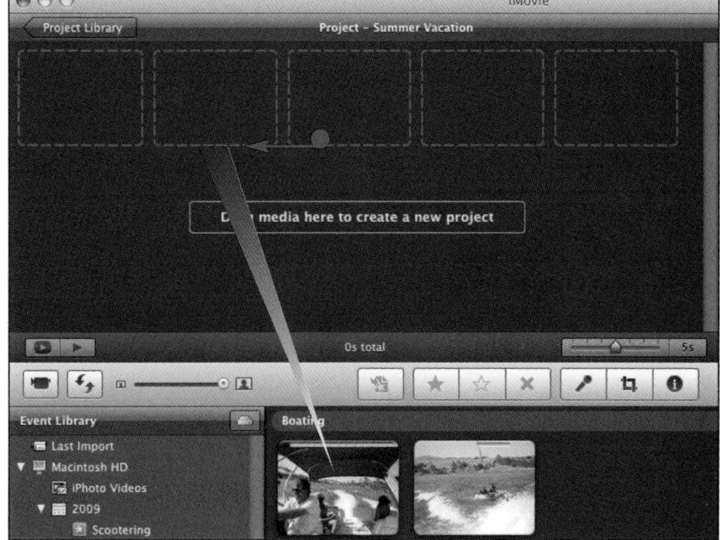

How can I preview a project in the project library?

1. Click to select a project in the project library.
   - You can click ▶ to play the project in the viewer.
   - You can click ▣ to play the project at full screen.
2. Drag the cursor across the clip thumbnails, a technique known as *skimming*.

   iMovie displays the project movie in the viewer and plays it as you drag.

Add a Clip to a Project

You can add video clips to a project to create a movie. You add clips from the event browser, which displays the clips you have imported from your camcorder and other sources. After you add your clips, you can add transitions and other special effects.

Add a Clip to a Project

1. Open a project. See "Create a Project" for details.
2. Display one or more video clips. See Chapter 7 for details about importing and displaying clips.
3. Click and drag to select a clip to add.

   You can drag across the entire clip or just a portion.

   You can also select the entire clip by ⌘-clicking it and selecting **Select Entire Clip** from the menu that appears.

A box surrounds the selection.

4. Click and drag the box edges to adjust the duration of your selection.

- To preview the selection, ⌘-click it and click **Play Selection** in the menu that appears.

5 Click and drag the selection to the project panel.

You can position the clip before or after existing clips in your project. To insert a clip within another clip, see "Insert a Clip."

- You can also click [icon] to add the selection to the end of the project.
- iMovie adds an orange stripe to clips that have been added to a project.

TIP

How do I delete a clip from a project?

1 Click and drag to select a clip in the project browser.

A selection box appears.

2 ⌘-click the selection and click **Delete Selection**.

You can also press Delete.

- You can click **Delete Entire Clip** to delete the whole clip.

iMovie deletes the clip from the project. The clip remains in the event library for you to use again.

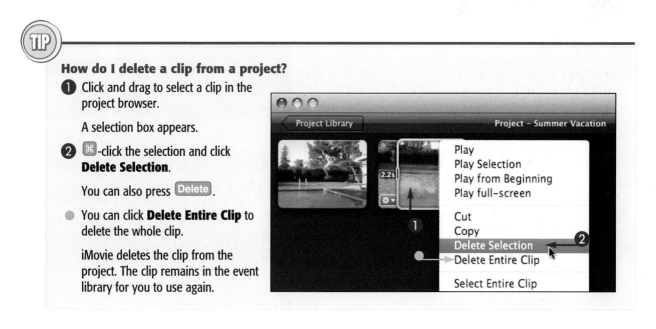

Rearrange Clips in a Project

You can rearrange clips to change the order in which they display in your movie. You change clip positions by clicking and dragging in the project browser.

Rearrange Clips in a Project

1. Click to select a clip.

***Note:** If you want to rearrange part of a clip, you can split the clip into parts before rearranging. See "Split a Clip" for details.*

2. Click and drag the clip to a different position.

3. Release the mouse button.

- iMovie rearranges the clip.
- You can click ▶ to play the edited project.

Trim a Clip in a Project

You can trim a clip to remove footage that you do not want to appear in your movie. You can also trim clips if you need to make the overall movie a shorter duration.

Trim a Clip in a Project

1. Click and drag to select the part of the clip you want to keep.

iMovie displays a selection box.

- You can click and drag the edges to adjust the selection.

You can ⌘-click the selection and click **Play Selection** to preview it.

2. ⌘-click the selection and then click **Trim to Selection**.

iMovie trims the clip.

- You can click ▶ to play the edited project.

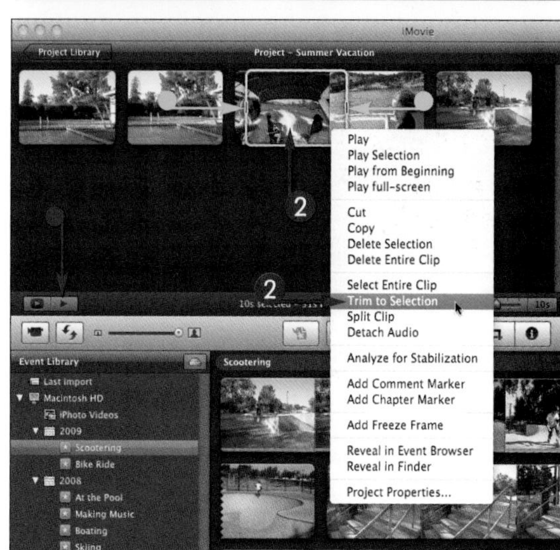

Insert a Clip

You can insert a video clip within another clip in your project. The second clip is divided in two and the first clip is placed in between.

Insert a Clip

1. Click and drag to select a clip to add in the event browser.

   You can drag across the entire clip or just a portion.

   You can also select the entire clip by ⌘-clicking it and selecting **Select Entire Clip** from the menu that appears.

2. Click and drag the clip inside a clip in your project.

   A red vertical line appears where the clip will be inserted.

   The scene is displayed in the viewer.

3. Release the mouse button.

iMovie displays a menu.

4. Click **Insert**.

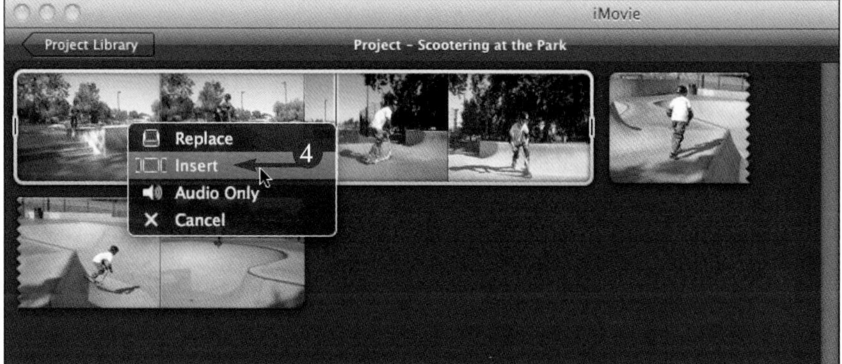

- The project clip is divided in two.
- The new clip is inserted in between.

How do I replace a clip in my project?

The steps for replacing a video clip are similar to inserting a clip.

1. Click and drag the replacement clip from the event browser onto the clip to replace in the project.
2. Release the mouse button.
3. In the menu that appears, click **Replace**.

   iMovie replaces the clip.

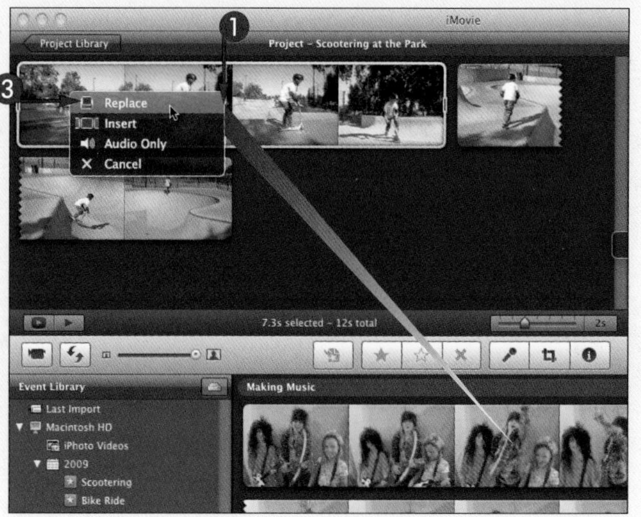

Split a Clip

You can split a clip into two. Then you can add a transition between the two new pieces, or add different effects to each of them.

Split a Clip

1. Click at the point where you want to split the clip and drag to make a selection.
2. Drag to the end of the clip and release the mouse button.

***Note:** If you make a selection in the middle of the clip instead of at the end, the clip will be split in three pieces.*

3. Click **Edit**.
4. Click **Split Clip**.

- iMovie splits the clip into two pieces.
- To join them together again after splitting, select one of the pieces and click **Edit** and then **Join Clips**.

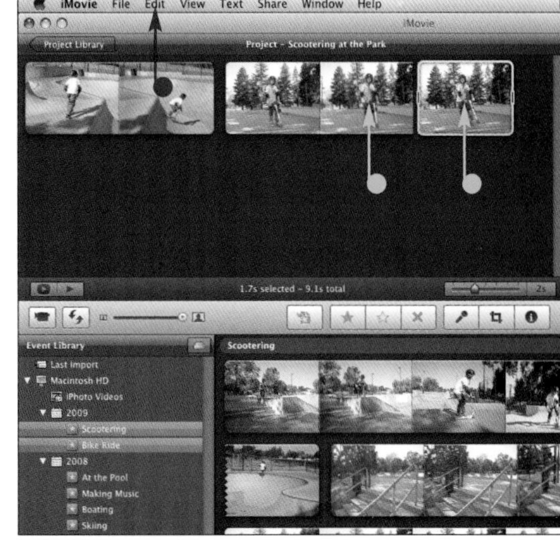

Find the Source of Clip

You can find the original source of a clip in the event browser. This can be useful if you want to locate similar clips to use in your project.

Find the Source of a Clip

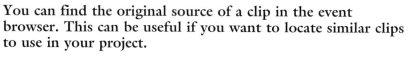

1. Click to select a clip in the project browser.
2. Click **Edit**.
3. Click **Reveal in Event Browser**.

- iMovie opens the associated event in the event browser and highlights the clip.

Add a Transition Between Clips

Transitions are special effects that blend the end of one clip with the beginning of another. iMovie offers a variety of transition types that you can add to your movies including fade-ins, page curls, and wipes.

Add a Transition Between Clips

1. Click [transitions icon] to open the transitions browser.

   iMovie displays a selection of predefined transitions.

- You can position your cursor over a transition thumbnail to see it played.

2. Click and drag a transition thumbnail between two clips in your project.

- A green line appears where the transition will be inserted.

3. Release your mouse button.

iMovie inserts the transition.

- A transition is represented in your project by a square icon.

4. Position your cursor to before a transition.

5. Press Spacebar.

- iMovie plays the movie in the viewer and displays the transition.

To delete a transition, you can ⌘-click its icon and click **Delete Selection** in the menu that appears.

How do I add a themed transition?

If you apply a theme to your project, iMovie makes available transitions that match that theme. For example, the Photo Album theme includes transitions that show clips taped to a photo album page. See Chapter 10 for more about themes.

1. Create a project with a theme.

Note: *See "Create a Project" for details.*

- For themed projects, special transitions appear at the top of the transitions browser.

2. Click and drag to place a themed transition between clips.

- You can click **Set Theme** to change the theme of a project.
- When you preview the transition, you can see the special styles and effects.

Edit a Transition

You can edit a transition to change its duration or effect. You might want to make changes to a transition to match the pace or mood of your movie.

Edit a Transition

❶ Double-click a transition icon in the project browser.

The Inspector appears.

❷ Type a transition duration in seconds.

● By default, the new duration is applied to all transitions in the project. Click to apply it only to the selected one (☑ changes to ☐).

❸ Click the transition effect.

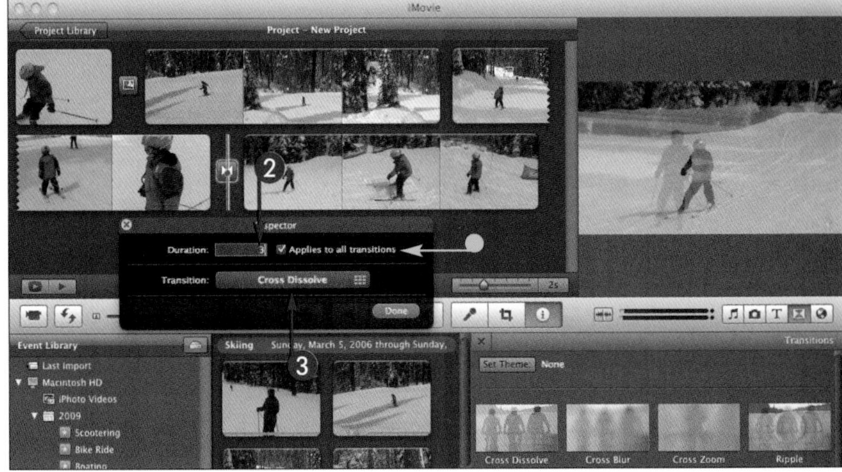

A Choose Transition dialog appears.

- You can drag the cursor across a thumbnail to preview the transition.

4 Click a thumbnail to select a new transition.

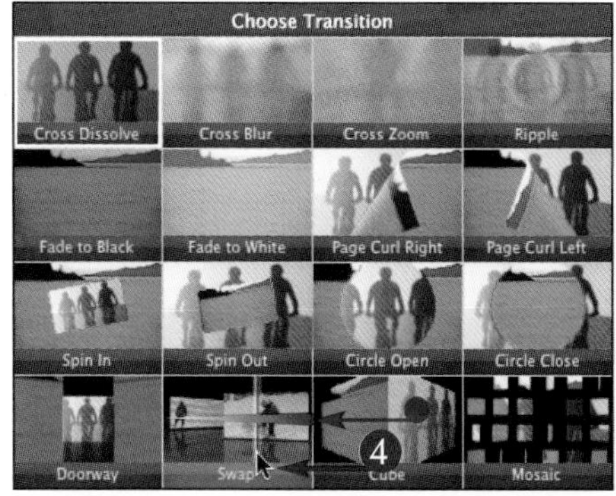

The Inspector appears.

5 Click **Done** to apply the changes.

How do I keep transitions from shortening my movie?

By default, iMovie overlaps the ends of your clips to create smooth transitions from one clip to another. This shortens the length of your movie slightly. You can change this behavior.

1 Open the Project Properties dialog by clicking **Set Theme** in the transitions browser.

2 Click to automatically add transitions between clips (☐ changes to ☑).

3 Click **Extend ends and maintain duration** (○ changes to ◉).

4 Click **OK**.

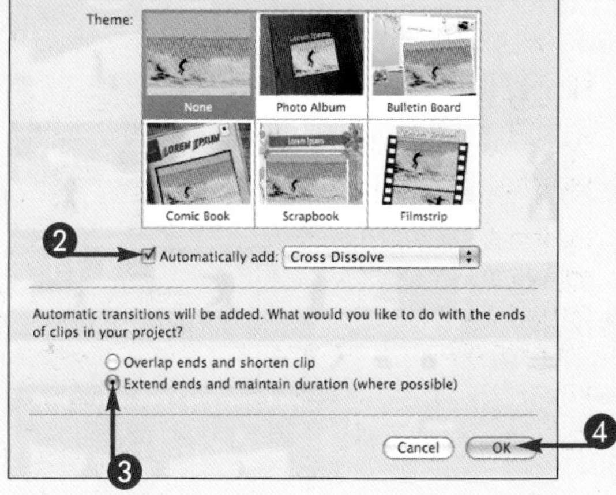

iMovie maintains movie duration by using a freeze frame at the end of clips when creating a transition. For more about freeze frames, see the tip section in "Add a Still Photo."

Use the Precision Editor

You can use the precision editor to magnify the view of a transition in order to fine-tune it. The editor lets you precisely trim or extend either clip in a transition so you can get just the right effect.

Use the Precision Editor

1. Add a transition to your project.

***Note:** See "Add a Transition Between Clips" for details.*

2. Position your cursor over the transition icon.

3. Click the edit icon (⚙) and click **Precision Editor** in the menu that appears.

iMovie opens the precision editor.

- The clip leading into the transition appears here.
- The transition appears here.
- The unused part of the clip, if present, appears here.
- The parts of the clip leading out of the transition appear here in the reverse order.

4. Drag the cursor to preview the transition.

A preview appears in the viewer.

5. Click and drag to adjust the clip leading in to the transition.

6. Click and drag to adjust the clip leading out of the transition.

- You can click and drag ⧓ to shift the transition independently of the clips.

iMovie makes the change to the transition.

7. Click **Done** to exit the precision editor.

TIP

How do I edit the transition duration in the precision editor?

Follow these steps:

1. Position the cursor over the left or right edge of the transition icon.

2. Click and drag left or right to shorten or lengthen the duration.

- iMovie changes the duration and displays the length in seconds on the icon.

Crop a Clip

You can use the Crop tool to highlight the main subject in a clip. Cropping a clip in a project does not alter the source clip, so you can still use the original version in other parts of a project.

Crop a Clip

1. Click to select a clip in your project.
2. Click **Crop** (⌗) or press C.

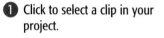

iMovie displays the Crop tool.

- You can click within the clip to view a specific frame.

3. Click and drag the corners to crop the clip.
4. Click and drag inside to move the Crop tool.

iMovie adjusts the crop area.

- You can click to preview the edited clip.

5 Click **Done**.

You can press Esc to exit the Crop tool without cropping.

iMovie crops the clip.

TIP

How do I change the default cropping when I add a clip?

You can change how iMovie crops a frame when you add a clip to a project.

1 Click **File** and then **Project Properties.**

2 Click **Timing** in the dialog that appears.

3 Click the **Initial Video Placement** menu.

- You can fit the entire clip in the frame. This may add black borders to the top and bottom or sides of the clip.
- You can fill the entire frame, which may crop the clip depending on the aspect ratios of the clip and the project.

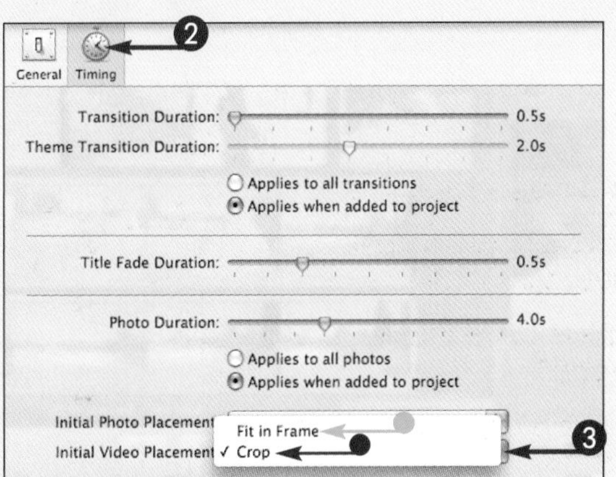

Rotate a Clip

You can use the Crop tool to rotate a video clip that you shot with your camera turned sideways. Rotating a clip in a project does not alter the original source clip.

Rotate a Clip

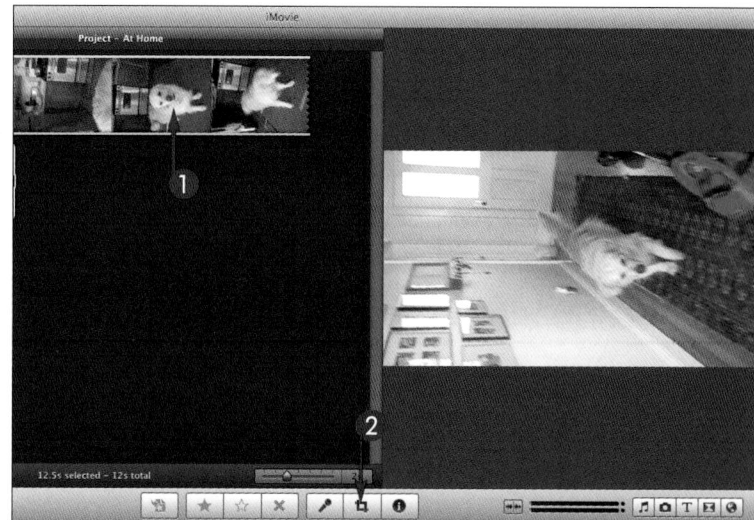

1. Click to select the clip in your project to rotate.
2. Click **Crop** (⌗) or press C.

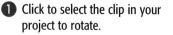

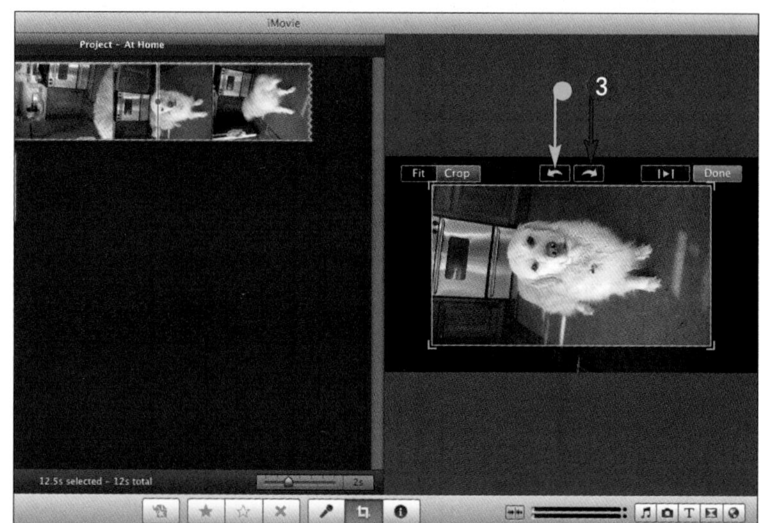

iMovie displays the Crop tool.

3. Click ↷ to rotate the clip clockwise.

- You can click ↶ to rotate the clip counterclockwise.

iMovie rotates the clip.

- You can click [▶|] to preview the edited clip.

4. Click **Done**.

You can press Esc to exit the Crop tool without rotating.

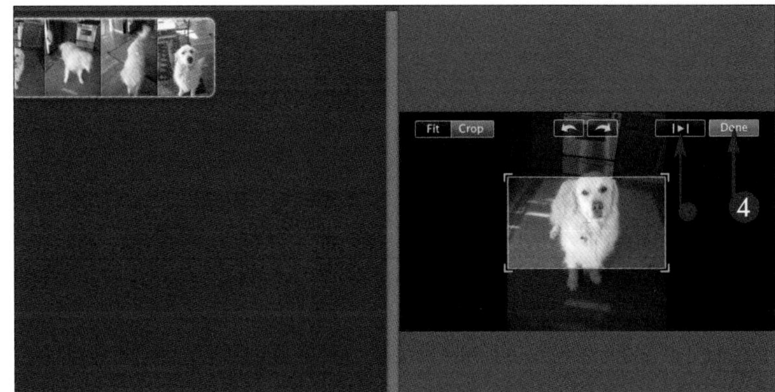

iMovie saves the change.

TIP

How do I turn the black bordering on and off in the Crop tool?

You can switch between the Fit and Crop modes in the Crop tool to turn black bordering on and off. You can see such bordering in the preview window.

1. Click **Fit** to fit the entire clip in the frame and add black borders if needed. These borders are called *letterboxes* on the top and bottom and *pillarboxes* on the sides.

- You can click **Crop** to fill the entire frame with the clip. This may crop your clip depending on the aspect ratios of the clip and the project.

Add a Title

You can add a title to your project to introduce your movie or describe a scene. Titles can exist on a separate background or be overlaid on a clip.

Add a Title

1. Click [T] to open the titles browser.

   iMovie displays its predefined titles.

- If a title includes animation, positioning your cursor over it plays the animation.

2. Click and drag a title to before or after a clip in a project.

   iMovie opens a selection of backgrounds.

- You can move your cursor across a background to preview it with sample text.

3. Click to select a background.

   iMovie adds the title and background.

- You can click and drag the edge of the title icon to change the duration.

4. Click here to select the title.

   The title editor appears in the viewer.

5. Click the title text.

   The title becomes editable.

6. Type the title text.

- You can click [▶|] to preview the title.

Note: To further customize the title, see "Edit a Title."

7. Click **Done** to close the title editor.

TIP

How do I add a title over a clip?

A title can appear over the content of a clip instead of over a background.

1. Click and drag the title onto a clip instead of before or after it.

- iMovie adds the title over the clip.

2. Click here to view and edit the title in the viewer.

Note: To further customize the title, see "Edit a Title."

Edit a Title

You can edit a title to change its font, color, size, and other properties. You can change your title text to make it contrast or blend in with its background.

Edit a Title

1. Add a title to your project.

Note: *See "Add a Title" for details.*

2. Click here to open the title editor in the viewer.

- You can click the text to edit the title content.

3. Click **Show Fonts**.

4. Click a font.
5. Click a color.
6. Click a size.

7 Click here to bold, italicize, or outline your text.

8 Click here to align your text.

- You can click **System Font Panel** to display more font choices.

9 Click **Done**.

You can click Esc to close the panel without making changes.

iMovie changes the title text.

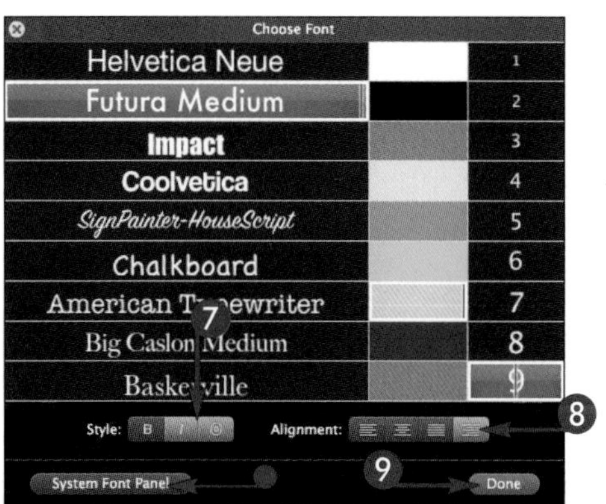

- You can click |▶| to preview the title.

10 Click **Done** to close the title editor.

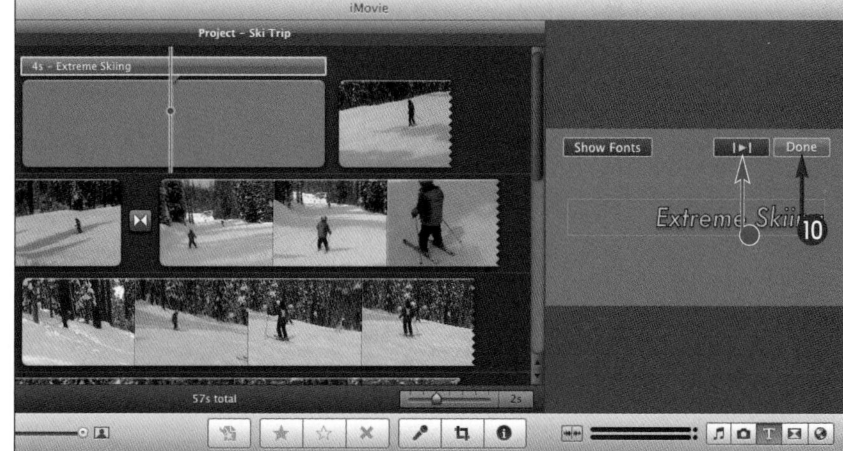

TIP

How do I control how a title fades in and out?

You can open the Inspector to control fading and other title properties.

1 Double-click the title icon.

The Inspector opens.

2 Click to manually adjust the fade in and out (○ changes to ◉).

3 Click and drag the slider to change the fade duration.

- The duration in seconds appears here.

- You can click here to change the title duration.

4 Click **Done** to close the Inspector and save the changes.

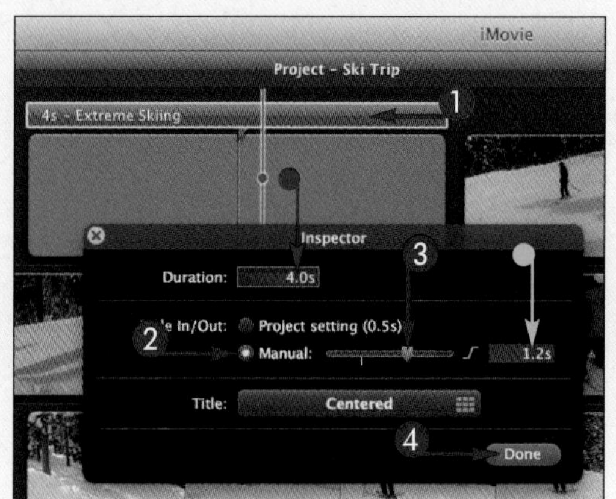

Add Closing Credits

You can add credits to the end of your project to list the people who created and starred in your movie. You can choose a background that matches the theme and mood of your movie.

Add Closing Credits

1. Click [T] to open the titles browser.

Note: Adding credits is similar to adding a title. See "Add a Title" for details.

2. Click and drag the **Scrolling Credits** thumbnail to the end of your project.

   You can drag the icon onto the final clip to have the credits scroll over the clip.

- Positioning your cursor over the thumbnail displays a preview of the credits.

iMovie opens a selection of backgrounds.

- You can move your cursor across a background to preview it.

3. Click to select a background.

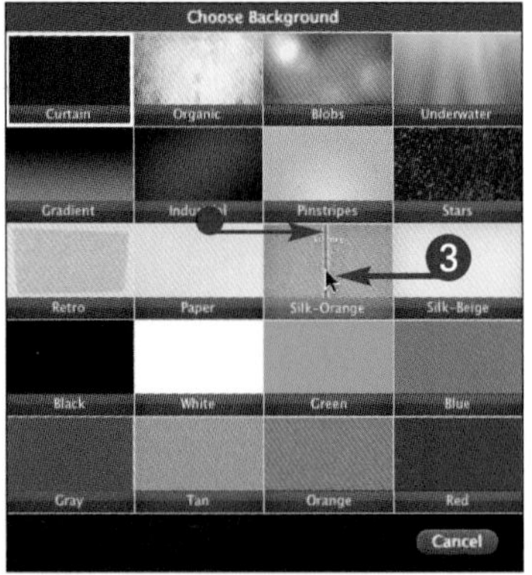

iMovie adds the credits and background to the project.

- You can click and drag the edge of the credits icon to change the duration.

4 Click here to select the credits.

The credits editor appears in the viewer.

5 Click and drag to select the text you want to change.

The text becomes editable.

6 Type your credits text.

- You can click ▶| to preview the credits.

Note: *To further customize the credits, see "Edit a Title."*

7 Click **Done** to close the credits editor.

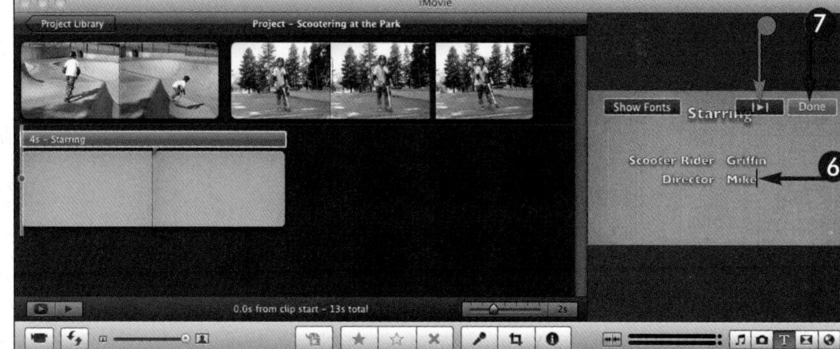

How do I check the spelling in my titles and credits?

You can use the built-in spell checker to have iMovie highlight misspellings and suggest alternatives.

1 Click a title or credits icon.

- iMovie displays the content in the viewer and underlines words that it cannot find in its dictionary.

2 Click **Edit**, **Spelling**, and then **Show Spelling and Grammar**.

iMovie displays spelling suggestions.

3 Click a suggestion and then click **Change** to replace a word.

- You can click **Learn** to add a correct word that iMovie thinks is misspelled to the iMovie dictionary.

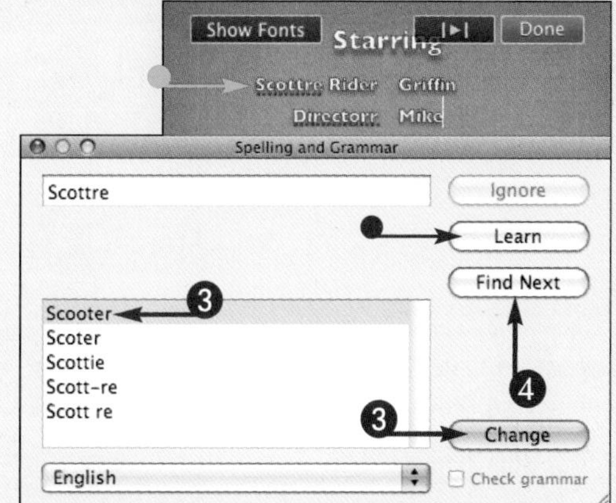

4 Click **Find Next** to look for the next misspelled word.

Add a Still Photo

You can add a still photo from iPhoto to your iMovie project. You can adjust the duration that the photo appears. For more about iPhoto, see Part II of this book.

Add a Still Photo

1. Click [camera icon] to open the photos browser.

   iMovie displays the iPhoto library.

2. Click the list to choose the photos to display.
3. Click and drag a photo thumbnail into the middle of a clip.
4. Release the mouse button.

A menu appears.

5. Click **Insert** to insert the photo as a still in your project.

- You can click **Replace** to replace the clip with the still photo.

Note: *If you drag the photo to before or after a clip, iMovie inserts the photo without displaying a menu.*

- iMovie inserts the still with a default duration of four seconds.

***Note:** By default, iMovie adds subtle panning and zooming, also known as a Ken Burns effect, to the inserted photo. See "Adjust the Ken Burns Effect" for details.*

6. Double-click the still photo.

iMovie opens the Inspector.

- You can type a number of seconds to change the duration of the still photo.
- You can click here to add a photo effect such as a color change or a vignette.

***Note:** For more about effects, see Chapter 10.*

7. Click **Done** to close the Inspector and save your changes.

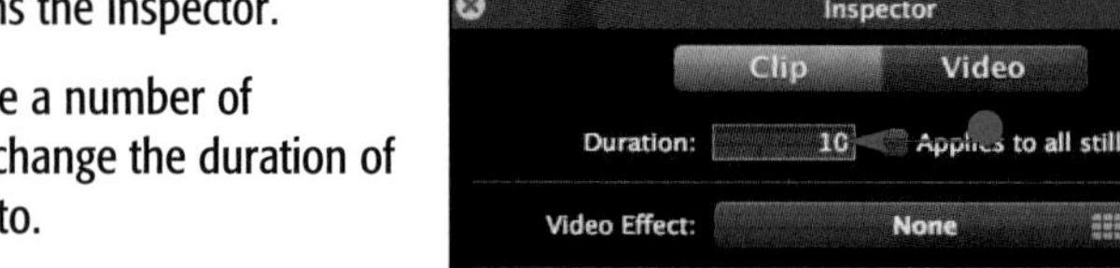

How do I add a freeze frame to my movie?

You can freeze a frame in your clip for a period of time to highlight an important moment in your project.

1. Drag your cursor over a clip to locate the frame you want to freeze.
2. ⌘-click the clip.
3. Click **Add Freeze Frame** from the menu that appears.

   iMovie adds a still photo to the project using the frame from your clip.

   You can use the techniques covered above to edit the still photo.

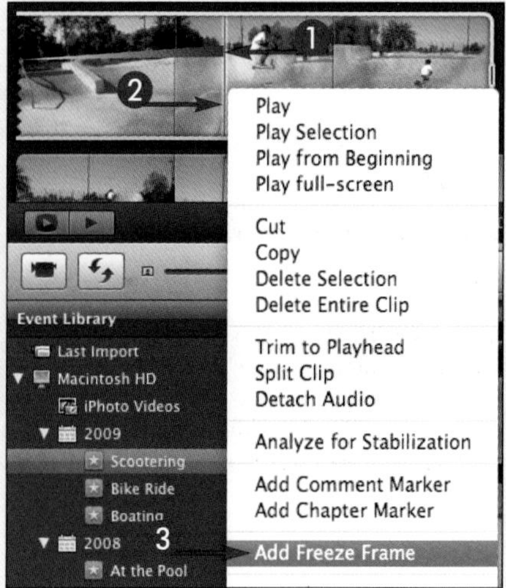

Adjust the Ken Burns Effect

When you add a still photo to a project, iMovie automatically adds a Ken Burns effect, which is a slight panning and zooming as the photo appears. This can make a normally motionless slide more interesting. You can adjust the panning and zooming in the effect or turn it off altogether.

Adjust the Ken Burns Effect

1. Add a still photo to a project.

Note: *See "Add a Still Photo" for details.*

2. Click to select the photo.
3. Position the cursor over the selection and double-click the crop icon (⊡).

iMovie displays the Crop tool with Ken Burns selected.

- The green box shows the starting position and zoom of the photo.
- The red box shows the ending position and zoom of the photo.

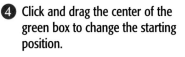

4. Click and drag the center of the green box to change the starting position.

5. Click and drag a corner handle of the green box to change the starting zoom.

6. Make the same adjustments to the red box to change the ending position and zoom.

7. You can click |▶| to preview the effect.

   You can turn off the Ken Burns effect by selecting a different display option.

- Click **Fit** to fit the entire clip in the frame and add black borders if needed. These borders are called *letterboxes* on the top and bottom and *pillarboxes* on the sides.
- Click **Crop** to fill the entire frame with the clip. This may result in cropping depending on the aspect ratios of the clip and the project.

8. Click **Done** to exit the Crop tool.

How can I swap the starting and ending positions in a Ken Burns effect?

You can click the swap icon (⇄) in the Crop tool to swap the starting and ending positions of a still photo in a Ken Burns effect.

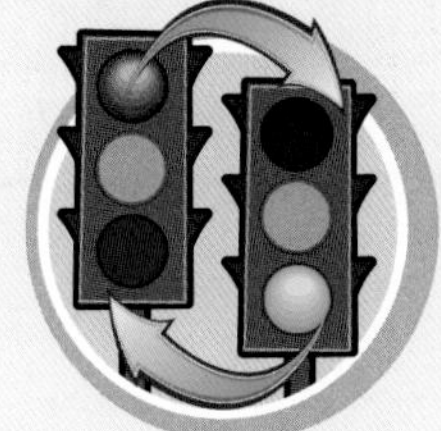

Why is it called a Ken Burns effect?

Ken Burns is a documentary director known for using panning and zooming when presenting old photographs in his movies.

Add Background Music

You can add background music to your iMovie project to complement the theme of your movie. You can use songs from iTunes or GarageBand for your background music.

For more about creating songs in GarageBand, see Part IV of this book.

Add Background Music

1. Click [music icon] to open the music and sound effects browser.
2. Click the list to view available songs.
   - You can click [play icon] to play a selected song.
   - You can type a song or artist name to search for a song.
3. Click and drag a song to the outside edge of the project browser.

Note: *To add a song as background music, do not drag it onto a clip.*

- The project browser background turns green or purple, depending on the type of song you are adding.

4. Release the mouse button.

   iMovie adds the song as background music.

- The name and how long the song plays appear here.

- You can click ▶ to play your movie with the new music.

5. If your movie is longer than the song, you can click and drag additional songs to fill the entire project with music.

***Note:** To change the volume of the background music and other audio in your project, see "Adjust Volume."*

How do I choose just part of a song to use as background music?

You can change when the background song begins and ends using the Clip Trimmer.

1. Click the edit icon (⚙).
2. Click **Clip Trimmer** in the menu that appears.
   - iMovie opens the Clip Trimmer and displays the song as a waveform, which is a graphical representation of the notes.
3. Click and drag the yellow handle to set when the song begins as background music.
   - You can click ▶| to preview the edited song.
4. To set when the song ends, scroll to the end of the song and adjust the ending handle.

Add a Sound Effect

You can choose from a variety of sound effects to accentuate the action occurring in your movie. After you add a sound effect, you can move it to just the right frame in your movie and also adjust the volume.

Add a Sound Effect

1. Click [music icon] to open the music and sound effects browser.
2. Click a list item to view the available sound effects.

- The sound effects appear here.
- You can click [play] to play a selected sound effect.
- You can type a keyword to search for a sound effect.

3. Click and drag a sound effect to the location in a clip where it plays.
4. Release the mouse button.

- iMovie displays a green icon where the sound effect is added.

  You can click and drag the icon to change when the effect plays.

  You can click the icon and press Spacebar to preview the new effect.

5. Click and drag to add more sound effects from the music and sound effects browser.

   Sound effects can overlap one another in a project.

***Note:** To change the volume of a sound effect and other audio in your project, see "Adjust Volume."*

TIPS

How do I turn the sound off when I skim clips?

Sometimes the audio accompaniment can be distracting when you are editing a project. You can click the **Audio Skimming** button (⧓) below the viewer to silence the audio when you drag your cursor across, or *skim*, clips in the project and event browsers.

How do I turn off audio from a video clip when the sound effect plays?

Reducing the volume of one source of audio as another one plays is called *ducking*. You can double-click a sound effect icon in your project and then click **Audio**. You can give the sound effect priority over other sounds using the ducking settings. For more about adjusting music and sound effects, see "Adjust Volume."

Adjust Volume

You can adjust the volume of the different sounds in your movie, including sounds from the video clips, background music, and sound effects. iMovie gives you control over overall volume as well as how audio fades in and out.

Adjust Volume

1. Double-click the music, sound effect, or clip whose volume you want to adjust.

   The Inspector opens.

2. Click **Audio**.

   The audio volume controls appear.

3. Click and drag the slider to adjust the overall volume of the music, sound effect, or clip.

   You can drag the slider all the way to the left to mute the clip.

4. Click to reduce the sound of other clips as a selected item plays (☐ changes to ☑).

- You can use the slider to adjust how much the other sounds are reduced.

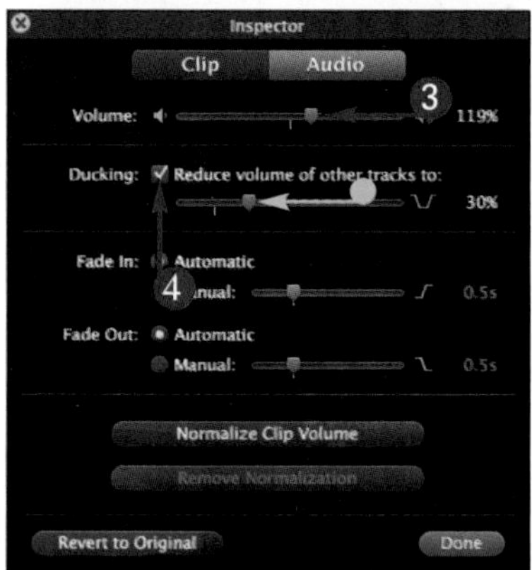

5. Click to adjust how the audio fades in (○ changes to ◉).
6. Click and drag the slider to the left to fade it in quickly or to the right to fade it in gradually.
7. Click to adjust how the audio fades out (○ changes to ◉).
8. Click and drag the slider to the left to fade it out quickly or to the right to fade it out gradually.
9. You can click **Normalize Clip Volume** to *normalize* the selection, making its volume consistent with the other audio in the project.
10. Click **Done**.

    iMovie adjusts the volumes.

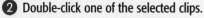

- You can click ▶ to play the project and listen to the results.

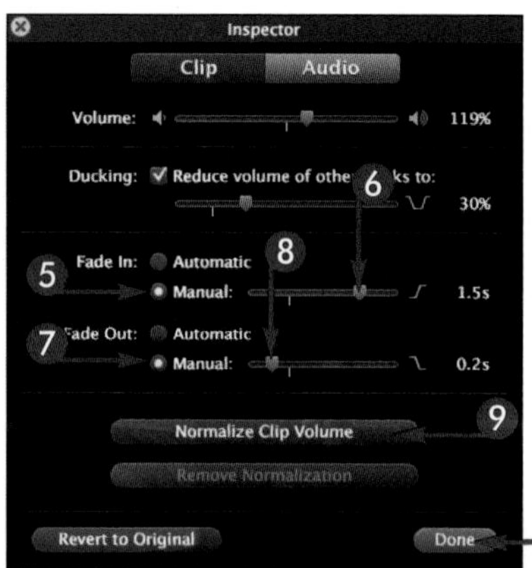

How do I change the volume of multiple clips in my project?

You can select multiple video clips and make changes to their audio all at once. Note that you cannot select multiple sound effects or background songs, only video clips.

1. ⌘-click to select multiple clips.
2. Double-click one of the selected clips.
3. In the Inspector, click **Audio**.
4. Make your audio adjustments.
5. Click **Done** to apply the adjustments to the selected clips.

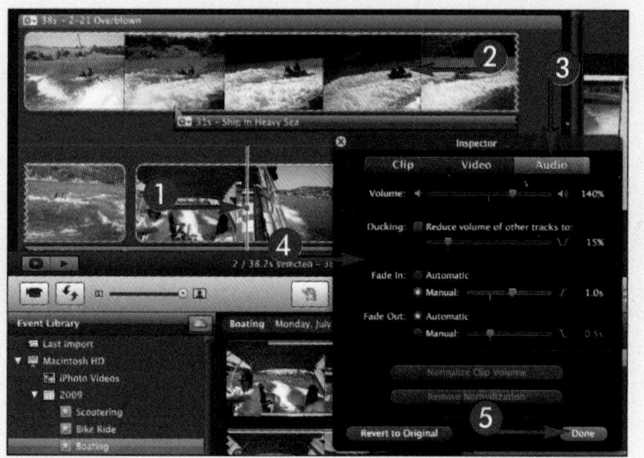

Add a Beat Marker

You can add beat markers where audio beats occur to synchronize action in the clip with the rhythm of the music. You add beat markers in the Clip Trimmer.

Add a Beat Marker

1. Click ⚙ for the audio you want to mark.
2. Click **Clip Trimmer**.

The Clip Trimmer opens.

- iMovie displays the music as a *waveform*, which is a graphical representation of the song.

You can move your cursor across the waveform to find the beats.

3. Click and drag ♪ to a beat in the song.

- You can also click ▶| to play the song and press M to add beat markers as it plays.

- iMovie adds a beat marker to the audio clip, which appears as a vertical white line in the waveform.
- If the audio overlays a clip, iMovie also splits the clip at the beat marker. This allows you to easily replace content between beats in your project.

How do I remove a beat marker?

Follow these steps:

1. Click and drag the vertical line representing the beat marker outside the Clip Trimmer.

   iMovie deletes the beat marker.

- You can also Control-click the waveform and then click **Remove All Beat Markers** to remove them all.

Synchronize Content to Beats

After you add beat markers to the beats in your song, you can easily synchronize your clips to play between the markers. When the snap-to-beats setting is turned on, iMovie automatically trims clips and still photos to fit between the next two markers.

Synchronize Content to Beats

1. Set beat markers in a song in your project. See "Add a Beat Marker" for details.

- In this example, beat markers have been added to the background music.

2. Click **View** and select **Snap to Beats** if the setting is not already checked.

3. Select a video clip to add. Make sure it is longer than the duration between beats.

Note: *For more about adding clips to a project, see Chapter 8.*

4. Click and drag the selection to add it to the end of the project.

   iMovie adds the clip to the project.

- The clip is truncated to fit between the next two beat markers.

5. Click [photo button] to open the photos browser.

6. Click and drag a photo to add it to the end of the project.

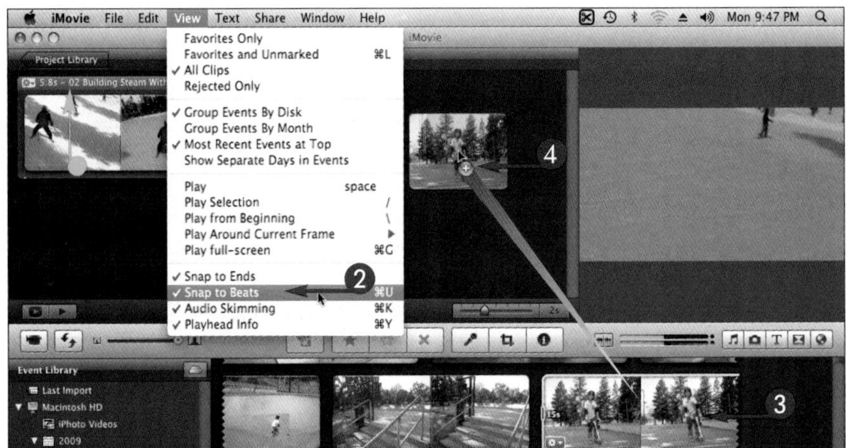

iMovie adds a still photo to the project.

- The photo is shown for the duration between the next two beat markers.

For more about adding still photos to a project, see Chapter 8.

7 Click to preview the project.

Because the content was snapped to the beats as it was added, the transitions match the rhythm of the background music.

How do I change the part of the clip that appears between the beat markers?

When iMovie shortens a clip to fit it between beats, it trims from the end of the clip. In the precision editor, you can shift your video so that a different part of the clip appears.

1. Position your cursor over the clip you want to edit.
2. Click and click **Precision Editor** in the menu that appears.

   The precision editor opens.
3. Click and drag the clip to the left to display a different part.
4. Click **Done** to save the change.

Record a Voiceover

You can add voiceover audio using a built-in or external microphone on your Mac. You record a voiceover within iMovie as your project plays. The recording is then added to your project.

Record a Voiceover

1. Click [microphone button] to open the voiceover settings.
2. Click here to select a microphone.
3. Speak into the microphone to adjust the recording levels.
4. As you speak, click and drag the slider so that your voice generates a strong green signal in the meter without turning the meter red.
5. You can click and drag the slider to control noise reduction, which can reduce background noise.

- You can click to turn off voice enhancement (☑ changes to ☐), which can electronically smooth your voice.
- You can click to play project audio as you record (☐ changes to ☑). Because your microphone can pick up this sound, you need to wear headphones if choosing this option.

6. Click a clip at the point where you want to start the voiceover.

iMovie counts down from three and then starts recording.

7. Speak into the microphone to create your voiceover.

- iMovie displays red where it has recorded in the project.

8. Click anywhere in the workspace to stop recording.

- iMovie adds the voiceover to your project as a purple icon.

9. Click ☒ to close the settings.

- You can click ▶ to play the project.

Note: *To change the volume of the voiceover, see "Adjust Volume."*

How do I add only the sound from a video clip, and not the video itself, to my project?

After selecting a video clip in the event browser, click and drag the selection onto an existing clip in the project browser. Click **Audio Only** from the menu that appears. iMovie adds the audio, which appears as a green icon in the project.

How do I mute the audio of a clip?

Select the clip in the project, click **Edit**, and then click **Mute Clip**. iMovie turns off the sound for that clip. You can mute video clips and audio clips this way. For more about changing the volume in your project, see "Adjust Volume."

Add a Video Effect to a Clip

You can add a video effect to a clip in your project to change its color or lighting. iMovie's effects allow you to quickly add an old-fashioned look, make your subjects glow, or add a shadowed vignette.

Add a Video Effect to a Clip

1. Double-click a video clip in your project.

   The Inspector opens with the clip adjustments showing.

2. Click **None**.

The Choose Video Effect panel appears.

- The None effect is selected.

3. Position your cursor over a video effect.

- iMovie previews the effect in the viewer.

4. Click an effect to apply it.

   This example shows the Heat Wave effect, which brightens and increases the contrast in a clip.

- You can click **Cancel** to close the panel without applying the effect.

The Inspector appears.

5. Click **Done** to close the Inspector and finish applying the effect.

- You can click to preview the video.

How do I turn off a video effect?

Follow these steps:

1. Double-click a video clip in your project to open the Inspector.
2. Click the **Video Effect** button. It will be labeled with the currently applied effect.
3. In the Choose Video Effect panel, click **None** to turn off the effect.

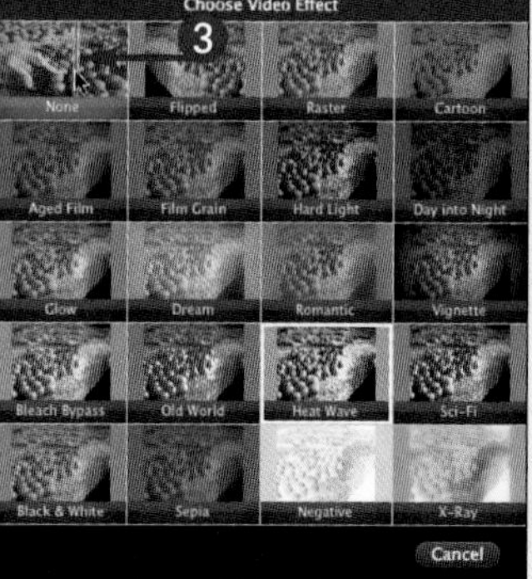

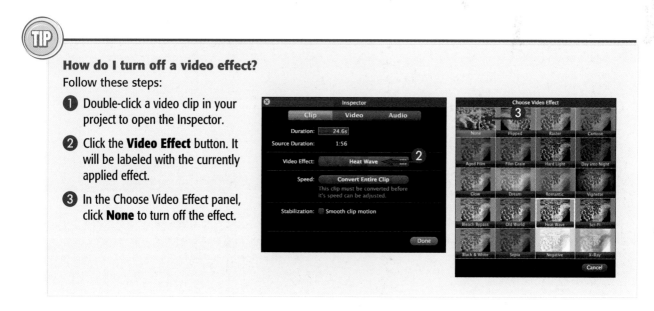

Adjust Color and Lighting in a Clip

You can use video settings to boost or dampen colors, brighten or dim lighting, and make other adjustments in your project. This can help you improve a poorly shot clip or add special visual effects to establish the mood in your movie.

Adjust Color and Lighting in a Clip

1. Double-click a video clip in your project to open the Inspector.
2. Click **Video**.

   iMovie displays the color and lighting settings.

3. Click and drag the Exposure slider to adjust the shadows and highlights.
4. Click and drag the Brightness slider to change the overall lighting.
5. Click and drag the Contrast slider to adjust the balance of the light and dark tones.

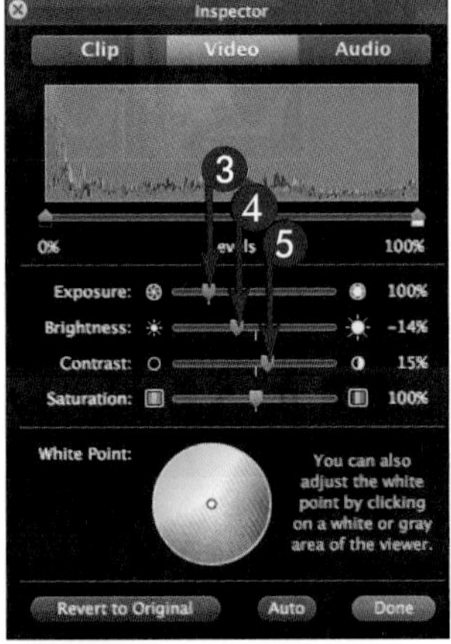

6. Click and drag the Saturation slider to change the color intensity.

   You can drag the Saturation slider to the right to make colors richer or to the left to remove color.

7. Click a color that should be pure white or gray color in the viewer.

- iMovie adjusts the white point to remove any color cast that may be present.

8. Click **Done**.

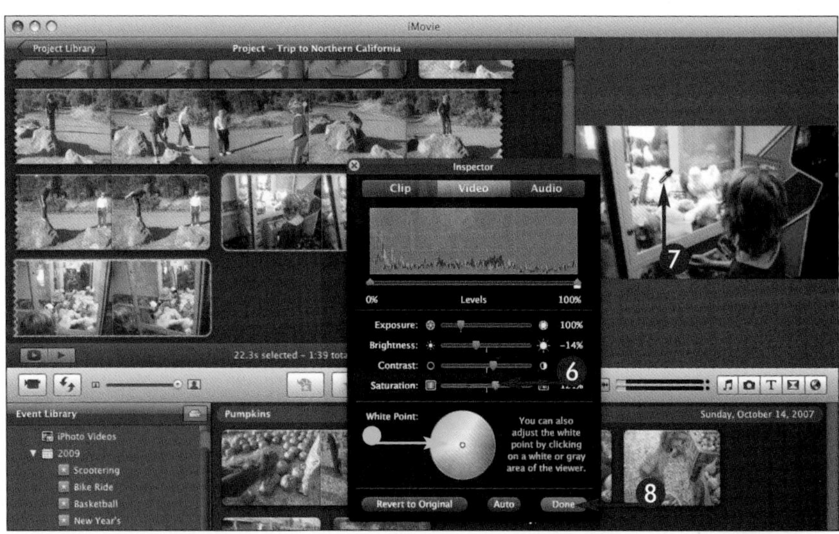

iMovie applies the adjustments to the clip.

- You can click ▶ to preview the video.

What are the Levels adjustments?

In the Video adjustments panel, Levels allow you to adjust dark and light tones in a clip more precisely.

- The Levels graph shows a color histogram that represents the distribution of colors in the clip. Darker colors are on the right and lighter colors are on the left.

1. You can click and drag the left slider to the right to boost the darker tones.

2. You can click and drag the right slider to the left to boost the lighter tones.

   Moving the left and right sliders toward the middle slightly can often improve the look of a clip by improving the color range.

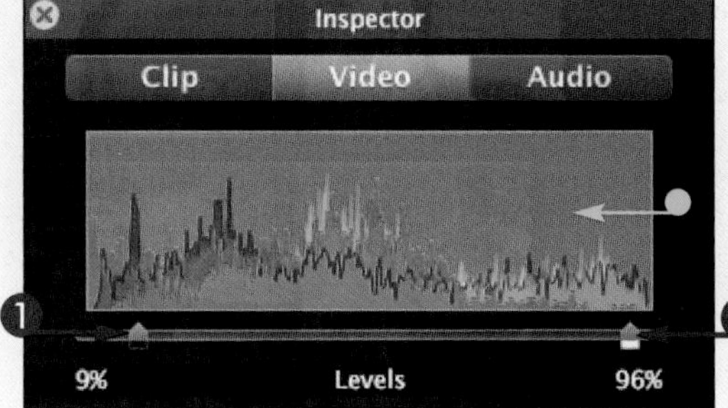

Adjust the Speed of a Clip

You can speed up or slow down a clip to emphasize the action occurring. You can boost the speed up to eight times the original rate or slow it down to one eighth the original rate.

Adjust the Speed of a Clip

1. Double-click a clip in your project.

   The Inspector opens.

2. Click **Convert Entire Clip**.

   iMovie must process a clip before it makes changes to the speed.

   The clip is converted and the speed controls appear.

3. Click and drag the slider to adjust the speed of the clip.

   Click and drag to the left to slow the clip down or to the right to speed it up.

- iMovie changes the length of the clip in the project to match the new speed.

  The clip lengthens if it is slowed down and shortens if it is sped up.

4. Click **Done**.

iMovie saves the changes to the speed of the clip.

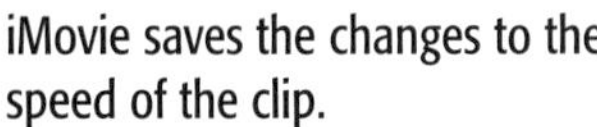

- You can click ▶ to play the movie with the adjusted speed.

How do I change the speed of action in the middle of a clip?

You can change the speed only of an entire clip in a project. To adjust action in the middle of a clip, first select the action and then split the clip.

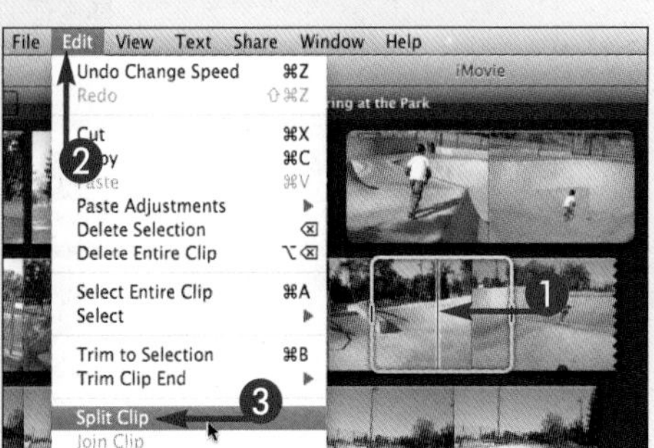

1. Click and drag to select only the action you want to change.
2. Click **Edit**.
3. Click **Split Clip**.

   iMovie divides the clip into new left, middle, and right clips.

4. Select the middle clip and follow the steps above to change the speed.

Reverse a Clip

You can reverse a clip to make action play backward. You can use this effect to add humor to your movie or to emphasize action in a scene by making it play back and forth.

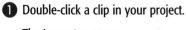

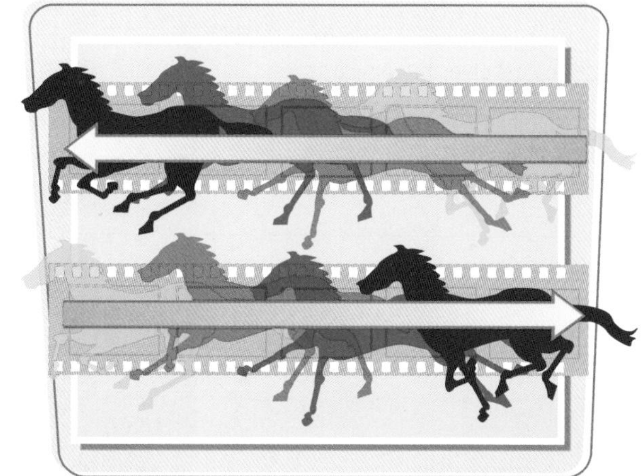

Reverse a Clip

1. Double-click a clip in your project.

   The Inspector opens.

2. Click **Convert Entire Clip**.

   iMovie must process a clip before it reverses the direction of the clip.

The clip is converted and the speed controls appear.

3. Click to reverse the direction of the clip (☐ changes to ☑).

- iMovie reverses the direction of the thumbnails in the project.

4 Click **Done**.

iMovie saves the changes to the direction of the clip.

- You can click ▶ to play your movie with the reversed clip.

TIP

How do I make a clip play forward and then backward?

You can duplicate a clip and then reverse the action in the second copy.

1 Click to select a clip.

2 Click **Edit**.

3 Click **Copy**.

4 Click **Edit** again and then click **Paste**.

- iMovie creates a second copy of the clip.

5 Select the second copy of the clip and follow the steps above to reverse the action.

Stabilize a Clip

iMovie can analyze the motion in a clip so that it can stabilize the action. This can often improve bumpy video shot from a moving vehicle, for example.

Stabilize a Clip

ANALYZE FOR STABILIZATION

1. Select a clip in the event browser.

   You can also select a clip in the project browser to stabilize it.

2. Click **File**.
3. Click **Analyze for Stabilization**.

- iMovie analyzes the clip and displays a progress bar.
- You can click **Cancel** to stop the stabilization analysis.

Note: *Stabilization is resource-intensive and takes time to complete. When analyzing a long video, you may want to let the process run overnight or while you are away from your computer.*

iMovie completes the analysis.

- Parts of the video where stabilization failed are marked with red squiggles.

ADD A STABILIZED CLIP

1. Click and drag to select an analyzed clip.
2. Click and drag the clip to your project.

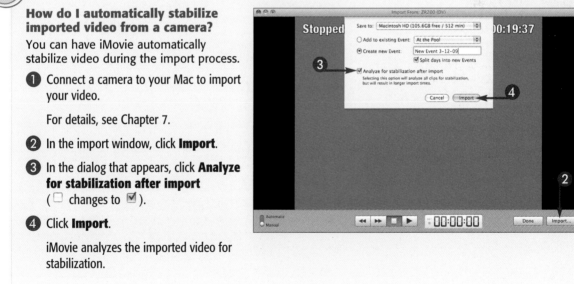

How do I automatically stabilize imported video from a camera?

You can have iMovie automatically stabilize video during the import process.

1. Connect a camera to your Mac to import your video.

   For details, see Chapter 7.
2. In the import window, click **Import**.
3. In the dialog that appears, click **Analyze for stabilization after import** (☐ changes to ☑).
4. Click **Import**.

   iMovie analyzes the imported video for stabilization.

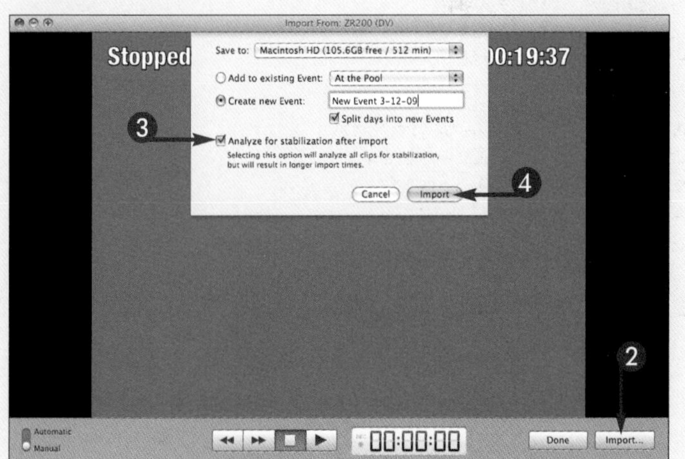

Stabilize a Clip *(continued)*

iMovie stabilizes the clip by analyzing the camera motion and then moving the video in the opposite direction to steady the action as it plays. The video is zoomed slightly so that the clip can be moved.

Stabilize a Clip *(continued)*

iMovie adds the clip to your project.

3. Click to select the clip.
4. Press Spacebar.

iMovie plays the stabilized clip.

- As the clip plays, it is zoomed and shifted to smooth any jerky movement.

TURN OFF STABILIZATION

1. Double-click a clip that has been stabilized.

The Inspector opens.

2. Click **Smooth clip motion** (☑ changes to ☐).

iMovie turns off the stabilization for the clip.

3. Click **Done**.
4. Select the clip and press Spacebar to view the change.

How do I limit the zooming that the stabilization feature applies?

You can limit the amount of zoom that iMovie applies during stabilization to view more or less of the scene.

1. Double-click a stabilized clip in the project.
2. In the Inspector, click and drag the slider to control the amount of zoom. Drag it to the left to lessen the zoom and to the right to increase the zoom.

   The clip adjusts in the viewer to show the amount of zoom.
3. Click **Done**.

Apply a Theme to a Project

You can add a theme to an iMovie project to automatically insert stylized graphics, transitions, and titles. You can edit the transitions and titles to further customize your project.

Apply a Theme to a Project

1. Click T to open the titles browser.

   The titles browser opens.

2. Click **Set Theme**.

Note: *You can also set the theme when you create a project. See Chapter 8 for details.*

3. Position your cursor over a thumbnail to preview the style of the theme.

4. Click a theme.

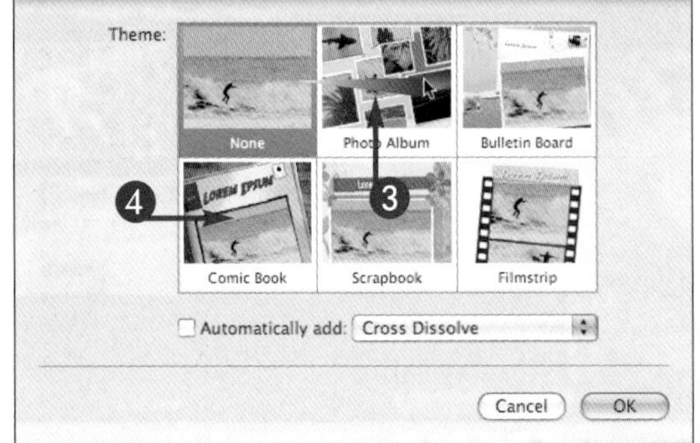

5 Click to add theme-related transitions and titles (☐ changes to ☑).

***Note:** Selecting this may replace transitions and titles already in your project.*

- You can choose how to create the transitions (○ change to ◉).

6 Click **OK**.

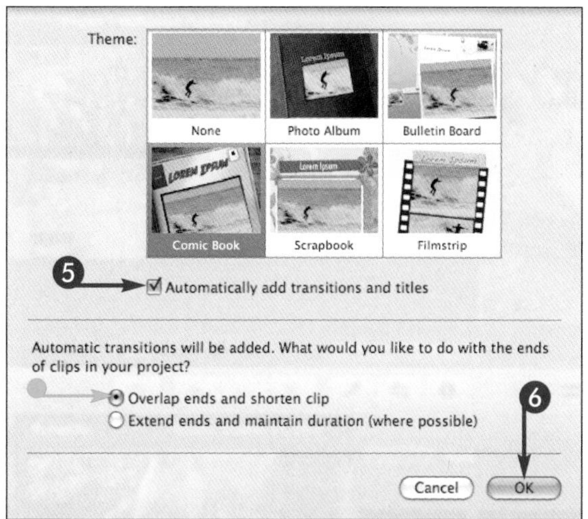

iMovie applies the theme to your project.

- Transitions are added between some clips.
- Titles are added to some clips.

7 Click  to preview the themed project.

TIP

How do I edit a themed title?

Editing a themed title is similar to editing a regular title.

1 Click here to select a title in your themed project.

The title appears in the viewer.

2 Click here to select the title text.

3 Type a new title.

***Note:** You cannot change the fonts in themed titles like you can in regular titles. For more about editing regular titles, see Chapter 8.*

4 Click **Done** to apply the edit.

Add a Picture-In-Picture Effect

You can embed a small version of a clip within another clip, known as a *picture in picture*, and have the clips play at the same time. This is useful when you want to present different perspectives of the same scene simultaneously or insert footage of someone commenting on the action.

You must turn on Advanced Tools in the iMovie preferences to use the picture-in-picture effect.

Add a Picture-In-Picture Effect

1. Click **iMovie** and then **Preferences**.
2. Click **Show Advanced Tools** (☐ changes to ☑).
3. Click ● to close the preferences.

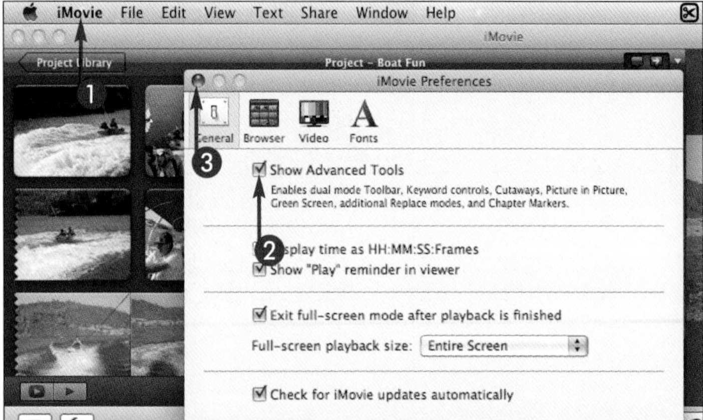

4. In the event browser, click and drag to select the clip you want to embed.
5. Click and drag the selection onto a clip in your project.

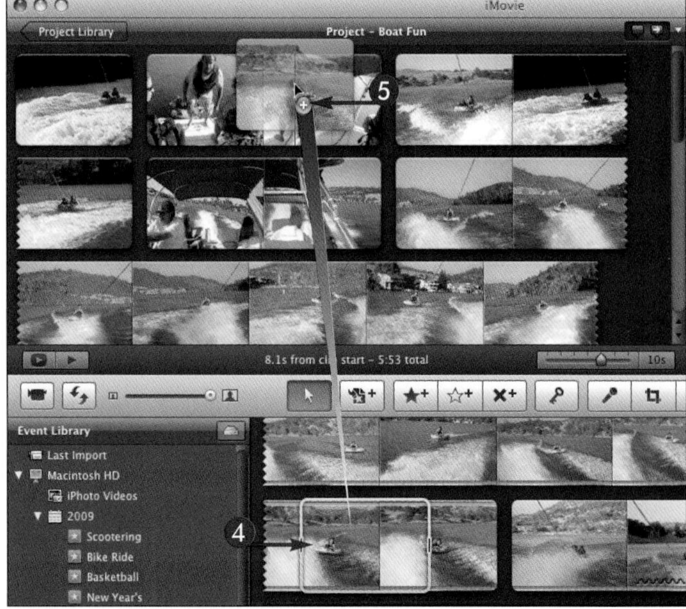

6 Click **Picture in Picture** in the menu that appears.

iMovie inserts the clip.

- The inserted clip appears as a thumbnail above the other clip.

7 In the viewer, click and drag the middle of the embedded clip to change its position.

8 Click and drag a corner to change its size.

9 Click **Done** to save the changes.

- You can select the embedded clip and press Spacebar to preview it.

How do I add a cutaway effect?

A cutaway is similar to a picture-in-picture effect except that the added clip takes up the entire screen. You can use a cutaway to show a person's response to action in the scene or to cover up imperfect footage. You must have the Advanced Tools turned on in iMovie's preferences to add a cutaway.

1 Click and drag the selection you want to use as the cutaway onto a clip in the project.

2 Click **Cutaway** in the menu that appears.

iMovie adds a cutaway to the project.

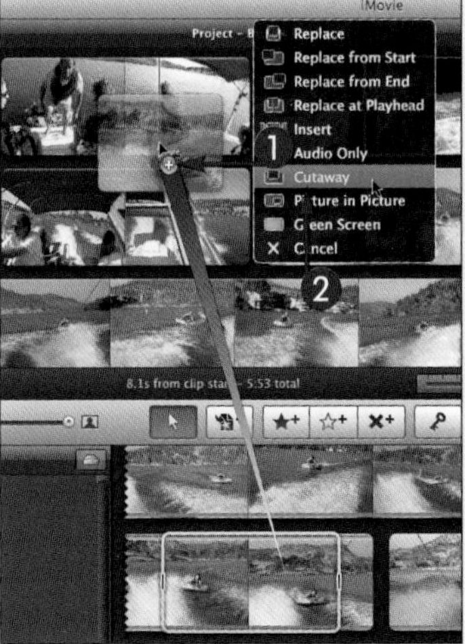

Add an Animated Travel Map

You can add a map to a travel-oriented project that shows starting and ending locations on the map. When you play the map, an animation connects the two locations. iMovie includes a database with thousands of geographic locations to help you illustrate places featured in your movie.

Add an Animated Travel Map

1. Click [globe icon] to view the maps and backgrounds browser.

   iMovie displays globe maps and flat maps for adding to your project.

2. Click and drag a map to between clips in your project.

   iMovie adds the map to your project and the Inspector opens.

3. Click the **Start Location** button.

The Choose City or Airport dialog appears.

4. Type a city or airport code.

   iMovie displays results for the search term.

5. Click a result to select it as a start location.

- You can optionally edit the label so it shows a different location, a landmark, or a person's name.

6. Click **OK** to return to the Inspector.

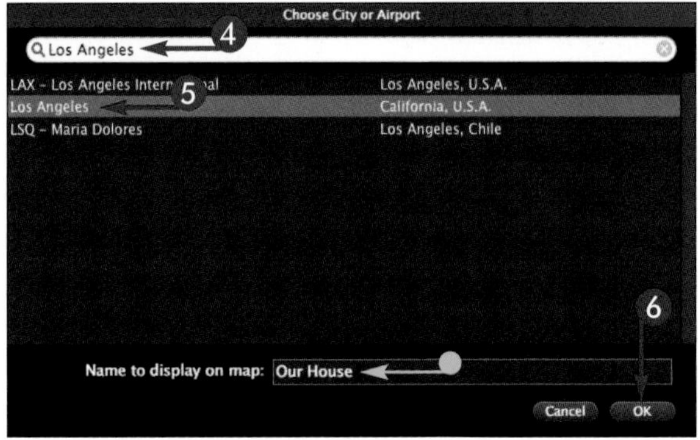

To feature a map that shows just a single location, skip to step **9**.

7. Click to include an end location (☐ changes to ☑).

8. Click here and repeat steps **4** to **6** to select an end location.

9. Click **Done** to save the new map.

- You can click the map and press Spacebar to preview the animated map.

Can I show a world map without displaying a specific location?

iMovie features several flat world maps without locations in the maps and backgrounds browser.

1. Click and drag a flat map from the third row in the browser to your project.

   iMovie adds a map without locations to your project.

2. Position the cursor over the map and double-click the crop icon (⌗) to open the Crop tool.

3. Click and drag the green and red boxes to adjust the Ken Burns effect, which is the panning and zooming that takes place when the map appears. For more about the Ken Burns effect, see Chapter 8.

Add a Green-Screen Effect

You can capture action in front of a green-colored backdrop and then use iMovie's tools to replace the backdrop with another image. You can use the effect to place people in famous locations, next to interesting animals, or against illustrated backgrounds.

The green-screen feature is one of the iMovie advanced tools. To turn on the advanced tools, see "Add a Picture-In-Picture Effect."

Add a Green-Screen Effect

1. Create a clip of your subjects against a solid green backdrop.

Note: You can buy green fabric from a video production supply store. The color used for this technique is called chroma key green.

2. Add the background on which you want your subjects to appear to your project.

Note: The background can be a video or a still photo. For more about adding still photos to a project, see Chapter 8.

3. Select the green-screen clip.

4. Click and drag the selection onto the background.

5 In the menu that appears, click **Green Screen**.

iMovie adds the clip as a green-screen clip, which appears above the background in the project browser.

6 Click to select the green-screen clip.

7 Click |▶| to preview the effect in the viewer.

The green backdrop is automatically removed from around the subjects.

How can I use cropping to improve the green-screen effect?

You can crop the subject in the clip to lessen the chance that unwanted artifacts appear around it, which can happen when the green backdrop is not perfectly solid. Click to select the green-screen clip in the project browser. iMovie displays the clip in the viewer. Click and drag the crop handles (◯) in the viewer to isolate just the subject of the clip and anywhere else the subject moves during the segment.

How can I subtract the final frame to improve the green-screen effect?

When shooting a clip, you can have the subjects move out of the frame at the end so that only the green backdrop is shown. You can then have iMovie analyze that final frame to improve the quality of the effect. Double-click a green-screen clip in the project browser to open the Inspector. Then select **Subtract last frame** (☐ changes to ☑) to apply the setting.

Organize Clips Using Keywords

You can assign keywords to describe the subject matter, location, and other characteristics of your clips. Then you can filter clips in the event browser by keywords to pull up the content you need for your projects.

The keywords feature is one of the iMovie advanced tools. To turn on the advanced tools, see "Add a Picture-In-Picture Effect."

Organize Clips Using Keywords

ADD A KEYWORD TO A CLIP

1. In the event browser, click and drag to select the clip to which you want to add a keyword.

   You can apply keywords to an entire clip or just part of a clip.

2. Click the keyword button to open the keywords panel.

   The keywords panel opens.

3. Click **Inspector**.

4. Click to add a keyword to the selection (☐ changes to ☑).

iMovie adds the keyword to the clip.

- You can click multiple check boxes to add multiple keywords to a clip.
- Clips with keywords are marked with a blue line.
- To remove a keyword, select a clip and click here (☑ changes to ☐).
- To add a new keyword to the list, type the term and press Enter.

FIND BY KEYWORDS

1. Click in the event library to select a collection of videos.
2. Click [icon].

   The Keyword Filter pane appears.
3. Click a keyword.

- [icon] appears next to the keyword.
- iMovie filters the clips, showing only the clips that have been assigned that keyword.
- You can click to toggle the filter on and off.

TIP

How do I apply more criteria in the Keyword Filter?
Follow these steps:

A green icon ([icon]) means a clip must have that keyword to be displayed.

- Click a keyword name to toggle the green icon on and off.

A red icon ([icon]) means a clip *must not* have that keyword to be displayed.

- Click to toggle the red icon on and off.
- Clicking **Any** displays clips that meet any of the criteria.
- Clicking **All** displays clips that meet all of the criteria.

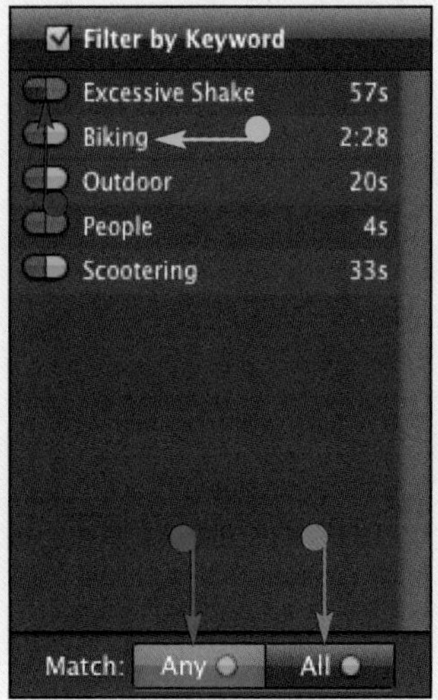

Save a Movie to Your Computer

You can save the clips, titles, transitions, and other content that you have assembled in a project as a single movie file on your computer. You can then play the movie on your computer, upload it to a Web site, or back it up to a CD-ROM or DVD.

Save a Movie to Your Computer

1. Open the project that you want to save.
2. Click **Share**.
3. Click **Export Movie**.

4. Type a name for the file.
5. Select the location where to save the file.

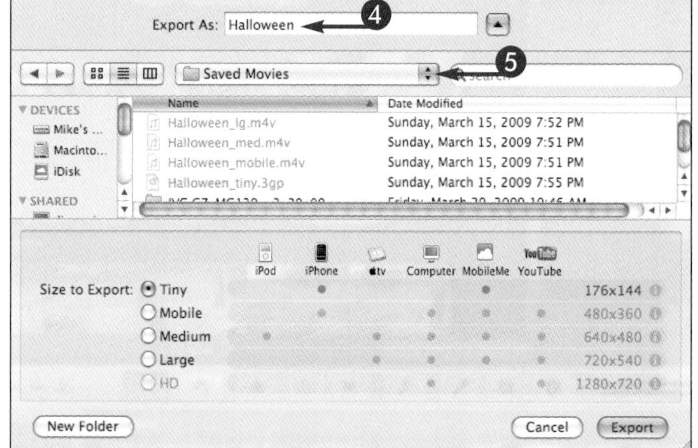

6 Click a size to export based on how you want to use the movie (○ changes to ◉).

- iMovie shows the devices and applications for which each size is appropriate.

7 Click **Export**.

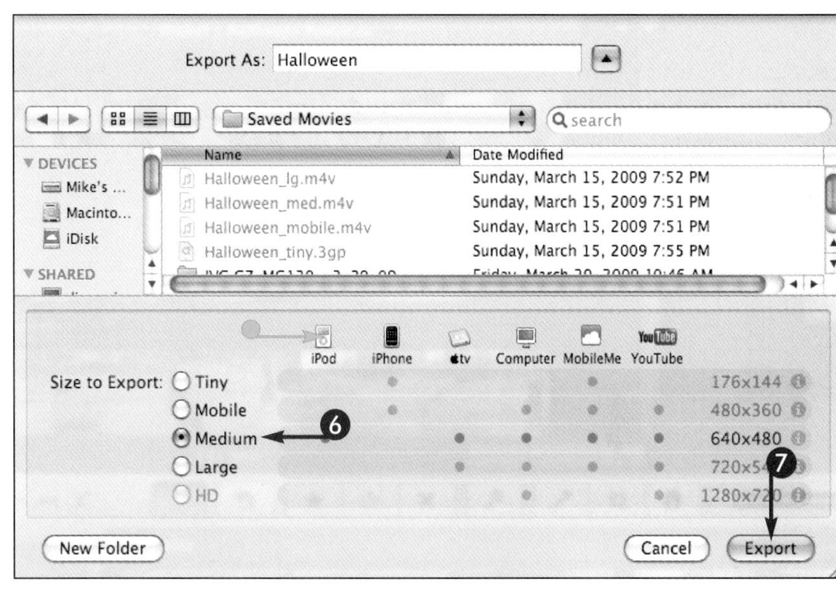

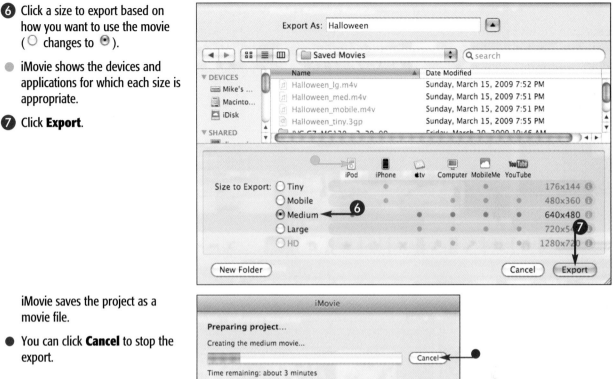

iMovie saves the project as a movie file.

- You can click **Cancel** to stop the export.

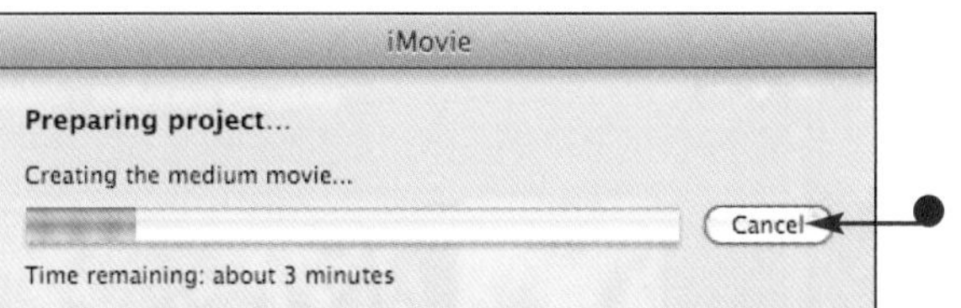

In what file format does iMovie save my exported movies?

When using the Export Movie command, the file format depends on the size.

- Selecting **Tiny** in the export options saves a 3GP file, which is a type of MPEG-4 format devised especially for mobile devices.
- Selecting **Mobile**, **Medium**, or **Large** saves a regular MPEG-4 (.m4v) file.

Note: *To save your movie in a variety of other formats, see the tip in "Publish a Movie to a MobileMe Gallery."*

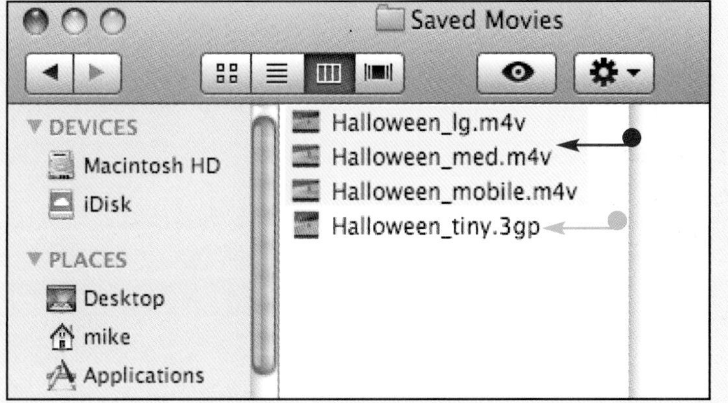

Publish a Movie to a MobileMe Gallery

You can publish your movie to your MobileMe gallery. You can then send your friends and family a Web address where they can access the movie on MobileMe.

To use this feature, you must have a MobileMe account. See Chapter 2 for details.

Publish a Movie to a MobileMe Gallery

1. Sign in to your MobileMe account.
2. Open the project that you want to publish.
3. Click **Share**.
4. Click **MobileMe Gallery**.

5. Type a title and description. These will appear on the movie page at your MobileMe account.
6. Select the sizes to publish (☐ changes to ☑). Viewers can choose from a size depending on their connection speed.
7. Select a privacy setting.
8. Click **Publish**.

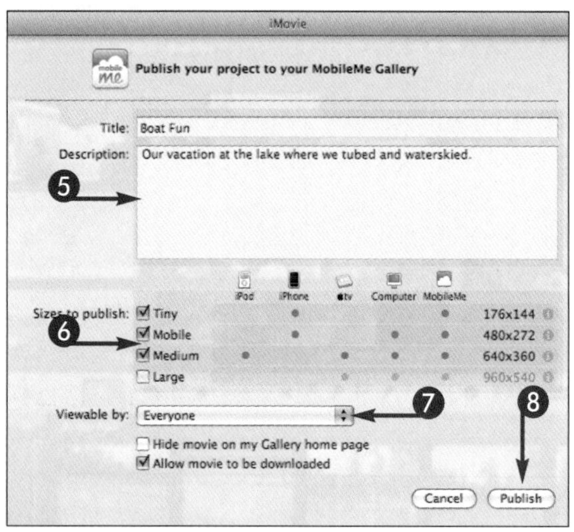

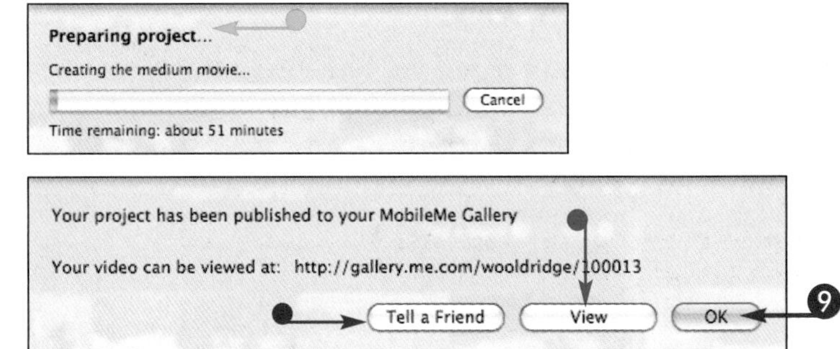

- iMovie publishes the movie. It may take minutes or hours to publish a project depending on the size of the movie and the speed of your Internet connection.

  After the movie is published, iMovie displays a confirmation dialog.

- Click **Tell a Friend** to invite others to view the movie.
- Click **View** to view the movie on the Web at your MobileMe account.

9 Click **OK** to close the dialog.

How can I have more control when exporting my project?

You can choose the Export Using QuickTime option and have precise control over the format and compression settings.

1 Click **Share** and then **Export Using QuickTime**.

The Save Exported File As dialog opens.

2 Select a file format.

3 Click **Options** to open the Movie Settings.

Note: *The settings available depend on the file format. This example shows settings for a QuickTime movie.*

4 Click **Settings** to adjust video compression and other video settings.

5 Click **Settings** to adjust audio compression and other audio settings.

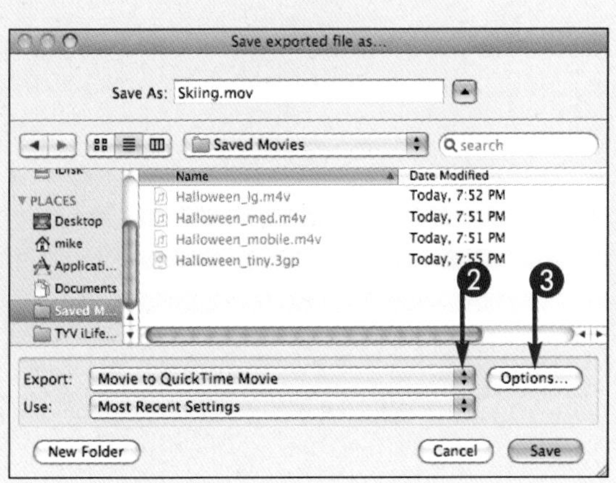

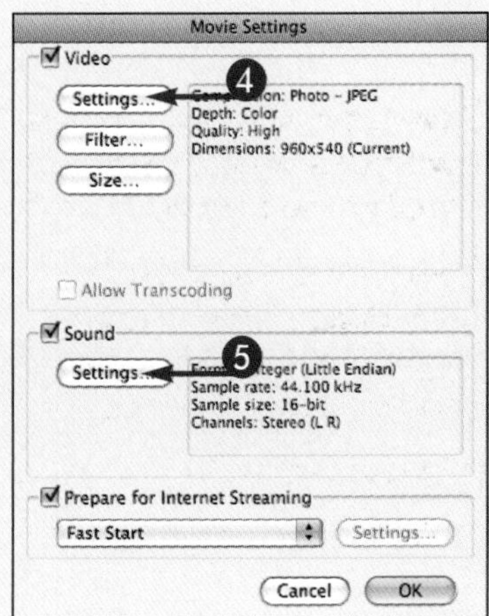

Publish a Movie to YouTube

You can publish your movie to YouTube, the popular video-hosting site. Once your movie is published to YouTube, you can send the YouTube Web address to friends and family. You can also make the movie publicly available to other YouTube viewers.

To use this feature, you must have a YouTube account. Visit www.youtube.com to sign up.

Publish a Movie to YouTube

1. Open the project that you want to publish.
2. Click **Share**.
3. Click **YouTube**.

4. Select your YouTube account.
   - The first time you publish, click **Add** to add your account to the menu.
5. Type your password.
6. Select a category.
7. Type a title and description.

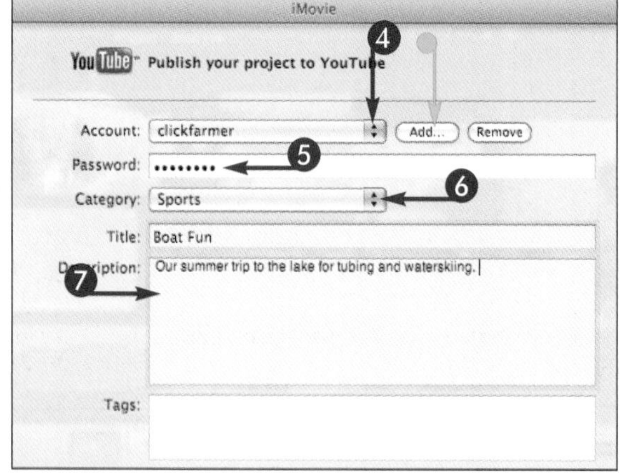

- You can add *tags*, or descriptive keywords, to further categorize your movie.

8 Select a size to upload (○ changes to ◉).

Selecting **Medium** results in better quality but a longer upload time.

- You can click to make the movie publicly accessible on YouTube (☑ changes to ☐).

9 Click **Next**.

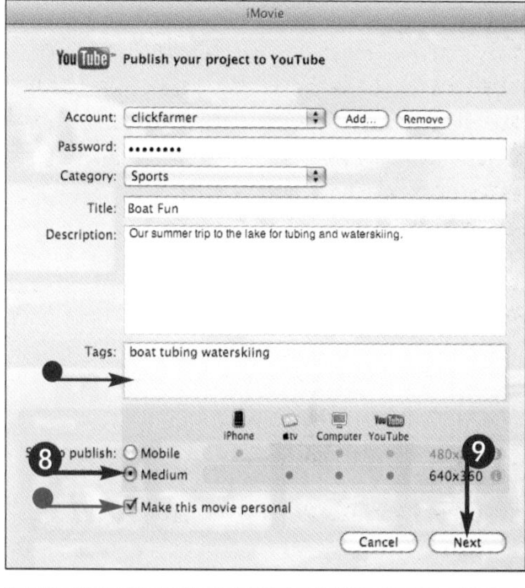

iMovie displays the terms of service.

10 Click **Publish** to accept the terms and upload the movie.

iMovie uploads the movie to YouTube. After the movie has been uploaded and processed, it is made available on the YouTube Web site.

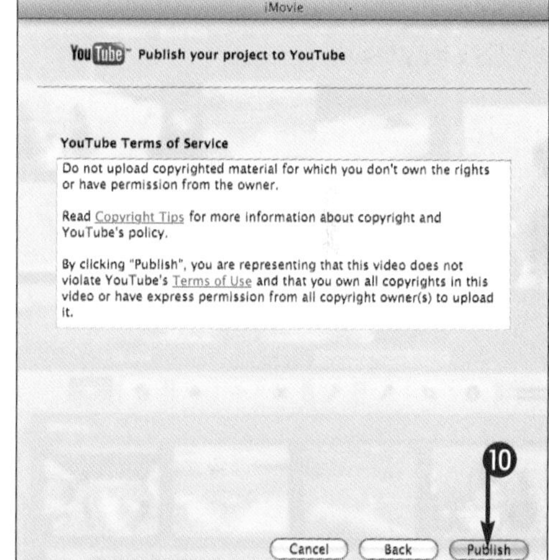

How do I publish my project to iTunes?

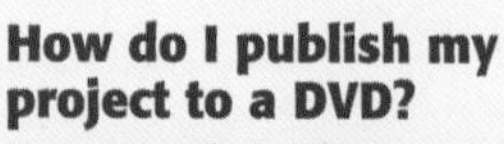

You can click **Share** and then **iTunes** to save your project as a movie in iTunes. This allows you to view the movie on iPods, iPhones, and other devices that connect to iTunes. You can also watch the movie on your computer through iTunes.

How do I publish my project to a DVD?

You can click **Share** and then **iDVD** to turn your project into a movie and then open it in the iDVD program. You can then publish the movie on a DVD with or without other movies. For more about iDVD, see Part VI of this book.

PART

IV

Working with GarageBand '09

This part teaches you about GarageBand '09, which lets you compose music on your Mac. The program lets you work with prerecorded loops or music that you record from real or software-based instruments. You can save your completed songs to iTunes, burn them to a music CD, or post them online in a blog or as podcasts. You can also get professional music instruction using the program's Learn to Play feature.

Understanding the GarageBand Workspace

GarageBand lets you assemble songs from prerecorded audio loops and music that you record yourself. You can adjust the volume and stereo placement of each instrument, also known as *mixing* a song, add special effects, edit individual notes, and more. Before starting a GarageBand project, familiarize yourself with the program workspace.

Timeline

The timeline is where you arrange music loops and recordings to create your GarageBand project. Each row in the timeline represents a *track* where you can place a different instrument. When you play a project, a vertical line called a *playhead* shows the progress along the timeline.

Tracks

GarageBand displays the types of instruments in your project as tracks. There are three types of tracks in GarageBand: real instrument tracks made up of instrument recordings or prerecorded loops of instruments, software instrument tracks where music is defined programmatically, and electric guitar tracks that can be modified using various guitar-specific settings.

Regions

When you add a segment of audio to your project, GarageBand creates a *region* in the timeline. You can arrange and rearrange the regions on the timeline to suit your tastes. Regions are colored differently depending on the type of music: Real instrument loops are blue, recorded real instruments are purple, software instruments are green, and imported audio files are orange. See "Add a Loop to the Timeline" for more details.

Track Info

Double-clicking a track opens a track info panel. Here you can make changes to the instrument that corresponds to the track. For example, you can add predefined special effects that change an instrument's sound. See "Add an Effect" for details.

Track Editor

The track editor gives you a low-level view of your project. Music is represented either as a waveform, for audio created from real instruments, or discrete notes, in the case of software instruments. In the editor you can change the pitch of a track to shift all the notes in a track or edit notes one at a time. See "Adjust the Pitch" or "Edit Musical Notes" for details.

Play Controls

You can preview your project to hear how the loops and recordings that you have assembled sound. See "Play a Project" for more information.

LCD

The *LCD*, or *liquid crystal display*, lets you monitor a song as it plays. It shows you the progress of the song in terms of time or musical measures. You can also display tuning, chord, tempo, and other basic information in the LCD.

Volume Controls

Volume sliders enable you to control the loudness of the music in your project. Besides controlling the overall volume, you can control the loudness of individual instruments in tracks. See "Change the Volume" for more details.

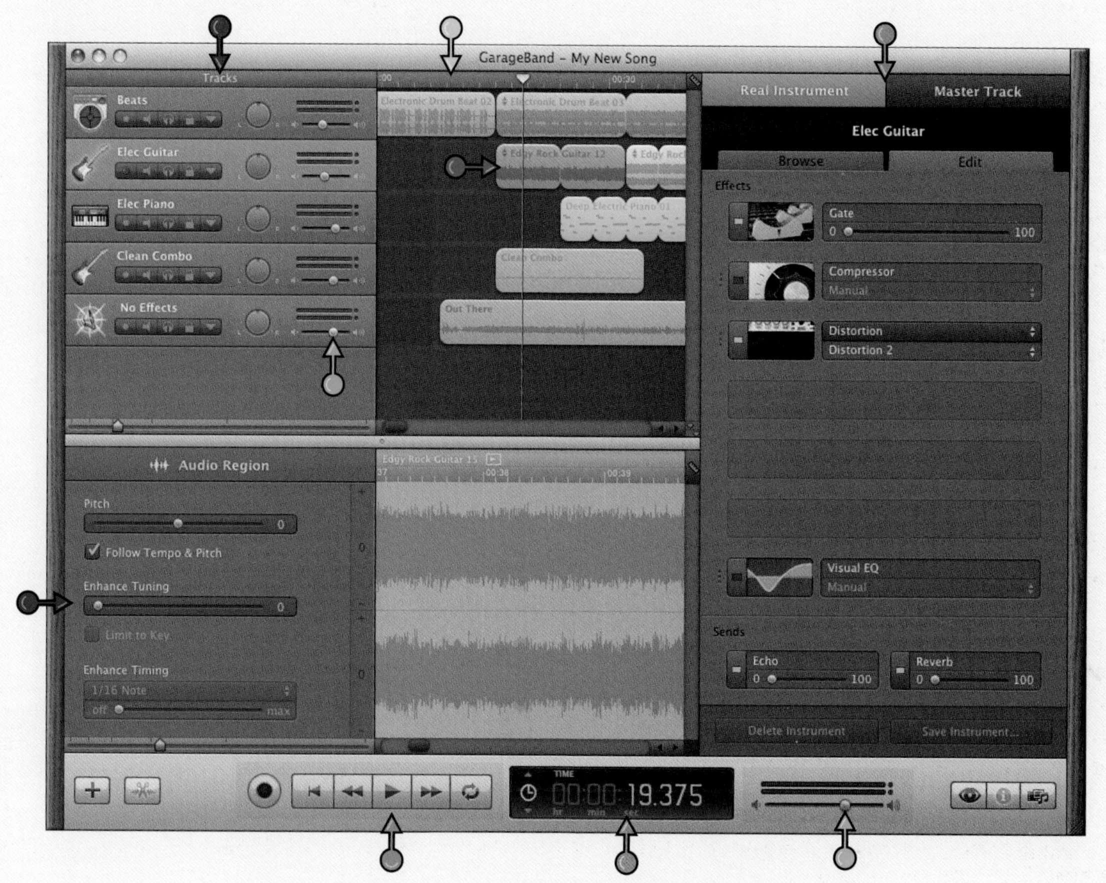

Create a New Project

You can start assembling music in GarageBand by creating a new project. You select a project template based on the type of audio you want to work with. You can work with GarageBand's predefined loops, work with a specific type of instrument, write a song for multiple instruments, or create a podcast.

Create a New Project

1. Click **File** and then **New**.

   The GarageBand window appears. This window also appears when you first start GarageBand.

2. Click **New Project**.
3. Click a project template.
4. Click **Choose**.

The New Project from Template window appears.

5. Type a name for your project.
6. Select where to save the project.

- You can click [▾] to save your project in other locations on your computer.
- You can optionally adjust the tempo, signature, and key settings for your project. See the tip for details.

7. Click **Create**.

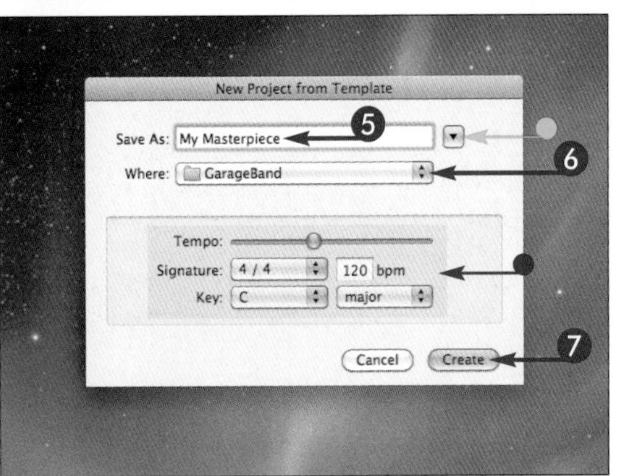

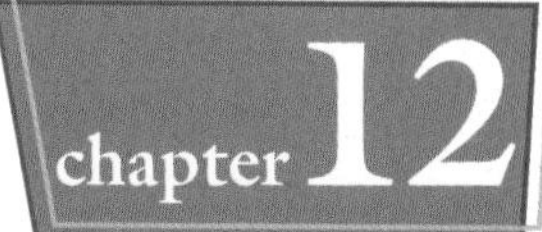

GarageBand creates a new project.

- You arrange the different loops and recordings that make up your song in the timeline.

  Tracks enable you to separately control the instruments in a song.

- In this example, a piano template was used, so GarageBand inserts a single piano track.
- You can click and drag loops from the loop browser to the timeline to add predefined music to your project.

Note: *See "Browse for and Preview Loops" for details.*

8. Click **File**.
9. Click **Save**.

GarageBand saves the project.

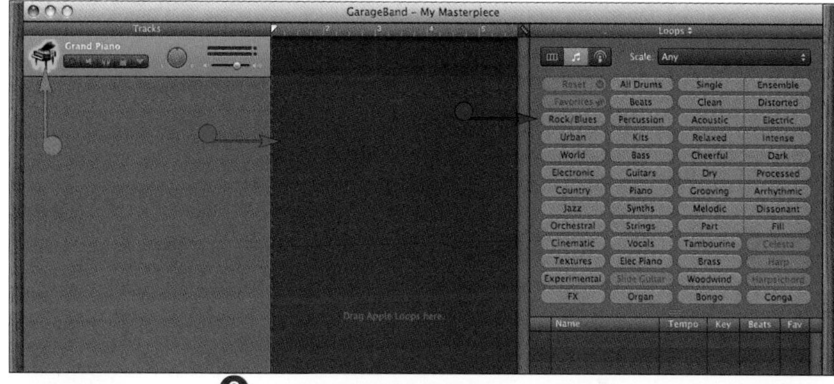

What are the tempo, time signature, and key settings?

These settings determine the timing and other fundamental aspects of your project. You can adjust them when you create a new project.

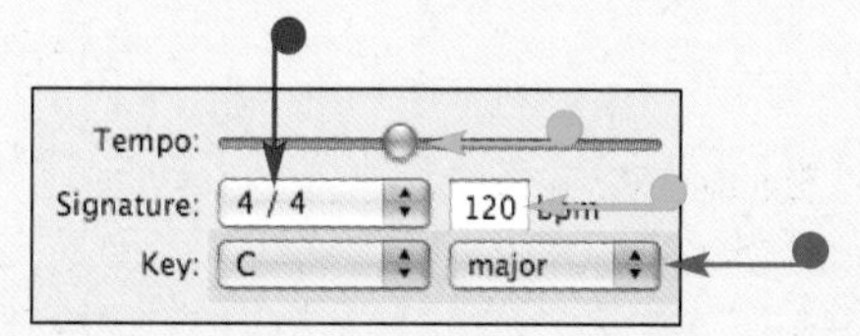

- The *tempo* is the rate at which beats occur. The tempo is measured in beats per minute (bpm). You can set the tempo for a project to between 60 and 240 bpm.
- The *time signature*, such as 4/4 or 6/8, determines the relationship between beats and measures. Measures are the divided sections in the project timeline. The first number is the number of beats in each measure and the second number the length of the note that gets one beat.
- The *key* defines the central note of a project. You can set the key to any note between A and G sharp (G#). Along with the key, you can choose to use either the major or minor scale.

Browse for and Preview Loops

GarageBand comes with hundreds of predefined music snippets, or *loops*, that you can combine to create a song. You can view the loops based on instrument, musical style, and more in the loop browser.

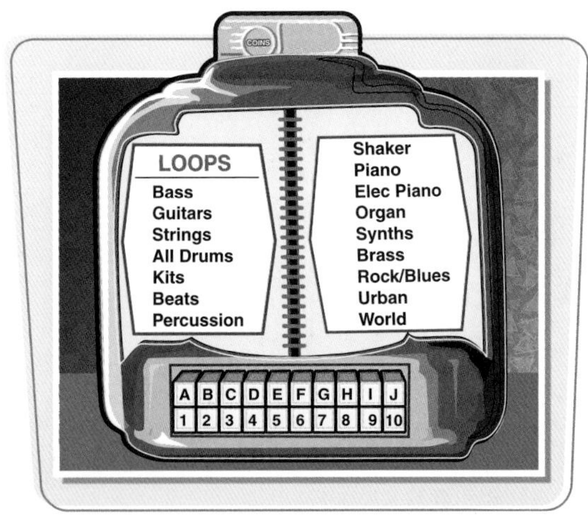

LOOPS
Bass
Guitars
Strings
All Drums
Kits
Beats
Percussion
Shaker
Piano
Elec Piano
Organ
Synths
Brass
Rock/Blues
Urban
World
A B C D E F G H I J
1 2 3 4 5 6 7 8 9 10

Browse for and Preview Loops

BROWSE IN BUTTON VIEW

1. Click [eye icon] to display the loop browser.
2. Click [musical note icon] to show musical button view.
3. Click a button to display loops in a category.
   - GarageBand displays the loops in the category.
4. Click another button.

   GarageBand filters the loops by the second category.
   - You can click **Reset** to reset the buttons.

BROWSE IN COLUMN VIEW

5. Click [column icon] to show column view.
6. Click a category.

   GarageBand displays a set of subcategories.
7. Click a subcategory.

   GarageBand displays a list of keywords.
8. Click a keyword.
   - GarageBand displays the loops.

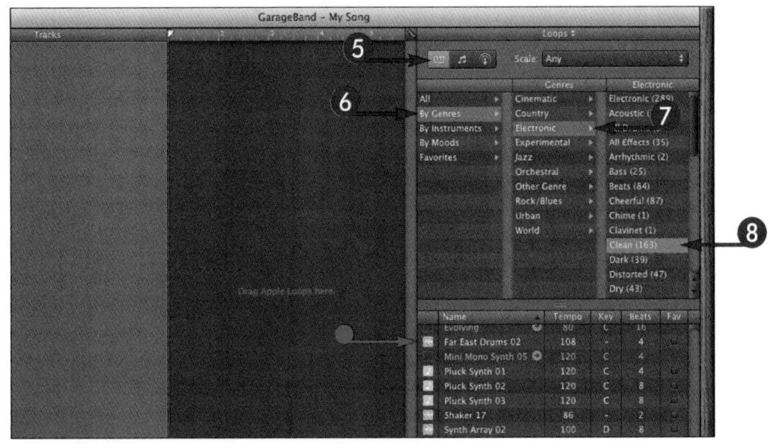

PREVIEW A LOOP

- Loops with colored icons are already installed and can be previewed and added to a project immediately.
- You can click the arrow (icon) to download and install a loop.

9 Click a loop.

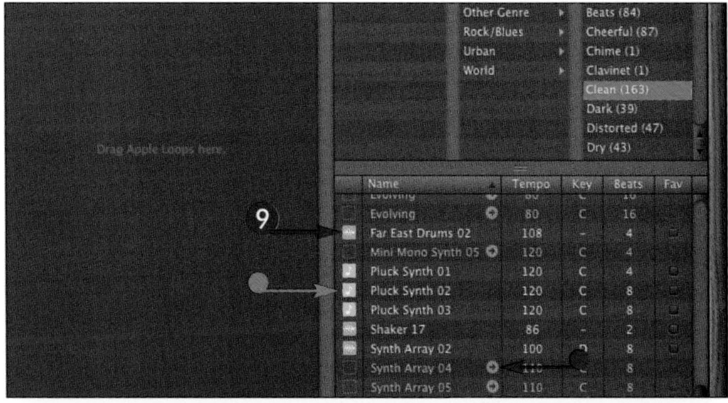

GarageBand plays the loop.

You can click the loop again to pause it.

- You can click the column headers to sort the loops by different criteria.
- You can click and drag the slider to adjust the volume.
- You can search for a loop by typing a keyword.

How do I mark a loop as a favorite?

Because hundreds of clips are available in GarageBand, it can be helpful to mark interesting ones that you find as you browse. Click the check box in the Fav column (☐ changes to ☑) for the loop you want to mark as a favorite. To view your favorite loops, click the Favorites button in musical button view or the Favorites category in column view.

What is the difference between a real instrument and software instrument?

There are two types of music in GarageBand. Real instrument music, which is marked with a blue icon (icon) in the browser, is a digital recording of a real instrument such as a guitar, a piano, or vocals. Software instrument music, which is marked with a green icon (icon) in the browser, is defined by code that describes how to play sounds, not actual recorded music. Real instruments and software instruments must be on separate tracks in the timeline.

Add a Loop to the Timeline

You can add loops to the GarageBand timeline to create a song. You can add loops in sequence so they play one after the other. You can also add them as separate tracks so that they play in parallel.

Add a Loop to the Timeline

ADD A LOOP TO A NEW PROJECT

1. Find a loop you want to add in the loop browser.

Note: *See "Browse for and Preview Loops" for details.*

2. Click and drag the loop to the timeline.

Note: *You can also add music that you recorded yourself. See Chapter 13 for details.*

- GarageBand adds the loop to your project.

  A loop added to the timeline is called a *region*.

  When you edit a region in your project, the edits do not affect the original loop.

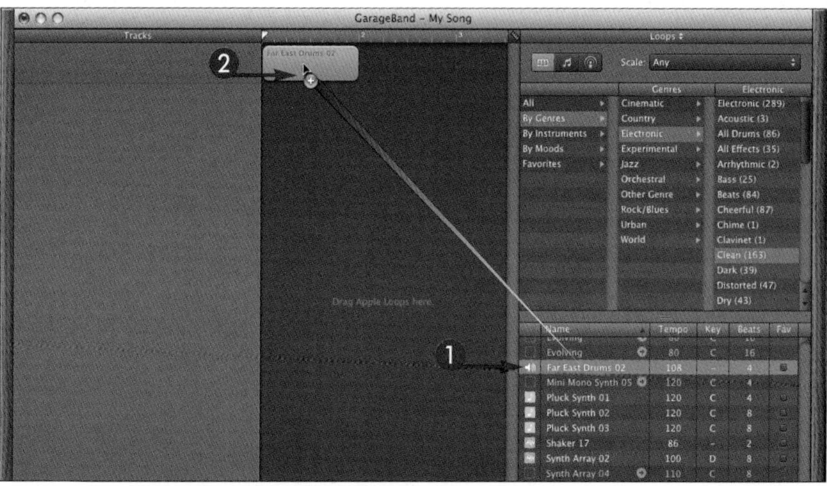

ADD A LOOP IN SEQUENCE

3. Click and drag the loop to the area just before or after an existing region.

   A track can only contain either real instrument loops or software instrument loops. For example, you can add real instrument loops only to loops that already contain real instruments.

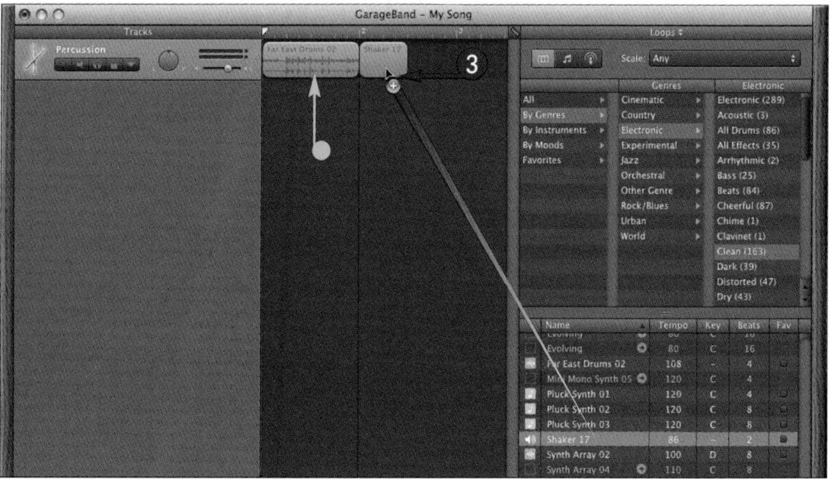

- GarageBand adds the loop to the existing track.

ADD A LOOP TO A NEW TRACK

4. Click and drag a loop to the area below any existing tracks.

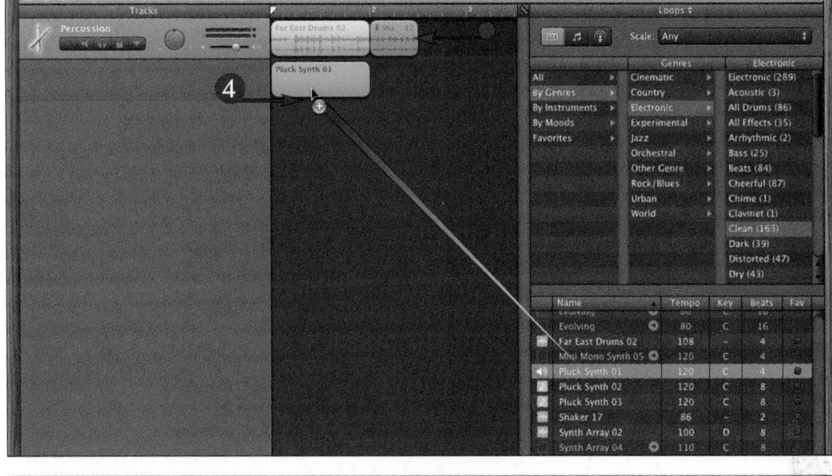

- GarageBand adds the loop to a new track.

  Regions that are above or below one another play at the same time.

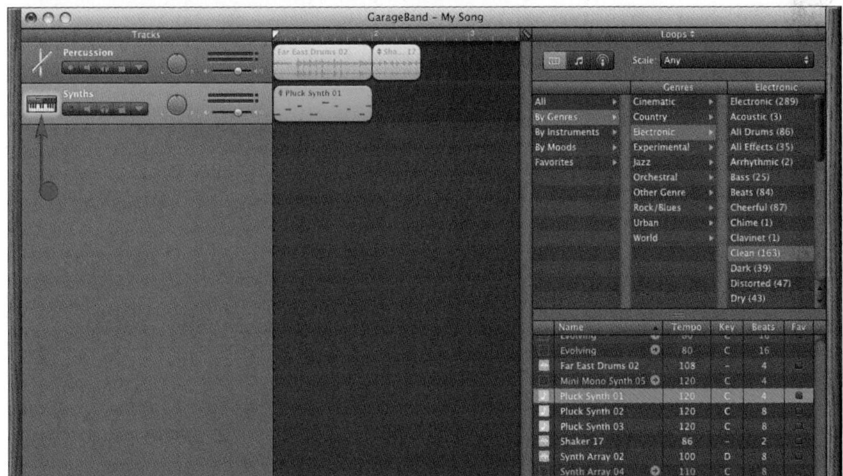

How do I rearrange regions in the timeline?

You can click and drag regions to rearrange them in the timeline. You can move regions within the same track or move them from one track to another. To delete a region, click to select it, click **Edit**, and then click **Delete**. To duplicate a region so that it repeats, see "Repeat a Region."

How can I make it easier to align my clips with one another?

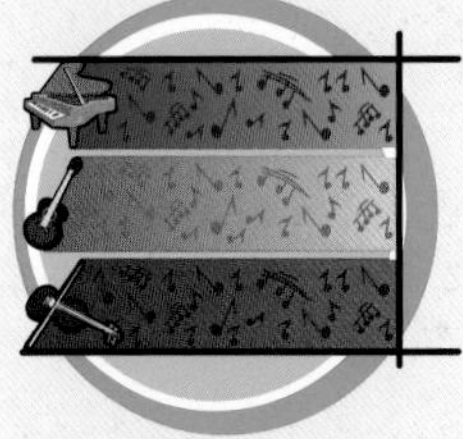

By default, the "snap to grid" feature is turned on in GarageBand. This means regions in the timeline automatically snap into alignment with beats and measures in the timeline. You can turn snapping on and off in the Control menu. You can also turn on alignment guides, which are vertical lines that appear when region edges align with one another. Click **Control** and then **Show Alignment Guides**.

Repeat a Region

You can make a region in the timeline repeat. This allows you to extend a drum beat or guitar riff throughout a song. You can cause a region to repeat by dragging its edge or by copying and pasting it.

Repeat a Region

BY CLICKING AND DRAGGING

1. Click and drag the zoom slider to view the area of the song you want to work with.
2. Move the cursor to the upper-right corner of a region (the cursor changes to the loop cursor).
3. Click and drag to the right.

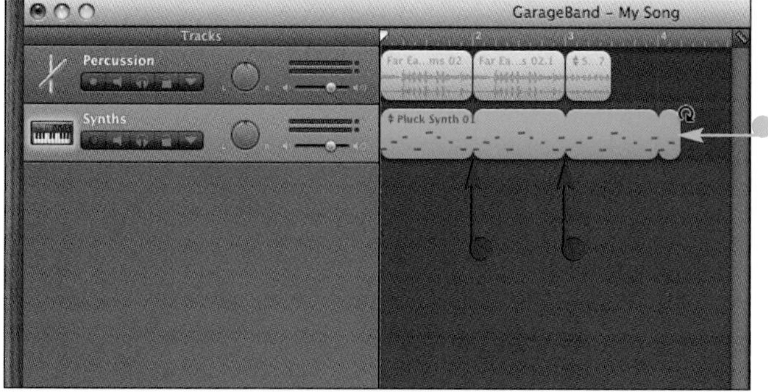

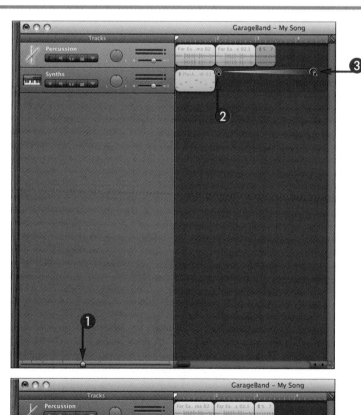

- GarageBand repeats the region.
- Notches appear where the region repeatedly starts and ends.

BY CUTTING AND PASTING

1. Click to select a region.
2. Click **Edit**.
3. Click **Copy**.

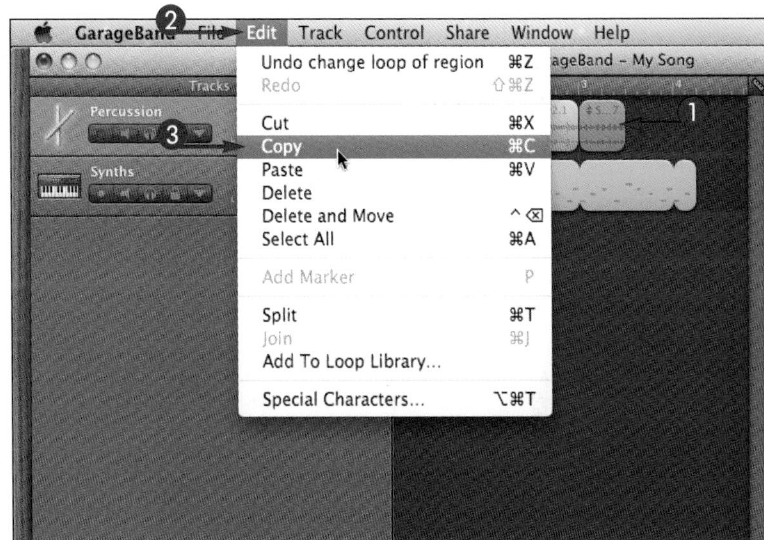

4. Click the track where you want to duplicate the region.
5. Click and drag the playhead to the place where you want to add the duplicate.
6. Click **Edit**.
7. Click **Paste**.

- GarageBand pastes the copy into the timeline.

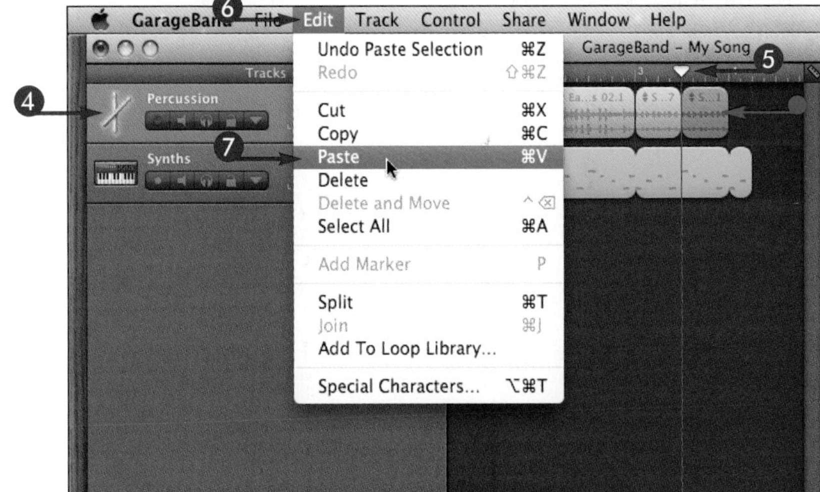

TIP

How can I change a region to a loop that is musically similar?

Some loops in GarageBand belong to a family of similar loops. Loops in a family have the same name but a different number at the end. You can easily change a region to another loop in the family.

1. Click the arrows (⇕).

   A menu showing related loops appears.

2. Click a loop name.

   GarageBand changes the region.

Split or Join Regions

You can split a region in two and then rearrange the split sections or apply different settings to each section. You can also join two regions to move the regions as a single unit or apply the same settings to the regions.

Split or Join Regions

SPLIT A REGION

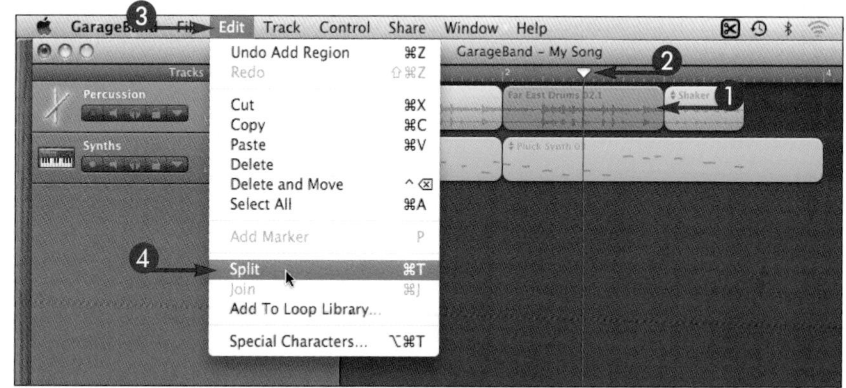

❶ Click to select a region.

You can split both real instrument regions (▦) and software instrument regions (♪).

❷ Click and drag the playhead to mark where to split the region.

❸ Click **Edit**.

❹ Click **Split**.

- GarageBand splits the region.

The split sections can be edited independently.

- You can select a region, click **Edit**, and then click **Delete** to remove it from the timeline.

JOIN REGIONS

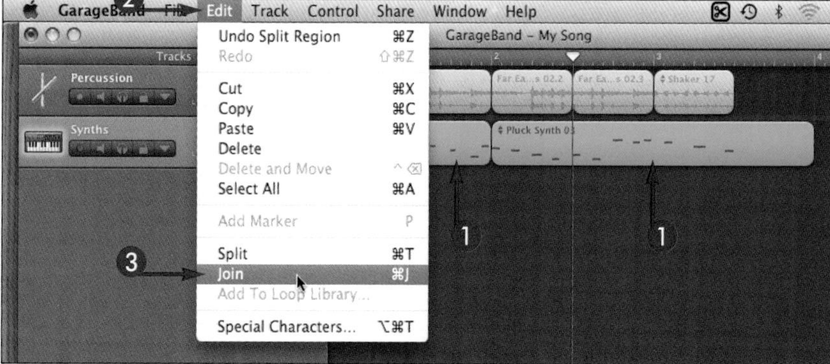

❶ Shift-click to select multiple regions in the timeline.

You can join regions created from software instrument loops (♪). The regions can be on the same or different tracks.

❷ Click **Edit**.

❸ Click **Join**.

- GarageBand joins the regions and applies the name from the leftmost region to the result.

  You can click and drag to move the joined region.

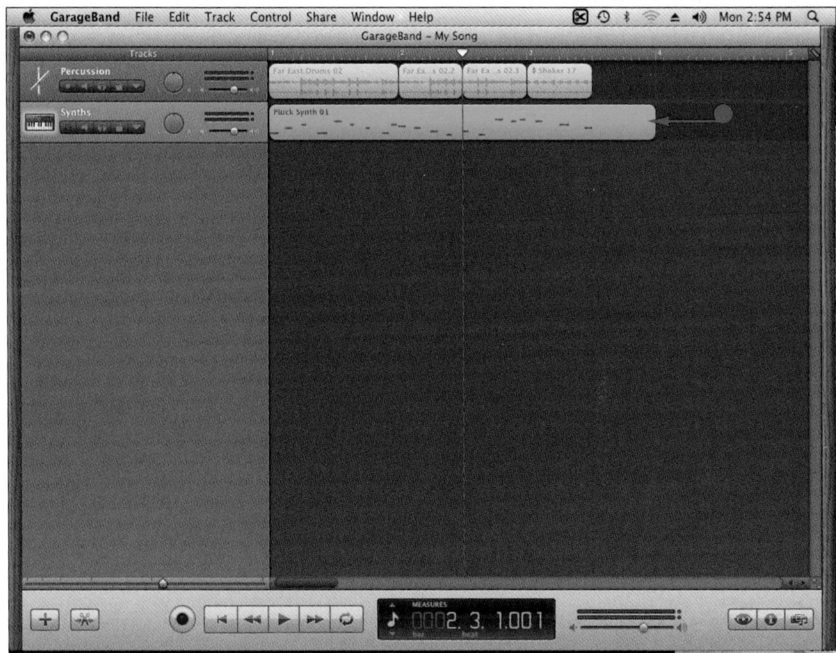

How can I adjust the resolution of the timeline to change how regions are shown?

You can drag the zoom slider to adjust how much of a region is shown in the timeline.

1. Click and drag left.
   - The timeline zooms out, showing more regions at once. This can be helpful when shuffling regions to different parts of a song.
2. Click and drag right.
   - The timeline zooms in, magnifying the regions. This can be helpful when precisely placing regions in a project.

Create an Arrange Region

You can create an arrange region to identify a section of the project containing multiple regions. You might create an arrange region to mark the introduction, verse, or chorus of a song.

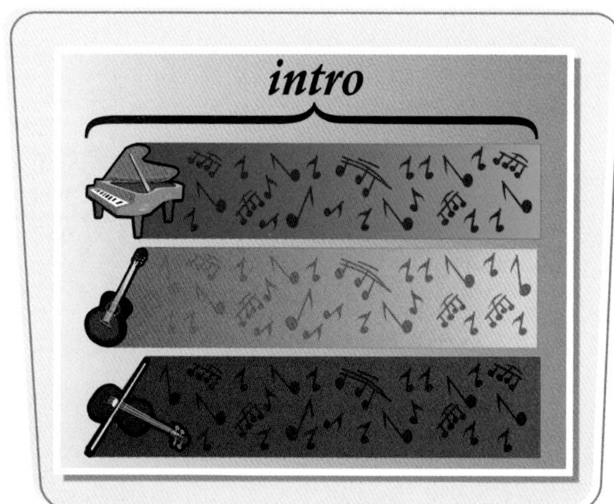

Create an Arrange Region

1. Click **Track**.
2. Click **Show Arrange Track**.

- GarageBand displays the arrange track.

3. Click the plus sign (■).

- GarageBand adds an arrange track to the beginning of the song.

4. Click and drag the edge of the arrange track to resize it.

   GarageBand resizes the arrange track.

5. Double-click the arrange track title.

The title becomes editable.

6. Type a name for the arrange track.
7. Press Enter.

- The arrange track is renamed.

TIP

How do I delete an arrange track?

Click to select the arrange track, press Backspace to delete all the regions within it and then press Backspace again to delete the arrange track itself.

How do I convert a software instrument to a real instrument when adding it to the timeline?

Real instrument loops require less processing power than software instruments, so converting software instruments can help your computer run more efficiently. You can press Option and then click and drag a software instrument from the loop browser to the empty area at the bottom of the timeline to convert the instrument.

Edit Using Arrange Regions

You can click and drag arrange regions in your project to quickly rearrange multiple music regions within a song. You can also duplicate arrange regions to extend the length of your project.

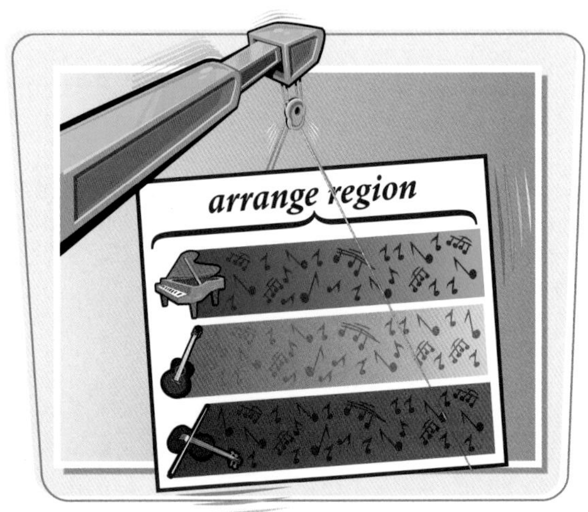

Edit Using Arrange Regions

MOVE AN ARRANGE REGION

1. If arrange regions are not visible, click **Track** and then **Show Arrange Track** to display them.
2. Click and drag an arrange region horizontally to another part of the song.

3. Release the mouse button.

- The arrange region and all of the regions within it are moved.

DUPLICATE AN ARRANGE REGION

4. Press Option and then click and drag an arrange region to another part of the song.

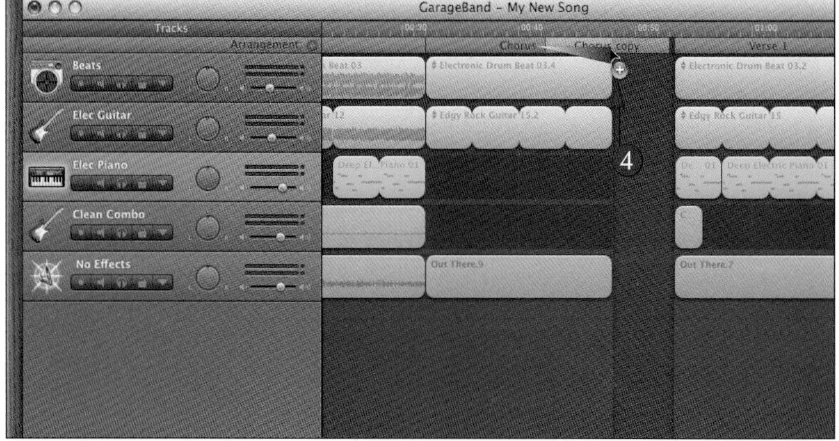

5. Release the mouse button.

- The arrange region and all the regions within it are duplicated in the new location.

How can I replace an arrange region in the timeline?

1. Press and hold ⌘.
2. Click and drag one arrange region directly over another arrange region.
3. Release the mouse button.

GarageBand replaces the second arrange region with the first one.

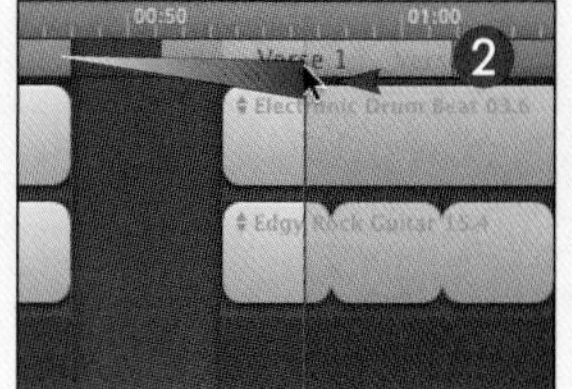

Play a Project

You can play a project to hear the music you have added to the timeline. A vertical line called a *playhead* moves along the timeline with the music showing the region currently being played. You can click and drag the playhead to a specific part of the song to hear it.

Play a Project

1. Click the **Play** button (▶).

   You can also press Spacebar to play a project.

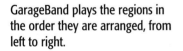

GarageBand plays the regions in the order they are arranged, from left to right.

- The playhead moves with the music as it plays.

2. Click the **Play** button (▶) or press Spacebar.

GarageBand pauses the music.

3. Click and drag the playhead to a different part of the song.

- You can also click to move the playhead to the beginning.
- You can click to move the playhead backward.
- You can click to move the playhead forward.

4. Click the **Play** button ( ) or press Spacebar.

GarageBand resumes playing the song.

- Click to repeat the song after it finishes.

How else can I monitor a song as it plays?

You can monitor the song as it plays using the LCD, which stands for *liquid crystal display*.

1. Click the clock icon ( ) to display the LCD modes.
2. Click a mode.

- Selecting **Time** displays the absolute time in hours, minutes, seconds, and fractions of a second.
- Selecting **Measures** displays musical time in measures, beats, and beat divisions.
- Selecting **Tuner** allows you to tune an instrument when it is connected through an instrument track.
- Selecting **Project** shows the tempo, key, and time signature information. See the "Create a New Project" tip for details.

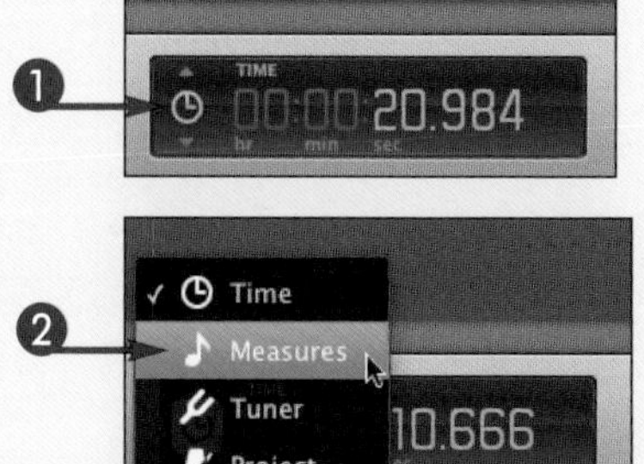

Change the Volume

You can adjust the volume of your project to change the loudness at which it plays. You can change the master volume to adjust the volume of all the tracks in the project. You can also change the volumes of individual tracks. Adjusting the volumes of the tracks in a song is also known as *mixing* a song.

Change the Volume

CHANGE THE MASTER VOLUME

1. Click the **Play** button.

   GarageBand plays the project.

2. Click and drag the master volume slider.

   Drag it to the left to lower the volume or to the right to raise the volume.

- You can click the mute icon to mute the project.
- You can click the maximum-volume icon to set the track to its maximum volume.

GarageBand changes the volume.

- When you play the project, the current volume levels are shown as colored bars. The volume from the left side is shown on the top and the volume from the right side on the bottom.

CHANGE THE VOLUME OF A TRACK

1. Click and drag a track volume slider.

   Drag the slider to the left to lower the volume or to the right to raise the volume.

- You can click to mute the track.
- You can click to set the track to its maximum volume.

- GarageBand changes the volume of the track.

Note: *For more about changing track volume, see "Mute Tracks."*

How do I set different volume levels at different points in a track?

You can set different volume levels using the automation curves for a track. Automation curves let you change track settings such as volume over time.

1. Click the automation icon ( ).
   - The automation curves appear.
2. Click here and select **Track Volume**.
3. Click on the curve where you want the volume to change.

   GarageBand inserts a control point ( ).
4. Click and drag the control point up or down to change the volume at that point in the track.

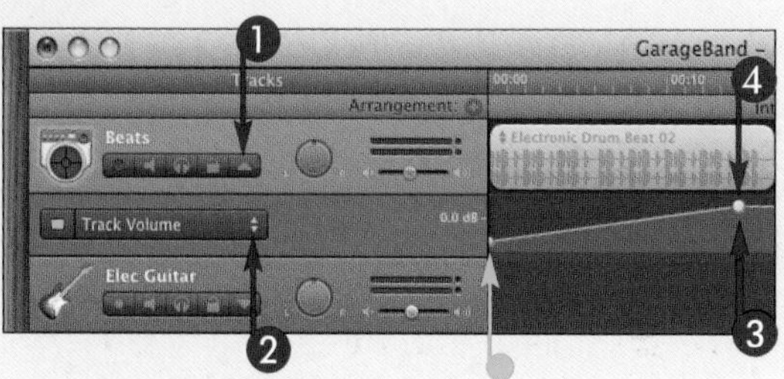

Mute Tracks

You can mute a track to listen to your project without a specific instrument playing. You can also mute all tracks except one, which is known as *soloing*. Soloing lets you make adjustments to a specific instrument without the distraction of other instruments.

Mute Tracks

MUTE A SPECIFIC TRACK

❶ Click **Mute Track** (🔈).

GarageBand mutes the track.

- When the project is played, the colored level bars for the track disappear.
- Regions in the track are grayed.

You can click the button again to unmute the track.

MUTE ALL TRACKS BUT ONE

1. Click **Solo Track** ( ).

GarageBand solos the selected track and mutes the others.

- When the project is played, only the colored level bars for the soloed track appear.
- Regions in the other tracks are grayed.

You can click the button again to unmute the other tracks.

How can I set the pan position?

The pan position for a track determines the left-to-right placement of a track in the stereo field. For example, you can adjust the pan of a track to play it mostly out of the left or right speaker. Adjusting pan positions is part of *mixing* a song.

1. Click and drag the pan dial counterclockwise to pan to the left or clockwise to pan to the right.

GarageBand adjusts the pan position.

- When you play the track, the colored level bars show the pan levels. The top bar displays the sound coming from the left side and the bottom bar the sound coming from the right side.

Adjust the Pitch

You can adjust the pitch of a track to make it play at a different key. This is also called *transposing* a track. Changing the pitch shifts all the notes in a track higher or lower.

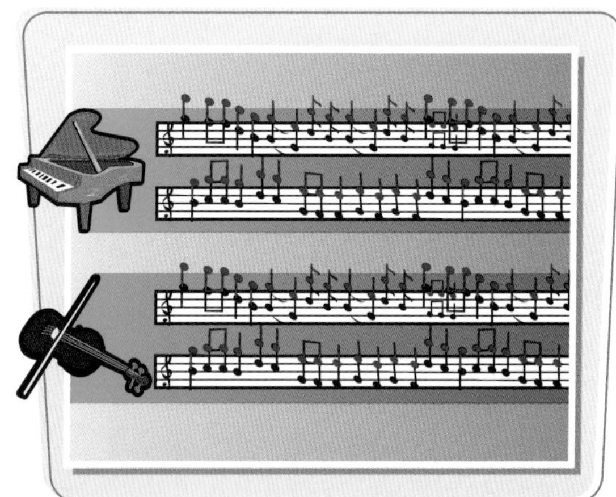

Adjust the Pitch

CHANGE A REAL INSTRUMENT

1. Select a real instrument region ( ).
   - You can also click a track to select an entire track of music.
2. Click the **Track Editor** button ( ).

The track editor opens.

- For real instruments, the music is shown as a *waveform*.
- Make sure **Follow Tempo & Pitch** is selected.

3. Click and drag the slider.

GarageBand adjusts the pitch.

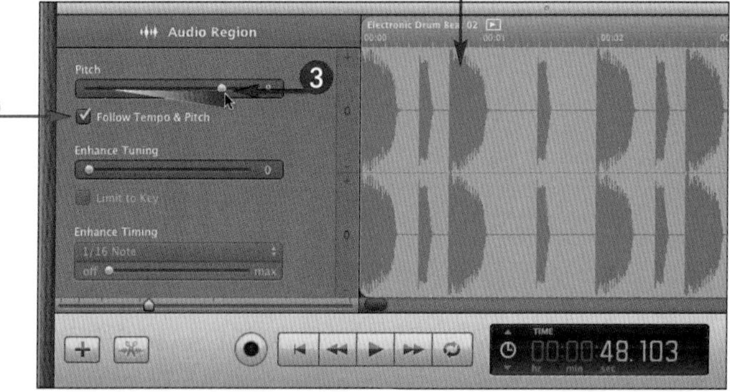

CHANGE A SOFTWARE INSTRUMENT

1. Select a software instrument region (□).

- You can also click a track to select an entire track.

2. Click the **Track Editor** button (✂).

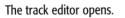

The track editor opens.

- For software instruments, the music is shown as discrete notes.

- You can click **Score** to view the notes as sheet music.

3. Click and drag the slider.

GarageBand adjusts the pitch.

How do I adjust the pitch of an entire project?

You can adjust the pitch of all the tracks at once using the Master Pitch setting.

1. Click **Track** and then click **Show Master Track**.

   The Master Track appears.

2. Click here and select **Master Pitch**.

3. Click where you want the pitch to change.

   GarageBand inserts a control point (■).

4. Click and drag the control point up or down to change the pitch of the project.

Edit Musical Notes

You can edit the individual notes of software instruments, making them higher or lower, changing where they are played in the song, and making the note duration longer or shorter.

Edit Musical Notes

PLAY A NOTE

1. Select a software instrument region (♪).
2. Click the **Track Editor** button (✂).

   The track editor opens.

- The music is shown as discrete notes in piano roll view.

3. Click a note to play it.

- You can click **Score** to edit the notes as sheet music.

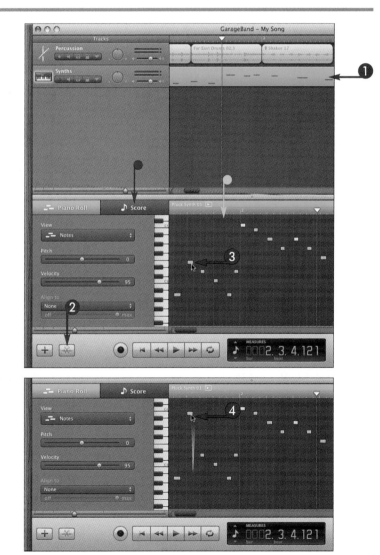

CHANGE THE PITCH

4. Click and drag a note up or down.

   GarageBand changes the pitch of the note, making it higher or lower.

CHANGE WHEN A NOTE IS PLAYED

5 Click and drag a note left or right.

GarageBand changes the position of the note in the song.

CHANGE THE NOTE DURATION

6 Click and drag the right edge of a note to the left or right.

GarageBand changes the how long the note is played.

- You can click and drag the slider to change the velocity, or loudness, of a selected note.

How do I add, copy, or delete a note?

To add a note, ⌘-click in the editor. You can then click and drag the note to adjust its pitch, position, and duration. To copy a note, ⌘-click it and then drag. To delete a note, click to select it and then press Delete.

How do I edit notes as music notation?

In the track editor, click **Score** (●) to view the region as music notation. You can click and drag notes to rearrange them just as you can in piano roll view. Right-clicking in score view displays a menu for adding different types of notes.

Add an Effect

You can apply echo, reverberation, distortion, and dozens of other special effects to tracks. You can fine-tune the effect settings or layer multiple effects to get the sound you want.

Add an Effect

1. Double-click a track.

- GarageBand opens the info pane for the track.

2. Click **Edit**.

The effects are shown.

- You can click to turn off an effect (changes to). You can click it again to turn it back on.

3. Click an empty box.

A menu appears.

4. Click an effect name.

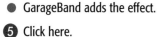

- GarageBand adds the effect.

5. Click here.

   A menu of effect presets appears.

6. Choose a preset to customize the effect.

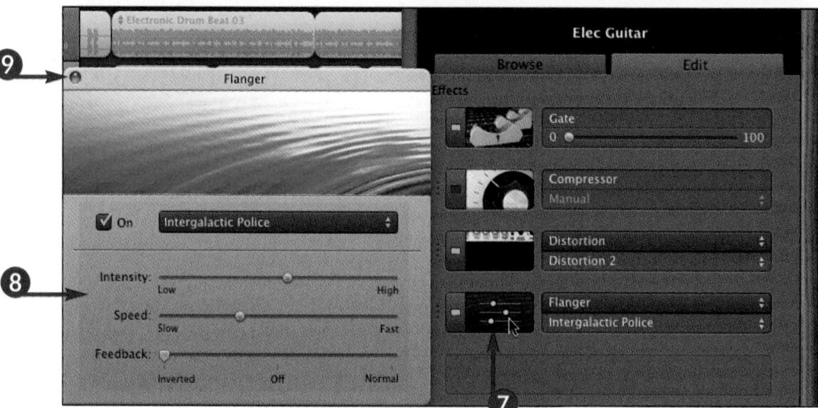

7. Double-click the effect icon.

   The effect settings appear.

8. Adjust the settings to customize the effect.

9. Click the close button to close the settings.

   GarageBand applies the effect to the track.

TIP

How do I apply effects to all the tracks in a project at once?

Follow these steps to use the Master Track settings:

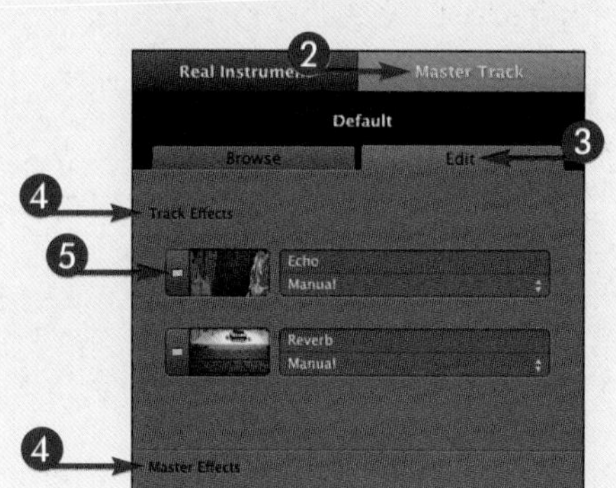

1. Click the info button to show the Track Info pane.
2. Click **Master Track**.

   The Master Track settings appear.

3. Click **Edit**.
4. Select from menus in the Track Effects and Master Effects areas to apply effects to the entire project.
5. Click to turn an effect on (on button) or off (off button).

Create a Magic GarageBand Song

You can use the Magic GarageBand feature to quickly record a song using a set of virtual instruments in one of nine genres. After you customize the instruments to get the sound you want, GarageBand builds the song and opens it in the editing interface.

Magic GarageBand can be useful when you are new to GarageBand and want to create a song to experiment with. You can also use it to quickly create background music for other iLife projects.

Create a Magic GarageBand Song

1. Click **File** and then click **New**.

   The GarageBand window appears.
2. Click **Magic GarageBand**.
3. Click a genre.

- You can position your cursor over a genre and click **Preview** to hear an example of a song.

4. Click **Choose**.

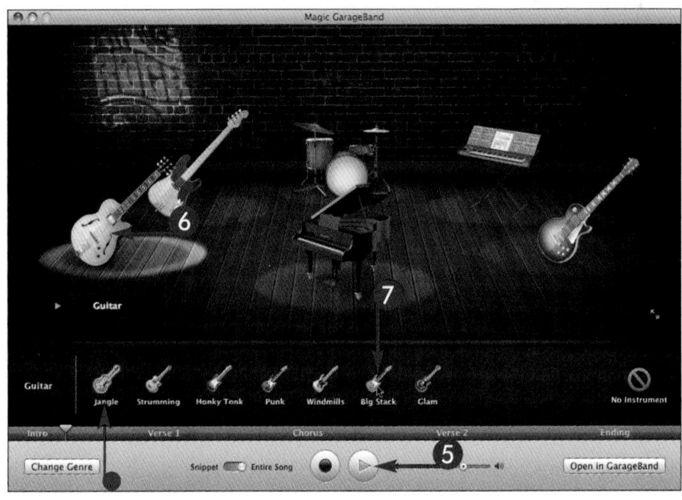

The Magic GarageBand window appears.

***Note:** It may take a moment to display the window and load the instruments.*

5. Click the **Play** button (▶).

   GarageBand plays the song.
6. Click an instrument.

- The current instrument type is highlighted.

7. Click another instrument type.

- GarageBand changes the instrument type and plays it in the song.
- You can click here to remove the selected instrument from the band.

8 When you are satisfied with the sound, click **Open in GarageBand**.

GarageBand creates the song and opens it in the project timeline.

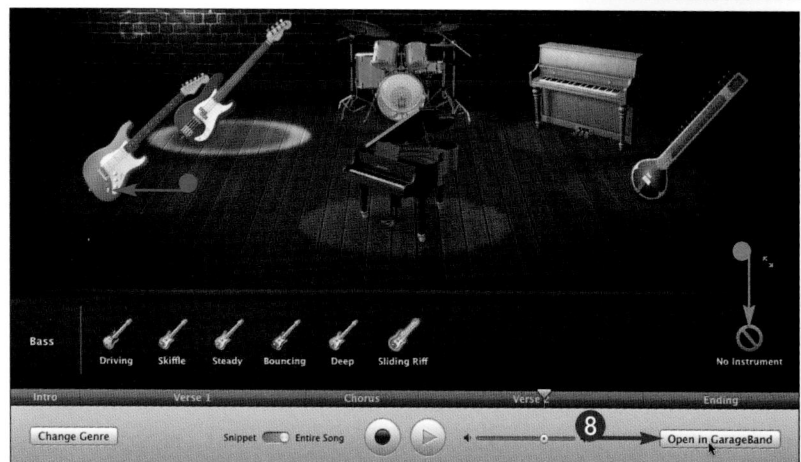

- Each instrument has a separate track.
- If you configured a My Instrument for the song, it appears as an empty track. See the tip below for details.

9 Click the **Play** button (▶) to play the song.

How do I record my own instrument along with a Magic GarageBand song?

1. In the Magic GarageBand window, click here to select **My Instrument**.
2. Click here to select the instrument you will record with.
3. Click here to customize the instrument.
4. Click the **Record** button (●), and the song plays.
5. Play your instrument along with the song to add accompaniment. For details about setting up an instrument to record with, see the other tasks in this chapter. Click the **Record** button (●) to stop recording.

Set Up an Electric Guitar Track

You can set up an electric guitar track that includes amp and stompbox effects. After creating the track, you can plug your electric guitar into your computer and record music using the settings.

See "Record an Instrument" for more about recording music for a track.

Set Up an Electric Guitar Track

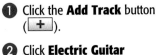

1. Click the **Add Track** button (+).
2. Click **Electric Guitar** (○ changes to ◉).
3. Click **Create**.

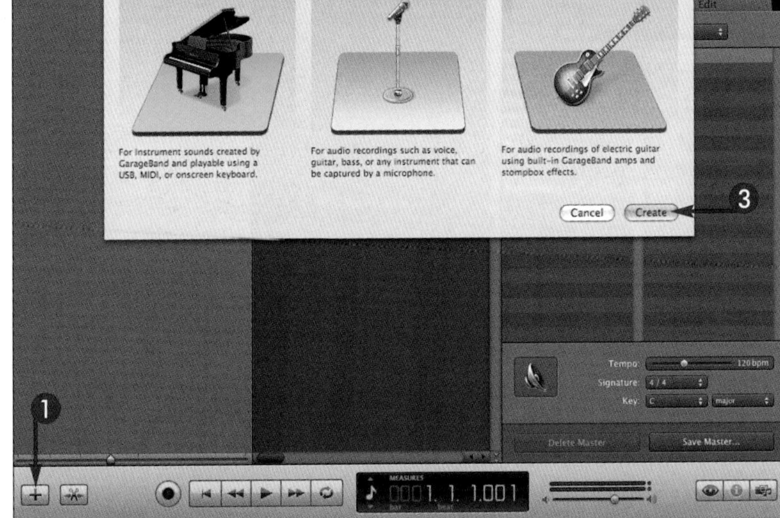

- GarageBand creates a new electric guitar track.

Note: *You can also create a new project and select* ***Electric Guitar*** *as the project type to create this type of track. See Chapter 12 for details about setting up a project.*

4. Click here and select a guitar preset.
5. Click the amp image.

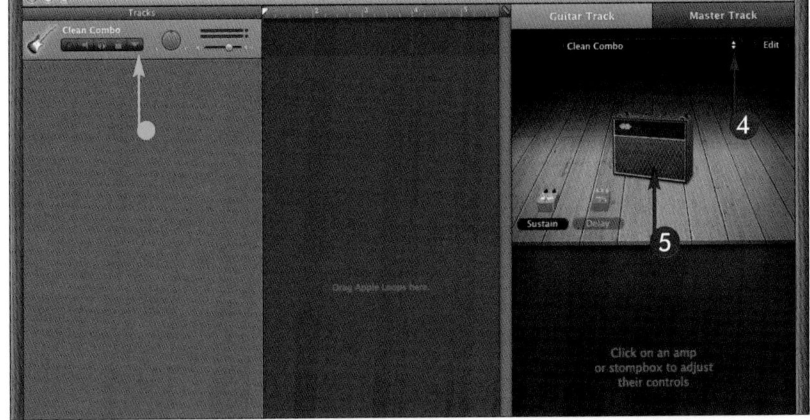

The amp settings appear.

6. Position your cursor over the amp and then click an arrow to cycle through the available amp types.
7. Click and drag up and down over an amp control to adjust it.
8. Click a stompbox.

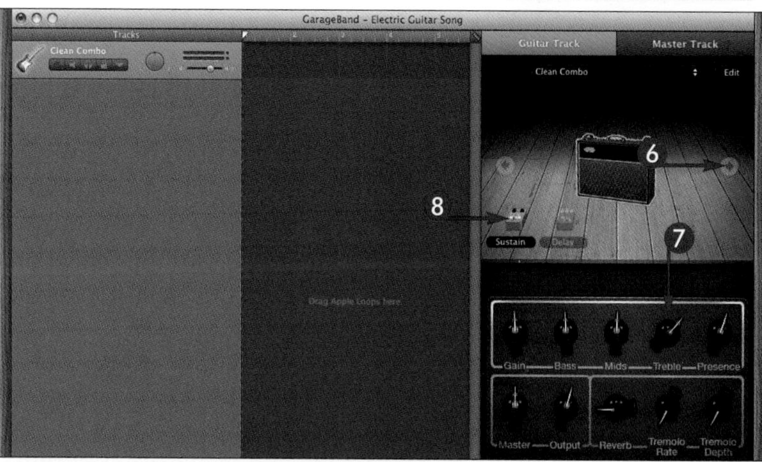

The stompbox settings appear.

9. Click and drag up and down over a stompbox control to adjust it.
10. To adjust other stompboxes on the stage, repeat steps **8** to **9**.

GarageBand adjusts the sound of the electric guitar track.

- You can click the Track Info button to close the Track Info pane.

How do I connect an electric guitar to my computer?

You can connect your guitar through several common input ports:

- **Audio Input Port**: If your computer has a built-in audio input port, you can connect an electric guitar to the port using an adapter cable. Be sure to set the Input Source to **Built-In Input** in the amp settings. To access this setting, open the Track Info pane, select the picture of the amp, and then click **Edit**.
- **USB or FireWire Port**: For a better quality recording, you can connect an audio interface to a USB or FireWire port on your computer. Then you can connect your electric guitar to the audio interface. To activate a connected audio interface, click **GarageBand**, **Preferences**, and then **Audio/MIDI**. Choose the name of the audio interface from the Audio Input menu. Also choose the audio interface from the Input Source menu located in the Track Info pane for the guitar.

Customize an Amp

You can customize the settings for your electric guitar amplifier, also called an *amp*, to get the sound you want. GarageBand features amp models that mimic the sound of classic setups, such as Blackface Combo and Vintage Stack.

In the real world, you plug an electric guitar into an amp to boost the instrument's loudness and modify its sound.

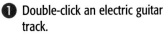

Customize an Amp

1. Double-click an electric guitar track.

Note: *See "Set Up an Electric Guitar Track" to create one.*

The Track Info pane appears.

2. Click the amp.
3. Click **Edit**.

The amp settings appear.

4. Click here to select a different model of amp.
5. Click the slider to adjust the master echo.
6. Click the slider to adjust the master reverb.

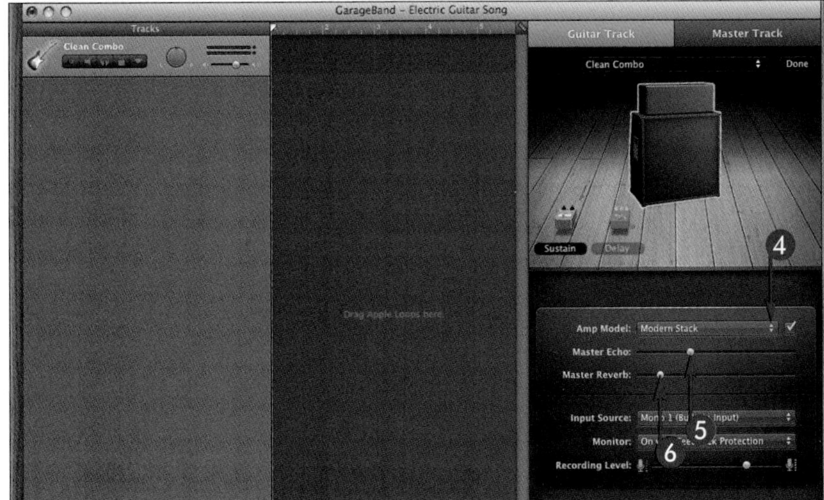

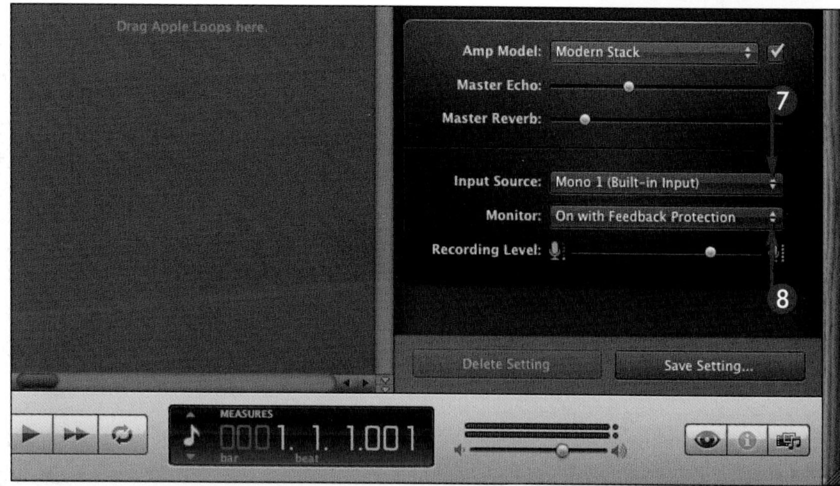

7. Click here to choose where the guitar is plugged into on your computer.

8. Click here to select a monitor setting.

   You can click **Off** to not play the guitar through the computer speakers.

   You can click **On with Feedback Protection** to hear the guitar but guard against its sound feeding back into the input.

   You can click **On** to have the guitar play without protecting against the possible echo effect.

9. Click and drag the slider to adjust the recording level of the electric guitar.

10. Click **Done**.

    GarageBand adjusts the amp settings.

- You can click the info button to close the Track Info pane.

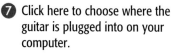

How do I turn my amp effects off?

You can deselect the bypass check box to turn off the amp effects.

1. Follow steps **1** to **3** above to open the amp settings.
2. Click the bypass check box (☑ changes to ☐).

   GarageBand turns off the amp effects for the electric guitar track. You can click the check box again to turn the effects back on.

Arrange Stompboxes

You can add and remove stompboxes from your electric guitar track to control the special effects applied by GarageBand. In the real world, stompboxes are foot-activated devices connected between your guitar and amp that customize the sound of a guitar.

Arrange Stompboxes

1. Double-click an electric guitar track.

Note: *See "Set Up an Electric Guitar Track" to create one.*

The Track Info pane appears.

2. Click a stompbox.
3. Click **Edit**.

A set of stompboxes appears.

4. Click and drag a stompbox to an empty position on the stage.

GarageBand adds the stompbox to the guitar track.

5 Click and drag a stompbox off of the stage.

GarageBand removes the stompbox from the guitar track.

You can have up to five stompboxes associated with a track at one time.

6 Click **Done**.

Note: *To adjust the settings of a stompbox, see "Set Up an Electric Guitar Track."*

What types of effects can I get from stompboxes?

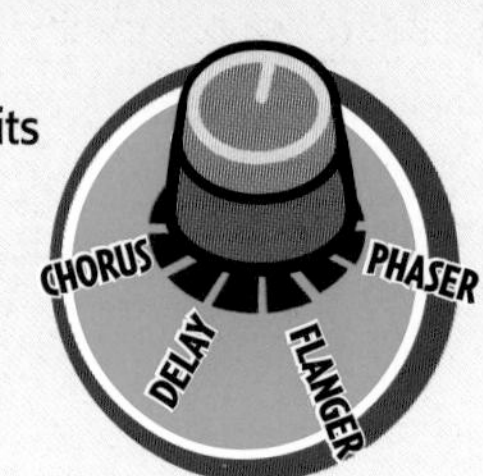

Here are descriptions of some of the stompbox effects. When you add a stompbox, its effect is listed in the Track Info pane.

- **Chorus**: Copies the original sound and plays it back later in time and slightly out of tune. This can mimic the sound of multiple instruments or voices.
- **Delay**: Copies the original sound and plays it back later in time. This can create a sense of the sound happening in a large space.
- **Flanger**: Similar to a chorus. Copies of the sound are played back later in time but more out of tune.
- **Phaser**: Copies of the original sound are played back slightly later in time and out of phase with the original. This can produce a whooshing effect.

Set Up a Real Instrument Track

You can add a real instrument track to your GarageBand project and then select an instrument type for the track. This allows you to record acoustic instruments, vocals, or any other instrument whose sound you can capture with a microphone.

See "Record an Instrument" for more about recording music for a track.

Set Up a Real Instrument Track

1. Click the **Add Track** button (+).

   The Add Track dialog appears.

2. Click **Real Instrument** (○ changes to ⊙).

3. Click **Create**.

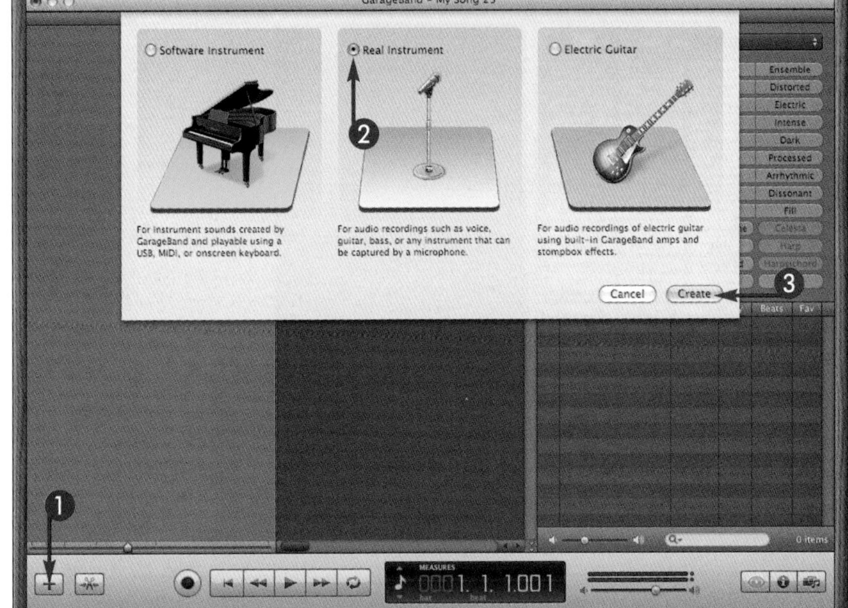

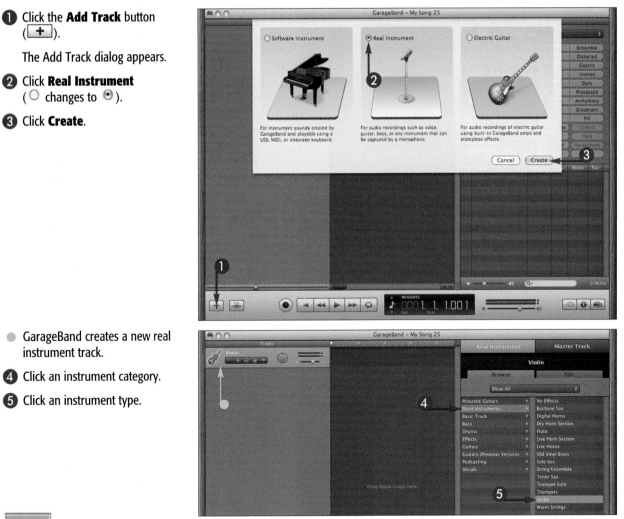

- GarageBand creates a new real instrument track.

4. Click an instrument category.

5. Click an instrument type.

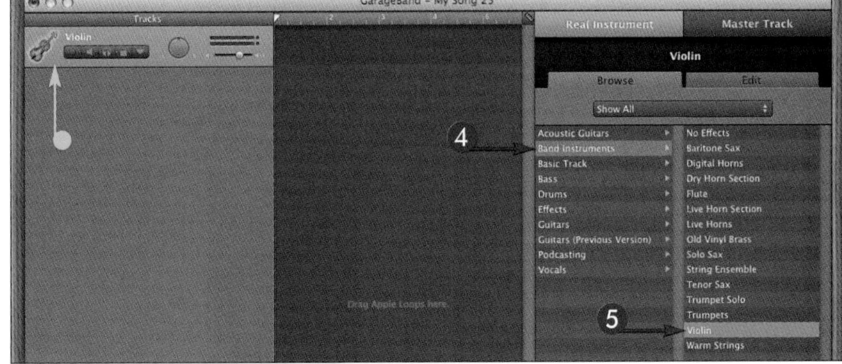

6 Click here to choose where the instrument microphone is plugged in to on your computer.

7 Click here to select a monitor setting.

You can click **Off** to not play the guitar through the computer speakers.

You can click **On with Feedback Protection** to hear the guitar but guard against its sound feeding back into the input.

You can click **On** to have the guitar play without protecting against the possible echo effect.

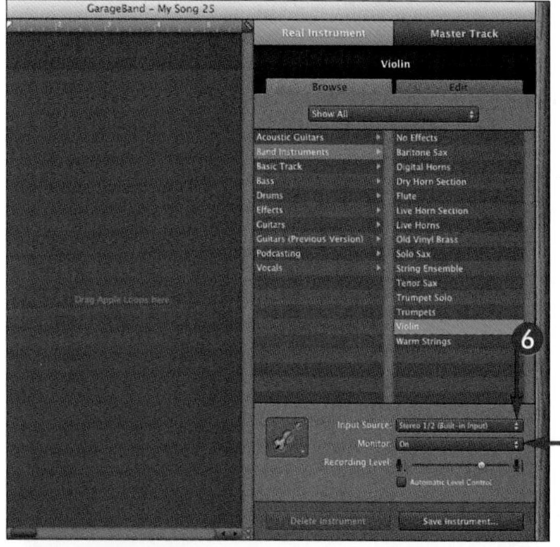

8 Click and drag the slider to adjust the recording level of the instrument.

- You can click **Edit** to edit the effects applied to the instrument. See "Add an Effect" in Chapter 12 for details.

GarageBand configures the real instrument track.

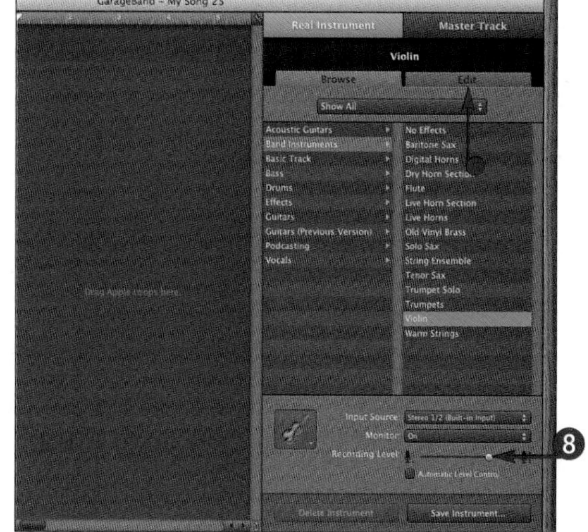

What is GarageBand doing when I select a specific instrument for a track?

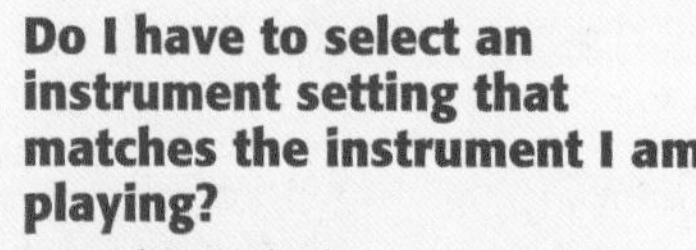

When you specify an instrument in the Track Info pane, GarageBand applies settings and effects to the track that are optimized for that instrument. You can view what GarageBand applies by clicking the **Edit** tab in the Track Info pane. The actual music added to the track comes from the instrument you play into the microphone.

Do I have to select an instrument setting that matches the instrument I am playing?

No. Although there is a good chance you will want to select a setting that matches, you can experiment with other settings to explore interesting effects. You can also adjust the instrument settings that GarageBand applies. See "Add an Effect" in Chapter 12 for details.

Set Up a Software Instrument Track

You can create a software instrument track to connect and record a MIDI keyboard or other software-based instrument with GarageBand. You can select a type of instrument for the track, such as a grand piano or string instrument, and then fine-tune the settings of the instrument.

See "Record an Instrument" for more about recording music for a track.

Set Up a Software Instrument Track

1. Click the **Add Track** button (+).

   The Add Track dialog appears.

2. Click **Software Instrument** (○ changes to ◉).

3. Click **Create**.

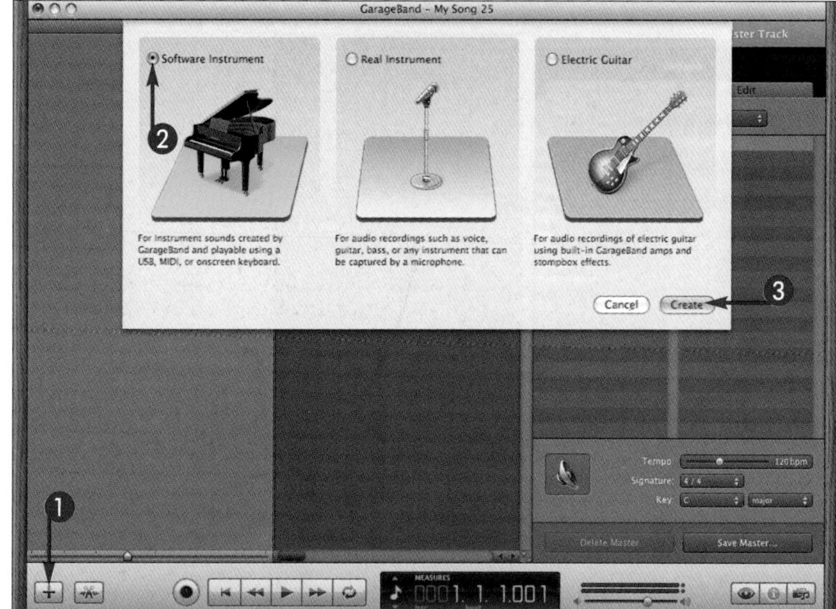

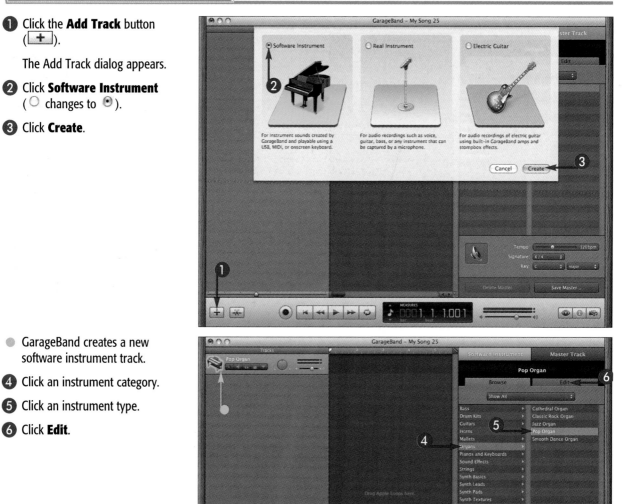

- GarageBand creates a new software instrument track.

4. Click an instrument category.

5. Click an instrument type.

6. Click **Edit**.

For software instruments, GarageBand uses a sound generator to create the instrument music.

7. Click here to change the generator.

   Some generators are based on real instruments, such as a guitar or piano, while others are synthesized sound.

8. Adjust the effects and settings that customize the generated music here.

   - You can click the Compressor effect to decrease the difference between the loudest and softest parts of the sound to give an instrument punch.
   - You can adjust the component frequencies of an instrument by clicking the Visual EQ (equalizer).

9. Click .

   GarageBand closes the Track Info pane and saves the instrument settings.

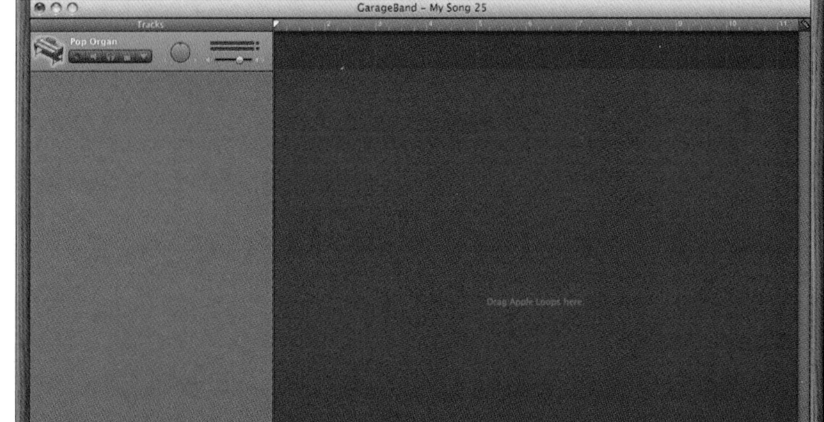

How do I connect a keyboard as a software instrument to my computer?

If the keyboard is USB-based, connect the keyboard to your computer using a USB cable. If the keyboard is a MIDI device, you can connect the keyboard to a MIDI interface using MIDI cables and then connect the interface to your computer.

How can I confirm that a software instrument is successfully connected?

You can switch the LCD at the bottom of the GarageBand workspace to Chord mode. When you play the software instrument, you should see note and chord names as you play. You can also click **GarageBand**, **Preferences**, and then the **Audio/MIDI** button. The MIDI status line should show that the device is connected.

Play Music with a Computer Keyboard

You can use the keys on your keyboard to play the notes of a software instrument. This is handy when you do not have a MIDI keyboard or other device but still want to play a software instrument. You can configure the keyboard to use different octaves and apply sustain and modulation effects.

Play Music with a Computer Keyboard

1. Select a software instrument track. Software instrument tracks are colored green.

Note: See "Set Up a Software Instrument Track" to create one.

2. Click **Window**.
3. Click **Musical Typing**.

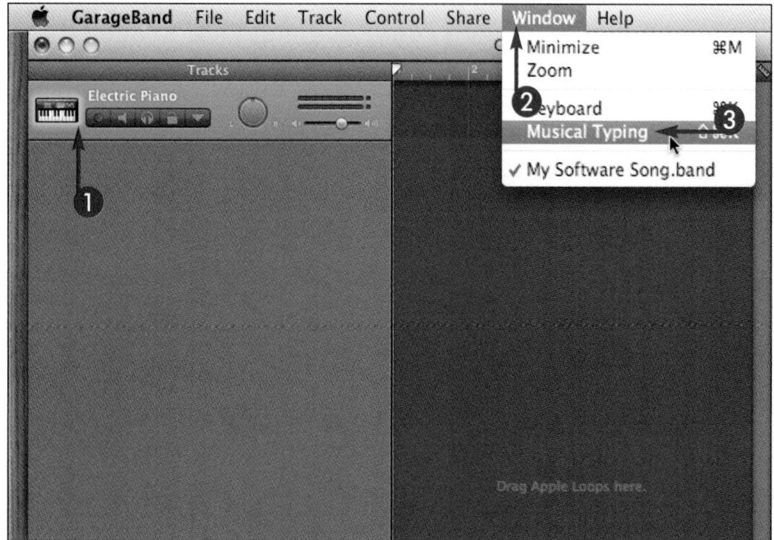

GarageBand opens the Musical Typing window.

- The keys in the window are labeled with letters and symbols corresponding to the keys of your keyboard.
- The octave to which the keys correspond is shown here.

4. Press a letter or symbol on the middle row of your computer keyboard.

   In this example F is pressed.

- GarageBand highlights the key.

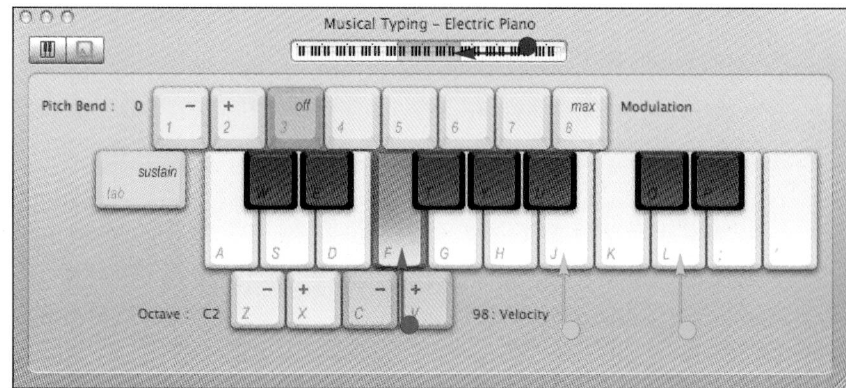

GarageBand plays the corresponding note. The instrument that plays depends on how the software track is configured.

- You can change the instrument by double-clicking the track to open the Track Info pane.

5 Click here one or more times to shift the keys up or down an octave.

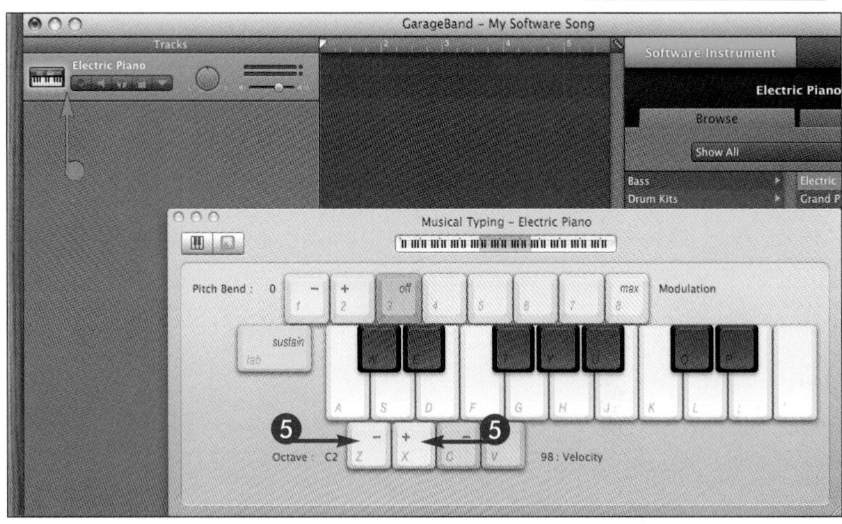

GarageBand shifts the octave up or down.

- In this example, the octave is shifted up.
- You can sustain a note as you play it by pressing and holding Tab.
- You can control the modulation of the instrument by pressing the number keys 3 through 8.

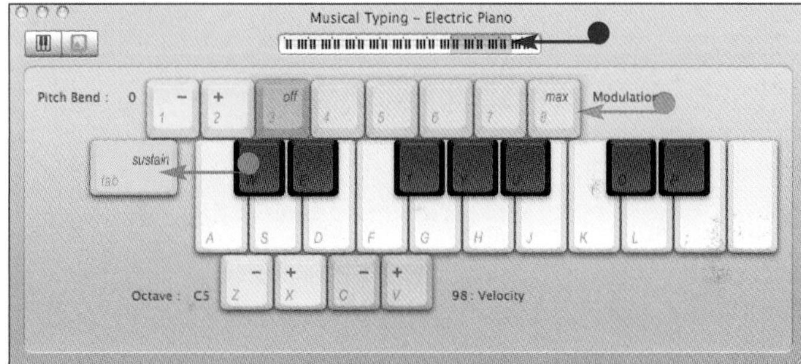

What is velocity on a software instrument keyboard?

Velocity refers to how hard you press keys as you play. This can change the loudness or other characteristics of a note. You can adjust the velocity on the Musical Typing keyboard by pressing C and V.

Can I display a keyboard on-screen that looks like a regular piano keyboard?

Yes. Click the keyboard button to display a piano representation of the musical keyboard. You can then click the keys with the cursor to play them. You can click and drag the corner of the keyboard window to change the size and range of the keys displayed.

Record an Instrument

After you connect your instrument or microphone to your computer and set up an instrument track, you can record the instrument as you play it. GarageBand creates a region on the timeline representing the recording. After you finish, you can edit the region to fine-tune the recorded piece.

Record an Instrument

1. Create a track for your instrument.
2. Connect your electric guitar, microphone, or software instrument to your computer.

Note: *See the other tasks and tips in this chapter for more about creating tracks and connecting instruments.*

3. Click the track for the instrument you want to record.

   If you have monitoring turned on, you can play the instrument to test its sound.

4. Click and drag the playhead to where you want to start recording on the timeline.
5. Click the **Record** button (●) to start recording.

- GarageBand starts recording, creating a red region as it records.

6 Play your instrument.

7 When you are done playing, click the **Play** button (▶).

You can click the **Record** button (●) to stop recording the instrument but continue playing the song.

GarageBand stops recording.

- The new recording is shown as a region in the timeline.

The region is purple for a real instrument.

The region is green for a software instrument.

- In this example, the blue region below represents a track created with an instrument loop. See Chapter 12 for more about loops.

How do I record multiple tracks at once?

You can record more than one track at a time. You need to have an audio interface for your computer that supports as many input channels as there are instruments.

1 Create tracks for the instruments and configure the audio interfaces for them.

2 For each track you want to record at once, click the **Record Enable** button (● changes to ●).

3 Click the **Record** button (●).

4 Play the instruments.

GarageBand records the instruments and creates new regions in the respective tracks.

Set the Metronome

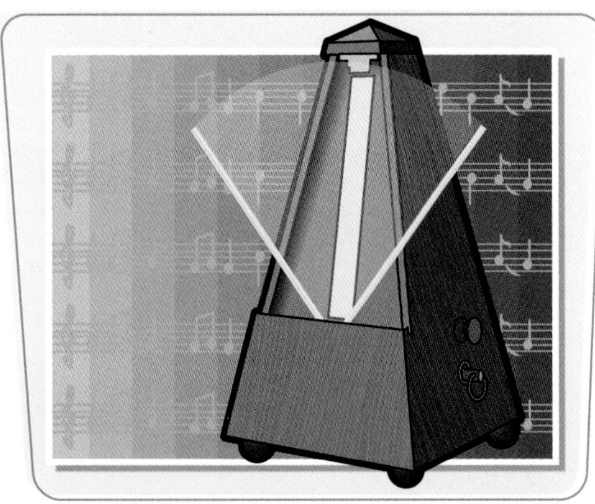

You can set up a metronome in GarageBand to play a steady beat as you record your music. This helps you keep time as you play. The speed at which the metronome plays depends on the tempo that you specify when you create a new project. See Chapter 12 for details about creating a project.

Set the Metronome

1. Click **Control**.

   The metronome is turned on by default.

- You can click **Metronome** to turn it off.

2. Click **Count In**.

3. Click the **Record** button to record a song.

   GarageBand plays a one-measure count-in before recording starts. This can help you time your playing with the song.

Note: *See "Record an Instrument" for more information about recording.*

4. Click the **Play** button (▶) to stop recording.

5 Click **GarageBand**.

6 Click **Preferences**.

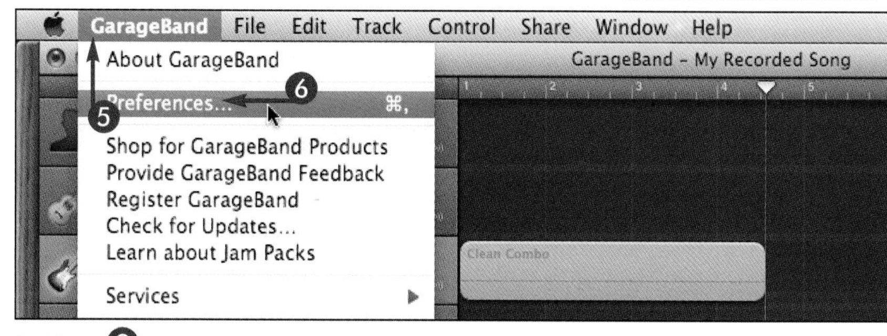

The Preferences window appears.

7 Click **General**.

8 Click a metronome preference (changes to).

Click **During recording** to play the metronome only when recording.

Click **During playback and recording** to play the metronome during regular playback and recording.

9 Click to close the Preferences window.

GarageBand saves the metronome settings.

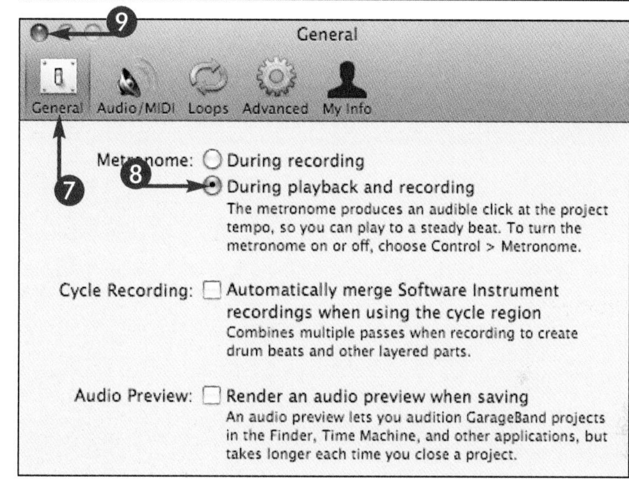

What is a songwriting project?

You can create a songwriting project to set up tracks for several common instruments.

1 Click **File** and then **New**.

2 In the GarageBand window, click the **Songwriting** project template.

3 Create the new project.

GarageBand opens the project workspace.

- Several instrument tracks are predefined.
- A drum track has music inserted as the backbeat for the project.

***Note:** You can select a track to record music for it. See "Record an Instrument" for details.*

Record Multiple Takes

When recording an instrument, you can have GarageBand repeat a section of your project so you can create multiple recorded versions, or *takes*, of that section. After recording the takes, you can review them and choose the best one for your finished recording.

Record Multiple Takes

1. Click [cycle icon] to turn on the cycle region.

   GarageBand displays the cycle region above the timeline.

2. Click and drag to resize the cycle region to set where recording starts and ends.

- You can drag the middle to move the entire region.
- You can drag an edge to resize the region.

3. Click the track for which you want to record multiple takes.
4. Click the **Record** button ([record icon]).

GarageBand starts recording.

5. Play your instrument.

- The playhead moves through the region and then repeats.

  A new take is recorded each time through.

6. Click the **Play** button (▶) to stop recording.

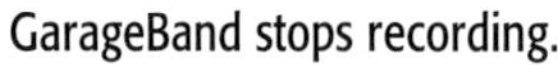

GarageBand stops recording.

- A number appears after the region name indicating the number of takes recorded.
- The number for the currently displayed take appears here.

How do I choose one of several recorded takes to use in a project?

1. Click the take number.

   A menu opens displaying the different takes for the region.

2. Click a take to use.

- You can click here to delete all unused takes for this region.
- You can click here to delete the currently selected take.

GarageBand displays the take in the timeline.

Save a Song to iTunes

You can save a song you create in GarageBand to iTunes. iTunes lets you manage music and other media on your Mac. From iTunes, you can play the song, transfer it to an iPod or iPhone, or burn it to a CD-ROM disc.

Save a Song to iTunes

1. Open the GarageBand project you want to save.
2. Click **Share**.
3. Click **Send Song to iTunes**.

4. Type a playlist for the song.
5. Type the artist, composer, and album information.

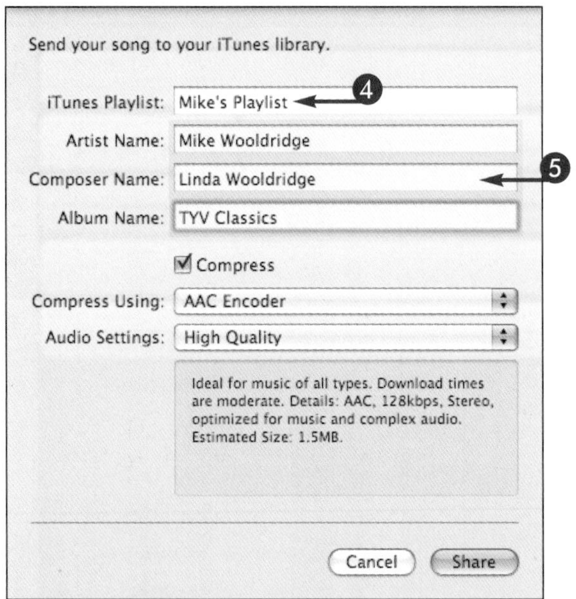

6 Select a compression scheme.

The AAC encoder saves files in the M4A format and offers better sound quality and smaller file size.

The MP3 encoder saves files in the MP3 format, which is a more widely supported audio standard.

7 Select the audio quality.

Higher quality settings result in larger file sizes.

- You can click here to turn off compression (☑ changes to ☐). GarageBand saves the file in AIFF format.

8 Click **Share**.

GarageBand processes the song and exports it to iTunes.

- iTunes opens and plays the song.
- Your playlist is selected.

9 Click here to stop playing the song.

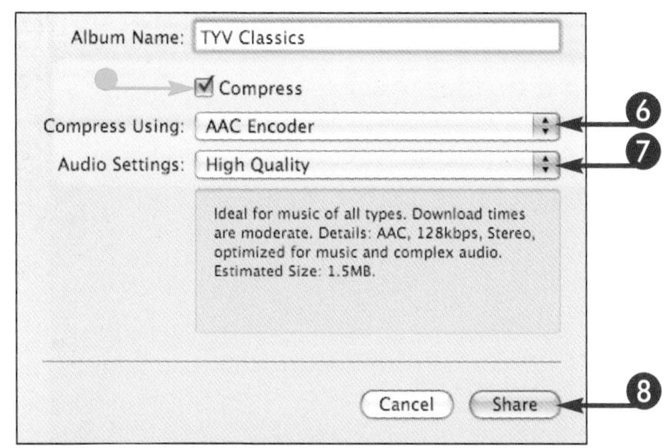

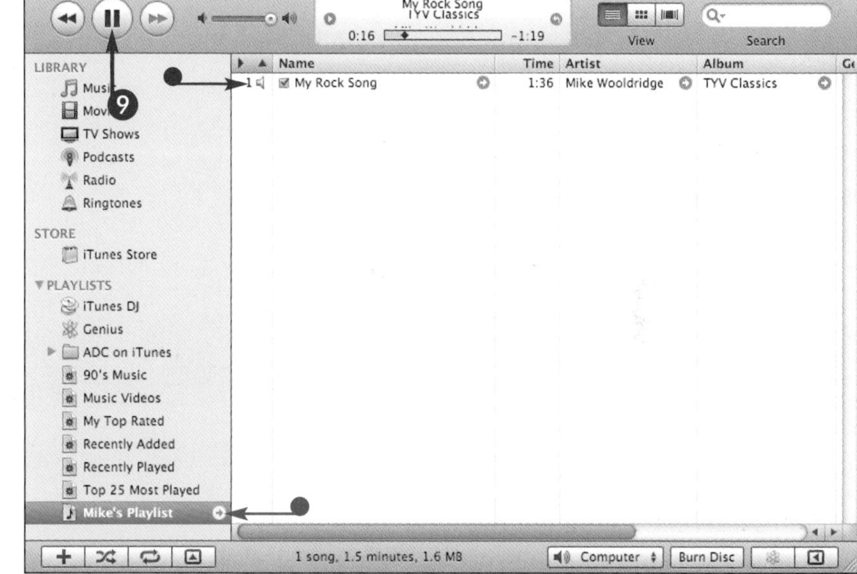

How do I set my information defaults for exports to iTunes?

You can set defaults for artist, composer, and other information in the GarageBand preferences.

1 Click **GarageBand** and then **Preferences**.

2 In the Preferences window, click **My Info**.

3 Type your default information.

4 Click ● to close the window.

GarageBand uses this information when exporting songs and podcasts to iTunes.

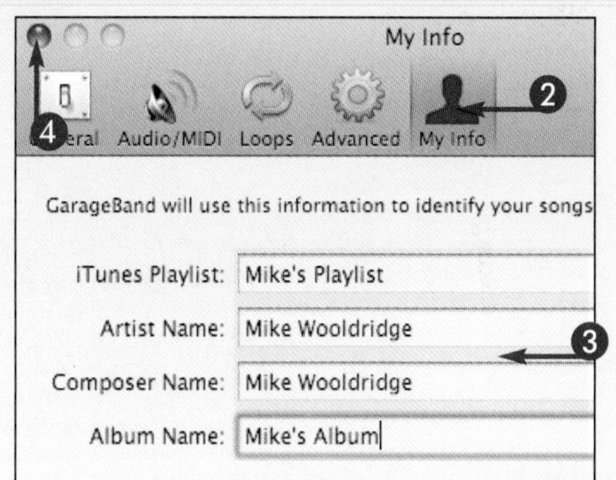

Export a Song to a File

You can export your song to a file on your computer. From there, you can use the file in another application, upload it to the Web with an FTP client, or burn the file to CD or DVD disc for backup.

Export a Song to a File

1. Open the GarageBand project you want to export.
2. Click **Share**.
3. Click **Export Song to Disk.**

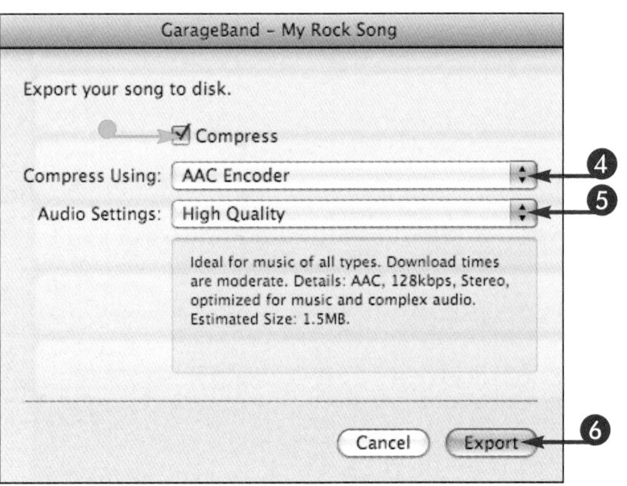

4. Select a compression scheme.

   The AAC encoder saves files in the M4A format and offers better sound quality and smaller file size.

   The MP3 encoder saves files in the MP3 format, which is a more widely supported audio standard.

5. Select the audio quality.

   Higher quality settings result in larger file sizes.

- You can click here to turn off compression (☑ changes to ☐). GarageBand saves the file in AIFF format.

6. Click **Export**.

7. Type a song name.
8. Select where to save the song on your computer.
9. Click **Save**.

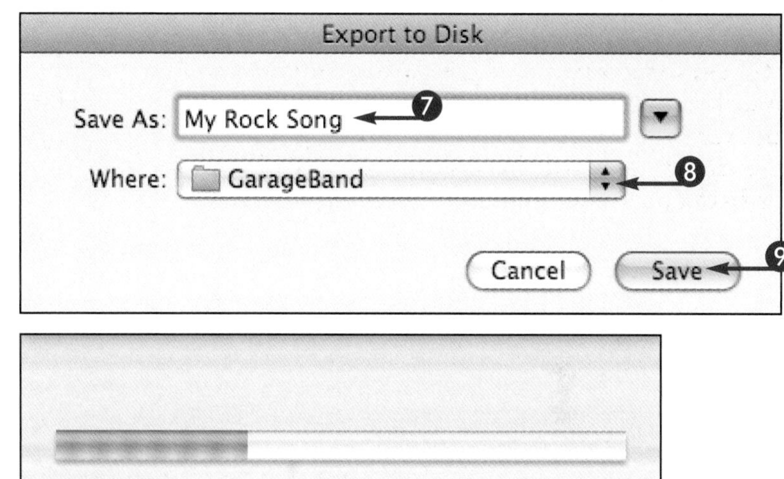

GarageBand saves the song.

How do I save or share just a segment of a song?

You can use the cycle region to define a part of the song that you want to save or share.

1. Click [cycle button] to display the cycle region.
2. Click and drag to define the segment you want to save or share.

   You can click and drag in the middle to move the region.

   You can click and drag at an edge to change the size of the region.
3. Click **Share** and then **Export Song to Disk**.

Note: *To save the segment to iTunes, click* ***Share*** *and then* ***Send Song to iTunes****.*

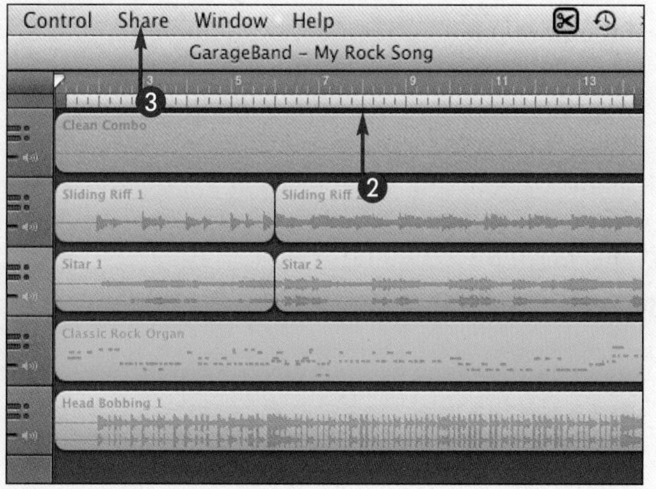

Create a Ringtone for an iPhone

You can select a part of your GarageBand song to use as a ringtone and then export it to iTunes. From iTunes, you can transfer the ringtone to your iPhone. Ringtones need to be 40 seconds or less. You can use the cycle region to define the part of your song to use.

Create a Ringtone for an iPhone

1. Click to display the cycle region.
2. Click and drag to define the segment you want to use as the ringtone.

   You can click and drag in the middle to move the region.

   You can click and drag at an edge to change the size of the region.

- You can click the **Play** button ( ) to preview the segment.

3. Click **Share**.
4. Click **Send Ringtone to iTunes**.

- GarageBand optimizes the segment as a ringtone and exports it to iTunes.

iTunes opens and plays the new ringtone.

5. Click **Ringtones**.

- iTunes displays your ringtone.

6. Click here to stop playing the ringtone.

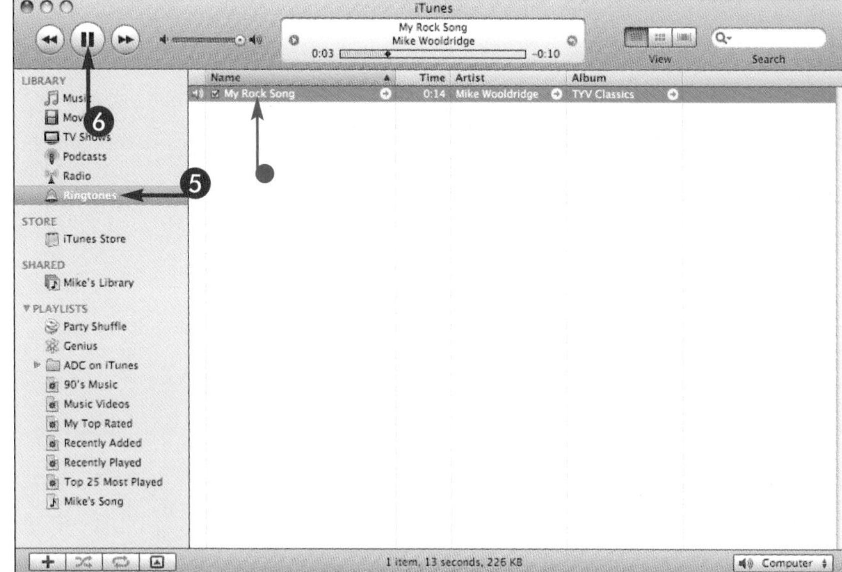

How do I add ringtones to my iPhone in iTunes?

Follow these steps:

1. Connect your iPhone to your computer and open iTunes.
2. In iTunes, click your iPhone in the Devices section.
3. Click **Ringtones**.
4. Click **Sync ringtones** (☐ changes to ☑).
5. Click **All ringtones** (○ changes to ◉).
6. Click **Apply**.

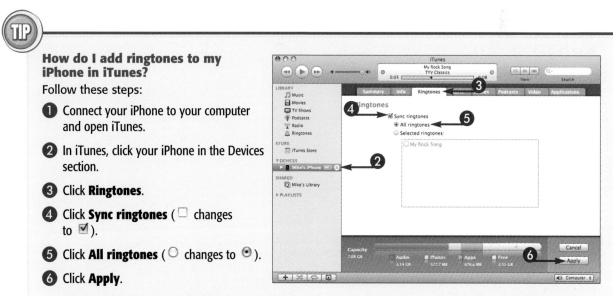

When you next sync your iPhone, iTunes adds ringtones in the iTunes library to your phone. For more about ringtones and syncing, see the iTunes documentation.

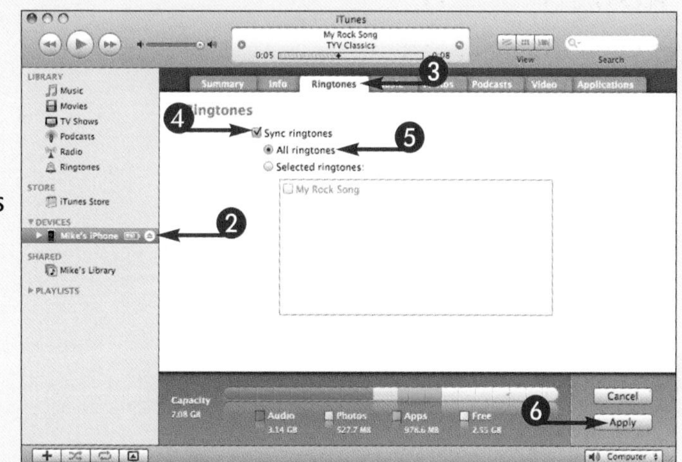

Burn a Project to CD

You can burn a music CD of your GarageBand project to create a disc that you can play in a CD player. Most newer Mac computers come with optical drives that can burn CD discs.

Burn a Project to CD

1. Open the GarageBand project you want to burn to CD.
2. Click **Share**.
3. Click **Burn Song to CD**.

4. Select the optical drive to burn with.
5. Insert a writable CD into the drive.

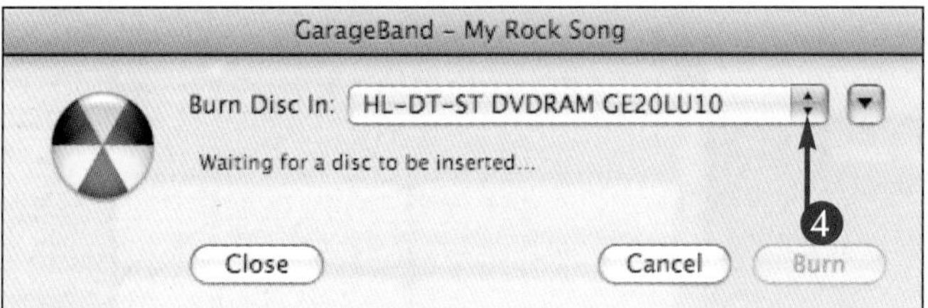

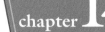

6 Click **Burn**.

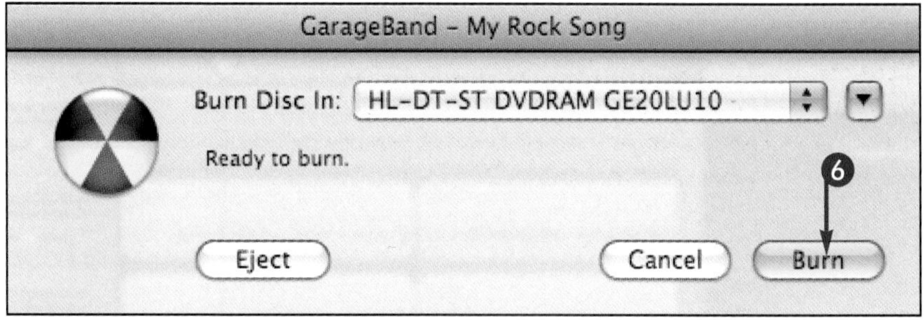

GarageBand burns the project to CD.

- You can click **Stop** to abort the burn.

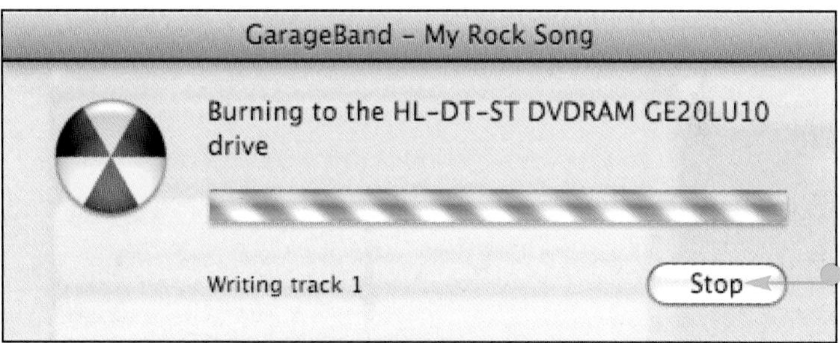

TIP

How do I save, export, or burn specific tracks from my song?

You can click the Mute or Solo buttons to select the tracks to be saved.

1 Click the **Mute** button to turn off a track and not have it used (changes to).

2 Click the **Solo** button to turn off every track except the selected one (changes to).

Note: For more about muting and soloing tracks, see Chapter 12.

3 Save your project. You can save it to iTunes, export it to a file, or burn it to a CD. See the other tasks in this chapter for details.

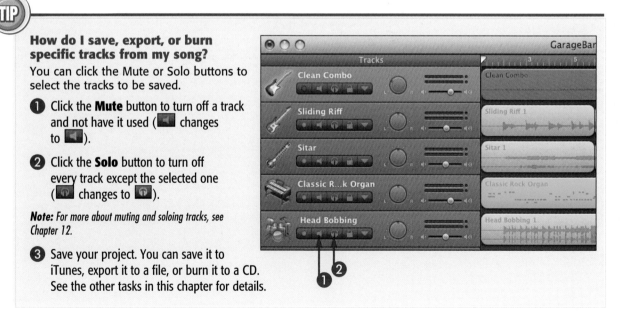

Create a Podcast

You can create a podcast to share your voice and music with accompanying imagery over the Internet. GarageBand makes creating podcasts easy with its podcast template. You can put a podcast online using iWeb.

Create a Podcast

CREATE A PODCAST PROJECT

1. Click **File** and then click **New**.
2. In the GarageBand window, click **New Project**.
3. Click **Podcast**.
4. Click **Choose**.
5. In the New Project from Template dialog, type a name for the project.
6. Select where to save the project.

- You can configure the tempo, signature, and key. See Chapter 12 for details.

7. Click **Create**.

GarageBand opens the podcast project template.

RECORD AUDIO

GarageBand sets up male and female vocal tracks by default.

8. Connect a microphone to your computer. See Chapter 13 for details.
9. Click a vocal track to record.
10. Click the **Record** button (●).

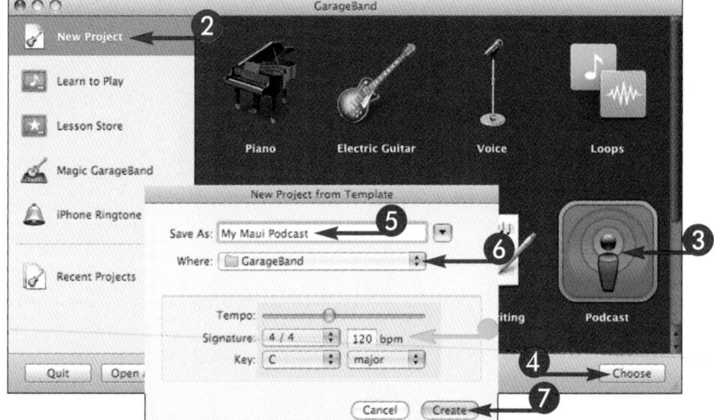

- GarageBand starts recording and the playhead moves across the timeline.

11. Speak into the microphone to record audio for your podcast.

- A new region is created in the timeline.

12. Click the **Play** button () when you are done recording.

How do I add music jingles to my podcast?

You can add jingles, or short snippets of music, to give your podcast a professional sound.

1. Click to open the loop browser.
2. Click to show loops for podcasts.
3. Click the Jingles category.
4. Click a keyword.

- GarageBand displays the loops.

5. Click and drag a loop to the Jingles track of the podcast.

GarageBand adds a jingle to play along with your other podcast recordings.

continued

Create a Podcast *(continued)*

You can add artwork to complement the audio of your podcast episode using the Podcast Track. By arranging the artwork on the podcast timeline, you can make different imagery appear during different segments of the podcast.

Create a Podcast *(continued)*

GarageBand stops recording.

- You can click [+] to create additional tracks, including instrument tracks, for your podcast. See Chapter 13 for details.

ADD ARTWORK

13. Click **Podcast Track**.
14. Click and drag the playhead to the point in the song where you want to add artwork.
15. Click **Add Marker**.
    - GarageBand adds a marker region.
16. If the media browser is hidden, click [icon].
17. Click **Photos**.
18. Click and drag an image to the podcast markers list.

    A thumbnail image appears in the Podcast Track.
19. Click and drag the center of the thumbnail to adjust when the image appears; click and drag the right edge to adjust the display duration.

⓴ You can repeat steps **17** and **18** to add more artwork to the podcast.

PREVIEW THE PODCAST

㉑ Click the preview icon in the Podcast Track.

● The Podcast Preview window opens.

㉒ Click the **Play** button (▶).

GarageBand previews the podcast.

How can I add artwork to represent my podcast episode when I publish it?

You can insert an image from the media browser to include representative artwork.

❶ Click **Podcast Track**.

❷ Click [media browser icon] to show the media browser.

❸ Click **Photos**.

● GarageBand displays images from the iPhoto library.

❹ Click and drag an image to the Episode Artwork box.

GarageBand creates episode artwork for the podcast.

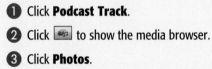

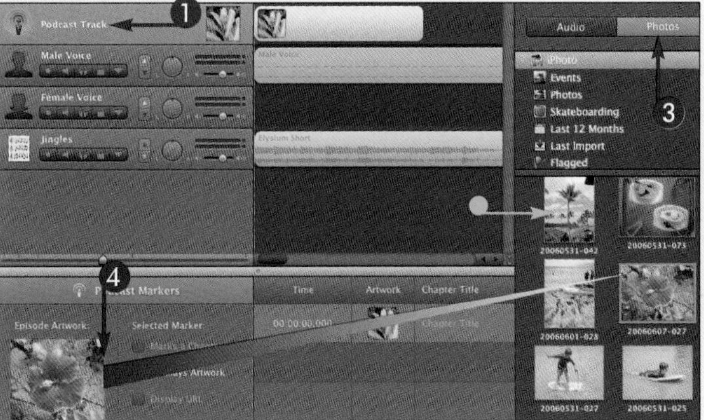

Add a Podcast to a Web Page

You can add a podcast created in GarageBand to a Web site in iWeb. After adding the podcast, you can publish it using the publishing features in iWeb. See Part V of this book for details.

Add a Podcast to a Web Page

1. Use the podcast project template to create a podcast.

Note: *See "Create a Podcast" for details.*

2. Click **Share**.
3. Click **Send Podcast to iWeb**.

GarageBand displays the export settings.

4. Select an encoding setting.

The AAC encoder saves files in the M4A format and offers better sound quality and smaller file size.

The MP3 encoder saves files in the MP3 format, which is a more widely supported audio standard.

5. Select an audio setting for your podcast.
6. Click **Share**.

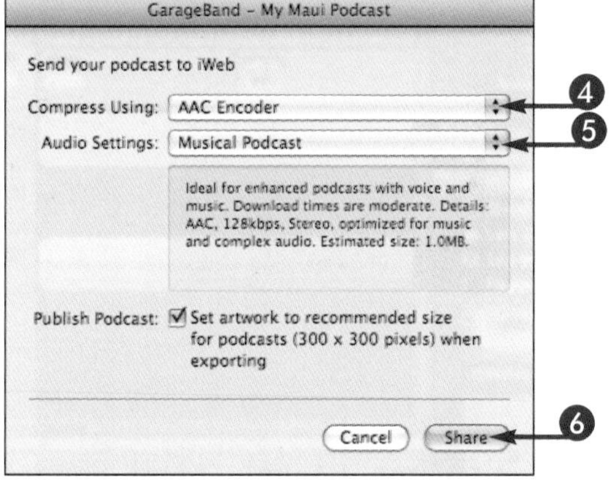

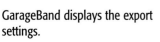

GarageBand processes the podcast and iWeb opens.

7. Select the page where you want the podcast to appear.

   You can add a podcast to a podcast page or blog page on any of your iWeb sites.

8. Click **OK**.

   iWeb adds the podcast to the Web page.

9. Click the play button to preview the podcast on the page.

Note: *See Part V of this book for more about iWeb and podcasts.*

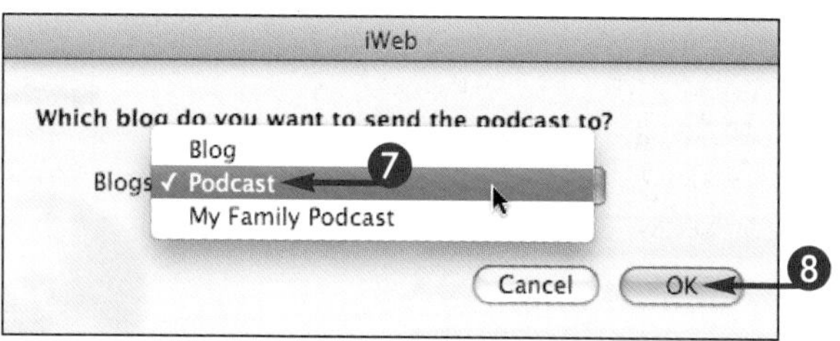

How can I export a podcast as a file?

You can export a podcast as a file to view on your computer, share with others, or publish on the Web. Click **Share** and then **Export Podcast to Disk**. GarageBand lets you select a compression setting and audio setting, and then where to save the file on your computer.

How do I add a movie to a podcast?

You have the option of adding movie clips to your podcasts instead of still artwork. You can click **Track** and then **Show Movie Track** to display a track for adding movies. You can open the media browser and then click **Movies** to access content to add to the track.

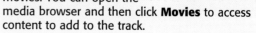

Understanding the Lesson Workspace

GarageBand lessons teach you how to play a piano or guitar through instructional videos and songs you can play along with. Musical notation, instrument graphics, a song timeline, and other features help you learn to play the instrument and understand musical concepts. Before starting a GarageBand lesson, familiarize yourself with the lesson workspace.

Lesson Chapters

A GarageBand lesson is divided into chapters. In Learn chapters, instructors explain musical concepts and demonstrate how to play instruments. In Play chapters, you can play along with songs to practice what you have learned.

Lesson Video

Lessons include videos of instructors playing instruments. The videos are shot at multiple angles to give you different views of the instrument you are learning. Musical notation and instrument graphics below the video are highlighted to show the notes, keys, and strings being played.

Notation

The notation area shows the notes of the song being played in the lesson. You can configure the notation in the settings to show chords, different piano hands, tablature, and more. See "Customize the Lesson Window" to learn about configuring the notation.

Instrument

The instrument area shows a representation of the instrument being played. It shows a piano keyboard for piano lessons and a guitar neck with strings for guitar lessons. Keys, strings, and frets are highlighted as different notes are played in the song. See "Customize the Lesson Window" to learn about viewing or hiding the instrument graphics.

Editing Your Lesson

You can click **Open in Garage Band** to open the lesson music, including any recordings you have made, in the GarageBand editor.

Volume

You can control the overall volume of the lesson here. To control the specific volumes of the instruction vocals and instruments being played, you can open the settings. See "Adjust Lesson Volumes" for more details.

Controls

You can use the main controls to play the lesson, record yourself playing along with the lesson, and repeat a part of a song.

Tempo

The lesson workspace includes a metronome that plays along with the song to help you keep time. The bottom of the metronome shows the tempo of the song. You can slow down a lesson song to make it easier to follow. See "Take a Piano Lesson" or "Take a Guitar Lesson" for details.

Timeline

The lesson workspace has a timeline that shows the parts that make up a lesson. A playhead moves along the timeline to show what part is currently being played. If you record yourself playing a lesson, the recording shows up as a colored bar on the timeline.

Take a Piano Lesson

You can take a piano lesson in GarageBand to learn the basics of using the instrument. Lessons involve instructional video and songs that you can play along with. An on-screen keyboard shows you what notes to play on your connected keyboard. To play along with the piano lessons, you must attach a USB or MIDI keyboard to your computer.

Take a Piano Lesson

1. Connect a MIDI music keyboard to your computer.
2. Click **File** and then **New**.

   The GarageBand window appears.
3. Click **Learn to Play**.
4. Click a piano lesson.

Note: GarageBand starts with one piano lesson and one guitar lesson. To access more lessons, see "Download a Lesson."

5. Click **Choose**.

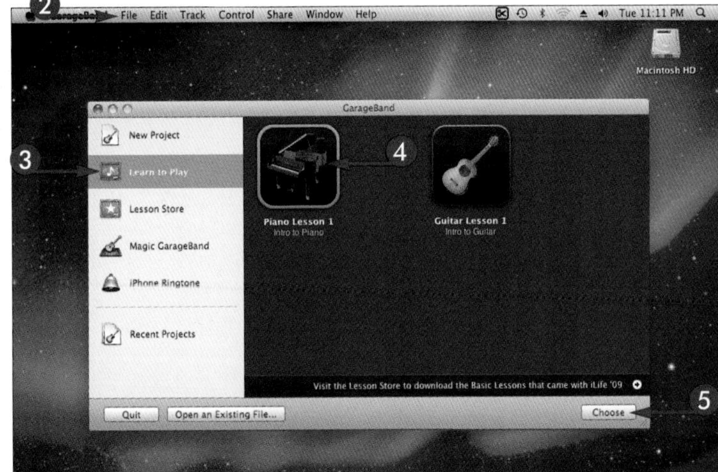

The lesson workspace opens. This example shows Piano Lesson 1.

6. Position the cursor over the main lesson area.

   Learn and Play chapters are displayed. Different chapter options may appear if you are completing a different lesson.
7. Click **Learn**.

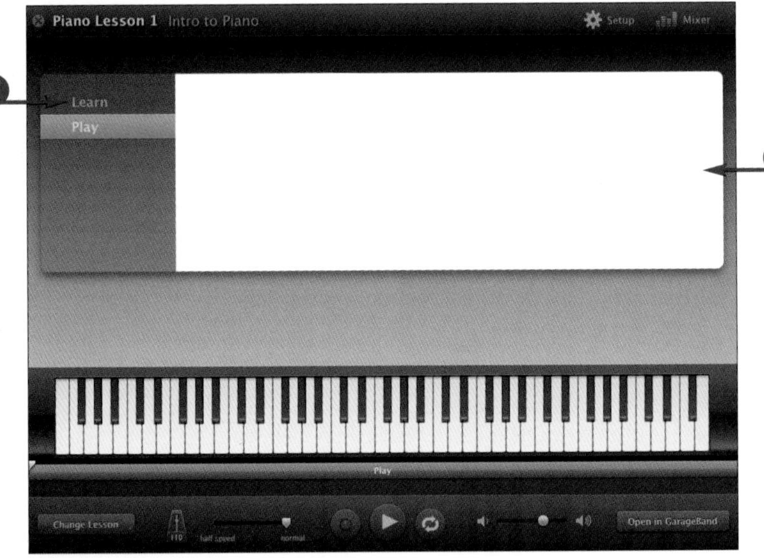

An instructional video plays, teaching you how to play a song.

- Keys on the keyboard are labeled to show the notes played during the lesson.
- You can click the timeline to skip to different parts of the lesson.
- You can click the **Play** button (▶) to pause the lesson.

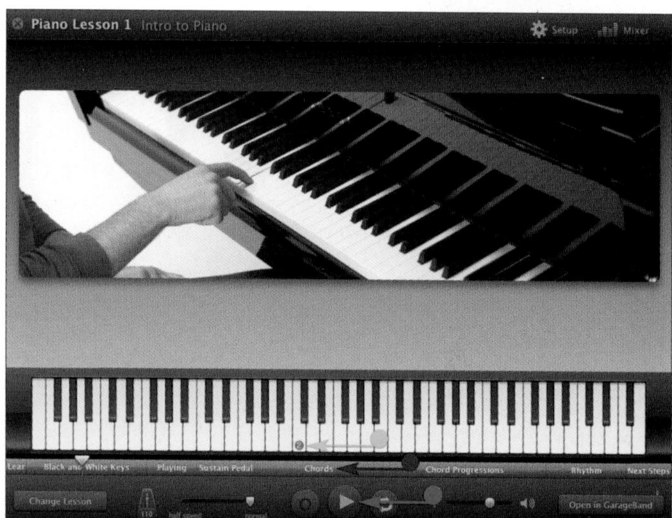

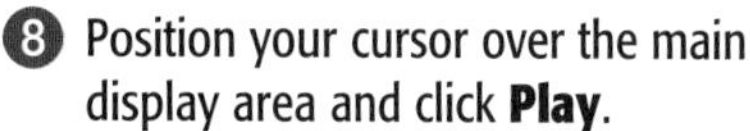

8 Position your cursor over the main display area and click **Play**.

GarageBand plays a song without instruction that you can play along with.

9 Play your keyboard to match the notes in the song.

10 Click the **Record** button (●) to record your playing.

TIPS

How does a MIDI keyboard talk to my computer?

MIDI stands for Musical Instrument Digital Interface. MIDI is a common standard that allows computers and musical instruments to communicate and synchronize with one another. MIDI keyboards are software instruments, which means instead of sending sound signals to a computer like a microphone does, they send software messages that specify the pitch, intensity, and other characteristics of each note.

How do I connect a MIDI keyboard to my computer?

You can connect your MIDI keyboard to the USB port of your computer using MIDI-to-USB cabling. This may come with your instrument or you can buy it separately. Some newer MIDI devices include USB ports on the instruments themselves, letting you use a USB-to-USB cable.

Take a Piano Lesson *(continued)*

As you follow along with a song in a lesson, you can adjust the tempo to slow the beat down or turn on a metronome to help you keep time. You can record yourself as you play and then open the recording in the GarageBand editor. As you improve, you can download more advanced lessons and complete them. See "Download a Lesson" for details.

- GarageBand records the playing, creating a red region in the timeline as it records.
- You can click and drag the slider to adjust the volume of the lesson.
- You can click and drag the playhead to move to another part of the song.

11. Click the **Play** button (▶) to stop recording and pause the song.

- The recorded region turns green. Green regions represent software instrument recordings.

12. Click and drag the slider to change the tempo of the lesson. You can drag to the left to slow the song down to make it easier to play along with.
13. If a warning dialog appears telling you the instructor's voice will be muted, click **OK**.

GarageBand changes the tempo.

- The new tempo is shown here.
- You can click here to turn on a metronome, which plays clicks along with the song to help you keep the beat.

14. Click the **Play** button (▶).

GarageBand plays the lesson with the new tempo.

Note: *You can play along with the song but cannot record when the tempo is set to other than normal.*

15. Click the **Play** button (▶) again to pause the song.
16. Click **Open in GarageBand**.

GarageBand opens the lesson in the editing view.

- The lesson instruments are placed in separate tracks.
- Your recording is placed in a track.

17. Click the **Play** button (▶) to play the lesson song.

Note: *For more about playing and editing music, see Chapter 12.*

How do I delete a recording from a lesson?

You can delete a recording from a lesson if you no longer have a need for it or want to record it over again.

1. Click a recorded region.

   GarageBand selects the region.

   You can Shift-click to select multiple regions at once to delete.

2. Press Delete.

- GarageBand deletes the recording.

Take a Guitar Lesson

You can take a guitar lesson in GarageBand to learn the basics of using the instrument. Lessons involve instructional video and songs that you can strum along with. An on-screen fret board shows you which strings to strum and where to place your fingers.

Take a Guitar Lesson

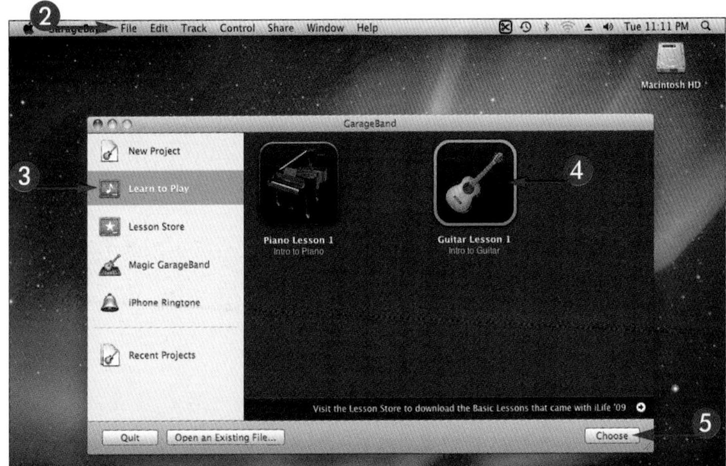

1. If you are using an acoustic guitar, connect a microphone to your computer to record the guitar.

   If you are using an electric guitar, connect the guitar directly to the computer.

***Note:** For more about connecting microphones and instruments, see the tip on the next page and the sections in Chapter 13.*

2. Click **File** and then **New**.

   The GarageBand window appears.

3. Click **Learn to Play**.
4. Click a guitar lesson.
5. Click **Choose**.

   The Lesson workspace opens. This example shows Guitar Lesson 1.

6. Position the cursor over the main lesson area.

   Learn and Play options are displayed. Different chapter options may appear if you are completing a different lesson.

7. Click **Learn**.

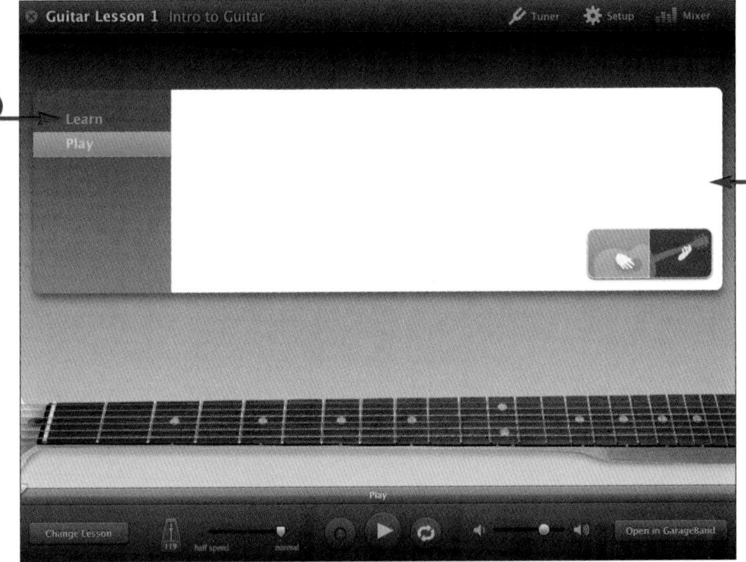

An instructional video plays, teaching you how to play a song.

- Guitar strings vibrate to show which ones are played during the lesson.
- The fret board is labeled to show finger placement.
- You can click the timeline to skip to different parts of the lesson.
- You can click the **Play** button (▶) to pause the lesson.

8 Position your cursor over the main lesson area and click **Play**.

GarageBand plays the song without instruction so you can play along.

9 Play your guitar to match the notes in the song.

10 Click the **Record** button (●) to record your playing.

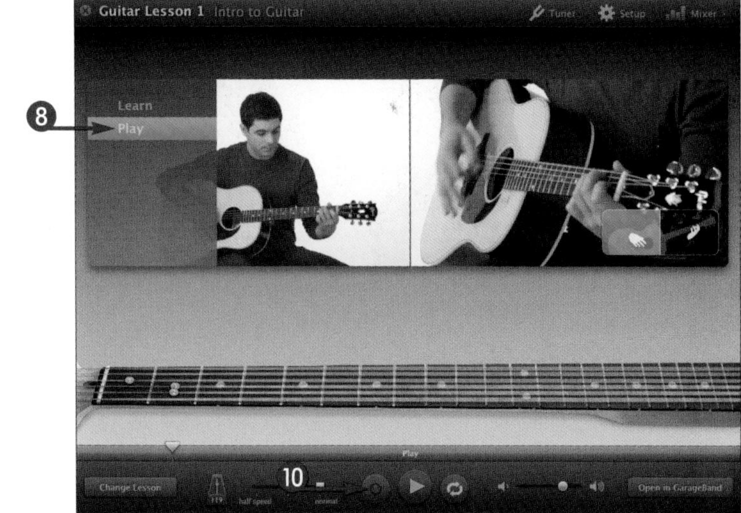

How do I specify how a guitar is connected to my computer?

When you are taking a lesson, you can click **Setup** and then choose from the My Input Device menu in the window that appears. Choose **Guitar** if you are connected through the audio input port, **Internal Mic** if you are playing through the built-in microphone of the computer, or **External Guitar** if your guitar is connected to an audio interface.

I get feedback when I record my lesson. How do I fix this?

Feedback is the high-pitched noise that can occur when recording with a microphone. You can click **Setup** and then select **Monitor Off** from the My Input Device menu to avoid feedback when recording during a lesson.

continued

Take a Guitar Lesson *(continued)*

As you follow along with a song in a lesson, you can adjust the tempo to slow the beat down or turn on a metronome to help you keep the beat. You can record yourself as you play and then open the recording in the GarageBand editor. As you improve, you can download more advanced lessons and complete them. See "Download a Lesson" for details.

- GarageBand records the playing, creating a red region as it records.
- You can click and drag the slider to adjust the volume of the lesson.
- You can click and drag the playhead to move to another part of the song.

11. Click the **Play** button (▶) to stop recording and pause the song.

- The recorded region turns purple. Purple regions represent real instrument recordings.

12. Click and drag the slider to change the tempo of the lesson. You can drag to the left to slow the song down to make it easier to play along with.
13. If a warning dialog appears telling you the instructor's voice will be muted, click **OK**.

    GarageBand changes the tempo.

- The new tempo is shown here.
- You can click here to turn on a metronome, which plays clicks along with the song to help you keep the beat.

14. Click the **Play** button (▶).

GarageBand plays the lesson with the new tempo.

Note: *You can play along with the song but cannot record when the tempo is set to other than normal.*

15 Click the **Play** button (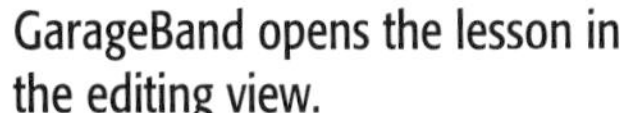) again to pause the song.

16 Click **Open in GarageBand**.

GarageBand opens the lesson in the editing view.

- The lesson instruments are placed in separate tracks.
- Your recording is placed in a track.

17 Click the **Play** button (▶) to play the lesson song.

Note: *For more about playing and editing music, see Chapter 12.*

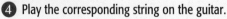

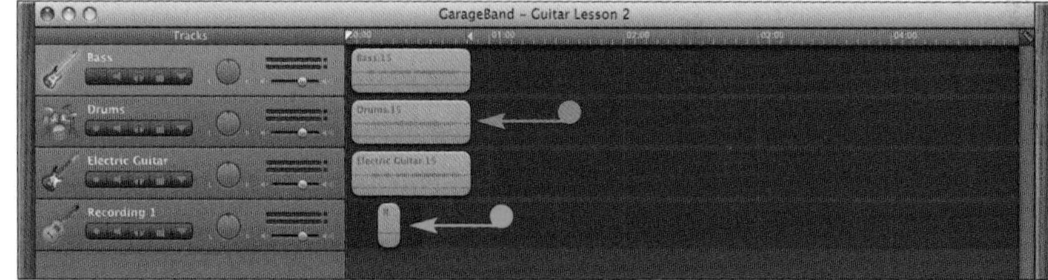

How do I tune my guitar with GarageBand?

Follow these steps:

1 Connect your guitar to the computer and open a guitar lesson.

2 Click **Tuner**.

The GarageBand tuner appears.

3 Click a string to tune.

4 Play the corresponding string on the guitar.

- If the string is out of tune, a note appears in red.
- A bar on either side also appears, indicating whether the note is flat or sharp.

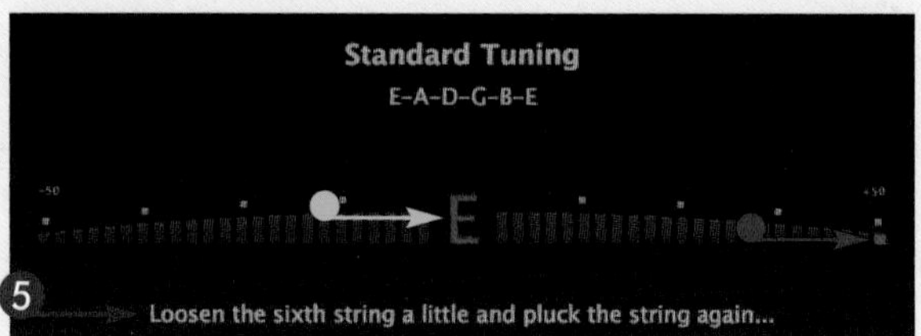

5 Adjust the tuning peg for the string on the guitar, following the directions on the screen.

When the string is in tune, the note appears in blue.

6 Repeat steps **3** to **5** for all the strings.

Download a Lesson

GarageBand comes with one piano lesson and one guitar lesson installed. You can download additional lessons of varying skill levels from the Internet into GarageBand.

Download a Lesson

1. Click **File** and then **New**.

   The GarageBand window appears.

2. Click **Lesson Store**.
3. Click **Basic Lessons**.

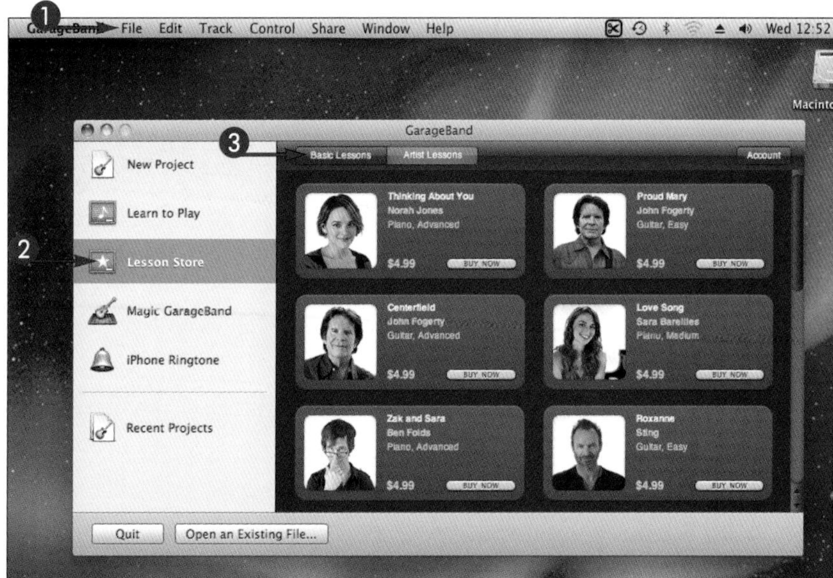

The basic lessons appear.

- You can scroll to view more lessons.

4. Click **Download**.
5. Click **Download** in the confirmation dialog that appears.

- GarageBand downloads and installs the new lesson.

6 To play the lesson, click to select it.

7 Click **Choose**.

GarageBand opens the lesson.

Note: *For more details about completing a lesson, see "Take a Piano Lesson" and "Take a Guitar Lesson."*

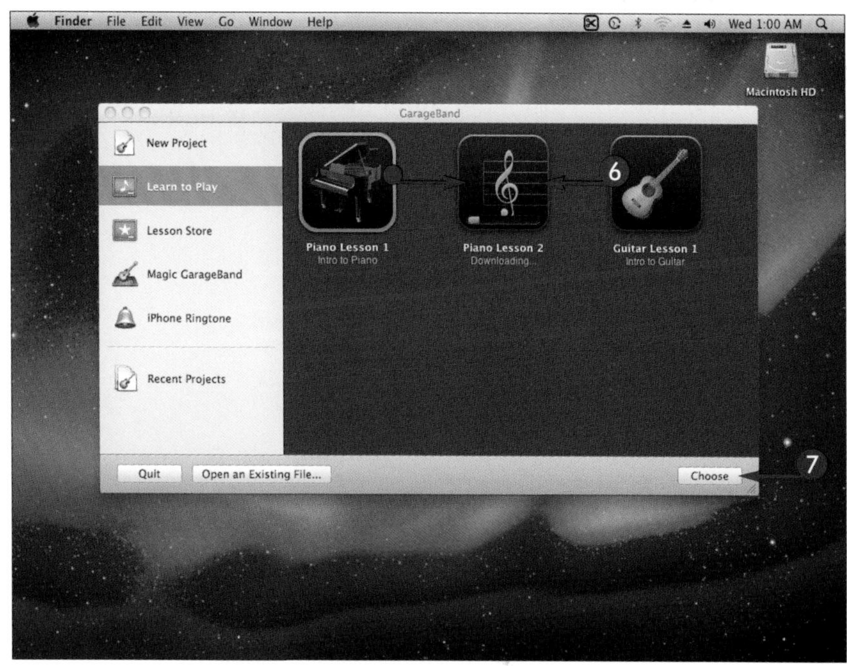

How do I purchase lessons from famous music artists?

You can purchase and then download piano and guitar lessons from famous music artists at the Lesson Store.

1 In the GarageBand window, click **Lesson Store**.

2 If Artist Lessons is not selected, click to select it.

GarageBand displays the artist lessons.

3 Click **Buy Now** for the lesson you want to purchase.

GarageBand prompts you to sign in to your Apple account or create one if you are a new customer.

After signing in or creating an account, you can follow the steps to purchase and download the lesson.

Adjust Lesson Volumes

You can change the volumes of the different tracks that make up the lesson audio, including the instructor voice, instructor instrument, band instruments, and your instrument. Giving your instrument higher volume can help you determine if you are playing along with the song.

Adjust Lesson Volumes

1. Open a piano or guitar lesson.

Note: *See "Take a Piano Lesson" or "Take a Guitar Lesson" for details.*

2. Click **Mixer**.

GarageBand opens the volume settings.

3. Click and drag the sliders to adjust the volumes.

- You can click [icon] to minimize the volume for a track.
- You can click [icon] to maximize the volume for a track.

4. Click [icon].

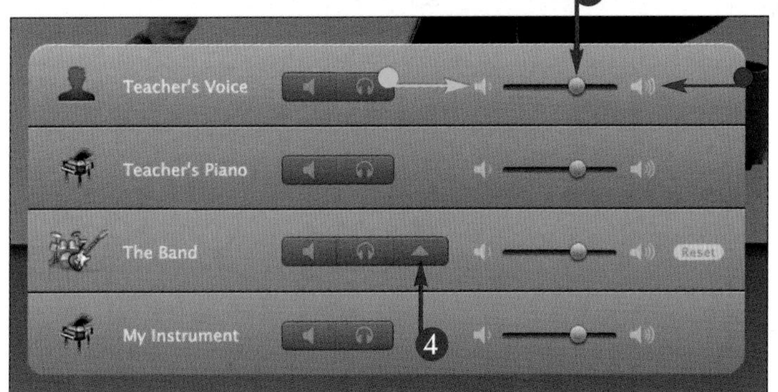

The band instrument volumes appear.

5 Click and drag the sliders to change the instrument volumes.

- You can click [mute] to mute a track.
- You can click [solo] to solo a track, which mutes every track but the selected one.

6 Click **Mixer**.

GarageBand saves the volume settings.

- You can click and drag the slider to adjust the overall volume of the lesson.

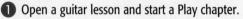

How do I change views of the guitar during a lesson?

You can change views of the guitar to focus on the guitar body or the guitar neck.

1 Open a guitar lesson and start a Play chapter.

2 Position your cursor over the main lesson area.

GarageBand displays view settings.

- Click here to view the body of the guitar.
- Click here to view the neck of the guitar.

Customize the Lesson Window

You can customize the lesson window to display different types of notation or to view an instrument, notation, or both. For example, users who cannot read music can show only the instrument during the lesson, whereas guitarists can display tablature notation.

Customize the Lesson Window

❶ Open a piano or guitar lesson.

Note: *See "Take a Piano Lesson" or "Take a Guitar Lesson" for details.*

❷ Click **Setup**.

❸ Click to select a notation setting.

The Automatic setting displays a notation type based on the content being shown.

For a piano lesson, you can also choose from Chords, Left Hand, Right Hand, and Both Hands settings.

For a guitar lesson, you can also choose from Chords, Chord Grid, TAB, and TAB & Standard settings.

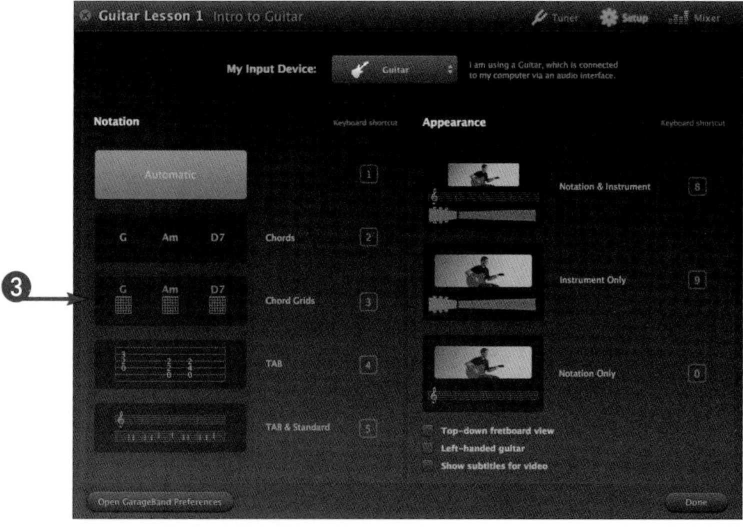

4 Click to select an appearance setting.

You can select from Notation & Instrument, Instrument Only, and Notation Only.

5 Click **Done**.

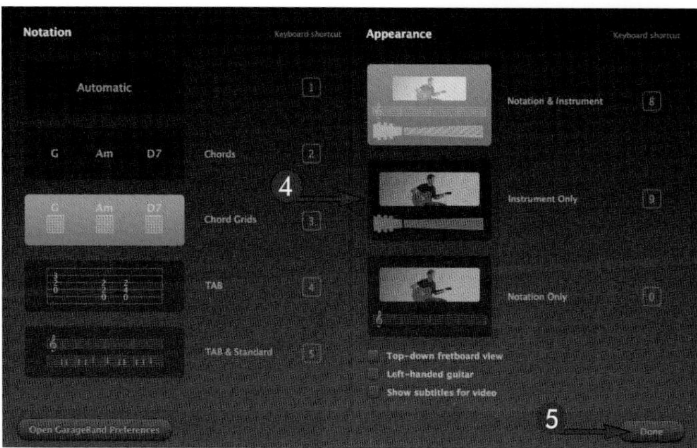

GarageBand saves the settings and displays the appropriate view.

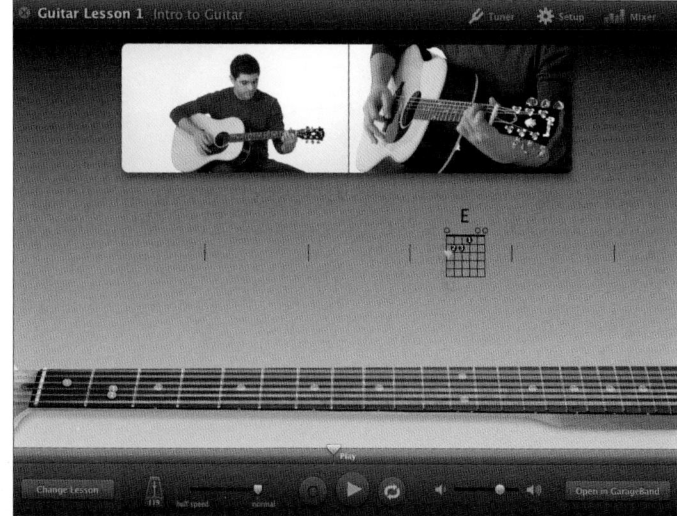

What are the keyboard shortcuts for customizing the lesson window?

You can customize the lesson window by pressing number keys on the keyboard.

Shortcut	*Notation/Appearance*
1	Automatic
2	Chords
3	Left Hand (piano), Chord Grids (guitar)
4	Right Hand (piano), TAB (guitar)
5	Both Hands (piano), TAB & Standard (guitar)
8	Notation & Instrument
9	Instrument Only

Turn On Easy View for Piano

You can turn on Easy View in a piano lesson to display the names of the notes on the instrument keyboard and in the musical score. This can help you match notes to the instrument if you are a new musician.

Turn On Easy View for Piano

1. Open a piano lesson.
2. Click **Setup**.
3. Check **Easy View** (☐ changes to ☑).
4. Click here to display both the notation and instrument in the lesson view.
5. Click **Done**.

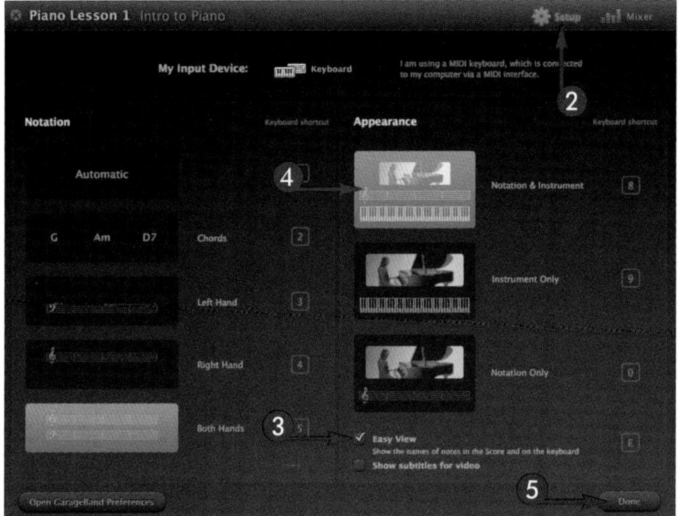

GarageBand applies the settings.

- Note names appear on the keyboard.
- Note names also appear in the score.

Switch to Left-Handed Guitar

If you play guitar left-handed, you can switch the orientation of the guitar neck in the lesson window.

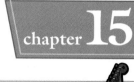

Switch to Left-Handed Guitar

1. Open a guitar lesson.
2. Click **Setup**.
3. Check **Left-handed guitar** (☐ changes to ☑).
4. Click **Done**.

- GarageBand displays a left-handed guitar neck.

Repeat Part of a Lesson

You can select a part of your lesson and then repeat it while recording or just playing. You might want to repeat a difficult part to practice it until you can play it just right. When recording, GarageBand saves each repetition, or *take*.

Repeat Part of a Lesson

1. Open a piano or guitar lesson.
2. Click the **Cycle** button (![]).

- GarageBand highlights the parts of the lesson.

3. Click the part of the lesson you want to repeat.

   GarageBand highlights the selected part.

4. Click the **Record** button (![]) to play and record the part repeatedly.

- Alternatively, you can click the **Play** button (![]) to play it repeatedly, without recording.

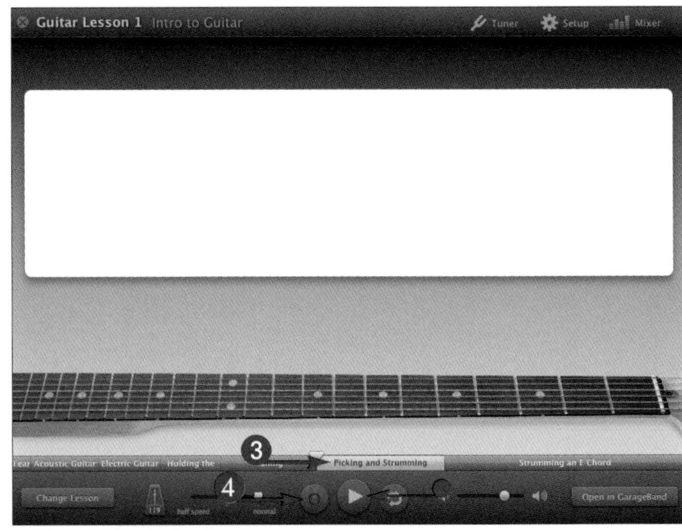

GarageBand plays the part of the lesson, repeating it after each time through.

5 Click the **Play** button (▶) to stop recording.

- GarageBand displays the number of takes recorded. For more about takes, see Chapter 13.

TIP

How do I listen to or delete a specific take?

You can click the take number in the recorded region to listen to or delete a take.

1 Record multiple takes of part of a song.

2 Click the number of takes.

A menu appears.

3 Click to select the take you want to hear.

- You can click here to delete takes.

4 Click the **Play** button (▶) to listen to the selected take.

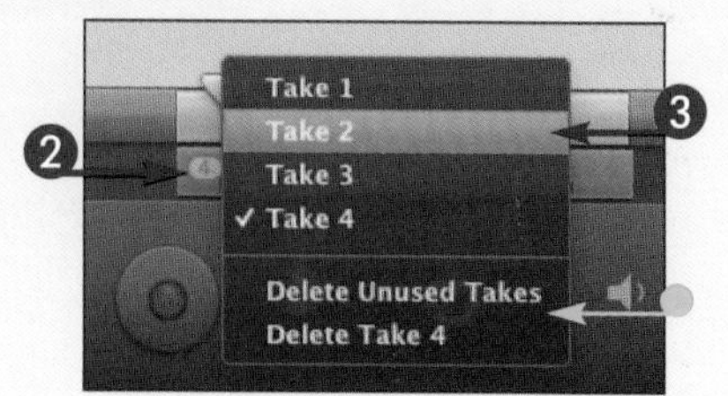

PART V

Working with iWeb '09

This part covers iWeb '09, which enables you to create Web sites using images, video, and audio from the other iLife programs. You can build professional-looking pages using dozens of page themes, without having to write HTML. Blog and podcast templates help you publish text and multimedia, whereas iWeb *widgets* let you integrate information from other Web sites. You can publish finished sites to your own Web server or to a MobileMe account.

Understanding the iWeb Workspace

iWeb enables you to create full-featured Web sites that you can publish online. You start with templates for common Web page types — such as Welcome pages, photo galleries, and blog pages — and fill in your own text and media to make the site your own. You construct pages using visual tools and without having to write HTML code. Before starting an iWeb project, familiarize yourself with the program workspace.

Sites and Pages

The iWeb sidebar displays a list of the sites you have created. Beneath each site name is a list of the pages in the site. Selecting a site displays publishing settings for the site in the main window. Selecting a page displays the page in the main window and allows you to add to and edit its content.

Adding New Pages

You can click **Add Page** to add new pages to your Web site, including Welcome and About Me pages, pages that feature photos and movies, and pages for blogs and podcasts. You can use a blank page template to start a page from scratch.

Publishing

You can publish your finished Web site to an Internet service provider via FTP or to your MobileMe account, if you have one.

Themes

iWeb offers dozens of themes to decorate your pages with predefined colors and graphics. There are themes for specific events such as vacations and road trips, colorful kids themes, and a variety of artistic themes. Each time you add a new page, you select a theme.

Editing Buttons

You can click different buttons to add text, shapes, and masks to your pages, rotate content, or adjust color. An Inspector window allows you to make precise adjustments to the dimensions of your page, customize fonts, configure RSS feeds, and more.

Media

You select content to add to your pages in the media pane. You can browse through photos from iPhoto, movies from iMovie, and music from iTunes and GarageBand. You can also add widgets, which are page containers for Google Maps, YouTube movies, iSight movies, and more.

Main Window

The main iWeb window displays your Web pages. You can click inside the window to select and edit text, images, and other page features. You can resize and reposition content containers and change backgrounds to get just the page design you want.

Create a New Site

You can create a new site in iWeb and then add different types of themed pages to it. Your pages can include text, images, multimedia, and more. iWeb allows you to easily maintain multiple Web sites at the same time. You can publish your finished Web sites to your MobileMe account or to your Internet service provider via FTP.

Create a New Site

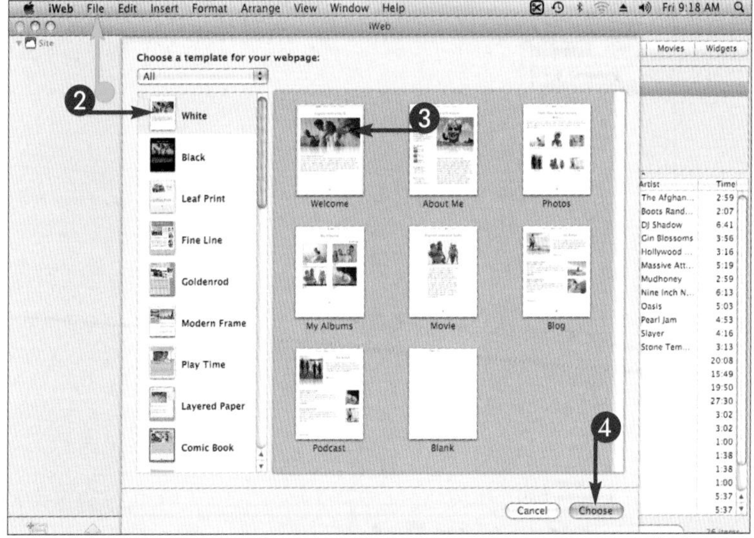

1. Start the iWeb program.

   The first time you run iWeb, the program prompts you to choose a template to start your site.

- You can also click **File** and then **New Site** to create a new site.

2. Click a theme to choose the style of your template.

Note: For more about themes, see "Change the Theme."

3. Click a template to determine the type of page to add.
4. Click **Choose**.

iWeb creates a new site with the chosen template as its first page.

- The site is listed in the sidebar.
- The page is listed under the site.
- The page is populated with generic text, images, and other media.
- You can click and drag content from the media pane to add it to the page.

Note: See Chapter 17 for details about adding and editing media.

5 Double-click the site name.

The site name becomes editable.

6 Type a new name for the site.

7 Press Enter.

iWeb renames the site.

You can rename page names similarly.

TIPS

Where does iWeb store Web sites on my computer?

iWeb stores your sites in a single file called Domain. To find it, open the Library folder in the Finder, then the Application Support Folder, and then the iWeb folder. You can transfer this file to work on your Web sites on another computer. Double-clicking the Domain file on your Mac opens iWeb.

How does my site name relate to its Web address?

If you publish your site to the MobileMe service, MobileMe uses your site name and member name to create the Web address — for example, http://web.me.com/membername/sitename. Keep in mind that if you change the name of a site published to MobileMe, your site Web address changes and external links to your site will no longer work. See Chapter 19 for more about publishing a site.

Create a New Page

You can add a new page to your iWeb site to publish new content. iWeb offers a variety of page templates for publishing text, photo galleries, blogs, and more. You can select graphics and colors for your page by choosing a theme.

Create a New Page

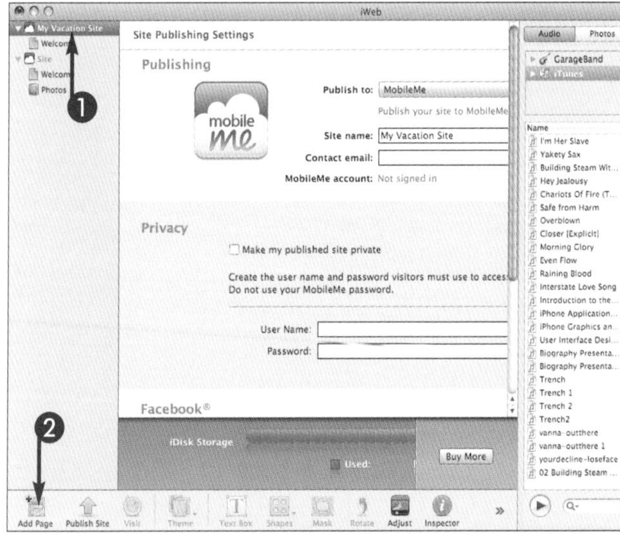

1. Click to select the site to which you want to add a page.
2. Click **Add Page**.

The template dialog appears.

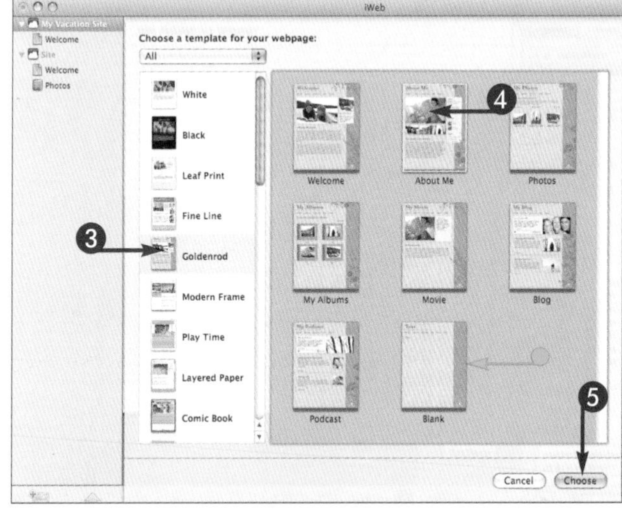

3. Click a theme to determine the style of your template.

   The pages of a site can have the same or different themes.

Note: *For more information about themes, see "Change the Theme."*

4. Click a template to determine the type of page to add.

- You can select a Blank template to start designing your page from scratch.

5. Click **Choose**.

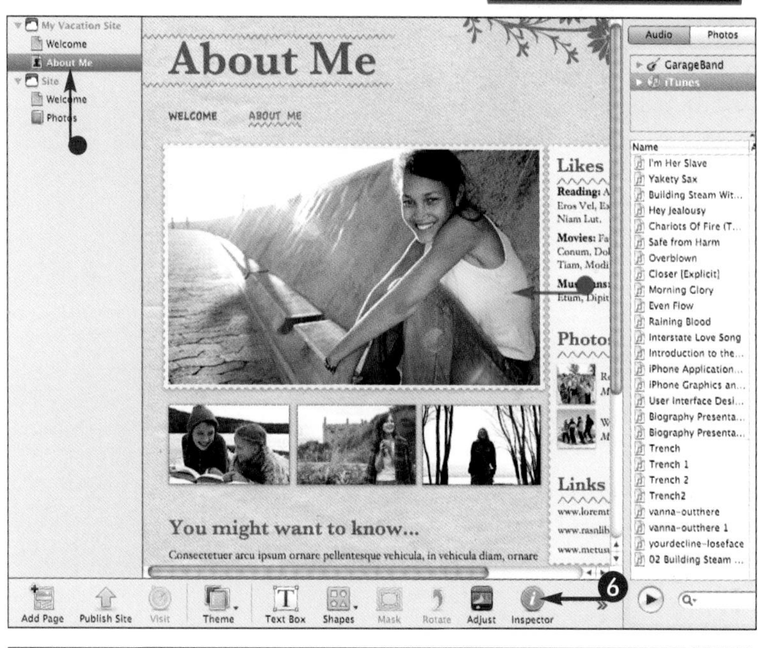

iWeb adds the page to your site.

- The page is listed under the site name in the sidebar.
- The page content appears here.

Note: See Chapter 17 for details about adding and editing page content.

6. Click **Inspector**.

The Inspector window appears.

7. Click the **Page Inspector** icon (📄).

iWeb lists the page settings.

8. Type a name for the page.

- This name appears in site navigation links.

Note: See "Control Navigation on a Page" for more about navigation.

9. Click ● to close the Inspector.

How do I duplicate a page?

You can duplicate a page to create a new page based on the design of an existing one.

1. Click a page in the sidebar.
2. Click **Edit**.
3. Click **Duplicate**.

iWeb duplicates the page and lists the copy in the sidebar.

Note: You can share pages between sites by clicking and dragging the pages in the sidebar.

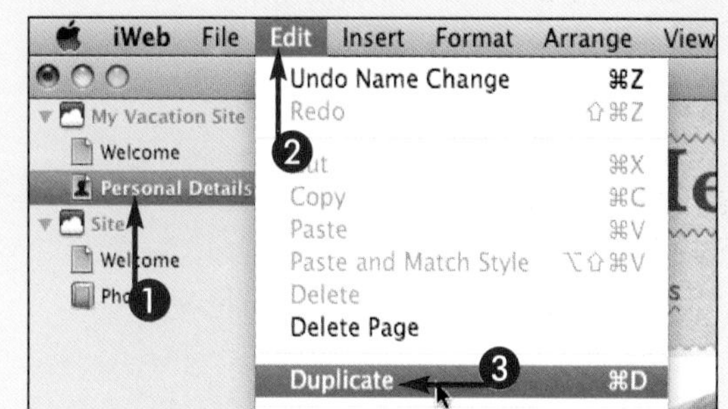

Change the Theme

You can change the theme of the page to make it suit its subject matter. iWeb offers two minimalist themes, titled White and Black, as well as dozens of other themes that include attractive color schemes and decorative graphics. Pages within a site can have the same or different themes.

Change the Theme

1. Select the page whose theme you want to change.
2. Click **Theme**.

A pane of themes appears.

3. Click a theme.

iWeb updates the page with the new theme.

Content on the page may rearrange, depending on the chosen theme.

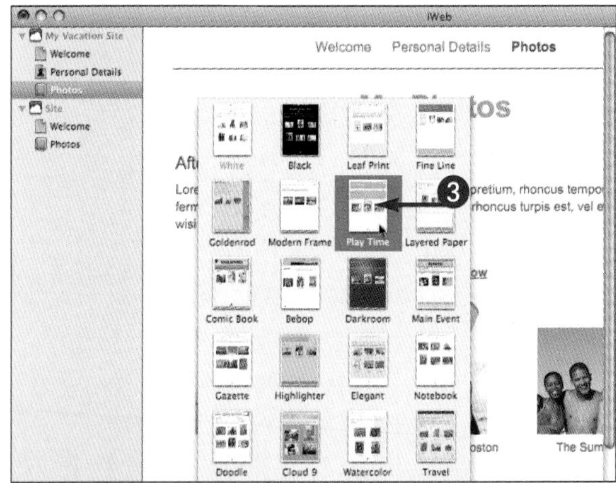

Control Navigation on a Page

You can hide or display navigation links on a page. Navigation links connect a page with other pages in the same site. You can also set whether a page is included in the navigation links.

Control Navigation on a Page

1. Select the page whose navigation you want to change.

- Navigation links typically appear near the top of the page.

2. Click **Inspector**.

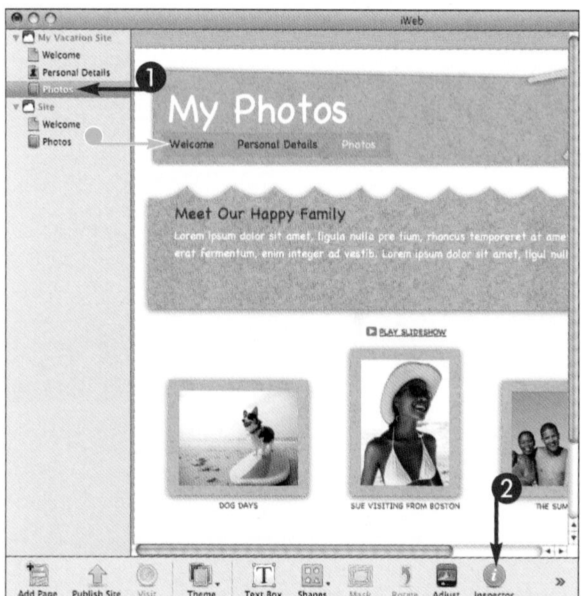

The Inspector window appears.

3. Click the **Page Inspector** icon ( ).

iWeb lists the page settings.

New pages have navigation turned on and are included in the site navigation.

- Click here to not display the page in the navigation links (changes to).
- Click here to hide navigation on a page (changes to).

4. Click to close the Inspector.

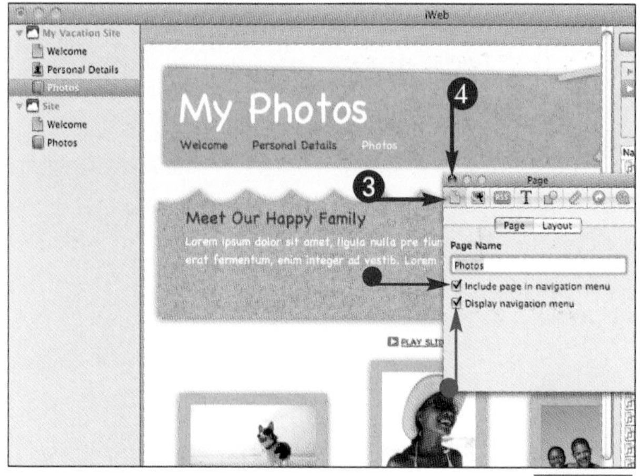

Change Page Dimensions

You can change the dimensions of your iWeb page and adjust the padding that surrounds it. You can also change the height of the header and footer, if the page has them. Changing dimensions can be useful if you want to accommodate viewers with different monitor resolutions.

Change Page Dimensions

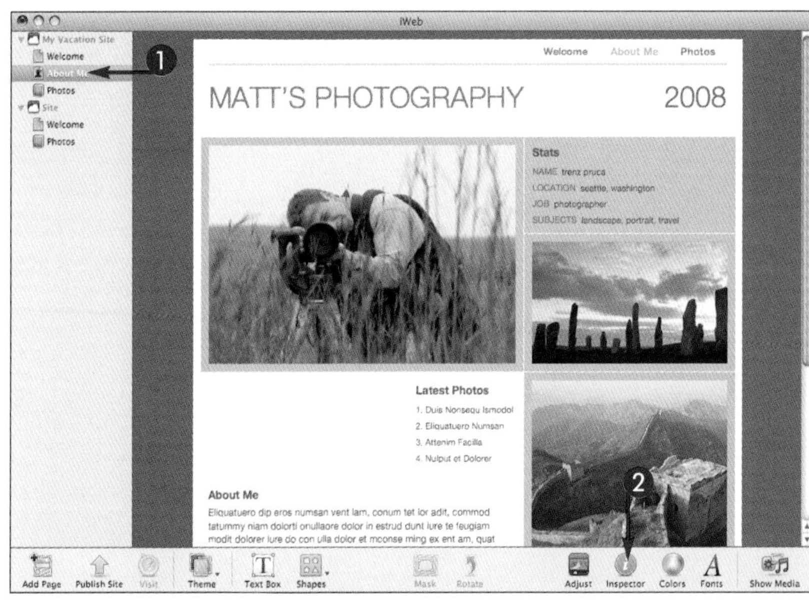

1. Select the page whose dimensions you want to change.
2. Click **Inspector**.

The Inspector window appears.

3. Click the **Page Inspector** icon ( ).
4. Click **Layout**.

Note: *Some layout settings may not apply to certain themes.*

5. Edit the value or click the arrows to change the padding above and below the page content.

- iWeb adjusts the padding.

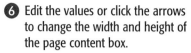

6 Edit the values or click the arrows to change the width and height of the page content box.

- iWeb adjusts the width and height.

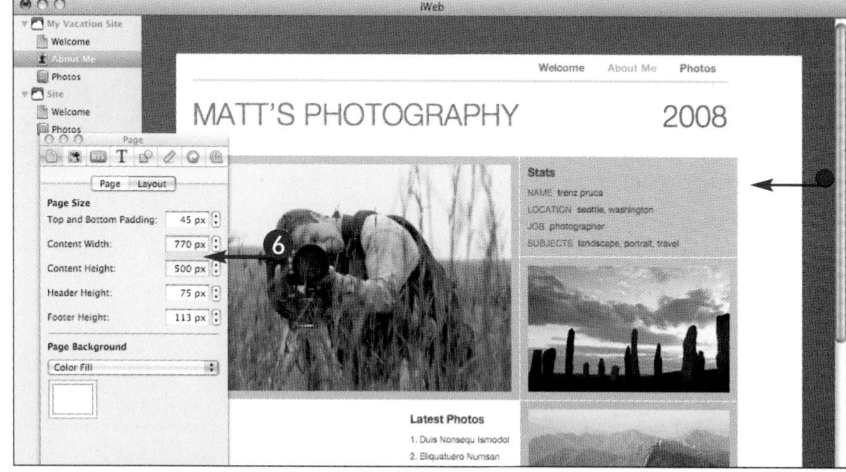

7 Edit the value or click the arrows to change the height of the header.

- iWeb adjusts the header.

8 Edit the value or click the arrows to change the height of the footer.

iWeb adjusts the footer.

9 Click  to close the Inspector.

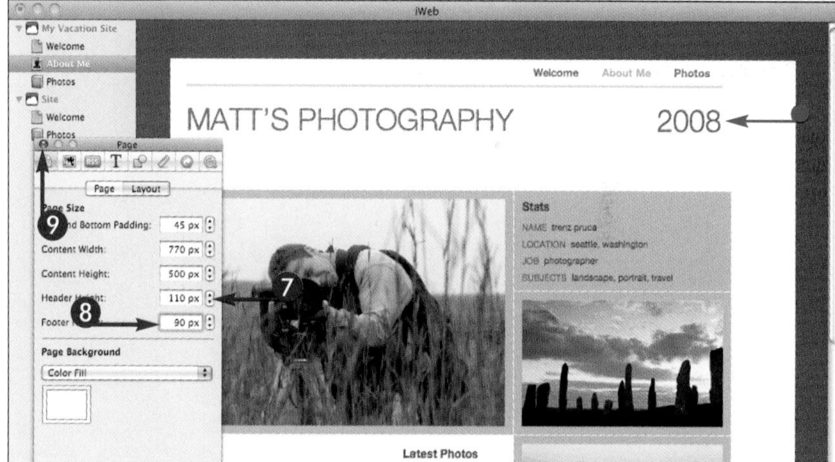

TIPS

What does px in the page measurements stand for?

The abbreviation *px* stands for pixels. Pixels are the tiny, solid-color elements that make up the images on a computer screen. Images and other objects on a Web page are often measured in pixels.

How do I show or hide the media pane?

The media pane on the right side of the workspace displays images, movies, and other content that you can add to your pages. You can hide it to make more room for displaying your pages. Click [»] and then click **Hide Media** from the menu that appears. After hiding the pane, you can click **Show Media** to display it again.

Change the Background

You can change the background of a page to give it a vibrant or subdued appearance. You can set the background as a color, a gradient, an image, or nothing at all. Most iWeb page themes feature two backgrounds: the page background on which the content appears and what iWeb calls the browser background, which shows under the page background.

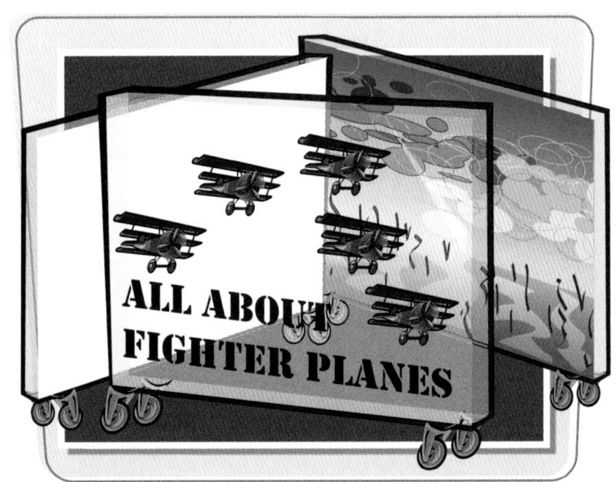

Change the Background

1. Select the page whose background you want to change.
2. Click **Inspector**.

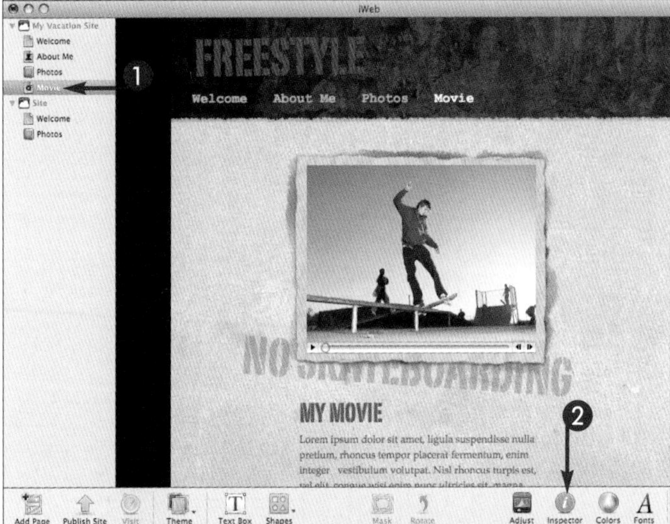

The Inspector window appears.

3. Click the **Page Inspector** icon ( ).
4. Click **Layout**.
5. Click here to select a page background type.

- For image fills, click to select background options.

  You can tile or stretch a small image to fill a larger background.

- The page background changes.

  For page backgrounds, you can also select Gradient Fill or None for the fill type.

6. Click here to select a browser background type.
7. For color fills, click here to select a color.

   The Colors dialog appears.
8. Click a color.
- The browser background changes.
9. Click ⬤ to close the Colors dialog.
10. Click ⬤ to close the Inspector.

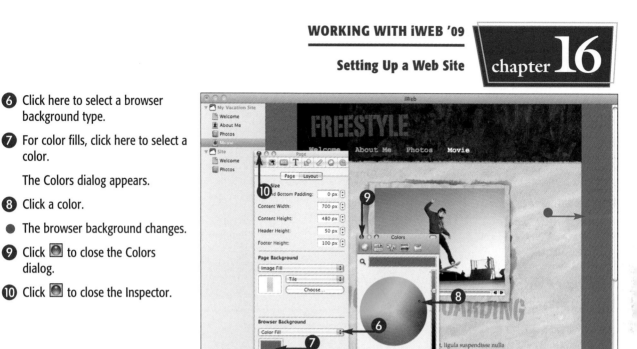

How can I tint a page background image?

You can add a color tint over a page background image to customize the appearance of the image. You can also adjust the opacity of the tint:

1. Select **Tinted Image Fill** for the page background.
- You can click **Choose** to change the background image.
2. Click the tint color icon.

   The Colors dialog opens.
3. Click to select a color.
4. Click and drag the slider to adjust the opacity. Dragging left makes the color more transparent and dragging right makes it more opaque.
5. Click ⬤ to close the Colors dialog.

Add a Text Box

You can add a text box to your Web page to add paragraphs, headings, and lists. You can adjust the size and position of the text box to make it fit in with the rest of the content on your page.

Add a Text Box

1. Select the page to which you want to add text.
2. Click **Text Box**.
   - A new text box appears in the middle of the page with a blinking cursor inside it.
   - To add text to a placeholder text box in a template, double-click it to select its text. Press Delete to remove the text and add your own.

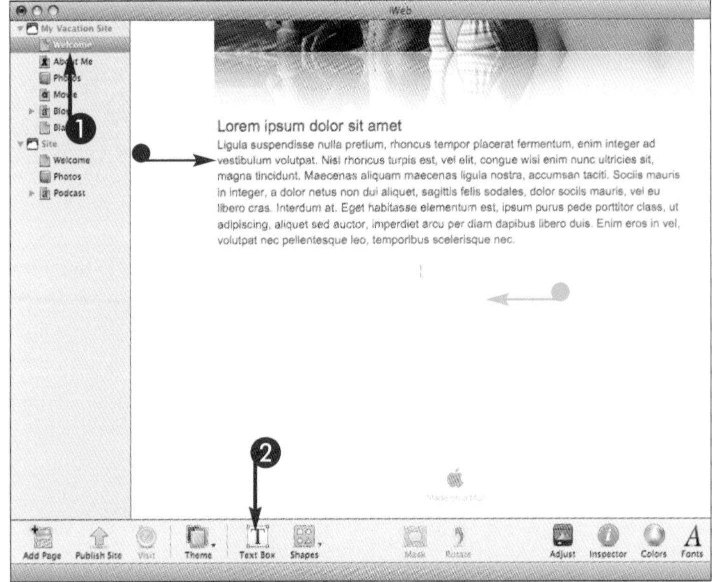

3. Type to add your text to the text box.

   You can also copy and paste text from another program.

   You can press Enter to start a new line.
4. Click the border of the text box.

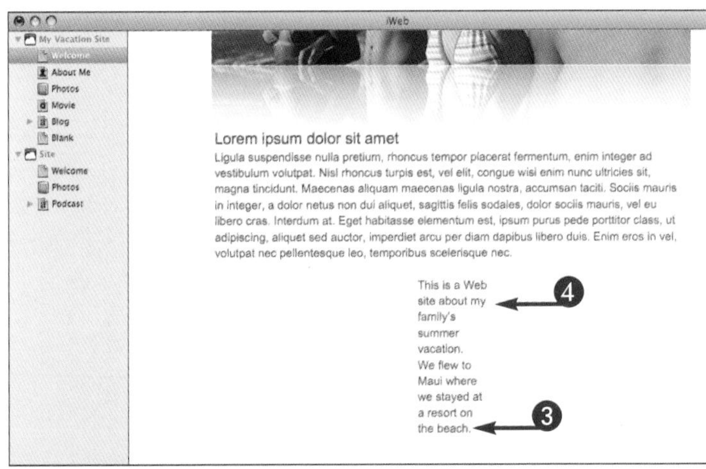

Handles appear on the sides and corners of the box.

5. Click and drag a handle to resize the text box.

   The box resizes.

***Note:** To change the alignment of text inside a box, see "Align Page Text."*

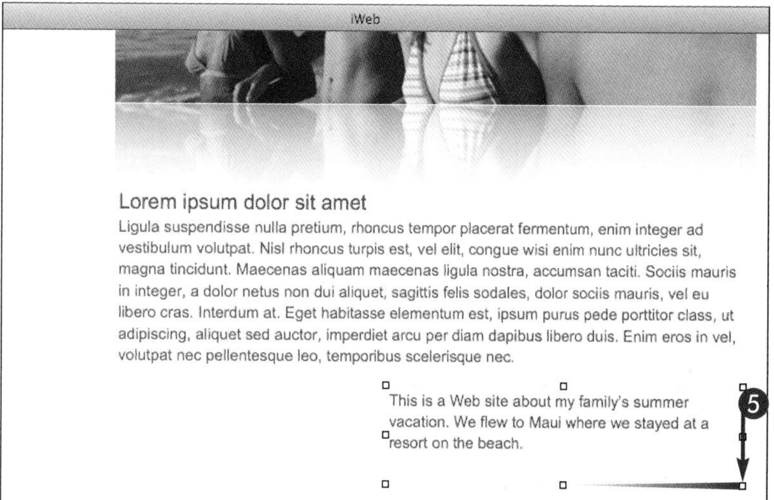

iWeb
Lorem ipsum dolor sit amet
Ligula suspendisse nulla pretium, rhoncus tempor placerat fermentum, enim integer ad vestibulum volutpat. Nisl rhoncus turpis est, vel elit, congue wisi enim nunc ultricies sit, magna tincidunt. Maecenas aliquam maecenas ligula nostra, accumsan taciti. Sociis mauris in integer, a dolor netus non dui aliquet, sagittis felis sodales, dolor sociis mauris, vel eu libero cras. Interdum at. Eget habitasse elementum est, ipsum purus pede porttitor class, ut adipiscing, aliquet sed auctor, imperdiet arcu per diam dapibus libero duis. Enim eros in vel, volutpat nec pellentesque leo, temporibus scelerisque nec.
This is a Web site about my family's summer vacation. We flew to Maui where we stayed at a resort on the beach.
5

6. Click and drag inside the text box to move the box to another place on the page.

- A yellow box appears displaying the coordinates of the box on the page as you drag.

   You can also press the arrow keys to change the position of a selected text box.

   To delete a text box, click the box to select it and then press Delete.

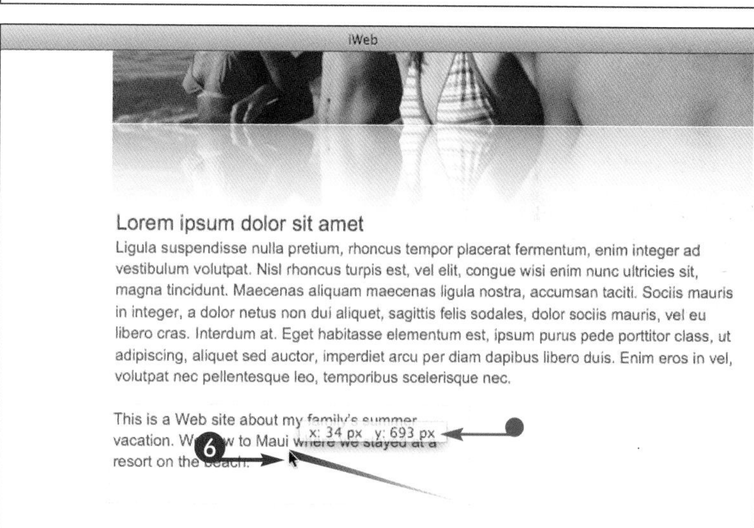

iWeb
Lorem ipsum dolor sit amet
Ligula suspendisse nulla pretium, rhoncus tempor placerat fermentum, enim integer ad vestibulum volutpat. Nisl rhoncus turpis est, vel elit, congue wisi enim nunc ultricies sit, magna tincidunt. Maecenas aliquam maecenas ligula nostra, accumsan taciti. Sociis mauris in integer, a dolor netus non dui aliquet, sagittis felis sodales, dolor sociis mauris, vel eu libero cras. Interdum at. Eget habitasse elementum est, ipsum purus pede porttitor class, ut adipiscing, aliquet sed auctor, imperdiet arcu per diam dapibus libero duis. Enim eros in vel, volutpat nec pellentesque leo, temporibus scelerisque nec.
x: 34 px y: 693 px
6

How do I move text boxes in and out of the header and footer?

iWeb pages are divided into regions, with a header at the top, a footer at the bottom, and the main content area in the middle. To move a text box *into* the footer, press ⌘ as you click and drag it. To move a text box *out of* the header, press ⌘ as you drag it. Some elements such as the navigation box in the header cannot be moved to another region. When selected, those elements are marked with gray handles.

How do I duplicate a text box?

To duplicate a text box within the same page, click to select it and then press Option as you click and drag. iWeb duplicates the text box. To create a duplicate that you can move to another page, select the text box and click **Edit** and then **Copy**. View the destination page and click **Edit** and then **Paste** to insert the copy.

Format Text

You can format text on your page to match the theme of the site or to emphasize the text. You can change the font color and size as well as how the text is spaced.

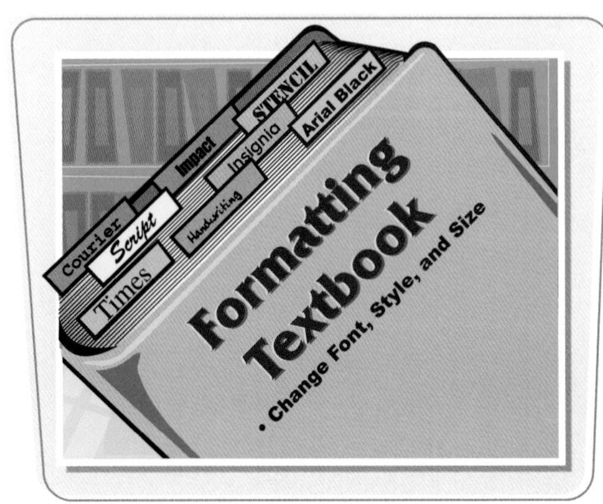

Format Text

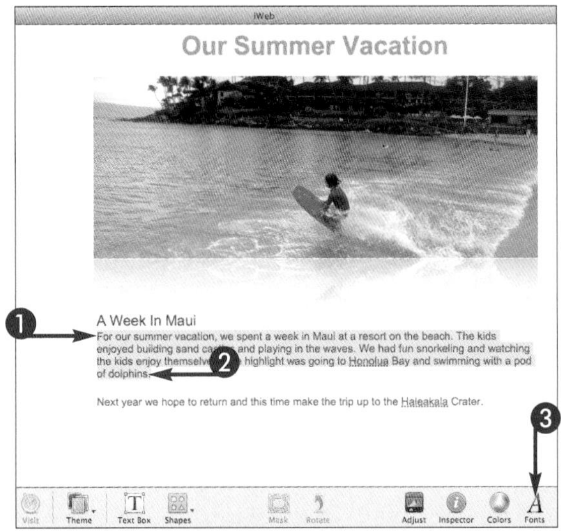

1. Double-click a text box.
2. Click and drag to select the text to format.
3. Click **Fonts**.

The Fonts dialog appears.

4. Click a font family.
5. Click a font typeface.
6. Click a size.

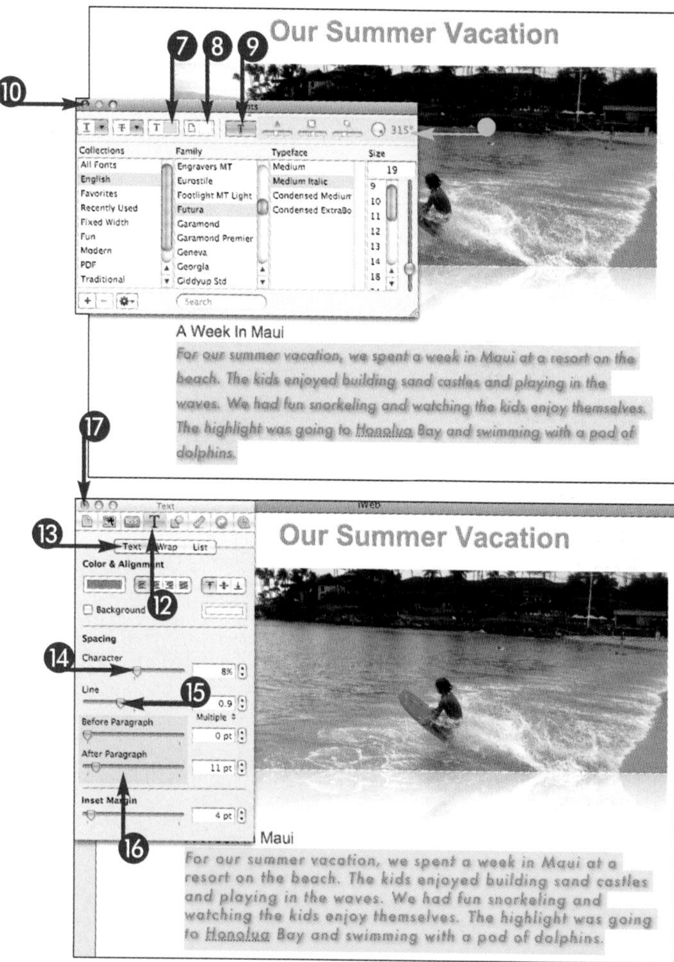

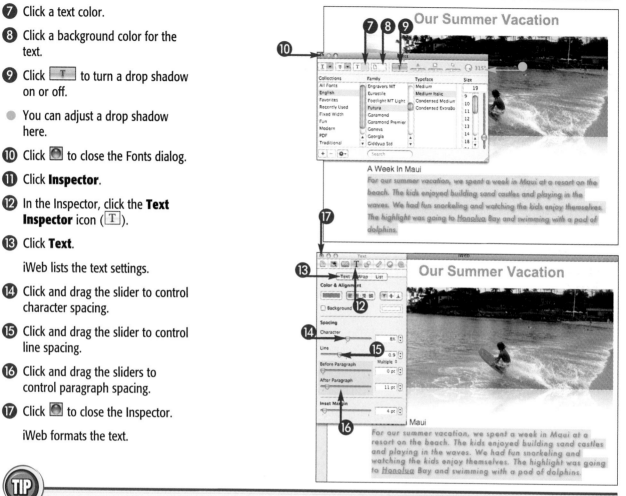

7. Click a text color.
8. Click a background color for the text.
9. Click [T] to turn a drop shadow on or off.

- You can adjust a drop shadow here.

10. Click the close button to close the Fonts dialog.
11. Click **Inspector**.
12. In the Inspector, click the **Text Inspector** icon ([T]).
13. Click **Text**.

    iWeb lists the text settings.

14. Click and drag the slider to control character spacing.
15. Click and drag the slider to control line spacing.
16. Click and drag the sliders to control paragraph spacing.
17. Click the close button to close the Inspector.

    iWeb formats the text.

How do I create a bulleted or numbered list of text items on my page?

1. Type the list items in a text box, one item per line, and then click and drag to select them.
2. Click **Inspector**.
3. Click the **Text Inspector** icon ([T]).
4. Click **List**.
5. Click here to select a list type.
6. Specify your list settings. The settings vary depending on the chosen list type.

   iWeb formats the items as a list.

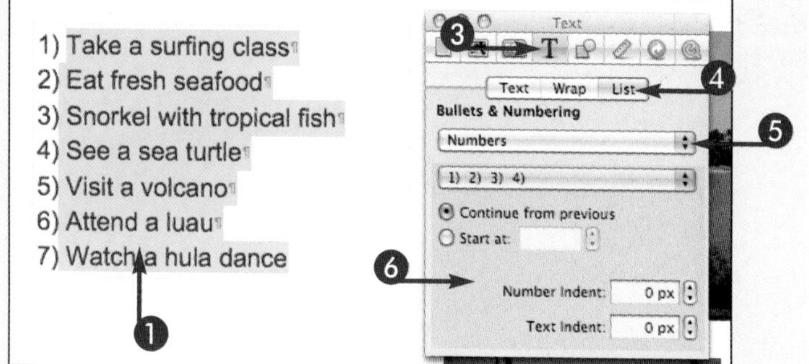

Align Page Text

You can control the horizontal or vertical positioning of text on your page. For example, you can align a bold heading in the center of the page or top-align several paragraphs beneath photo.

Align Page Text

ALIGN TEXT HORIZONTALLY

1. Click to select the text box whose text you want to align.
2. Click **Inspector**.

   The Inspector appears.
3. Click the **Text Inspector** icon (T).
4. Click **Text**.

5. Click a horizontal alignment.

   You can horizontally align text to the left, right, or center. You can also justify text, which aligns it to both the left and right.

   iWeb aligns the text.

- In this example, the heading text is center-aligned.

ALIGN TEXT VERTICALLY

1. Click to select the text box whose text you want to align.
2. Click **Inspector**.

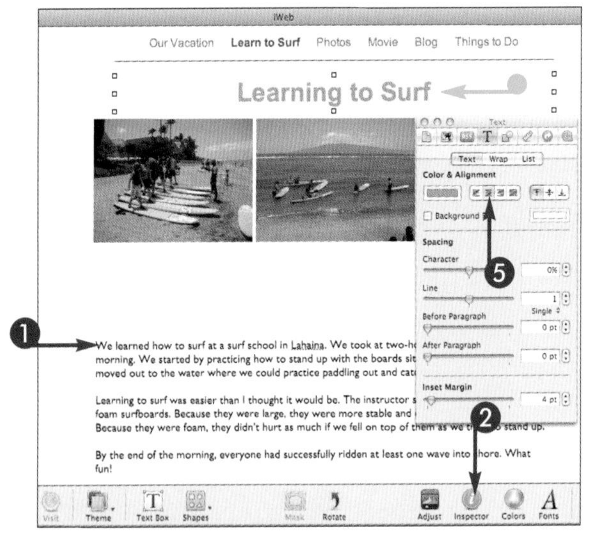

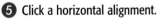

The Inspector appears.

3. Click the **Text Inspector** icon (T).
4. Click **Text**.
5. Click a vertical alignment.

   You can vertically align text to the top, middle, or bottom of a text box.

   iWeb aligns the text.

- In this example, the body text is top-aligned.

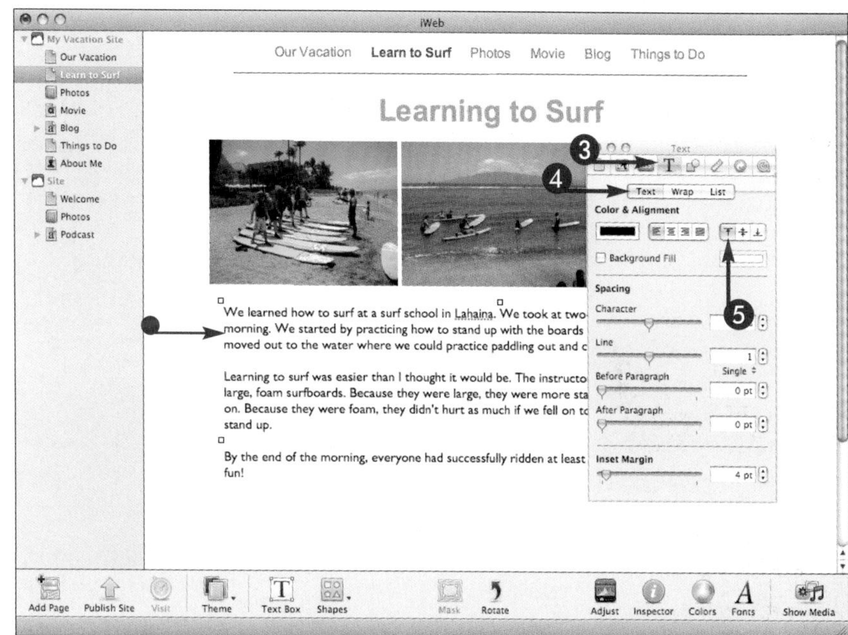

How do I add space around text in a text box?

You can add space between text and the text box margin, also known as *padding*, by adjusting the inset margin.

1. Click to select a text box.
2. Click **Inspector**.

   The Inspector appears.

3. Click the **Text Inspector** icon (T).
4. Click **Text**.
5. Click and drag the slider to adjust the padding.

- iWeb adjusts the padding.

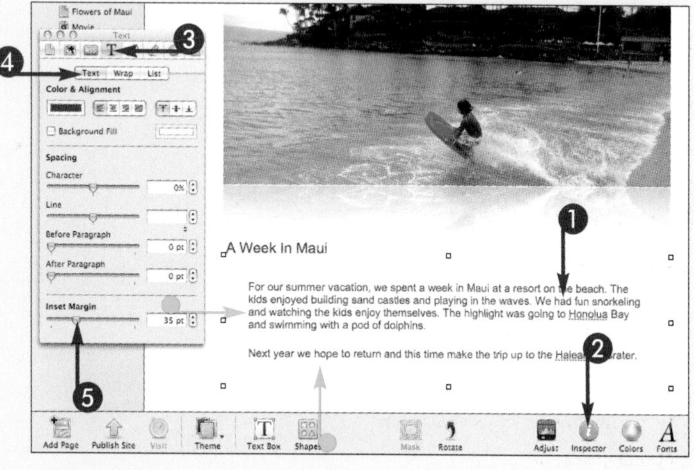

Add a Hyperlink

You can connect your Web page to another page by turning text or other objects on the page into *hyperlinks*, also known as links. Hyperlinked text on a page is usually distinguished with a different color and underlining. You can create a link to another page in your site, an external page on the Web, or an e-mail address.

Add a Hyperlink

LINK TO A PAGE IN YOUR SITE

1. Select the text or object you want to turn into a hyperlink.
2. Click **Inspector**.

   The Inspector appears.
3. Click the **Link Inspector** icon ( ).
4. Click **Hyperlink**.

- You can also click **Insert**, **Hyperlink**, and then **Web Page**.

5. Click **Enable as a hyperlink** (☐ changes to ☑).
6. Click here and select **One of My pages**.
7. Click the **Page** and select the destination page.

- iWeb creates a hyperlink.

Note: *You can also add links to other pages in your site with page navigation. See Chapter 16 for details.*

LINK TO AN EXTERNAL PAGE

8. With additional text selected, click here and select **An External Page**.
9. Type the Web address for the external page.

   To get the Web address for a page, you can view the page in a Web browser and copy the address from the browser address box.

- You can click here to cause the destination page to be opened in a new browser window (☐ changes to ☑).
- iWeb creates the hyperlink.

CREATE AN E-MAIL LINK

10. With additional text selected, click here and select **An Email Message**.

    You can also click **Insert**, **Hyperlink**, and then **Email Message**.

11. Type the e-mail address.
12. Type an e-mail subject.

- iWeb creates the hyperlink.

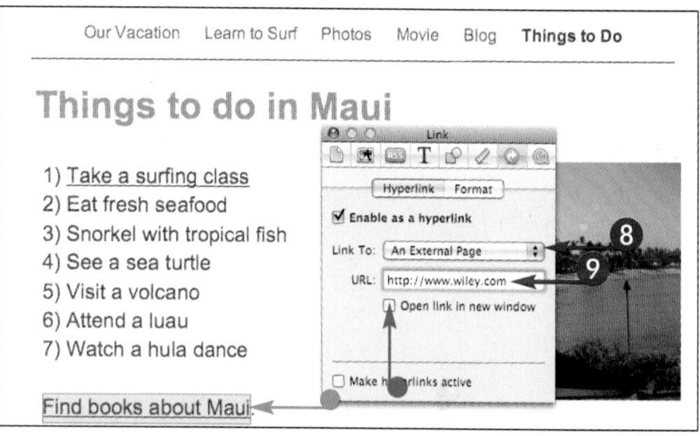

How do I change the color of a hyperlink?

1. In the Link Inspector, click **Format**.
2. Click a link color for normal links.
3. In the Colors dialog, click a color.
4. Click colors for other types of links.
5. Click ◉ to close the Colors dialog.
6. Click U to turn underlining on and off on links. Underlining is turned on by default.

- iWeb formats the hyperlink.

***Note:** To add other formatting to a hyperlink, see "Format Text."*

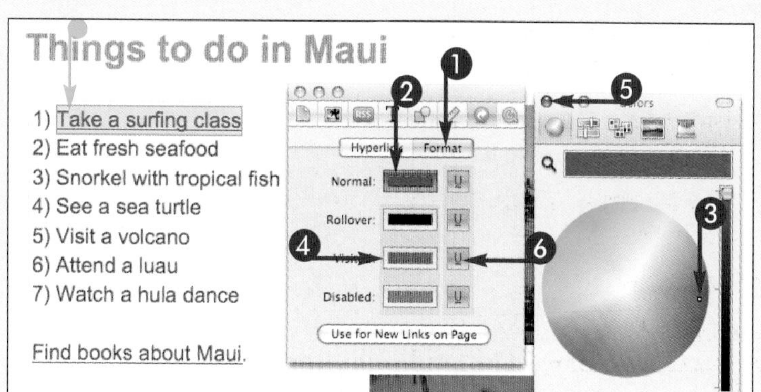

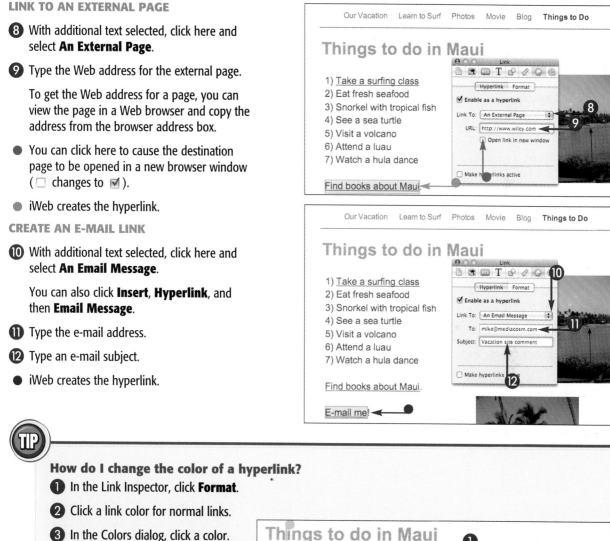

Add an Image

You can add an image to illustrate a passage of text or to add decoration to a plain-looking page. You can choose images from your iPhoto library. To easily add a collection of photos as an album to your Web site, see Chapter 18.

Add an Image

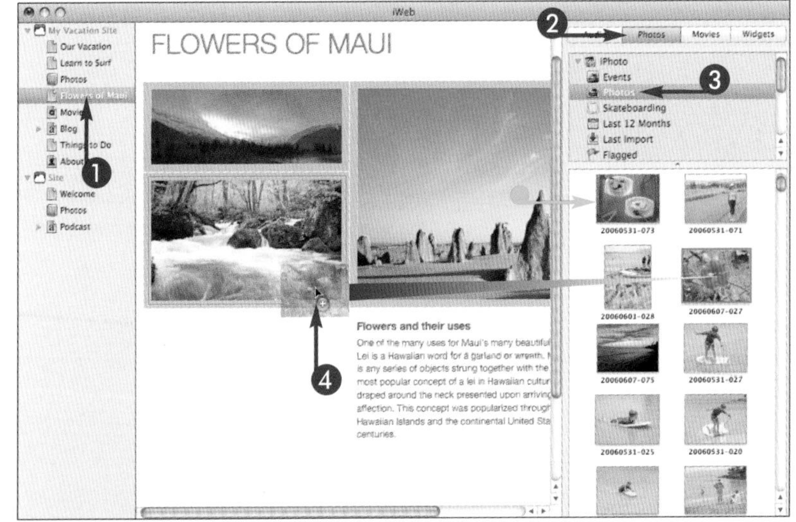

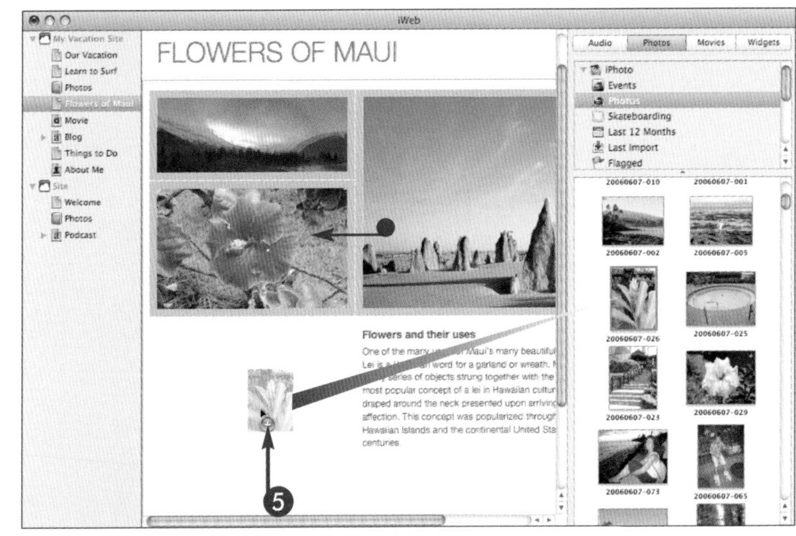

1. Select the page to which you want to add an image.
2. Click **Photos** in the media pane.

Note: *If the media pane is not visible, click* ***Show Media*** *at the bottom of the workspace to display it.*

- iWeb displays images from the iPhoto library.

  To make more photos available, you can drag folders containing images from the Finder to the media pane.

3. Click a list item to display images from iPhoto. For more about organizing images, see Chapter 4.
4. Click and drag an image to an image placeholder.

   Placeholders are the generic content items that appear when you create a page from a template.

- iWeb replaces the placeholder image.

5. Click and drag an image to an empty area of the page.

- iWeb adds the image to the page.

  You can click and drag the image to reposition it.

Note: *To customize the image, see "Resize an Image" and "Mask an Image."*

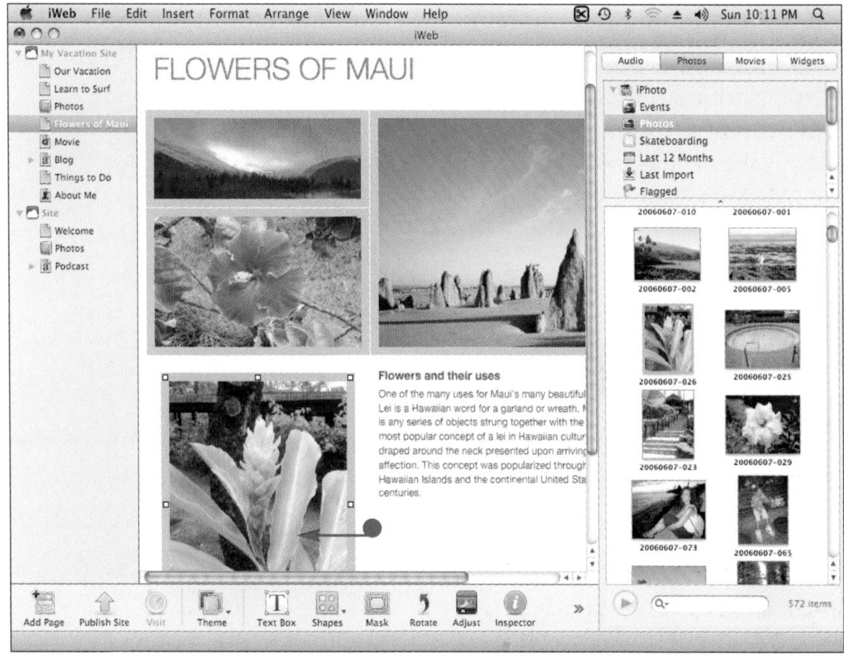

How do I add a frame to an image?

You can add a decorative picture frame to an image and adjust the size of the frame.

1. Click to select the photo.
2. In the Inspector, click the **Graphic Inspector** icon ( ).
3. Click here and select **Picture Frame** for the stroke type.

   If you want a plain, solid-color border, you can select **Line**.
4. Click the arrow and select a frame style.
5. Click and drag the slider to select the size of the frame.

- iWeb adds a picture frame around the image.

Resize an Image

You can resize an image on your page to emphasize or de-emphasize it, or to make it fit in with the other page content. You can control the size of your image, as well its position on the page, using the Metrics Inspector. Note that resizing an image to greater than its original size can make it look blurry.

Resize an Image

USE IMAGE HANDLES

1. Click to select an image.

   Handles appear on the edges of an image.

2. Click and drag a side handle to change one dimension of the image.

3. Click and drag a corner handle to change two dimensions of the image at once.

   To keep the image at the same proportions, press Shift as you click and drag a corner handle.

- iWeb resizes the image.

  In this example, the bottom left corner handle was used to shrink the image.

***Note:** You can click **Edit** and then **Undo** to revert to the previous size.*

USE THE METRICS INSPECTOR

1. Click to select an image.
2. Click **Inspector**.

   The Inspector opens.
3. Click the **Metrics Inspector** icon ( ).
4. Type new dimensions here.

Note: *Image sizes are measured in pixels (px). Pixels are the tiny, solid-color squares that make up digital images.*

- You can click **Constrain proportions** (☑ changes to ☐) to change one dimension at a time. This will distort the image.
- iWeb resizes the image.

Note: *You can click* ***Edit*** *and then* ***Undo*** *to revert to the previous size.*

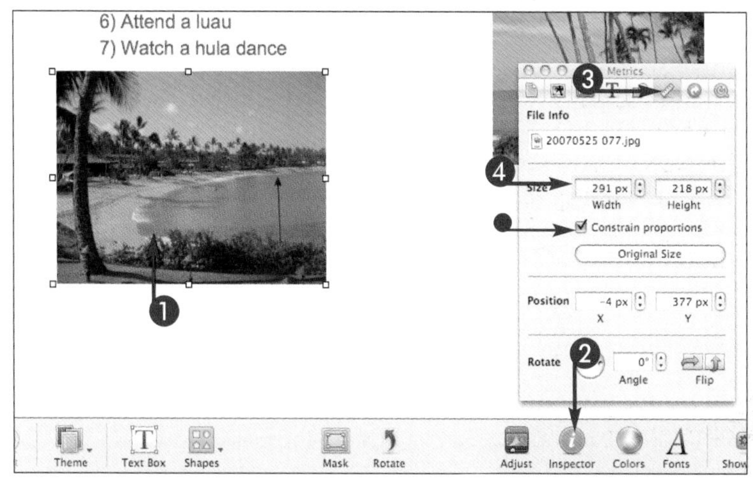

How do I adjust the color, lighting, and other attributes of an image?

You can open the Adjust Image panel to make changes to different image settings.

1. Click to select an image.
2. Click **Adjust**.
3. In the Adjust Image panel, click and drag the sliders to adjust the brightness, contrast, and other image settings.

- The panel displays a *histogram*, which shows the distribution of shadows and highlights in an image.

4. Click and drag the sliders to adjust the lighting.
5. Click **Enhance** to automatically optimize the color and lighting in the image.

Note: *For more about adjusting the color and lighting in images, see Chapter 5.*

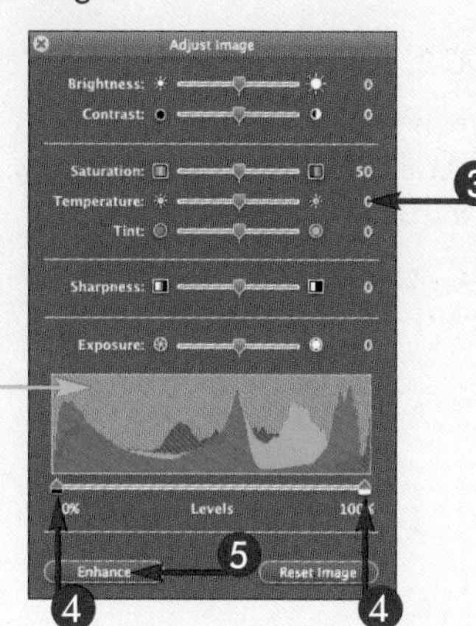

Mask an Image

You can mask an image to crop it, which removes unwanted areas of the image from view. iWeb hides the masked areas without removing them from the original image, so you can still crop the image differently later. You can also zoom the image within the masked area.

Mask an Image

1. Click to select an image.
2. Click **Mask** (Mask changes to Unmask).

   iWeb adds a mask to the image.
3. Click and drag the handles to adjust how the image is cropped.

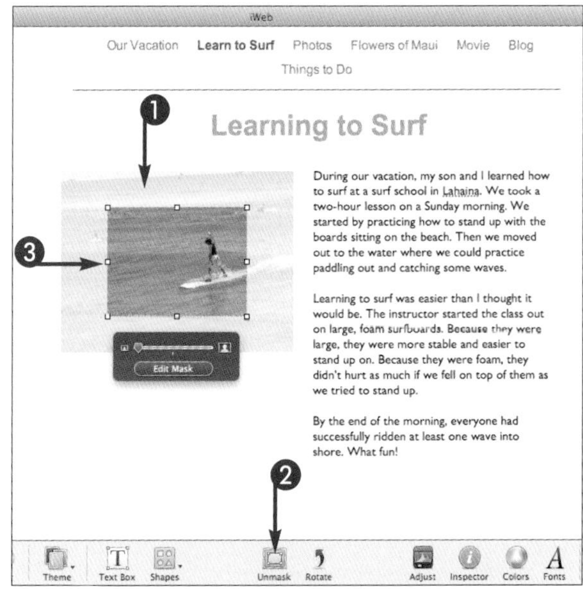

4. Click and drag the slider to zoom the image. Drag left to zoom out or right to zoom in.

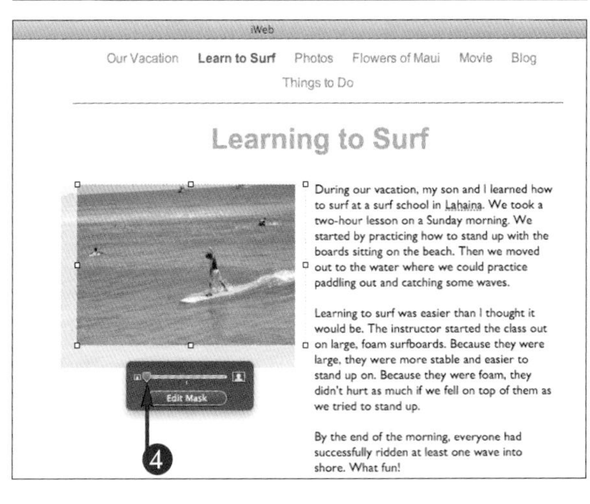

iWeb zooms the image under the mask.

5 Click and drag inside the tool to adjust the position of the image.

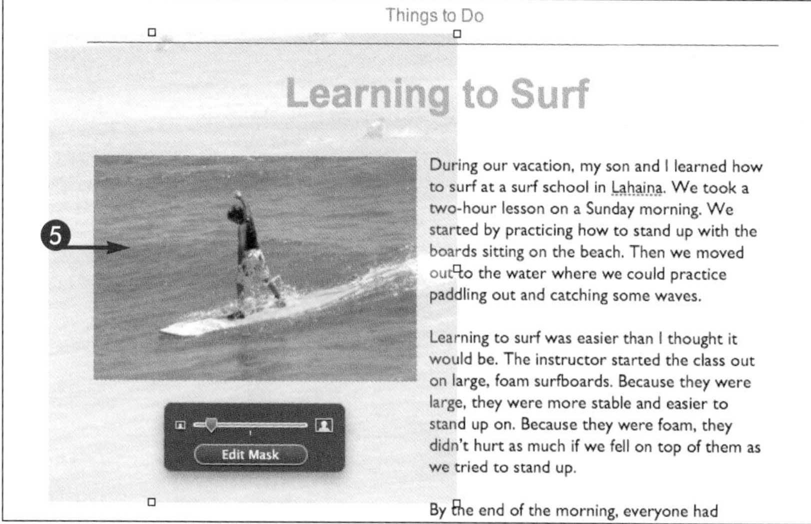

Things to Do
Learning to Surf
During our vacation, my son and I learned how to surf at a surf school in Lahaina. We took a two-hour lesson on a Sunday morning. We started by practicing how to stand up with the boards sitting on the beach. Then we moved out to the water where we could practice paddling out and catching some waves.
Learning to surf was easier than I thought it would be. The instructor started the class out on large, foam surfboards. Because they were large, they were more stable and easier to stand up on. Because they were foam, they didn't hurt as much if we fell on top of them as we tried to stand up.
By the end of the morning, everyone had
Edit Mask
5

6 Click away from the masking tool.

- iWeb displays the masked image.

You can click the image again to display the masking tools and adjust the image further.

Learning to Surf
During our vacation, my son and I learned how to surf at a surf school in Lahaina. We took a two-hour lesson on a Sunday morning. We started by practicing how to stand up with the boards sitting on the beach. Then we moved out to the water where we could practice paddling out and catching some waves.
Learning to surf was easier than I thought it would be. The instructor started the class out on large, foam surfboards. Because they were large, they were more stable and easier to stand up on. Because they were foam, they didn't hurt as much if we fell on top of them as we tried to stand up.

TIP

How do I add a reflection to an image on my Web page?

1 Click to select an image.

2 Click **Inspector**.

3 Click the **Graphic Inspector** icon ( ).

4 Click **Reflection** (☐ changes to ☑).

- iWeb adds a reflection below the image.

5 Click and drag the slider to control the opacity of the reflection.

- You can click and drag the slider to control the opacity of the entire image.

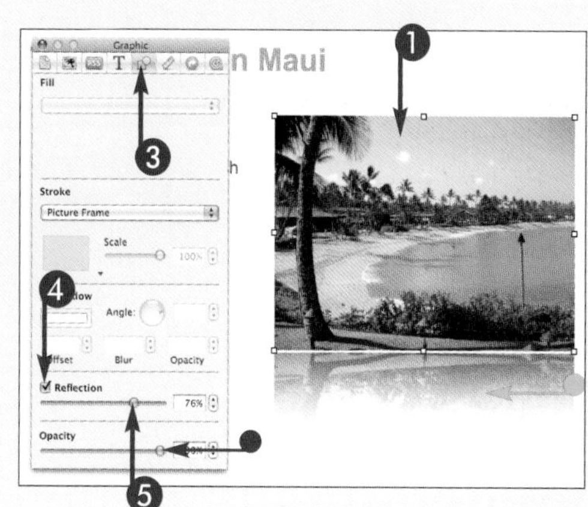

Insert a Shape

You can insert a shape to use as a text box or to decorate your page. To customize the shape, you can fill it with a color, gradient, or image. You can also stroke the outside edge with a color or add a drop shadow.

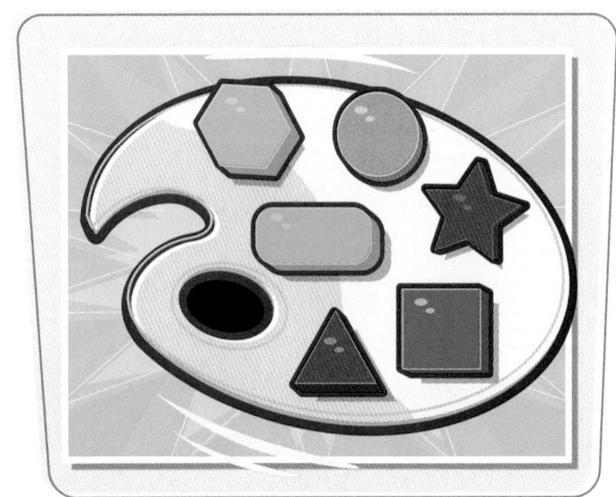

Insert a Shape

1. Select the page to which you want to add an image.
2. Click **Shapes**.

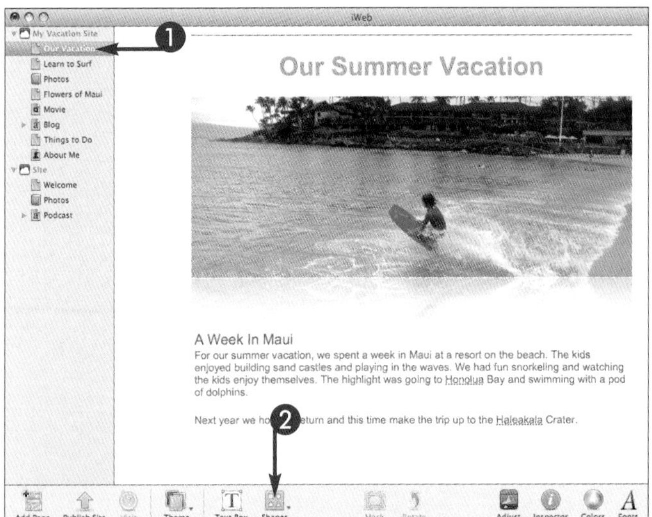

A list of shapes appears.

3. Click a shape.

iWeb adds the shape to the page.

4. Click and drag the side and corner handles to resize the shape.
5. Click the shape and drag to reposition it.

- You can customize some shapes using additional settings.

6. Click **Inspector**.

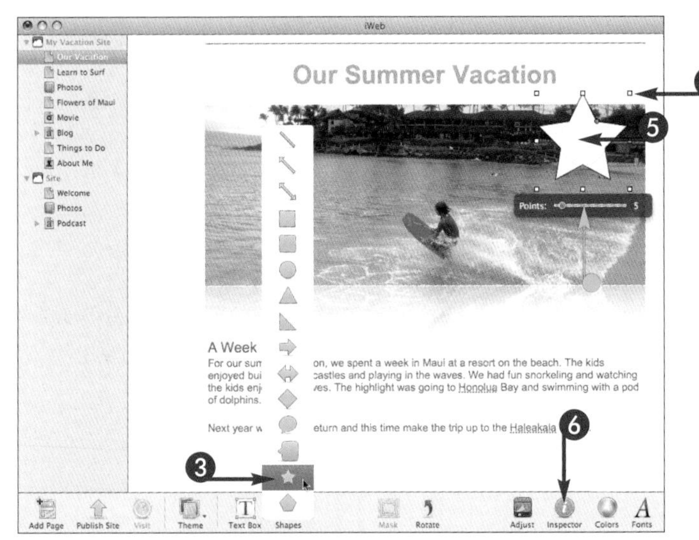

The Inspector opens.

7 Click the **Graphic Inspector** icon ( ).

8 Use these settings to fill the shape with a color, gradient, or image.

9 Use these settings to outline the shape.

10 Use these settings to apply a drop shadow.

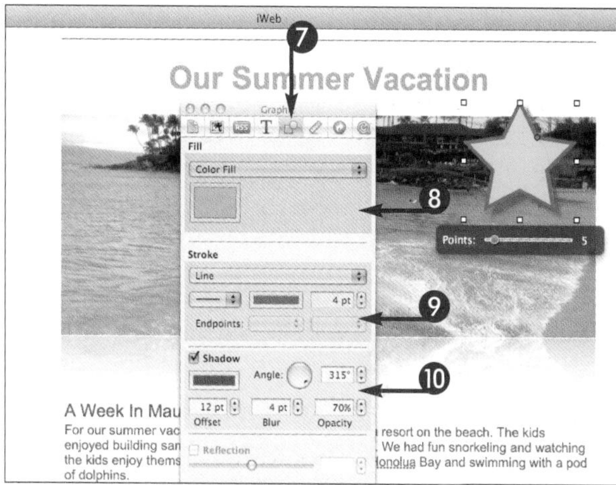

11 Double-click the shape.

A blinking cursor appears in the shape.

12 Type to add text inside the shape.

Note: *To format the text, see "Format Text."*

How do I mask images with different shapes?

You can mask an image with a shape other than a rectangle and then make crop and zoom adjustments.

1 Click to select a photo.

2 Click **Format** and then click **Mask With Shape**.

3 Click a shape.

Note: *You can add a shape only if the image does not currently have a mask applied.*

- iWeb masks the shape and displays the masking settings.

Note: *For more about adding masks, see "Mask an Image."*

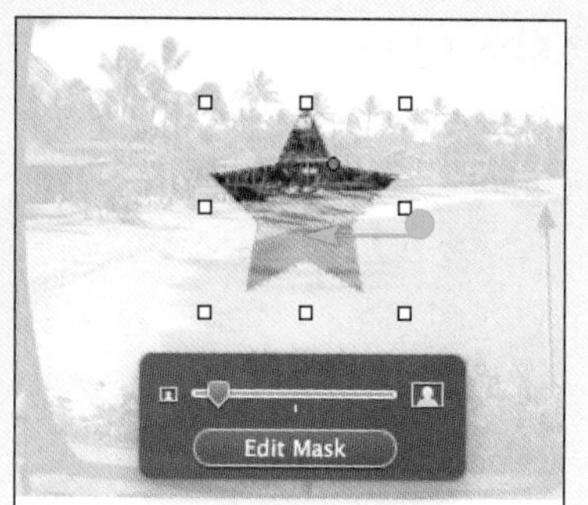

Wrap Text Around an Image

You can wrap text around an image to fit more content on your page or to associate an image with descriptive text. To wrap text around an image, you insert the image in a text box and then select the alignment settings.

Wrap Text Around an Image

1. Click **Photos** in the media pane.

Note: If the media pane is not visible, click ***Show Media*** *at the bottom of the workspace to display it.*

- iWeb displays images from the iPhoto library.

2. Press and hold ⌘.
3. Click and drag an image to a text box.

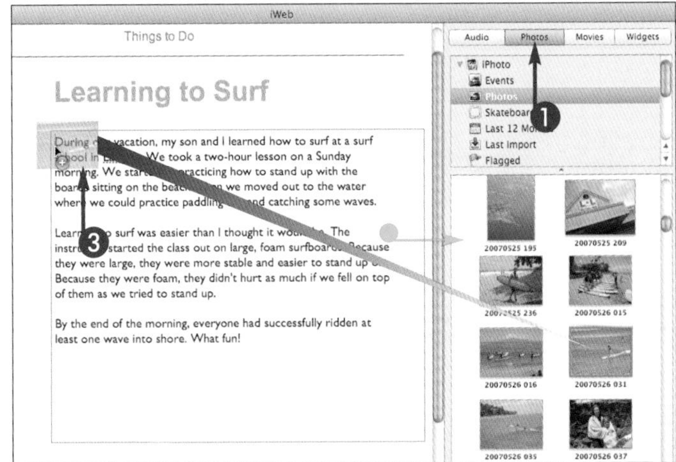

- iWeb inserts the image into the text box.

4. Click **Inspector**.

   The Inspector opens.

5. Click the **Text Inspector** icon (T).
6. Click **Wrap**.

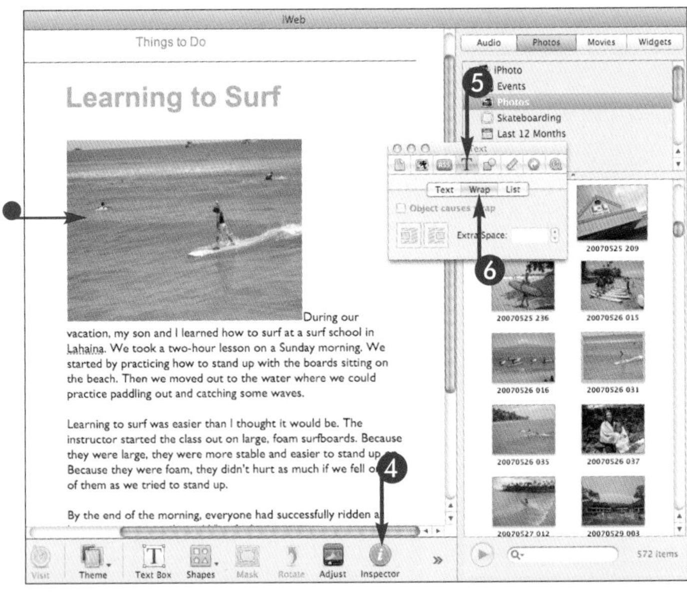

7. Double-click the image to select it.
8. Click **Object causes wrap** (☐ changes to ☑).
9. Click an alignment; this example aligns the image to the left.

- Click here to align the image to the right.

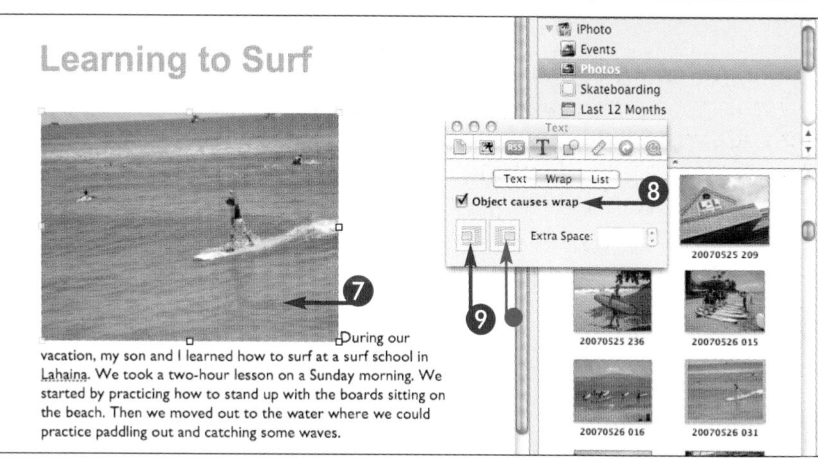

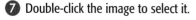

- iWeb aligns the image.
- The text is wrapped to the opposite side.

10. Adjust the space between the image and the text here.

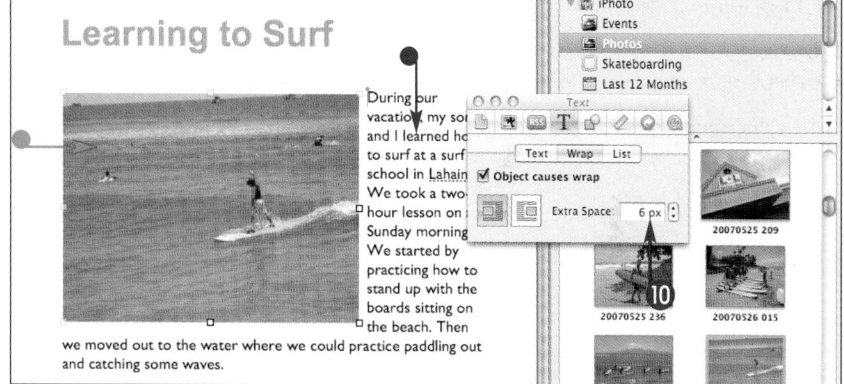

TIP

How do I rotate or flip an object on a page?

1. Click to select an object.
2. Click **Inspector**.
3. Click the **Metrics Inspector** icon (✎).
4. Click to rotate the object.

- You can type a degree value from 0 to 359.9 to rotate it precisely.

5. Click ⇄ to flip the object horizontally.
6. Click ⇅ to flip the object vertically.

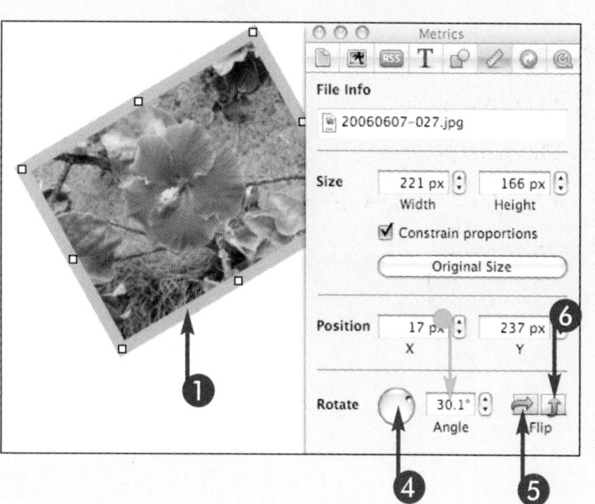

Add an E-mail Button

You can add an e-mail button to your page to allow viewers to send you feedback or comments about your site. You can reposition the button to make it fit in with the rest of your page content.

Add an E-mail Button

ADD AN E-MAIL BUTTON

1. Select the page to which you want to add an e-mail button.
2. Click **Insert**.
3. Click **Button**.
4. Click **Email Me**.

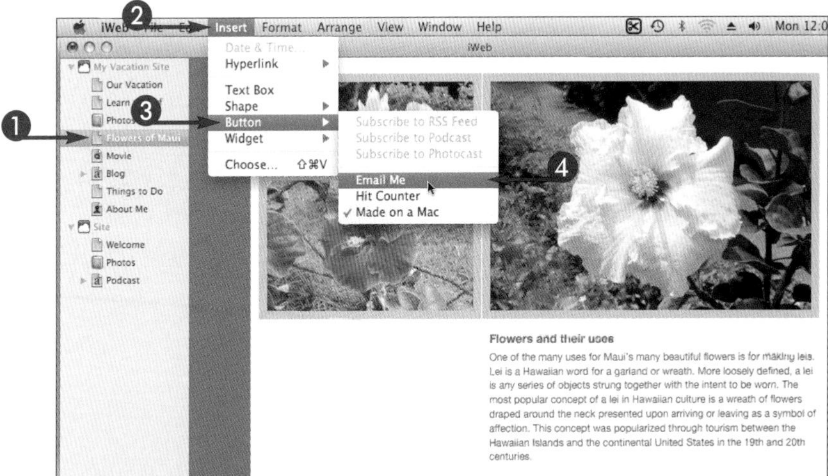

iWeb inserts an e-mail button.

5. Click and drag the button to position it.

- iWeb repositions the button.

USE AN E-MAIL BUTTON

1. Click the button on a published Web page.

Note: *See Chapter 19 for details about publishing your Web pages.*

- An e-mail message opens in the default e-mail program.

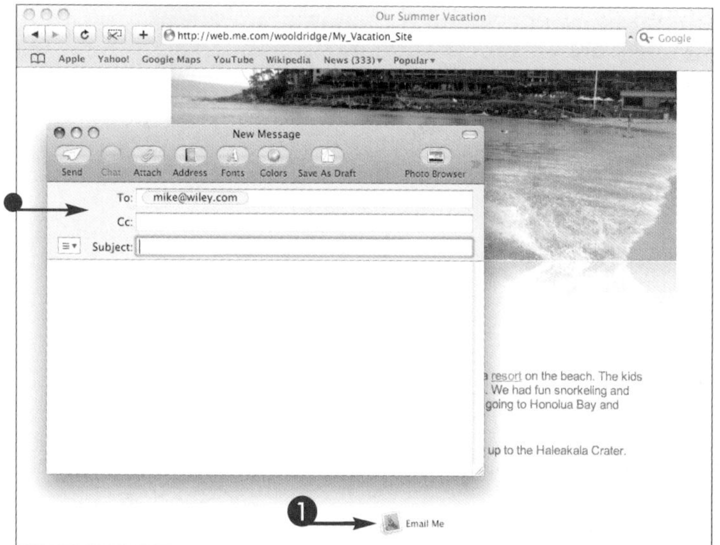

What e-mail address does the button use when creating the message?

Messages are addressed to the e-mail address listed in the site publishing settings. For details about specifying these settings, see Chapter 19.

Can I customize the Email Me button?

No, you cannot change or resize the button image or make any other adjustments other than repositioning it. An alternative to using the button is to turn an image that you insert on your page into an e-mail link. For details about inserting images and creating e-mail links, see Chapter 17.

Insert a Movie

You can add a movie to your Web page to allow users to view vacation highlights, product demonstrations, and more. You can choose movies from your iMovie library. You can use the Movie template to create a page designed for displaying a movie. You can click and drag to add a movie to other pages as well.

Insert a Movie

ADD TO A MOVIE TEMPLATE

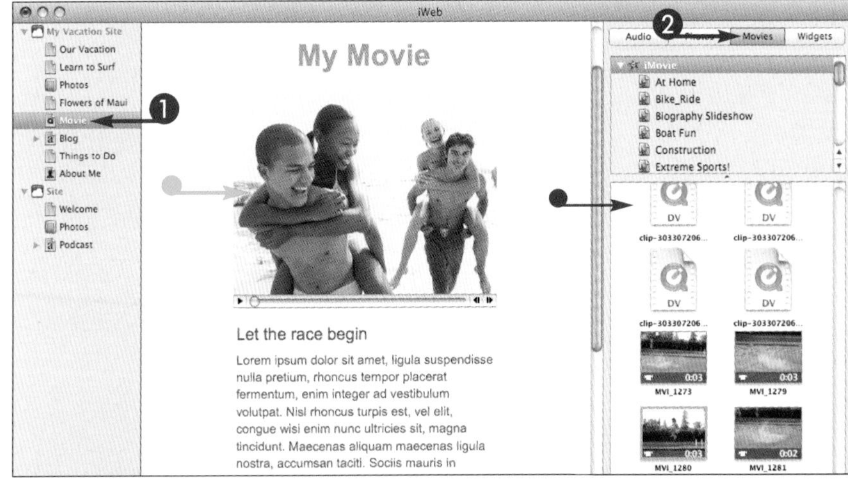

1. Add a new page to your site using the Movie template.

- iWeb creates a page with a movie placeholder on it.

Note: For more about adding a new page, see Chapter 16.

2. Click **Movies** in the media pane.

Note: If the media pane is not visible, click ***Show Media*** *at the bottom of the workspace to display it.*

- iWeb displays movies from the iMovie library.

3. Click an iMovie event to display a set of movie clips.

Note: See Chapter 7 for more about organizing iMovie clips into events.

4. Click and drag a movie to the movie placeholder.

- iWeb replaces the placeholder movie.
- You can click the controls to test the movie.

ADD TO A REGULAR PAGE

5 Click and drag a movie to an empty area of the page.

- iWeb adds the movie to the page.

  You can click and drag the movie to reposition it.
- You can click and drag the handles to change the movie's size.

TIPS

How do I add a YouTube movie to my page?

You can add a YouTube video using the YouTube widget. Click **Widgets** in the media pane and then click and drag the **YouTube** icon to your page. iWeb prompts you for the Web address for the YouTube video. You can find this address by viewing the video on YouTube and then copying the text in the Embed field.

How do I add an iSight movie to my page?

You can add video captures from your Mac's iSight video camera using a page widget. Click **Widgets** in the media pane and then click and drag the **iSight Movie** icon to your page. iWeb displays the view from your iSight camera. You can click the record button to capture a movie with the camera. You can also add an iSight snapshot photo to your page using the iSight Photo widget.

Insert an Audio Clip

You can add an audio clip to a page to include musical accompaniment to your other site content. You can add songs from your GarageBand or iTunes libraries. Audio settings enable you to automatically start the clip when the page loads, repeat the clip when it finishes, and more.

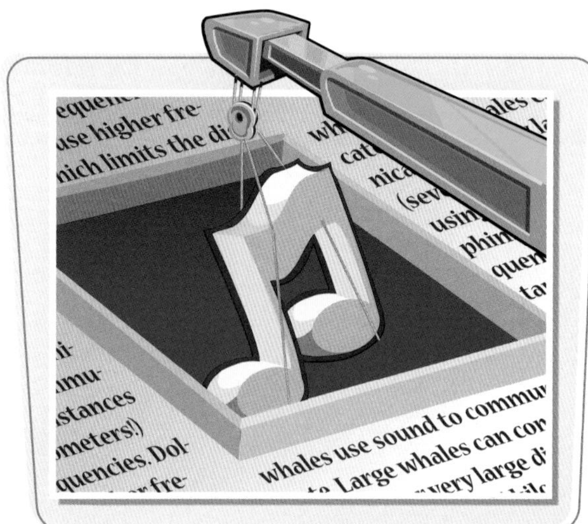

Insert an Audio Clip

1. Select the page to which you want to add an audio clip.
2. Click **Audio** in the media pane.

Note: *If the media pane is not visible, click* ***Show Media*** *at the bottom of the workspace to display it.*

- iWeb displays music from the GarageBand and iTunes libraries.

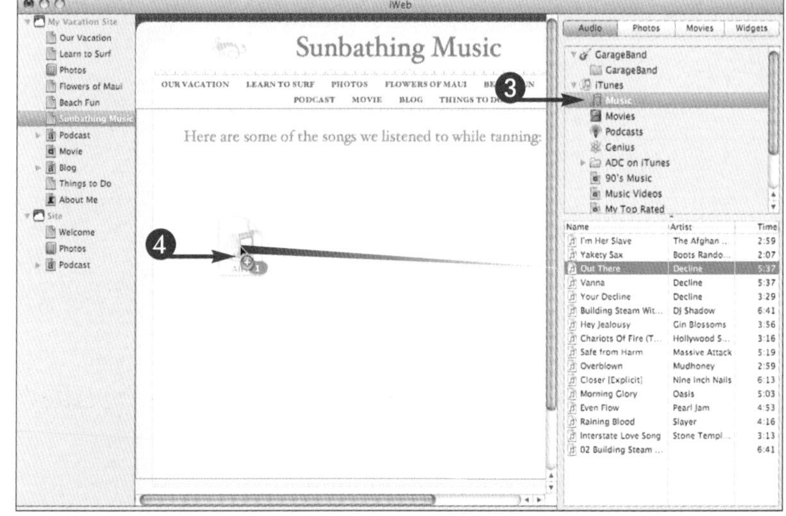

3. You can click a list item to display categories of music from GarageBand or iTunes.

Note: *iTunes includes categories for movies and other types of content as well as music.*

4. Click and drag an audio clip to the page.

- iWeb adds the clip to the page with a placeholder image.

5 Click **Photos** in the media pane.

- iWeb displays the images from the iPhoto library.

6 Click and drag an image to accompany the audio clip to the placeholder.

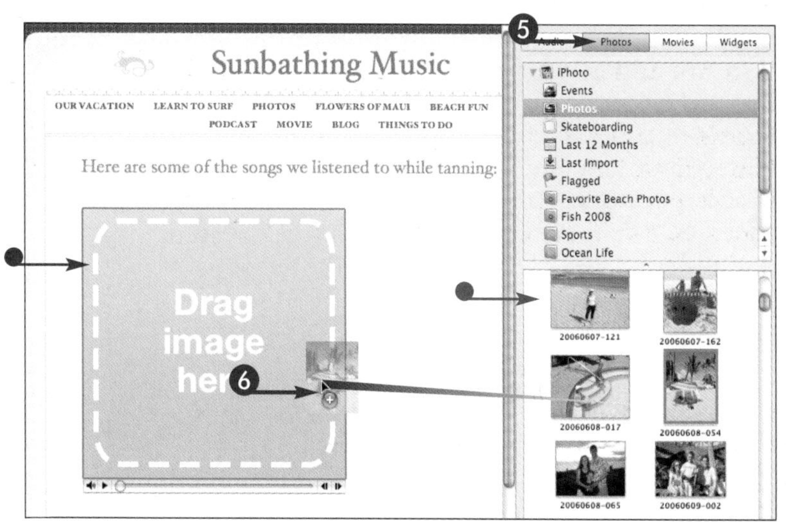

iWeb inserts the image.

- You can click the controls to play the audio clip.

7 Click the image.

- You can click and drag the handles to resize the image and controls.

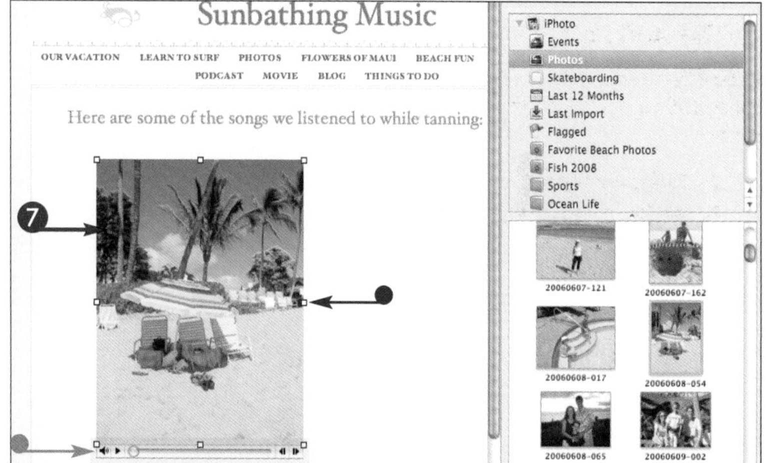

How do I change the audio settings?

1 With an audio clip selected, click **Inspector**.

2 Click the **QuickTime Inspector** icon ( ).

3 Click to play the audio automatically when the page loads (☐ changes to ☑).

4 Click to repeat, or loop, the music after it ends (☐ changes to ☑).

5 Click to hide the controller (☑ changes to ☐).

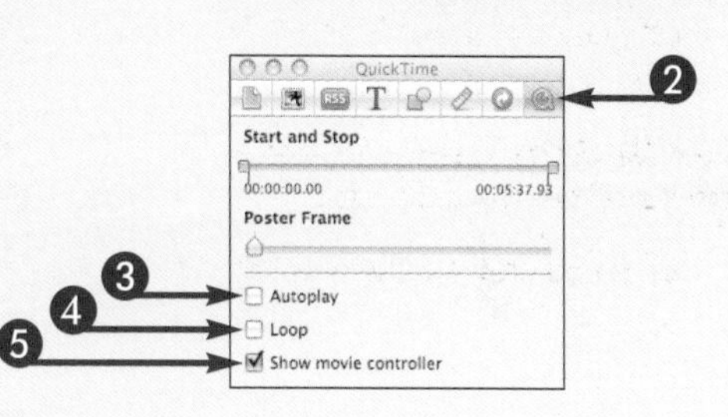

***Note:** These settings also apply to movie clips. See "Insert a Movie" for how to add movies to pages.*

Create a Blog

You can add a blog, which is short for *web log*, to your site to create an online journal that you can write in and others can read. You can use a blog for a variety of purposes. For example, you can keep friends up to date on your daily activities or make your opinions known about current events.

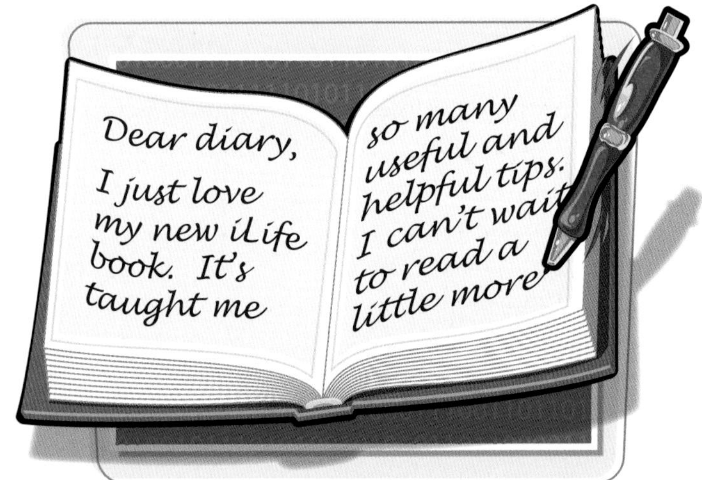

Create a Blog

1. Click **Add Page**.

   The template dialog appears.

2. Click a theme to determine the style of your blog.

Note: *For more information about themes, see Chapter 16.*

3. Click the Blog template.
4. Click **Choose**.

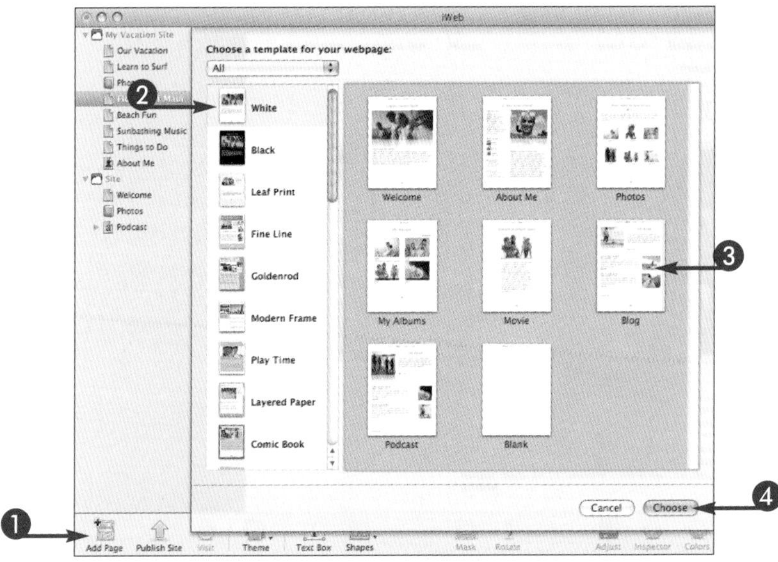

- iWeb creates your blog.
- It displays your first entry in the main window below a list of all entries.

5. Click **Photos** in the media pane to display images from your iPhoto library.
6. Click and drag an image to replace the placeholder image.
7. Double-click the entry title and then type your own title.
8. Double-click the description and then type your own description.

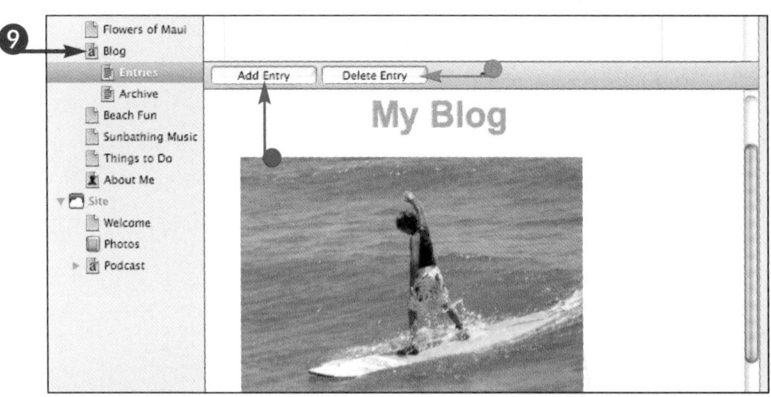

iWeb updates the blog entry.

- You can click **Add Entry** to post new information to your blog.
- You can select an entry in the list and click **Delete Entry** to delete information from your blog.

9. Click the blog summary page in the sidebar.

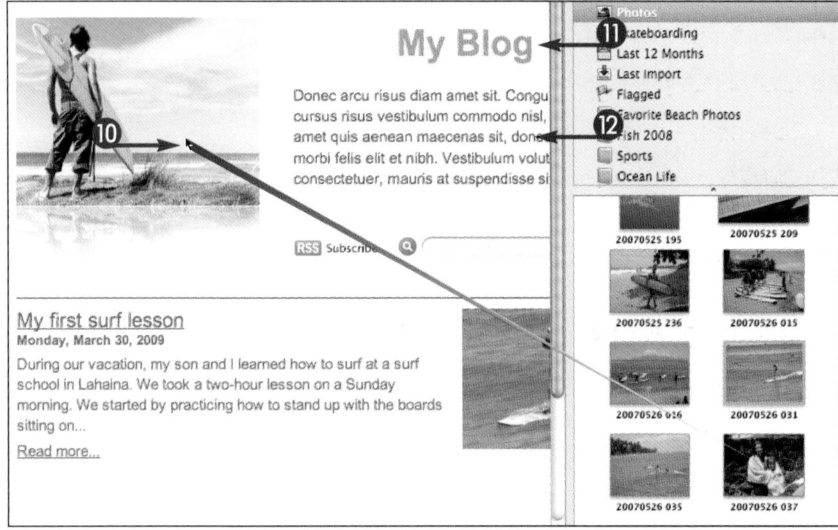

iWeb displays the blog summary, which is what users see when they click a link to the blog in the page navigation.

10. Click and drag an image to replace the placeholder image.
11. Double-click the blog title and then type your own title.
12. Double-click the description and then type your own description.

Can I change how entries appear on the blog summary?

Yes. You can change the size and orientation of the photo as well as how much space is added between summaries.

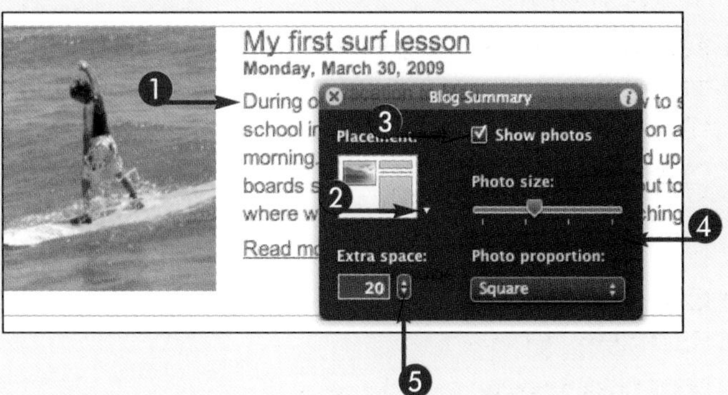

1. Click the blog summary text.
2. In the Blog Summary panel, click the Placement menu to select how the image is aligned.
3. Click to hide the photo (☑ changes to ☐).
4. Click to set the photo size and cropping.
5. Click here to set the spacing between summaries.

continued

Create a Blog (continued)

Blog entries are listed in reverse chronological order on the summary page of a blog. You can click the titles to view the entries. You can customize how the information is summarized on the main page and also turn on comments.

Create a Blog *(continued)*

iWeb updates the blog summary.

- Recent blog entries are listed on the summary page.
- Viewers can click a title to view the entry.
- Viewers can subscribe to an RSS feed for a blog or search the blog entries here.

13. Click **Inspector**.

The Inspector appears.

14. Click the **Blog & Podcast** icon (RSS).
15. Click **Blog**.
16. Click here to set how many entry summaries appear on the summary page.
17. Click and drag the slider to set the length of the excerpt.

    iWeb updates the summary page.

18. Click the close button to close the Inspector.

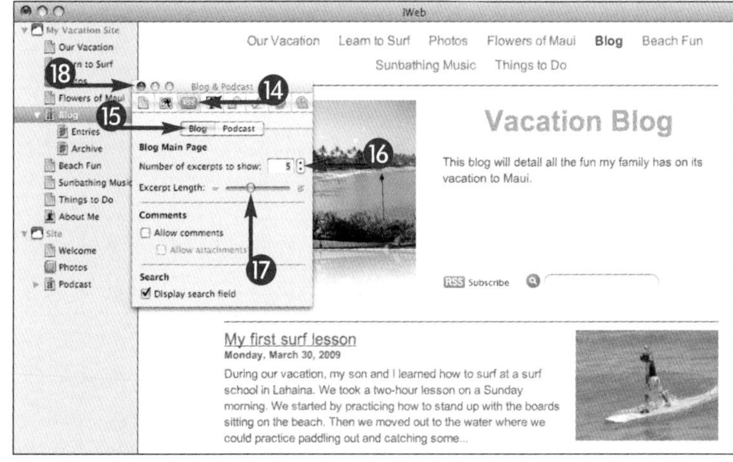

19 Click the archive page for the blog in the sidebar.

iWeb displays the blog archive.

All blog entries, including old ones, are listed in the archive.

- Viewers can click a title to view an entry.

20 If you have already published your Web site, click **Publish Site** to update the blog and other information on your site.

You must publish your site for new blog entries to appear online.

***Note:** For details about publishing a site, see Chapter 19.*

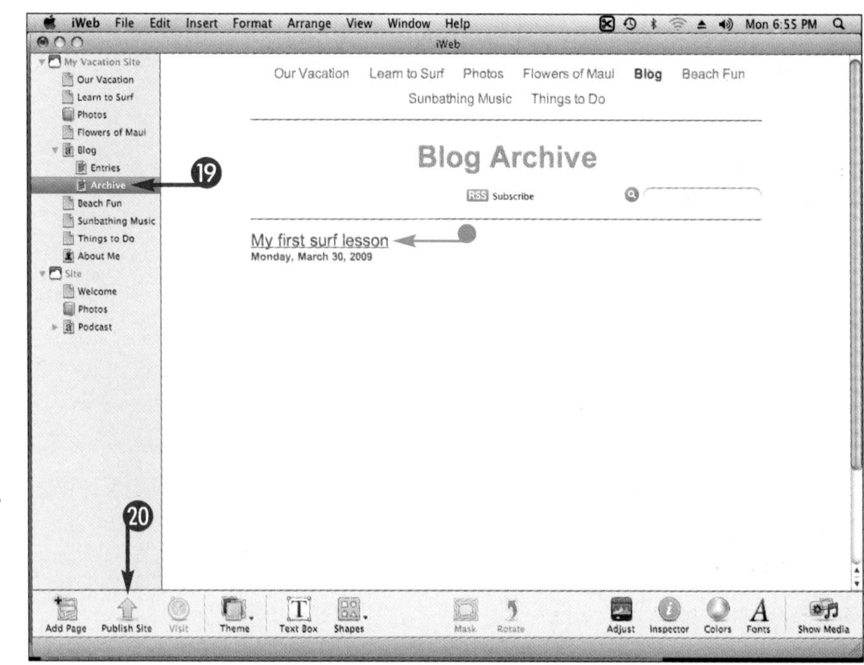

How do I allow comments on my blog?

If you publish your site to the MobileMe service, you can activate comments on your blog. This allows viewers to add related information or tell you what they think about your entries. You can use similar steps to turn on comments in a podcast.

1 View a blog entry.

2 Click **Inspector**.

The Inspector appears.

3 Click the **Blog & Podcast** icon (RSS).

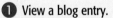

4 Click **Blog**.

5 Click to activate comments (☐ changes to ☑).

- iWeb adds a comment link to the bottom of each blog entry. Submitted comments appear below the entry.

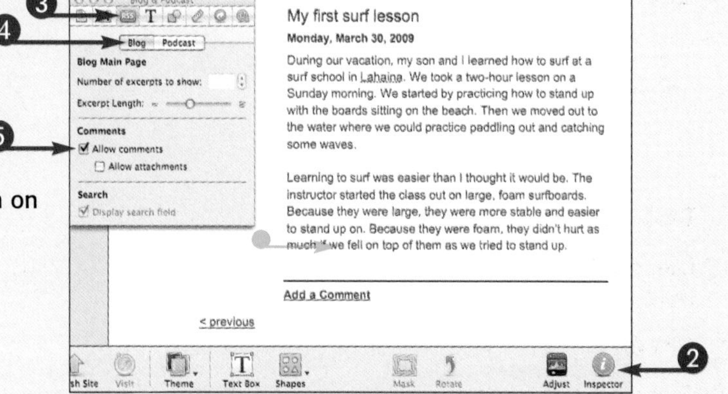

Create a Podcast

You can add a podcast, which is an audio or video file that can be downloaded, to your site. iWeb offers a podcast template that enables you to add podcasts to your site on an ongoing basis. You can create podcast videos in iMovie and podcast audio clips in GarageBand.

Create a Podcast

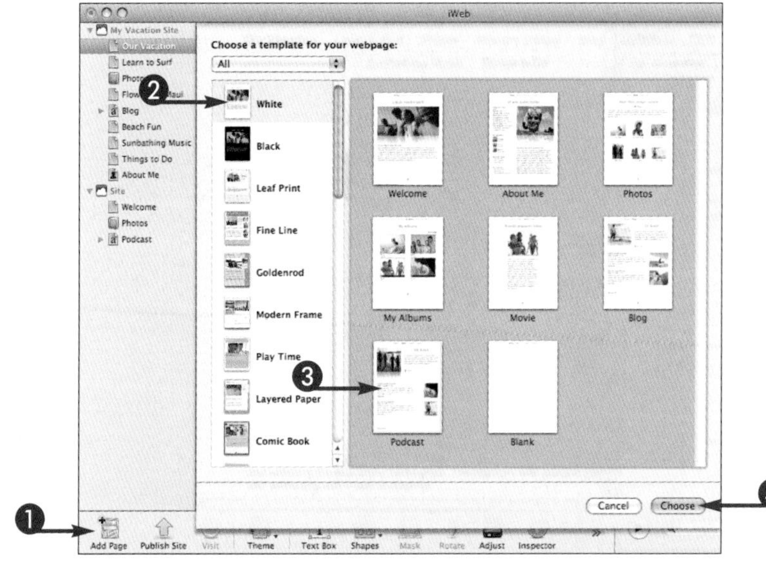

1. Click **Add Page**.

   The template dialog appears.

2. Click a theme to determine the style of your podcast.

Note: *For more information about themes, see Chapter 16.*

3. Click the Podcast template.
4. Click **Choose**.

- iWeb creates your podcast.
- It displays your first entry in the main window below a list of all entries.

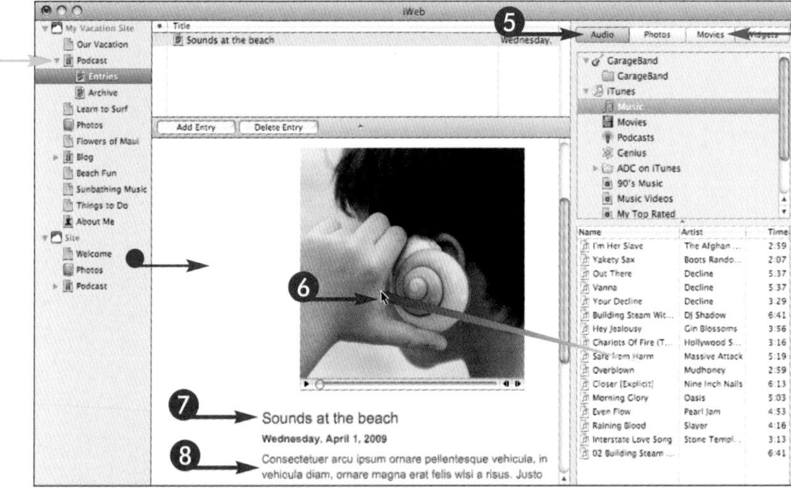

5. Click **Audio** in the media pane to display media from your iTunes and GarageBand libraries.

- You can click **Movies** to display media from your iMovie library.

6. Click and drag a media file to replace the placeholder.
7. Double-click the entry title and then type your own title.
8. Double-click the description and then type your own description.

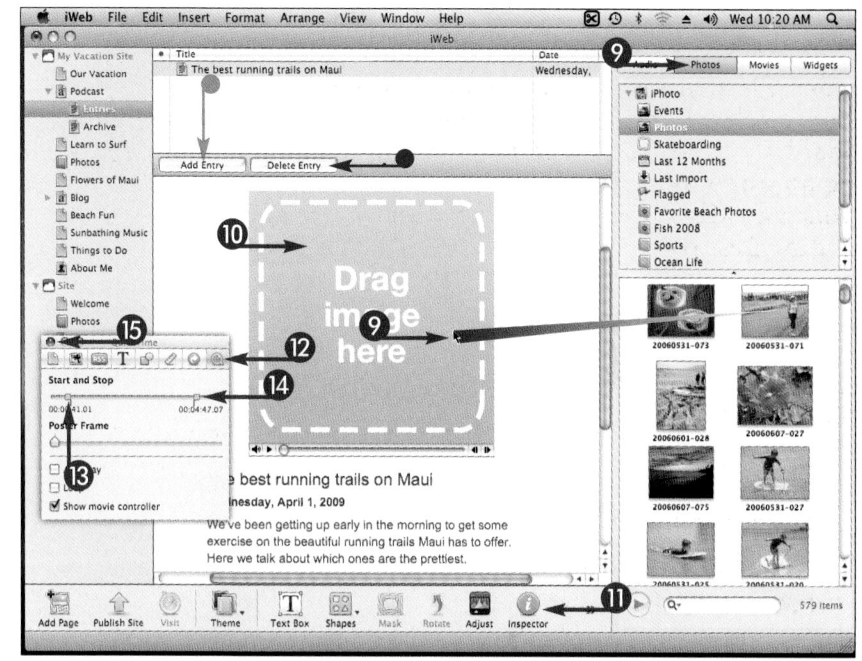

iWeb updates the podcast entry.

9 If you added an audio file, click **Photos** and click and drag an image to replace the placeholder.

- You can click **Add Entry** to post new media to your podcast.
- You can select an entry in the list and click **Delete Entry** to delete media from your podcast.

10 Click to select the media clip.

11 Click **Inspector**.

The Inspector appears.

12 Click the **QuickTime Inspector** icon ( ).

13 Click and drag the slider to specify where the media clip starts when played.

14 Click and drag the slider to specify where the media clip ends.

15 Click to close the Inspector.

How do I submit a podcast to the iTunes Store?

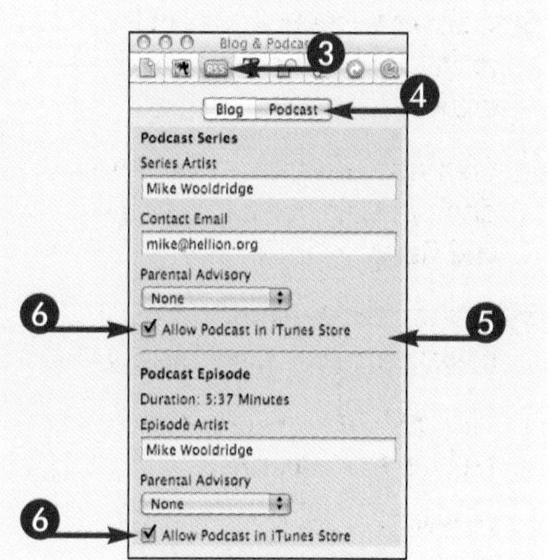

1 View a podcast entry.

2 Click **Inspector**.

3 Click the **Blog & Podcast** icon ( ).

4 Click **Podcast**.

5 Describe your podcast.

6 Make sure the **Allow** box is checked for the series or episode, depending on what you want to publish (☐ changes to ☑).

7 Click **File** and then click **Submit Podcast to iTunes**.

iWeb submits the podcast for consideration.

continued

Create a Podcast *(continued)*

Podcast entries are listed in reverse chronological order on the summary page of a podcast. You can click the titles to view the entries. You can customize how the information is summarized on the main page and also turn on comments to give viewers a voice.

Podcast Entries
1. Spin Me Right Round
2. Round in Circles
3. Jukebox Hero
4. Turntable Two-Step
5. Prop Me Up Against the Jukebox

Create a Podcast *(continued)*

⑯ Click the podcast summary page in the sidebar.

iWeb displays the podcast summary, which is what viewers see when they click a link to the podcast in the page navigation.

⑰ Click **Photos** to display images from your iPhoto library.

⑱ Click and drag an image to replace the placeholder image.

⑲ Double-click the podcast title and then type your own title.

⑳ Double-click the description and then type your own description.

iWeb updates the podcast summary.

- Recent podcast entries are listed on the summary page.
- Viewers can click a title to view the entry.
- Viewers can subscribe to an RSS feed for a podcast or search the podcast entries here.

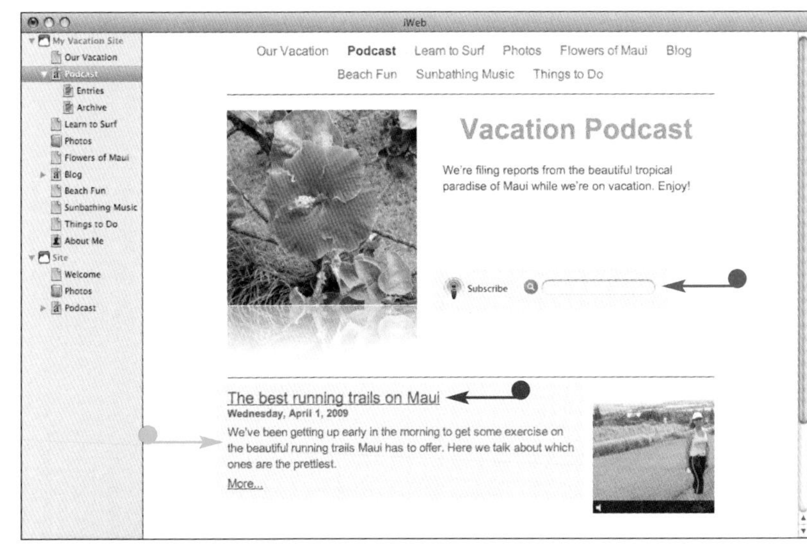

21 Click the archive page for the podcast in the sidebar.

iWeb displays the podcast archive.

All the podcast entries, including old ones, are listed in the archive.

- Viewers can click a title to view an entry.

22 If you have already published your Web site, click **Publish Site** to update the podcast and other information on your site.

You must publish your site for new podcast entries to appear online.

Note: *For details about publishing a site, see Chapter 19.*

TIP

How do I change the still image that appears with a movie clip on my page?

The still image that appears above the movie controls is called the *poster frame*. You set the poster frame by choosing a frame from your movie.

1. Click to select the movie on a page.
2. Click **Inspector**.

   The Inspector appears.

3. Click the **QuickTime Inspector** icon ( ).
4. Click and drag the slider to display the frame to use as the poster frame.
5. Click to close the Inspector.

   iWeb sets the poster frame.

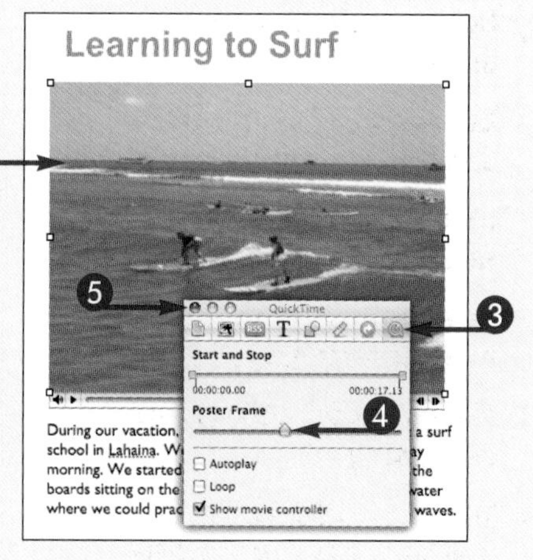

Create a Photo Album

You can create a photo album to present a collection of photos from an event on your Web site. iWeb organizes small versions of the photos into a grid. You can click a small version to view a larger version. iWeb can create multiple pages if you have a large number of photos in the album.

Create a Photo Album

1. Click **Add Page**.

   The template dialog appears.

2. Click a theme to set the style of your album.

Note: *For more information about themes, see Chapter 16.*

3. Click the Photos template.
4. Click **Choose**.

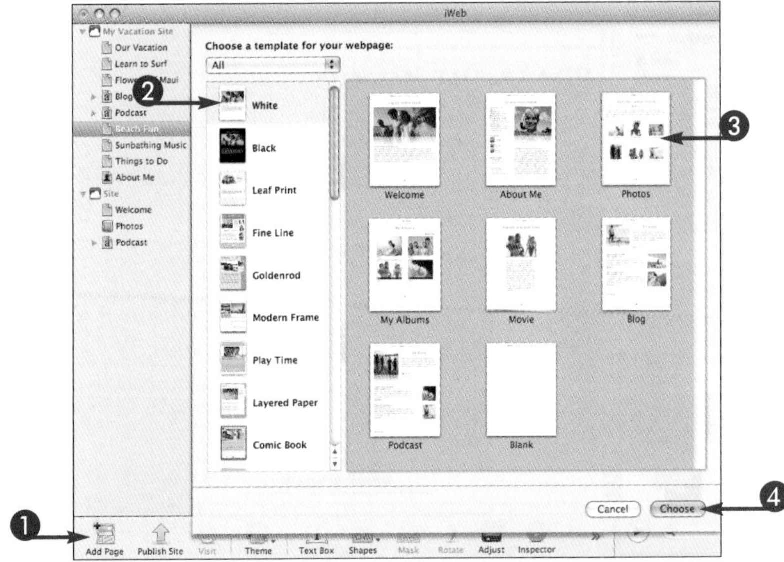

iWeb creates your photo album page.

5. Click **Photos** in the media pane to display images from your iPhoto library.
6. ⌘-click to select one or more images.
7. Click and drag the selected images to the photo album.

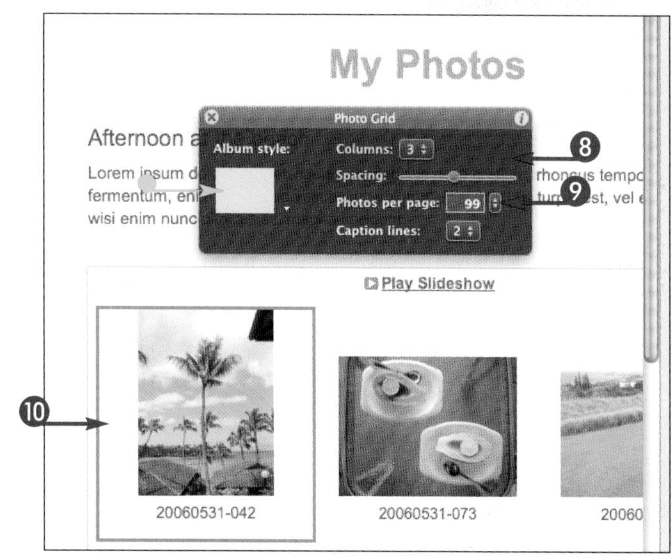

iWeb adds the images to the album.

The Photo Grid panel appears.

8. Click to set the number of columns and the spacing of the photos.
9. Click here to set how many photos appear on a page.

- You can change the album style by clicking the style menu.

10. Double-click a photo in the grid to view it.

Viewers on your Web site can single-click the photo to view it.

iWeb displays the photo detail page.

- Clicking thumbnail versions of the photos enable viewers to view other photos in the album.
- Viewers can click an icon to hide (■) or display (■) the thumbnails.
- Viewers can click **Play Slideshow** to play the photo album as a slideshow.
- You can double-click the title and description to edit them.

How do I add movies to a photo album?

You can click and drag movie clips to an album from the media pane to add them alongside photos.

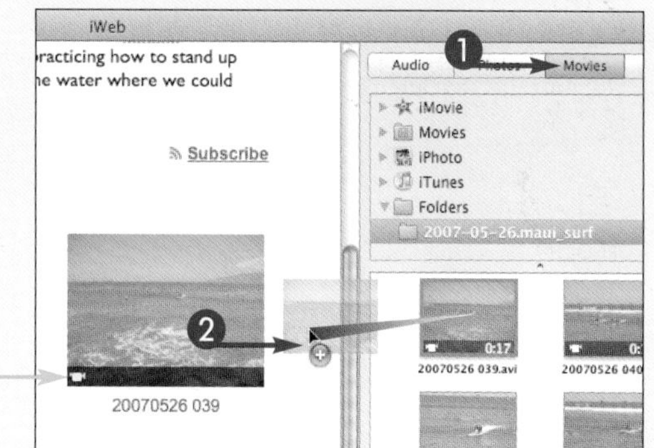

1. Click **Movies** in the media pane to display clips from your iMovie library.

*Note: If the media pane is not visible, click **Show Media** at the bottom of the workspace to display it.*

2. Click and drag a movie clip to the photo album.

- iWeb adds the movie clip.

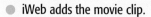

Organize Multiple Albums

If you have more than one photo album in a site, you can organize them using the My Albums template. Your albums are arranged in a grid and viewers can click to view them.

Organize Multiple Albums

1. Click **Add Page**.

   The template dialog appears.

2. Click a theme to determine the style of your album.

***Note:** For more information about themes, see Chapter 16.*

3. Click the My Albums template.
4. Click **Choose**.

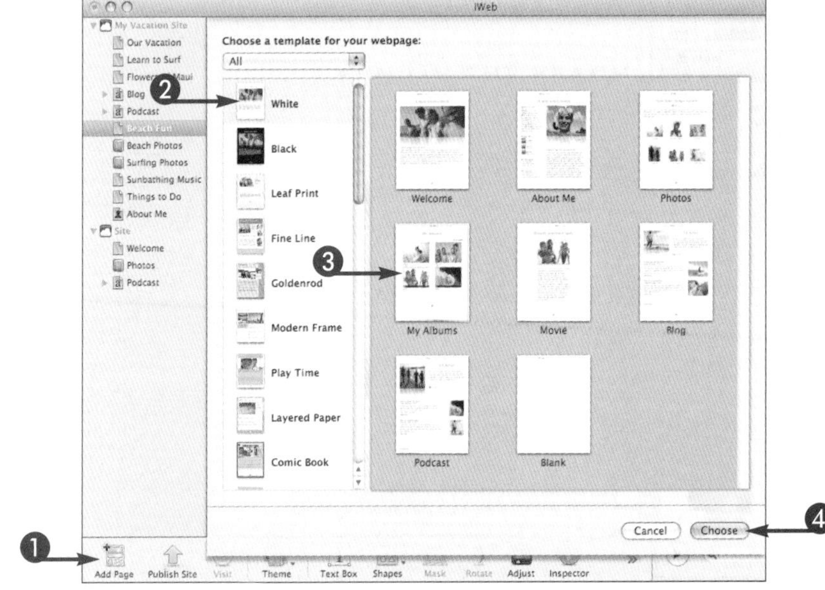

iWeb creates your albums page.

5. Click and drag a photo album page to the placeholder.

***Note:** For details on creating photo albums, see "Create a Photo Album."*

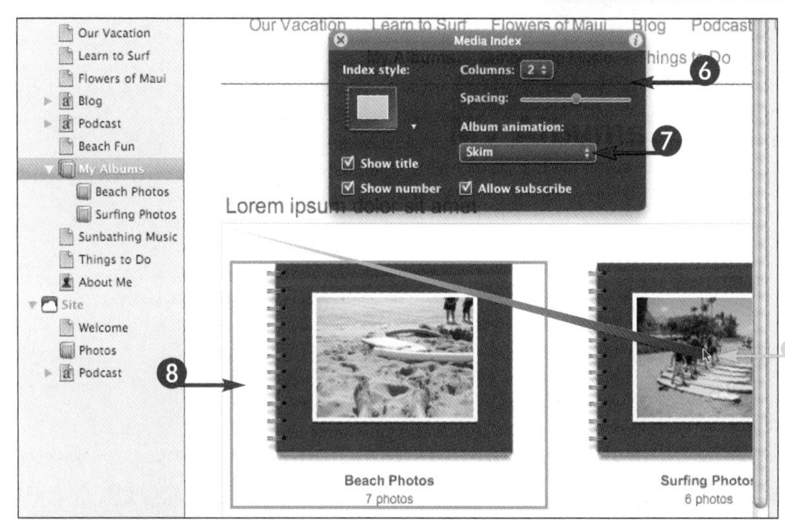

iWeb adds the album to the page.

- You can click and drag additional albums to add more.

iWeb displays the Media Index panel.

6. Click to set the number of columns and the spacing of the albums.
7. Click here to set the type of animation to appear.

A skim animation enables the viewer to position the cursor over the album to preview the photos.

8. Double-click an album in the grid to preview it.

Viewers on your Web site can single-click the album to view it.

iWeb displays the photo album.

- Viewers can click **Back to Index** to return to the albums page.

How can viewers subscribe to my photos?

Viewers can subscribe to a photo album or albums page on your site. New photos can then be automatically downloaded via RSS into their iPhoto library or RSS reader. For more about RSS, see "Insert an RSS Feed."

1. Open a Photos or My Albums page.
2. Click **Inspector**.
3. Click the **Photos Inspector** icon ( ).
4. Click **Allow visitors to subscribe** (☐ changes to ☑).

- iWeb adds a subscribe link to the page. The link gives viewers access to the RSS information for that page, which tells which photos are new.

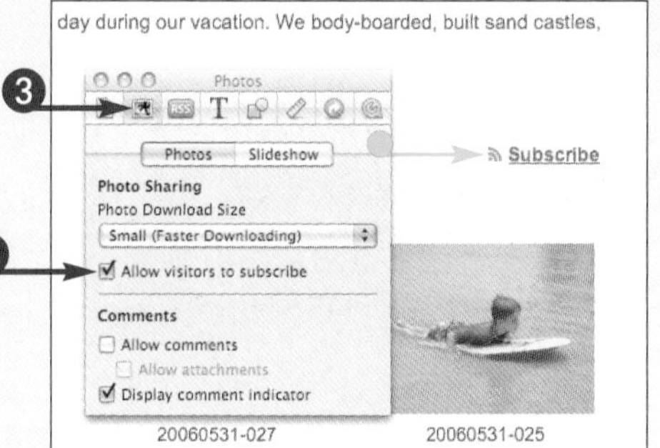

Create a MobileMe Photo Gallery

You can publish an album to your MobileMe account to make your photos available online. You can then send your friends and family a Web address where they can access the photos on MobileMe.

To use this feature, you must have a MobileMe account. See Chapter 2 for details.

Create a MobileMe Photo Gallery

1. Make sure you are connected to the Internet so your MobileMe gallery can be accessed.
2. Click **Widgets** in the media pane.

Note: If the media pane is not visible, click ***Show Media*** *at the bottom of the workspace to display it.*

3. Click and drag the **MobileMe Gallery** icon to a page.

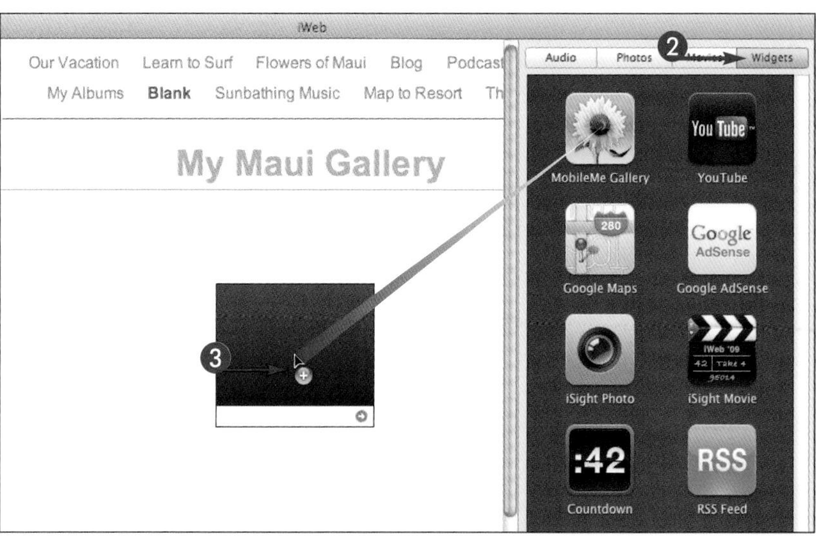

- iWeb inserts a box on your Web page and plays a slideshow of the images inside it.

4. Click here to select the MobileMe gallery to display.

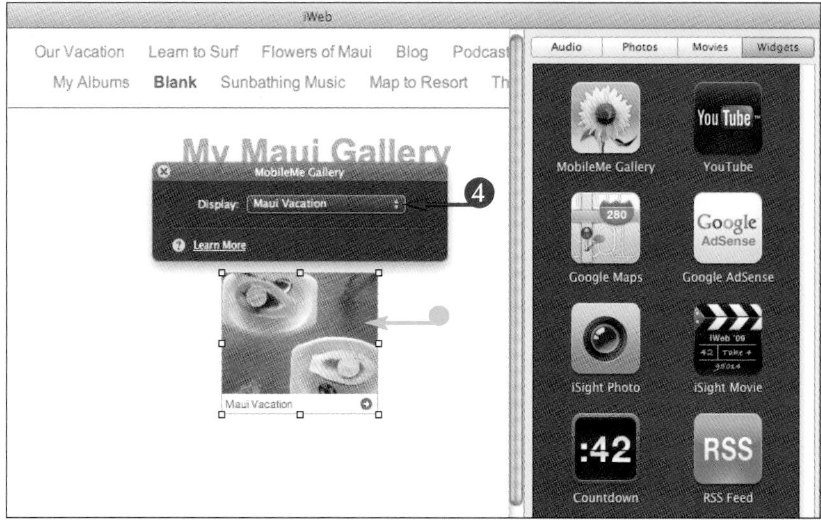

- You can click and drag in the center to reposition the gallery.
- You can click and drag a handle to resize the gallery.

5 Click ⊠ to close the settings.

iWeb saves the page settings.

- The title of the gallery appears here.
- Viewers can click ⊡ to cycle through the photos in the gallery.

How do I edit captions for photos in an album?

Each photo in an album includes a caption that you can use to describe the subject matter. Captions also appear on the detail page for the photo.

1 Open a photo album page.

Note: *To create a photo album using the Photos template, see "Create a Photo Album."*

- iWeb uses the file name of a photo for its caption by default.

2 Click the caption to make it editable, and type a photo description.

3 Click away from the caption.

iWeb saves the caption.

Insert a Google Map

You can add an interactive Google Map to your page to show a location of an event or business on your Web site. Viewers can click controls on the map to pan, zoom, and view satellite versions of the map. You must be connected to the Internet to configure the features of a Google Map.

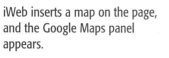

Insert a Google Map

1. Click **Widgets** in the media pane.

*Note: If the media pane is not visible, click **Show Media** at the bottom of the workspace to display it.*

2. Click and drag the **Google Maps** icon to a page.

iWeb inserts a map on the page, and the Google Maps panel appears.

3. Type the address of the location you want to map.

You can also type common landmarks such as "Golden Gate Bridge."

4. Click **Apply**.

- If found, the address appears in the map.

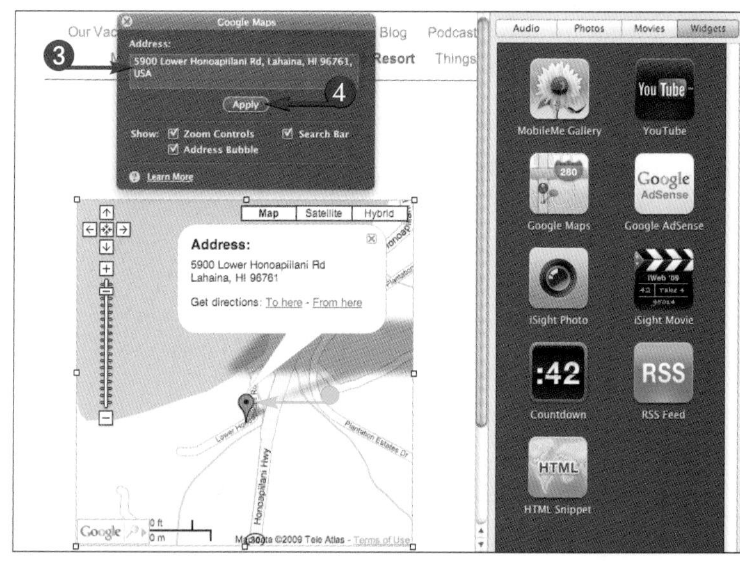

5 Click to select the features to appear on the map (☐ changes to ☑).

6 Click to select the view displayed.

***Note:** Clicking **Satellite** or **Hybrid** displays a map made up of satellite images.*

7 Use the zoom and pan controls to adjust the area displayed initially. You can also click and drag within the map to pan.

8 Click away from the map.

iWeb saves the map settings.

You can click and drag to reposition the map on the Web page.

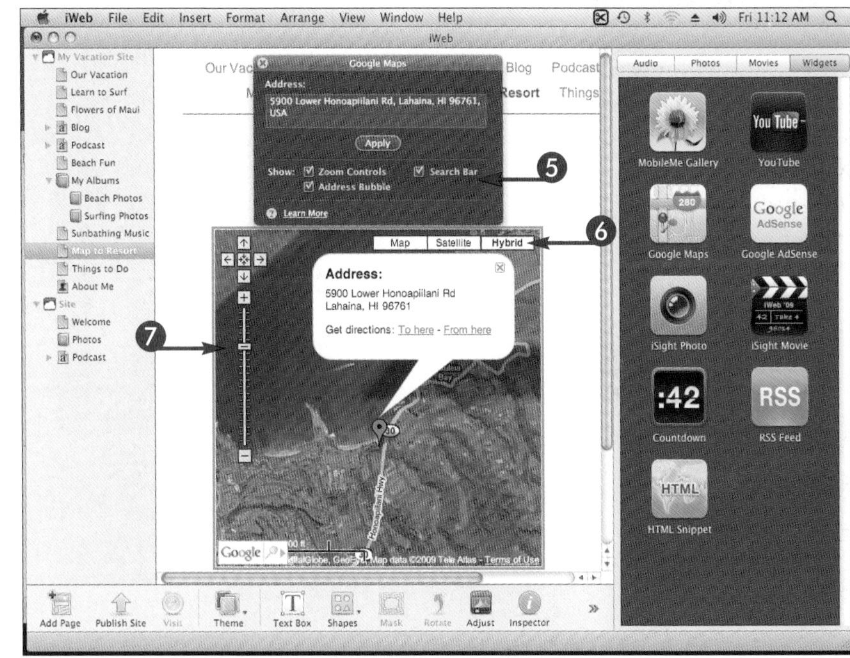

What is an HTML snippet?

An HTML snippet allows you to add content from another Web site to your own site. Often, Web sites offer snippets for dynamic content such as news headlines, stock quotes, and weather reports. To view snippet content in iWeb, you must be connected to the Internet. Another way to add external content is with an RSS feed.

1 Click **Widgets** in the media pane.

2 Click and drag the **HTML Snippet** icon to a page.

3 Type or paste the HTML snippet from another site here.

4 Click **Apply**.

- If you are connected to the Internet, iWeb downloads the HTML content from the Web and displays it.

Insert a Countdown Clock

You can insert a countdown clock to display the time remaining before a specific date and time. You can use it to build excitement before an event or encourage viewers to meet a deadline.

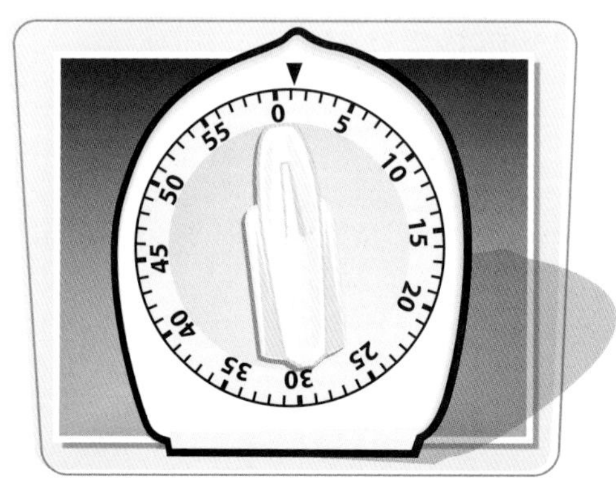

Insert a Countdown Clock

1. Click **Widgets** in the media pane.

Note: If the media pane is not visible, click ***Show Media*** *at the bottom of the workspace to display it.*

2. Click and drag the **Countdown** icon to a page.

iWeb adds a countdown clock.

3. Click the clock menu to select a clock and digits style.
4. Click and drag here to specify what digits to display.
5. Select the countdown date and time.

- You can click the calendar icon to select a date.

6. Click away from the clock.

iWeb saves the settings.

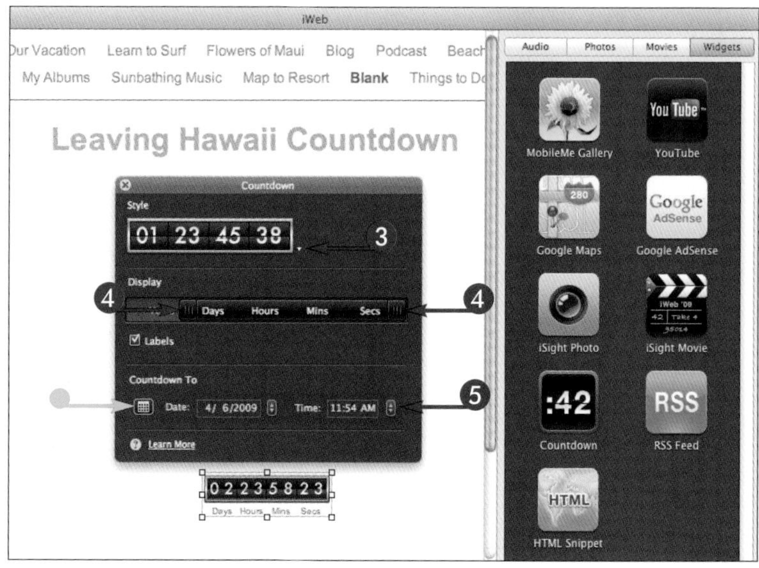

Insert an RSS Feed

You can insert an RSS feed to display a summary of the latest content from a news, blog, or other Web site with changing information. To set it up, you need the feed address from the other site. You can customize how much content is displayed on your page.

Insert an RSS Feed

1. Click **Widgets** in the media pane.

Note: If the media pane is not visible, click ***Show Media*** *at the bottom of the workspace to display it.*

2. Click and drag the **RSS Feed** icon to a page.

iWeb adds an RSS feed.

3. Type or paste the address of an RSS feed here.

Note: Look for an RSS icon (RSS icon) to access RSS feeds on Web sites.

4. Click **Apply**.

iWeb loads the feed.

5. Click to adjust how the content is displayed.

6. Click here to change how many entries are displayed.

- You can click and drag the handles to adjust the display area.

Test Your Web Pages

You activate the hyperlinks in your pages to ensure that they work before publishing your site and making it public. You can also view your pages in iWeb to ensure that they appear as you want them to appear.

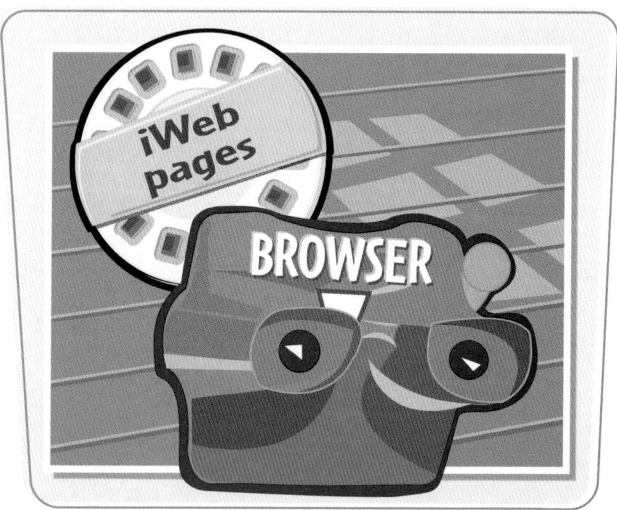

Test Your Web Pages

1. View the Web page you want to test.
2. Click **Inspector**.

   The Inspector window appears.
3. Click the **Link Inspector** icon ( ).
4. Click **Hyperlink**.

   iWeb lists the hyperlink settings.
5. Click **Make hyperlinks active** (changes to).

iWeb activates the hyperlinks on your pages.

***Note:** To create a hyperlink, see Chapter 17.*

6. Click a hyperlink on your Web page (changes to).

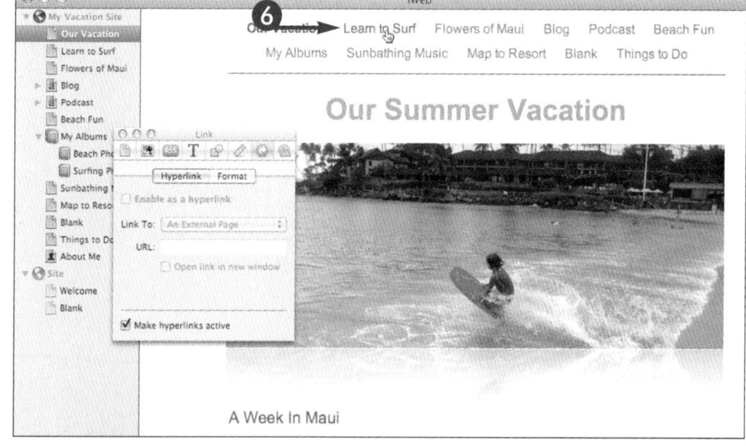

- iWeb opens the destination page.

  In this example, the destination is another page in the Web site.

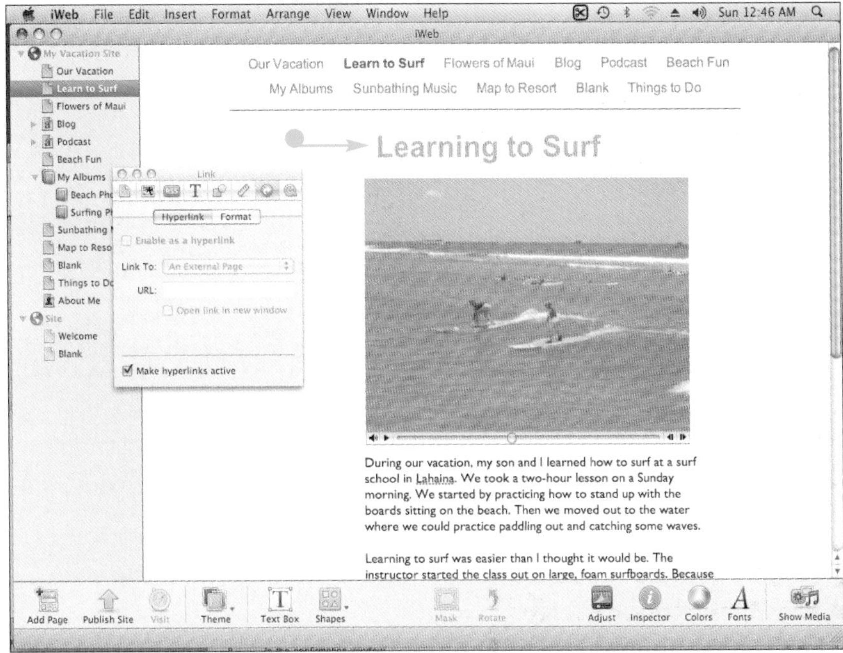

How can I test hyperlinks to external pages?

If you activate hyperlinks for your site and have an Internet connection, you can test links to pages on other sites.

1. Complete steps **1** to **5** above to turn on hyperlinks.
2. Click a hyperlink to an external page.

- The external page opens in a new window in your Web browser.

  If you do not have an active Internet connection, a browser window opens but it does not display the page.

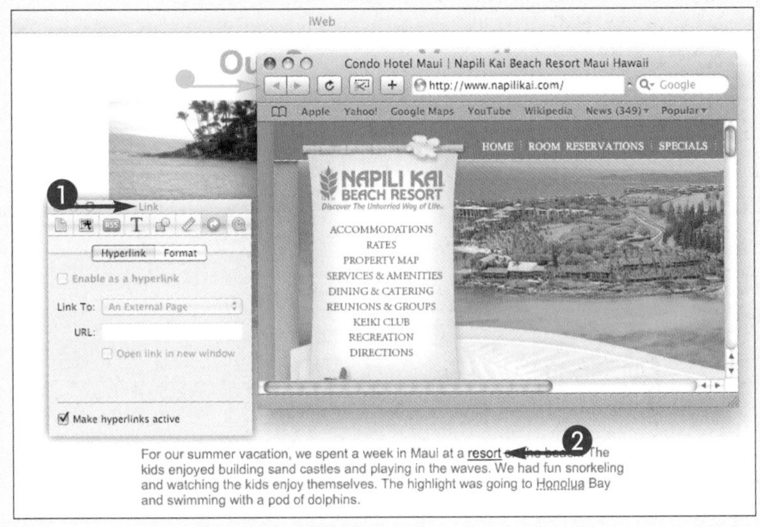

Publish a Site Using FTP

If you have a Web host, you can transfer your iWeb pages to a Web server at the host using *FTP*, which stands for File Transfer Protocol. After your pages are transferred, people can view them on the Web. To make the transfer, you need to obtain the server login information.

Publish a Site Using FTP

1. Click the site you want to publish.

   iWeb displays the publishing settings.

2. Select **FTP Server**.
3. Type a contact e-mail address.

Note: *The address is used for any Email Me buttons on your site pages. See Chapter 18 for details.*

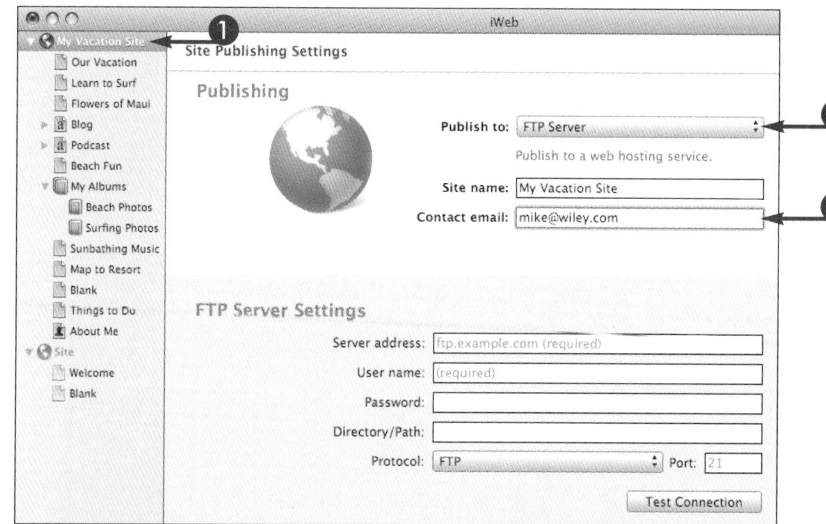

4. Type the server address at your Web host.
5. Type your user name.
6. Type your password.

- If necessary, type the path to the directory where your Web content is stored on the server.
- Select from this menu if your server requires FTP with extra security features.

  Check with your Web host for the server, user name, password, and other settings to use.

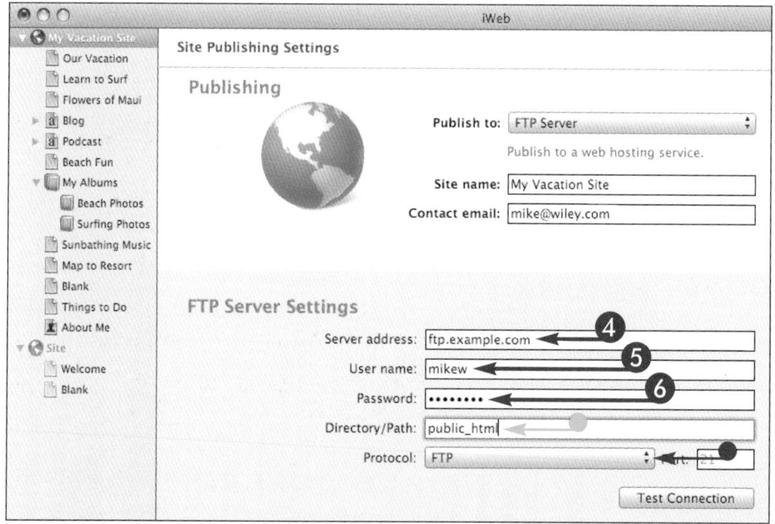

- Click **Test Connection** to test the login settings.

7. Type the root Web address of your site, which is typically the address for your home page.

   iWeb needs this to build certain types of links as well as any RSS feeds on your site.

Note: *See Chapter 18 for more about RSS.*

8. Click **Publish Site**.
9. If iWeb displays a dialog about content rights, click **OK**.
10. If iWeb displays a dialog about publishing in the background, click **OK**.

    iWeb uploads the Web site. How long it takes depends on the amount of site content. iWeb displays a confirmation when the upload is complete.

11. Click **Visit Site Now** to visit your site in a Web browser.

- You can also click **Visit** to visit a published site.

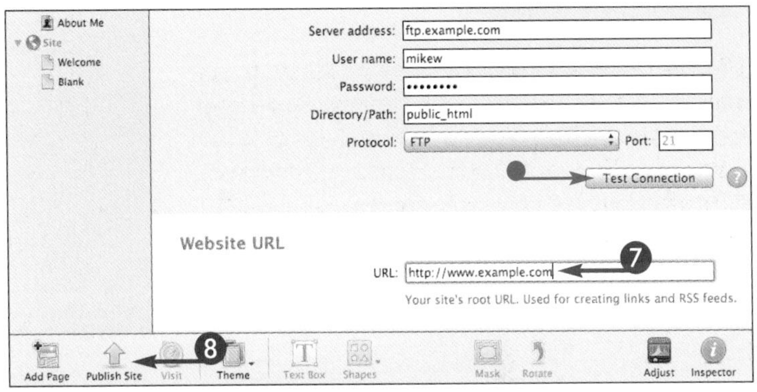

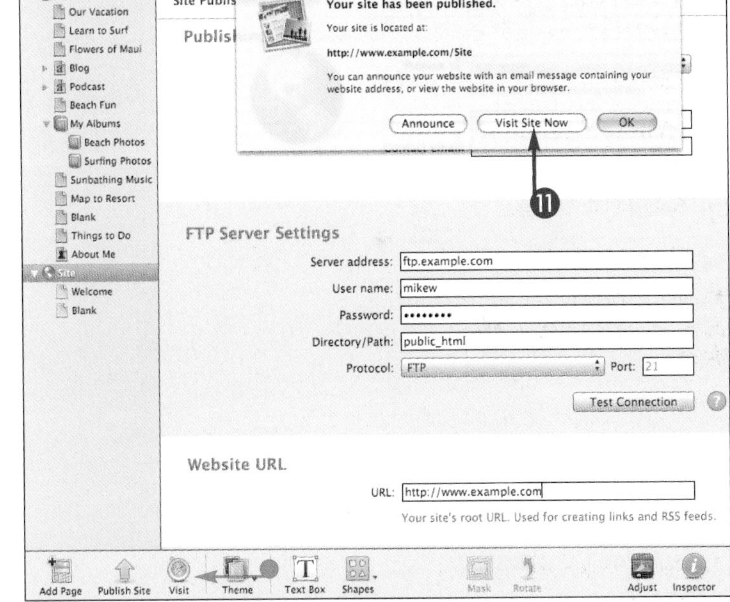

How can I republish my entire site to my Web server in iWeb?

If you remove site files from your Web server, for example using an FTP client program, you must republish your site for it to function properly.

1. Click your site in the sidebar.
2. Click **File**.
3. Click **Publish Entire Site**, and iWeb uploads all of the site files.

Note: *Clicking **Publish Site** at the bottom of the workspace as in step **8** uploads only content that iWeb sees as changed since the previous upload.*

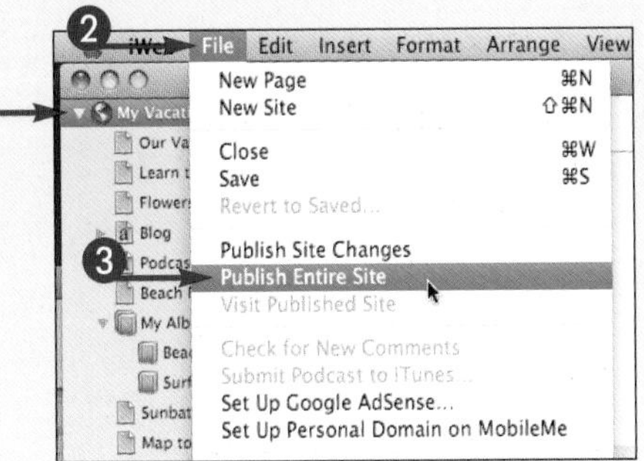

Publish a Site to MobileMe

You can publish a Web site to your MobileMe account to make your content available online. You can then send your friends and family a Web address where they can access the site on MobileMe.

To use this feature, you must have a MobileMe account. See Chapter 2 for details.

Publish a Site to MobileMe

1. Sign in to your MobileMe account.
2. Click the site you want to publish.

   iWeb displays the publishing settings.
3. Select **MobileMe**.
4. Type a contact e-mail address for any Email Me buttons on your site pages. See Chapter 18 for details.

- Your MobileMe account user name appears here.
- You can click here to protect your site with a user name and password (☐ changes to ☑).
- If you protect your site, type a user name and password. Do not use your own MobileMe user name and password.

  The password must be between 6 and 20 characters and is case-sensitive.

5. Click **Publish Site**.

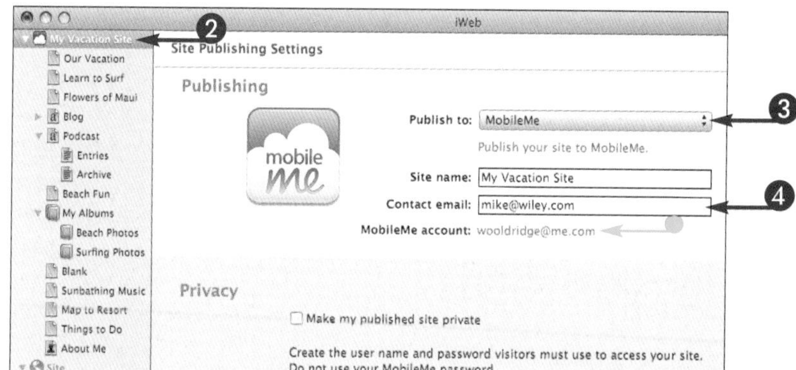

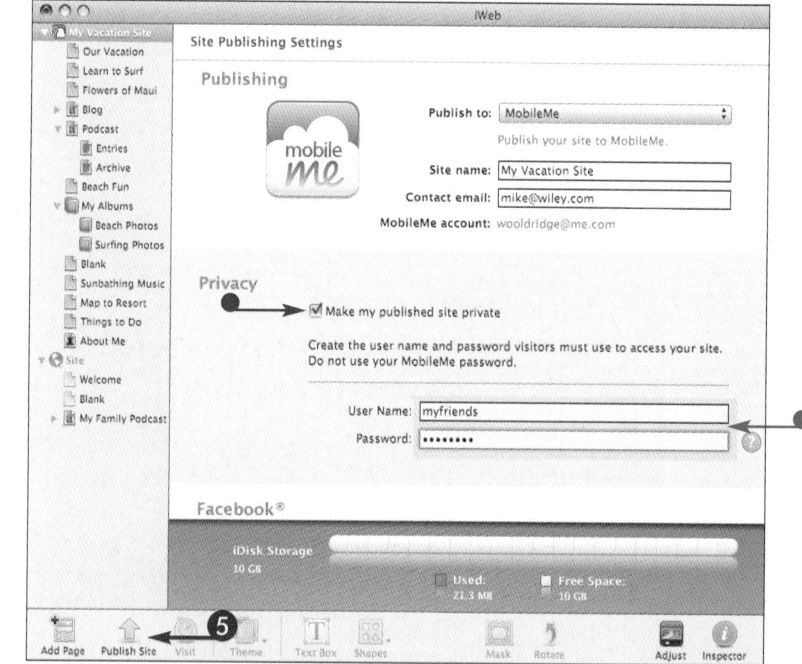

If a Content Rights dialog appears, click **Continue**.

- iWeb publishes your site to your MobileMe account.

If a dialog appears telling you the site will be published in the background, click **OK**.

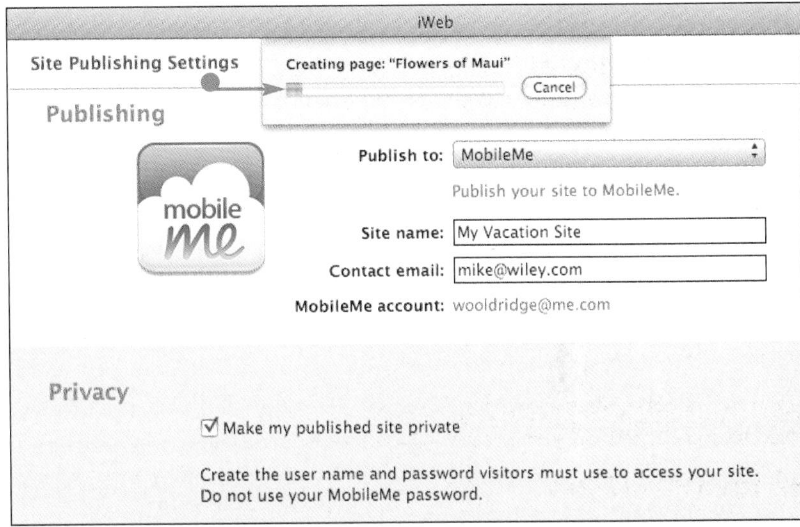

After the site is published, iWeb displays a confirmation dialog.

- Click **Announce** to announce the publication and invite others to view the site.
- Click **Visit Site Now** to view the site at your MobileMe account.

6 Click **OK** to close the dialog.

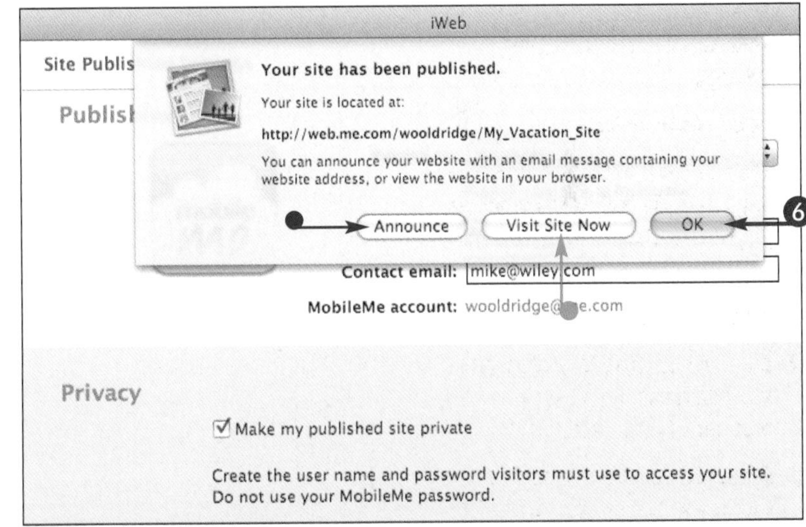

What Web address do I use to access my sites published to MobileMe?

You can use your MobileMe user name and site name to create the Web address for your site.

1. In the Web browser address box, type **http://web.me.com**.
2. Then type a / (forward slash) followed by your MobileMe user name.
3. Then type another / (forward slash) followed by the site name. Replace any spaces in the site name with _ (underscore) characters and remove any apostrophes.

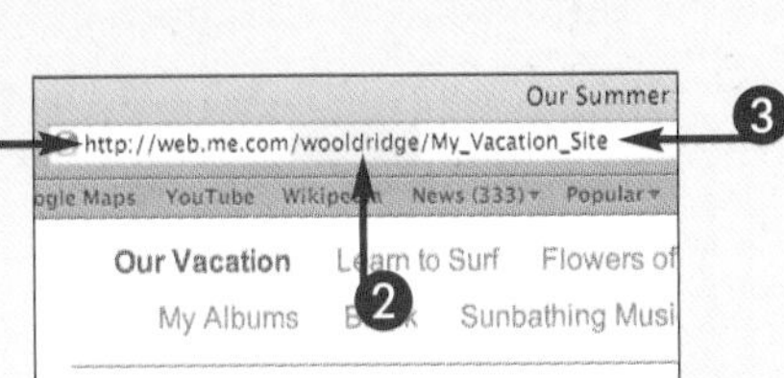

Note: *iWeb may convert or remove other nonalphanumeric characters in the site name as well. See the confirmation dialog that appears after publishing for the exact address.*

Share Site Updates on Facebook

You can announce updates to your Web site on your Facebook account. iWeb makes the announcements every time you make changes to your site and publish them.

Facebook is a popular social networking Web site where users can connect with friends and share information. To share site updates on Facebook, you must already have a Facebook account.

Share Site Updates on Facebook

1. Specify your publishing settings for your FTP server or MobileMe account.

Note: *For details about specifying settings, see the other tasks in this chapter.*

This example shows the settings for publishing using an FTP server.

2. At the bottom of the publishing settings, click **Update my Facebook profile when I update this site** (☐ changes to ☑).

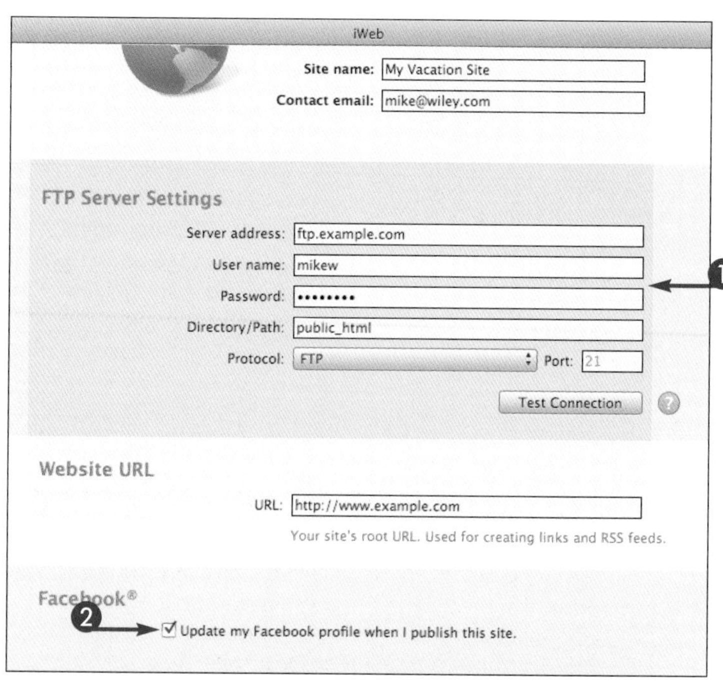

The Facebook window appears in iWeb.

3. Type the e-mail address associated with your Facebook account.

Note: *To set up a Facebook account, visit www.facebook.com.*

4. Type your password.
5. Click **Login**.

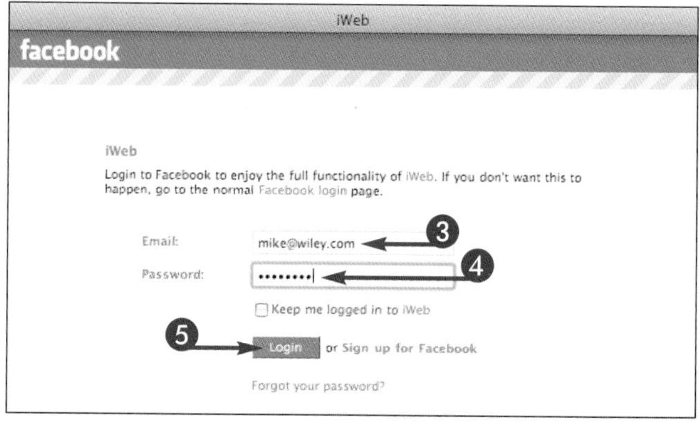

iWeb displays a confirmation page.

6 Click **Finish**.

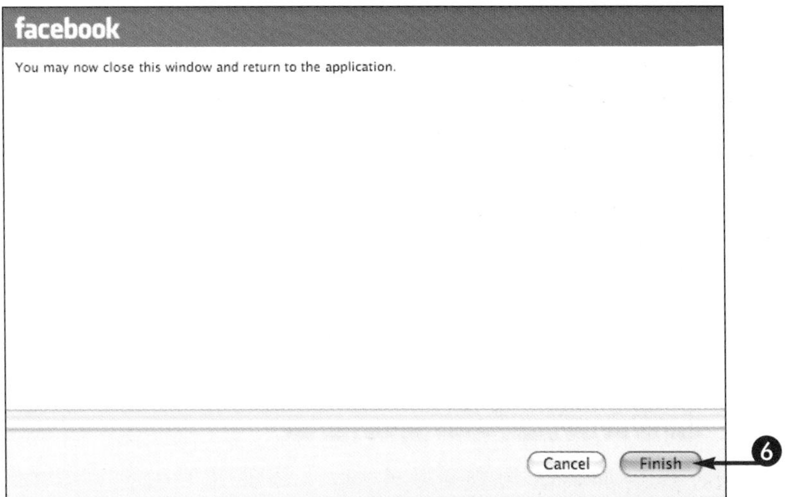

iWeb updates your Facebook account when you update your site.

- You can click here to temporarily disable the updating (☑ changes to ☐).
- You can click **Remove Account** to remove the connection to your Facebook account. You can reestablish it later if you want.

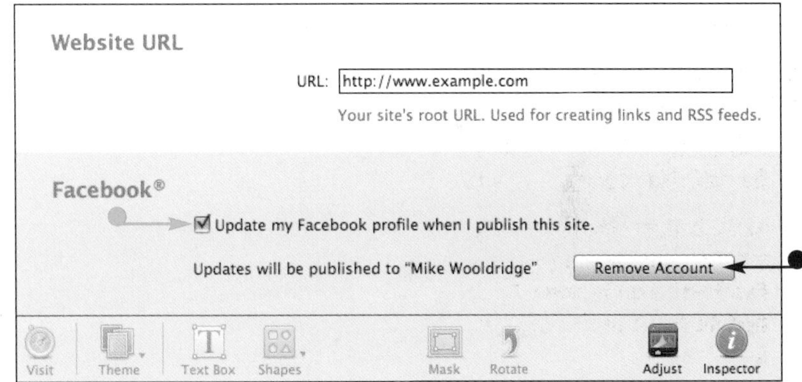

I want to publish my site to a Web server on my local network or computer. How do I do this?

You can publish your site to a location on your computer or network just like you can to a server at a Web host. This is useful when you maintain your own Web server.

1. In the publishing settings, select **Local Folder** in the Publish To menu.
2. Click **Choose** to select the Web server folder on your computer or on your network.
3. Type your Web site URL.
4. Click **Publish Site**.

iWeb copies the site to the folder.

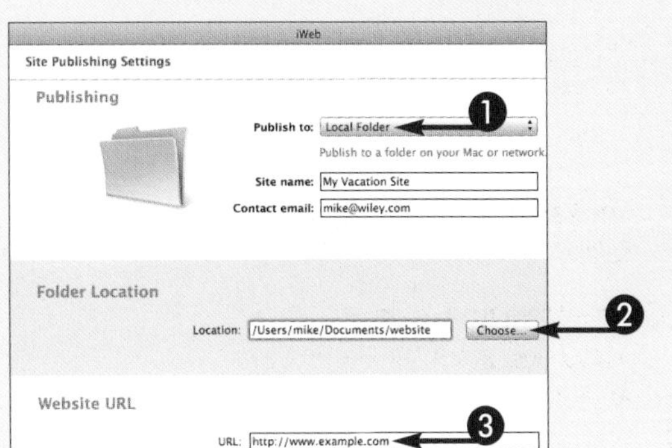

PART VI

Working with iDVD

iDVD lets you create DVD productions that showcase movies, images, and music from the other iLife applications. You can choose dozens of themes to create stylish DVD menus that match the mood of your digital content. This part shows you how to use iDVD to build a DVD project and then burn it to disc.

Understanding the iDVD Workspace

iDVD allows you to author professional-looking DVDs that feature your movies and photos. iDVD makes it easy to assemble content from the different iLife applications. Before starting an iDVD project, familiarize yourself with the program workspace.

Menus

An iDVD project is made up of one or more menus. A menu is a page that features buttons that link to content such as movies and photo slideshows. iDVD menus can include decorative graphics, animations, and background music. When you play a DVD, you navigate menus and click buttons using the DVD player's remote control.

Themes

Each menu in a project has a theme that determines the graphics and animation that appear with it. iDVD comes with dozens of different themes. You can select a theme to establish a mood for your DVD project. You access the iDVD themes by clicking **Themes** in the lower-right area of the workspace.

Buttons

Clickable buttons in menus let users access movies, slideshows, and other menus on your DVD. You can customize buttons with underlining, bullets, and shapes. You access button styles by clicking **Buttons** in the lower-right area of the workspace.

Media

To create a DVD, you add movies, photos, and audio from iMovie, iPhoto, iTunes, GarageBand, and the folders on your computer. You click and drag files from the media pane to the main window to add them. You access media files by clicking **Media** in the lower-right area of the workspace. See Chapter 21 for more about adding and editing media in your DVD project.

Map View

iDVD makes it easy to author complex DVDs by letting you view projects in a hierarchical map view. Map view shows movies, slideshows, and other content as boxes connected by lines. You can rearrange content by clicking and dragging.

Drop Zones

You can click the **Edit Drop Zones** button to customize the preview areas in iDVD menus. The number and layout of drop zones in menus are determined by the theme you choose for the project. For more information about drop zones, see Chapter 21.

Previewing

After you add content to your project, you can preview it to see what the end users will see in their DVD player.

Burning

You can burn your project to a DVD by clicking the **Burn** button. iDVD can burn to a variety of disc formats including DVD-R, DVD-RW, DVD+R, and DVD+RW single-layer discs. It can also burn DVD+R DL double-layer discs. For more details, see Chapter 22.

Create a New Project

You can create a new project in iDVD and then add movies, photos, menus, and buttons to the project. iDVD comes with a variety of professionally designed themes that add graphics and animations to your project and establish a mood.

Create a New Project

1. Start the iDVD program.
2. Click **Create a New Project**.
   - You can also click **File** and then **New** from within a project in iDVD.

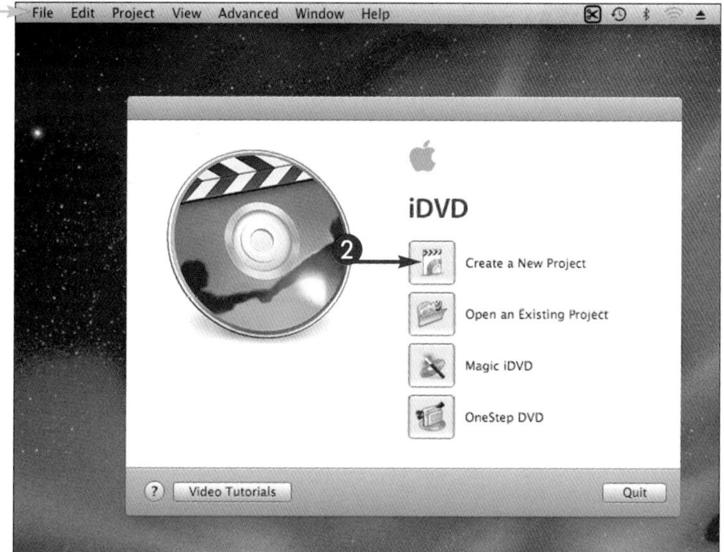

3. Type a name for your project.
4. Specify where to save the project.
5. Select an aspect ratio.

   Some themes in iMovie are available only for a certain aspect ratio.

   - You can change the aspect ratio later by clicking **Project** and then **Switch to**.
6. Click **Create**.

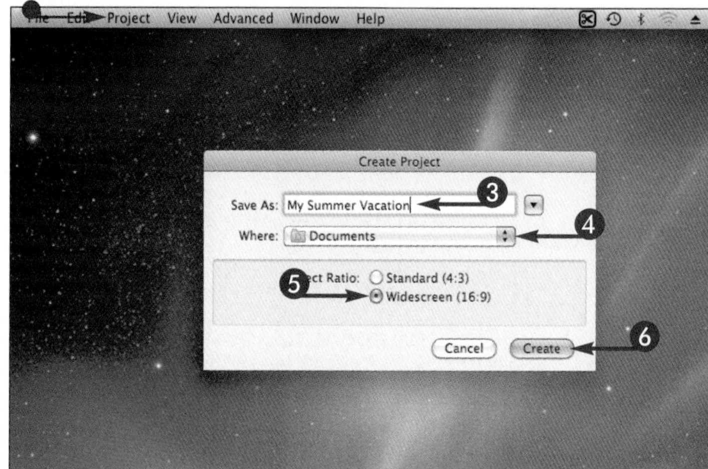

7 Select a set of themes.

8 Click a theme to apply to your DVD project.

A theme determines the graphics and animation that appear in your project menus.

- You can click the arrow to access different versions of the same theme (▶ changes to ▼).

Add movies, slideshows, and menus to your project. See Chapter 21 for details.

9 Click the **Preview** button (▶).

- iMovie previews the project.
- A controller enables you to control the playback of the project.

10 Click **Exit** to stop the preview.

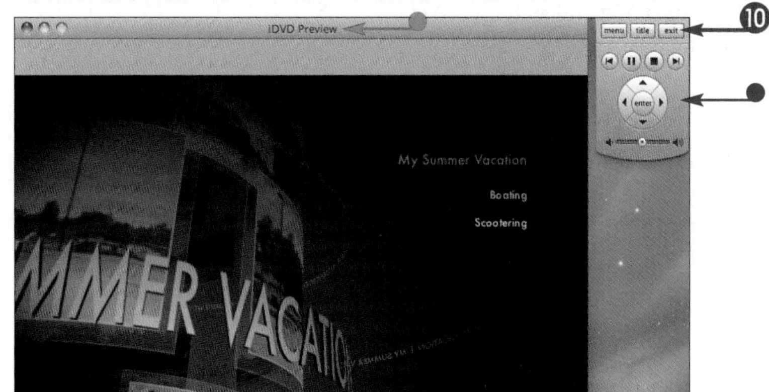

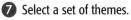

How do I change the theme of a menu in my project?

1 Click **Themes** in the lower-right area of the workspace.

2 Select a theme set.

3 Click the arrow to view the variations for a theme (▶ changes to ▼).

- You can click a large thumbnail to change the current menu and the other menus in the project.

Note: *See Chapter 21 for more about adding menus.*

- You can click a small thumbnail to change only the theme of the menu being displayed.

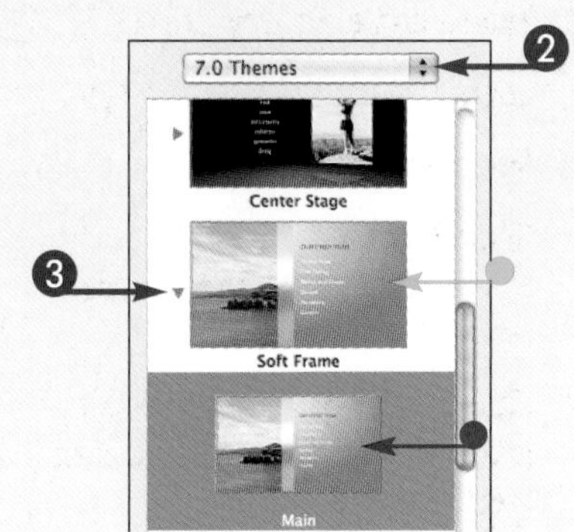

Change Preferences

You can edit the iDVD preferences to change what appears in the project window, how the content is processed prior to burning to disc, and more. Reviewing the settings before you begin can help you become familiar with the program and save you time later.

Change Preferences

1. Click **iDVD**.
2. Click **Preferences**.

   The General preferences open.

- You can click to hide the text that appears on drop zones (☑ changes to ☐).

Note: See Chapter 21 for more about drop zones.

- You can click to hide the Apple logo that appears on your project menus (☑ changes to ☐).

3. Click **Projects**.

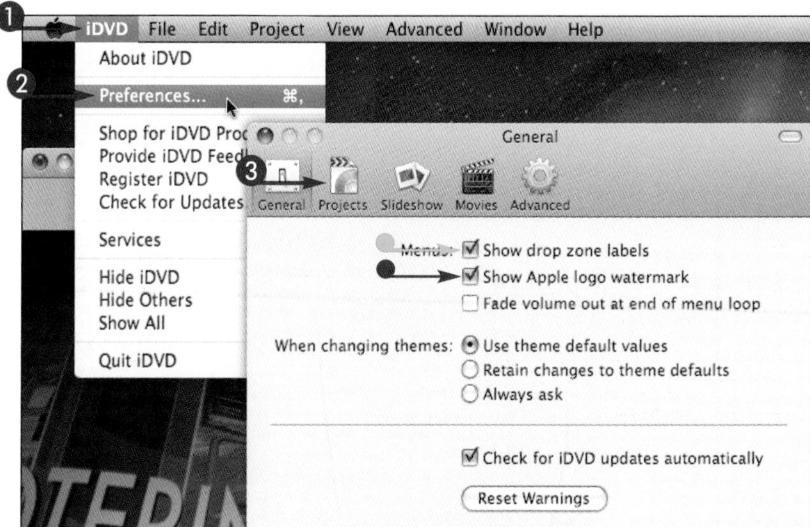

The Projects preferences appear.

- You can click to change the video mode (○ changes to ⦿).

Note: NTSC is the mode used in most of North and South America and Japan, whereas PAL is used in most European countries.

- You can select an encoding option, which determines how content is processed prior to burning. See the tip on the next page for details.

4. Click **Slideshow**.

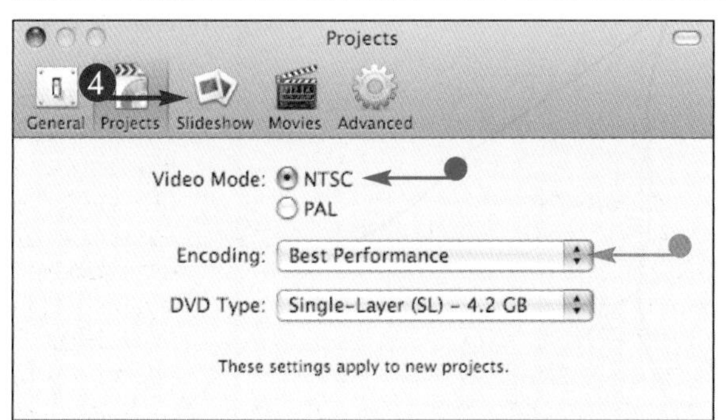

The Slideshow preferences appear.

- You can click to configure how iDVD presents still photos as slideshows in your projects (☐ changes to ☑).

5 Click **Movies**.

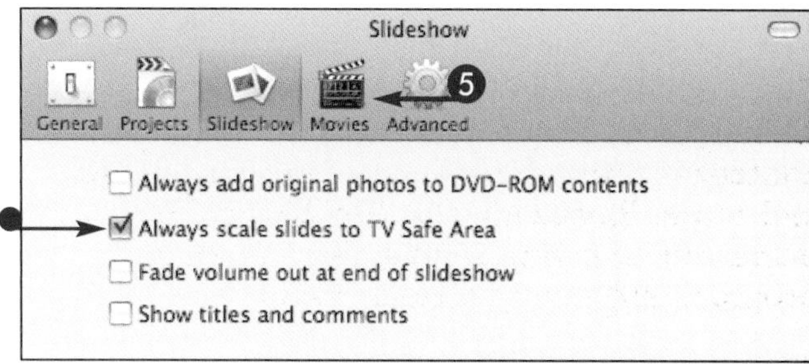

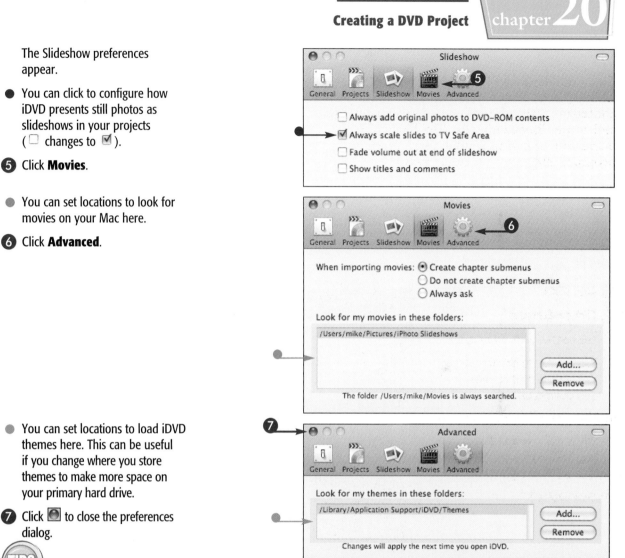

- You can set locations to look for movies on your Mac here.

6 Click **Advanced**.

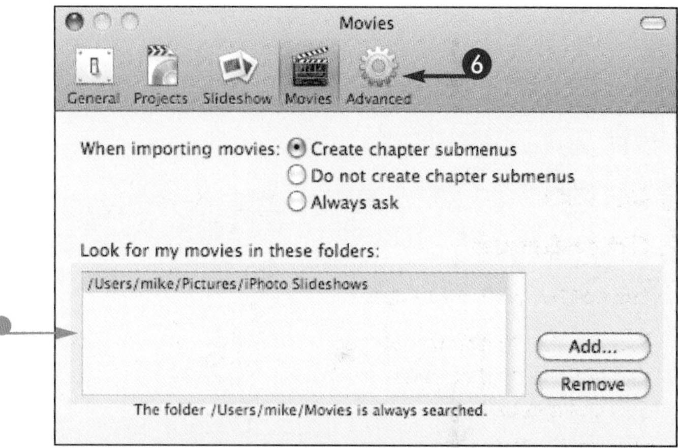

- You can set locations to load iDVD themes here. This can be useful if you change where you store themes to make more space on your primary hard drive.

7 Click ● to close the preferences dialog.

How do I view a summary of the content that has been added to a project?

You can click **Project** and then **Project Info** to view a content summary. A dialog appears showing the different types of content in the project – for example movies, slideshows, and menus – and how much space each type takes up. The amount of content you can put on a disc depends on the encoding setting for the project and whether you use a single-layer or double-layer DVD.

What encoding option should I choose?

Encoding is the processing and digital compression that occurs prior to writing content to a DVD. Choosing **Best Performance** encodes the DVD content as you work and provides the quickest burn time. It is good for projects with less than 60 minutes of content being written to a single-layer DVD. **High Quality** encodes at burn time and is good for projects with between one and two hours of content when using single-layer discs. **Professional Quality** also encodes at burn time and is good for up to two hours when using single-layer discs, but takes the longest time to complete.

Create a Magic DVD

You can create a Magic iDVD to automatically build a project with a theme, a set of movies, and a set of slideshows. iMovie organizes the content into the menus and submenus of a project that you can burn right away. With a Magic iDVD, you do not have the option of editing the menus, buttons, and other details like you do with a standard project.

Create a Magic DVD

1. Click **File** and then **Magic iDVD**.

   The Magic iDVD dialog appears.

   You can also click **Magic iDVD** in the iDVD start window.

2. Type a name for the DVD.
3. Select a set of themes.
4. Click a theme to choose the graphics and menu styles for your project.

5. Click **Movies**.
6. Click a list item to display movies from an iMovie event.
7. Click and drag to add movies to your project.

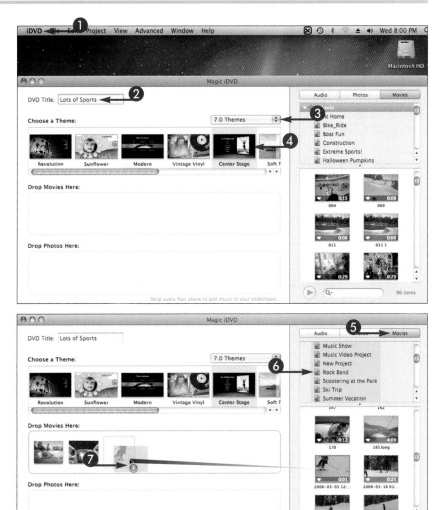

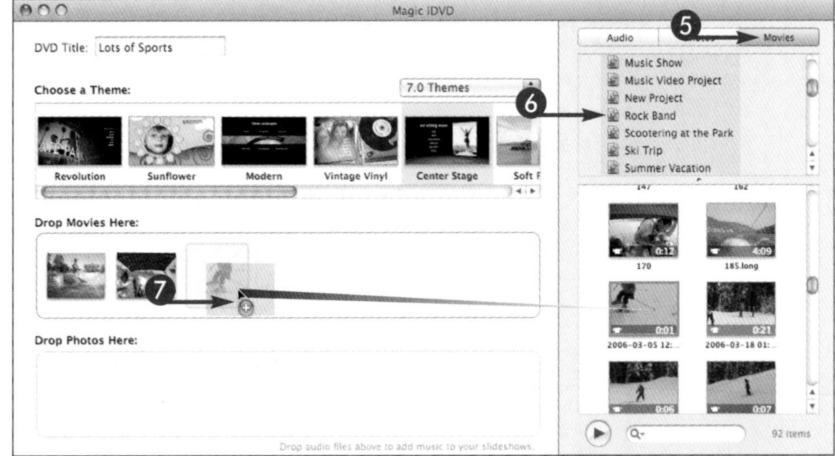

8 Click **Photos**.

9 Click a list item to display photos from an iPhoto category.

10 ⌘-click to select one or more photos.

11 Click and drag to add the selected photos to the DVD as a slideshow.

You can repeat steps **10** and **11** to add additional slideshows.

You can also drag an iPhoto Event icon or folder from the Finder to add a group of photos as a slideshow.

12 Click **Audio**.

13 Click a list item to display the available audio files from GarageBand or iTunes.

14 Click and drag to add background music to a slideshow.

15 Click **Create Project** to automatically assemble an iDVD project.

iDVD creates the project. To burn the project to disc, see Chapter 22.

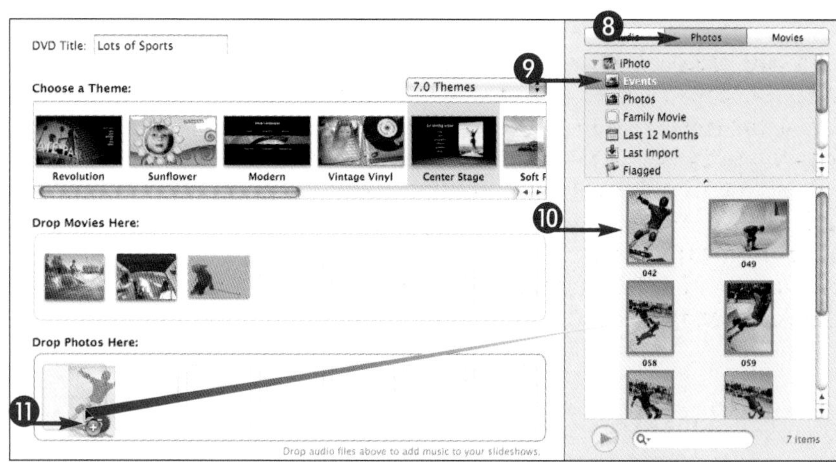

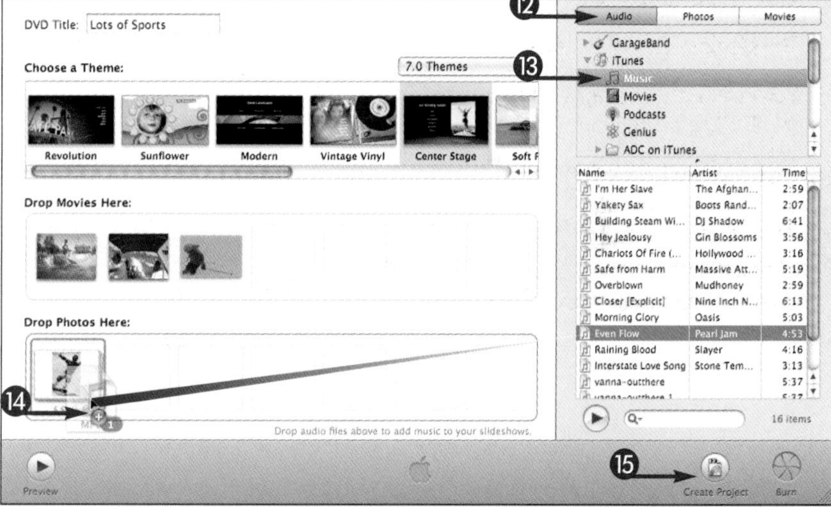

Some of my iMovie projects are not available to use in iDVD. What can I do?

iMovie projects that have not been previously shared can be shared with iDVD using the media browser. To get the best quality on your resulting DVD, share the project at the largest possible size.

1 Open the project you want to use in iDVD in iMovie.

2 Click **Share** and then **Media Browser**.

iMovie displays a dialog enabling you to choose the size of the project to publish.

3 Select one or more sizes (☐ changes to ☑).

4 Click **Publish** (not shown).

iMovie publishes the project and makes it available in iDVD.

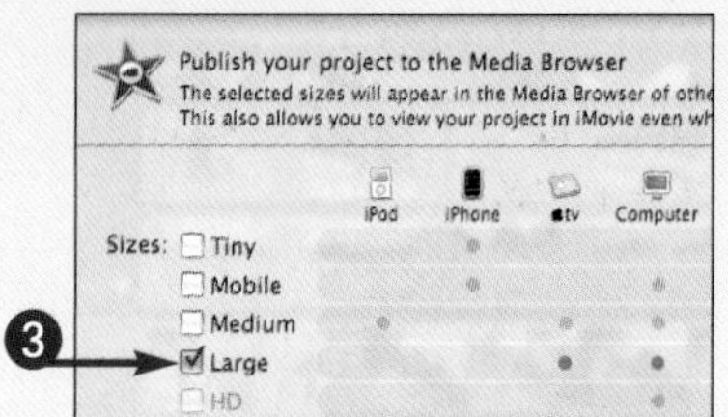

Create a OneStep DVD

You can burn the content from a videotape to a DVD in one step. A OneStep DVD automatically plays when you insert it into a DVD player. It does not include the menus or other formatting of a regular DVD project or Magic DVD.

Create a OneStep DVD

1. Turn your camcorder on and connect it to your Mac.

   Connect the camera using a FireWire cable.

   Make sure your camcorder is switched to VTR, VCR, or Play mode. The terminology may vary depending on the model of your camcorder.

2. Start the iDVD program.
3. Click **OneStep DVD**.

- You can also click **File** and then **OneStep DVD** from within a project in iDVD.
- If you do not have a blank DVD already in your DVD drive, a dialog appears prompting you to insert one.

4. Insert a blank DVD.

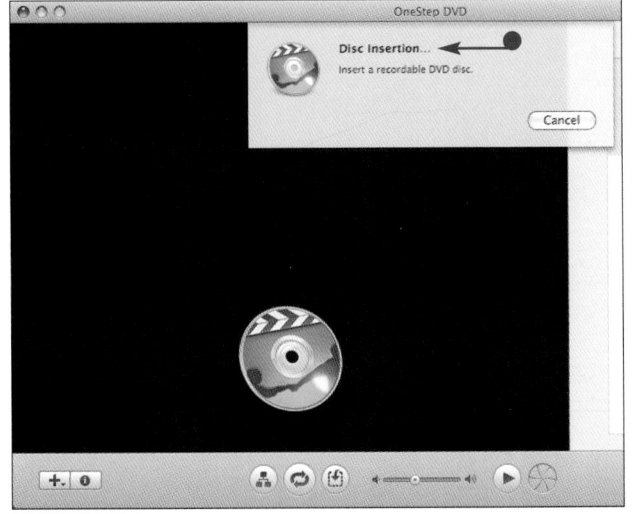

iDVD rewinds the tape to the beginning and then begins to play the tape.

- iDVD captures the video from the tape as it plays.
- You can click **Stop** to stop the capture and then either complete the OneStep DVD or cancel it.

iDVD stops capturing at the end of the tape and prepares the DVD, processes the captured content, and burns the content to the DVD.

- iDVD finishes the OneStep DVD and displays a dialog.

5 Click **Done**.

You can play the completed DVD to view the content from the videotape.

- To create a OneStep DVD from a movie saved on your computer, you can click **File** and then **OneStep DVD from Movie**.

How do I start my OneStep DVD from somewhere in the middle of the tape?

By default, iDVD adds your video content from the beginning of your videotape. To start it from somewhere else, set the videotape to the place where you want to begin in the camcorder. When you make your OneStep DVD, press play after you insert your DVD in step **4**. iDVD starts recording from where you press play.

How do I end my OneStep DVD from somewhere in the middle of the tape?

By default, iDVD plays your videotape to the end and captures all the video on the tape. To stop capturing before the end, click **Stop** in the iDVD capture window. Then, in the dialog that appears, click **Continue** to burn the DVD with the content that was captured.

Add a Movie

You can include a movie in your iDVD project and view the movie when you play your DVD. When you add a movie, iDVD creates a clickable button in your project menu. You can choose movies from iMovie, iPhoto, iTunes, or folders on your computer.

Add a Movie

CLICK AND DRAG

1. Click **Media**.
2. Click **Movies**.
3. Click a list item to display the available movies from an iMovie event.
4. Click and drag a movie to the project menu.

- iDVD adds a button to the menu labeled with the movie file name.

Note: *To edit the button, see "Customize a Button."*

5. Double-click the button to play the movie.

USE THE ADD ICON

1. Click the add icon (+).
2. Click **Add Movie** in the menu that appears.

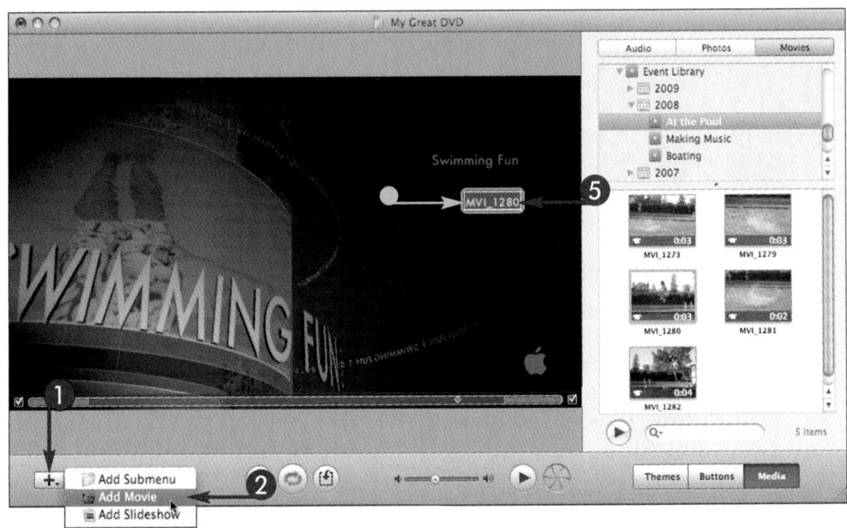

- iDVD adds an empty button to the menu.

3. Click and drag a movie from the media pane to the empty button.

   iDVD associates the movie with the button.

Note: *To edit the button, see "Customize a Button."*

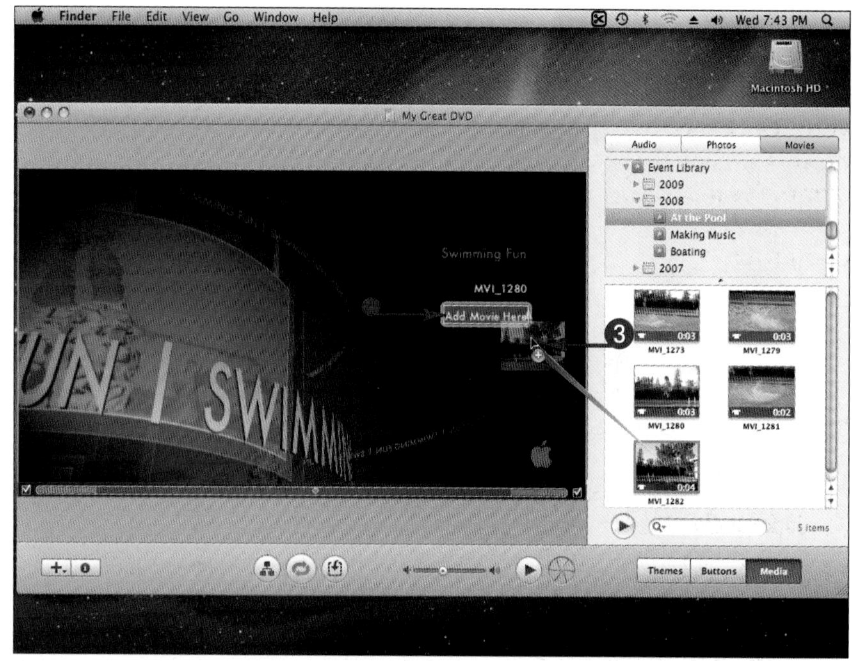

TIP

How can I make more content available in the media pane?

The media pane lists the movies, photos, and music that you can add to your DVD project. You can add specific folders from the Finder to the media pane to make them accessible.

1. Click **Media**.
2. Click the type of media to which you are adding.
3. Access the folder you want to add in the Finder.
4. Click and drag the folder to the media pane.

   iDVD adds the folder to the media pane inside a folder titled Folders.

Add a Slideshow

You can include still photos in your iDVD project as a slideshow. You can view the slideshow when you play your DVD. iDVD creates a clickable button for the slideshow in your project menu.

Add a Slideshow

1. Click the add icon (+).
2. Click **Add Slideshow** in the menu that appears.
   - iDVD adds a button to the menu labeled My Slideshow.

Note: *To edit the button, see "Customize a Button."*

3. Double-click the button.

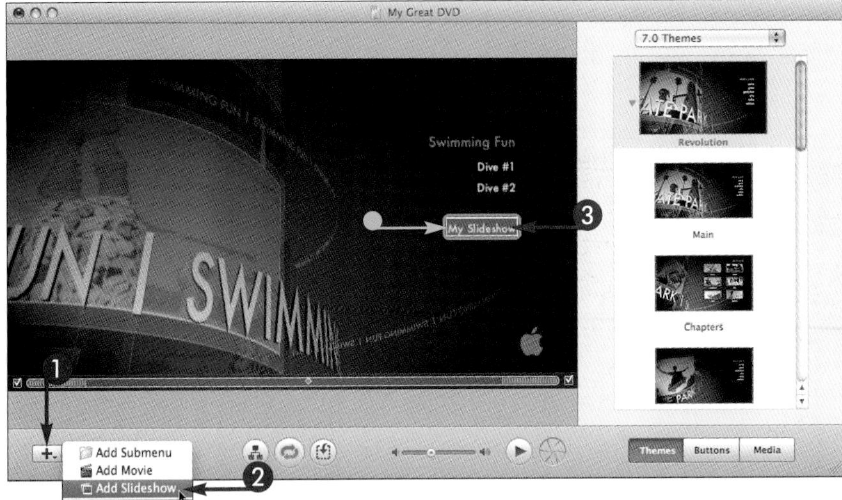

iDVD opens the slideshow editor.

4. Click **Media**.
5. Click **Photos**.
6. Click a list item to display the available photos in an iPhoto category.
7. Click and drag to add photos to the slideshow.

   You can ⌘-click to select multiple photos.

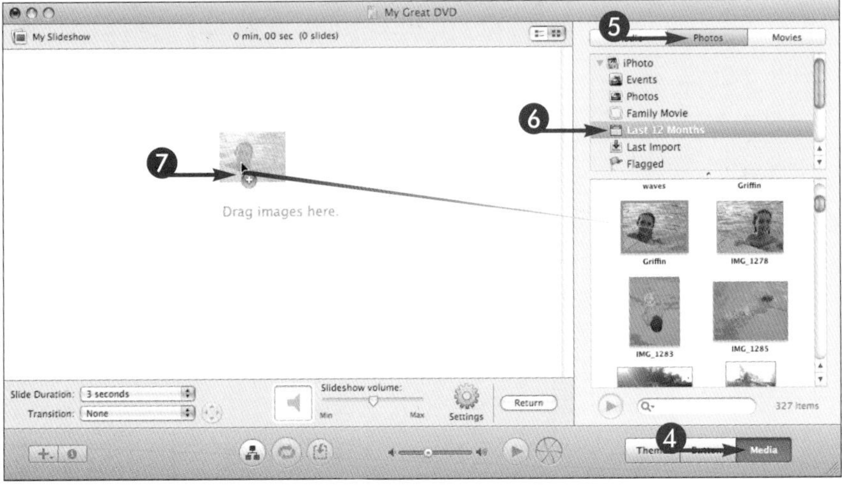

- You can click and drag in the editor to rearrange the order of the slides.

8. Select the slide duration.
9. Select a transition to play between slides.

- You can click **Settings** to change additional settings.

10. Click the **Preview** button (▶).

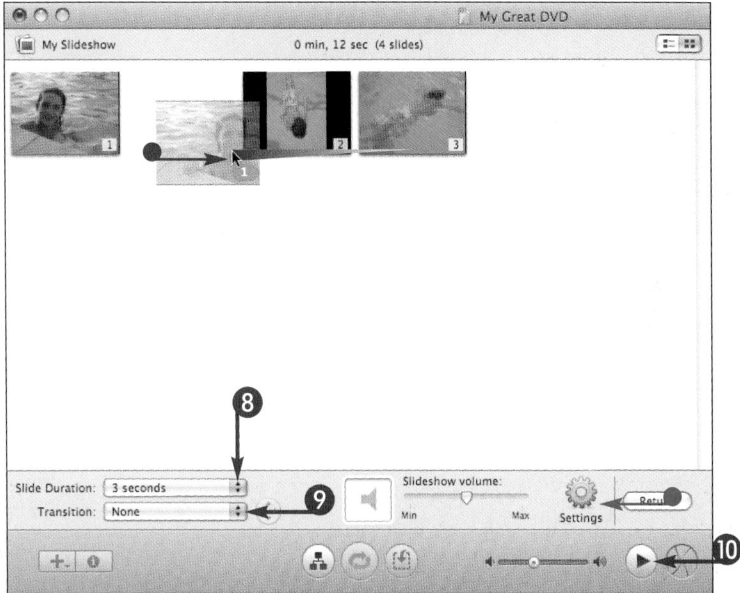

iDVD displays the slideshow and a controller.

- You can click ⏮ and ⏭ to move through the slides.
- You can click ⏸ to pause the slideshow.
- You can click **Exit** to return to the slideshow editor.

11. Click ⏹ to stop the slideshow and return to the menu.

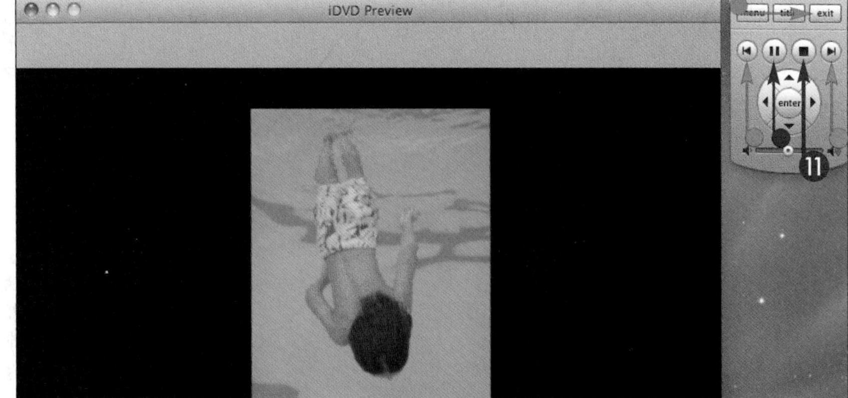

How do I add text to the slides in my slideshow?

You can add titles and comments to your slides.

1. In the slideshow editor, click **Settings**.
2. Click to show titles and comments (☐ changes to ☑).

   iDVD displays file names for titles.

3. Click here to edit a title.
4. Click here to edit a comment.

   The titles and comments appear in your slideshow.

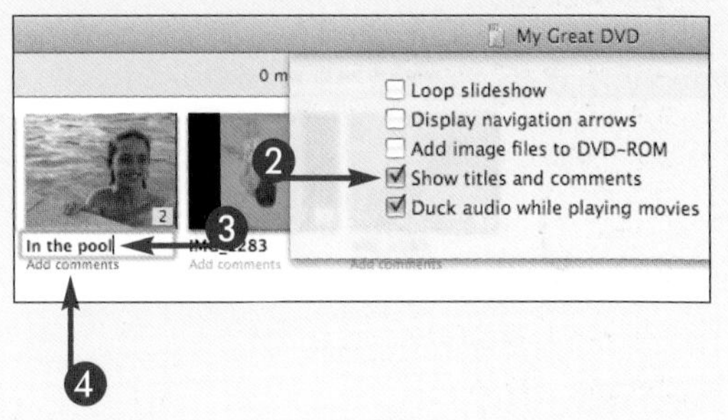

Add Music to a Slideshow

You can add a song from iTunes or GarageBand as background music for your slideshow. This can help add a mood to your slideshow and make it more interesting. You can automatically time the slideshow duration so that it is the same as that of the song.

Add Music to a Slideshow

1. Double-click a slideshow button.

Note: *To create a slideshow, see "Add a Slideshow."*

iDVD opens the slideshow editor.

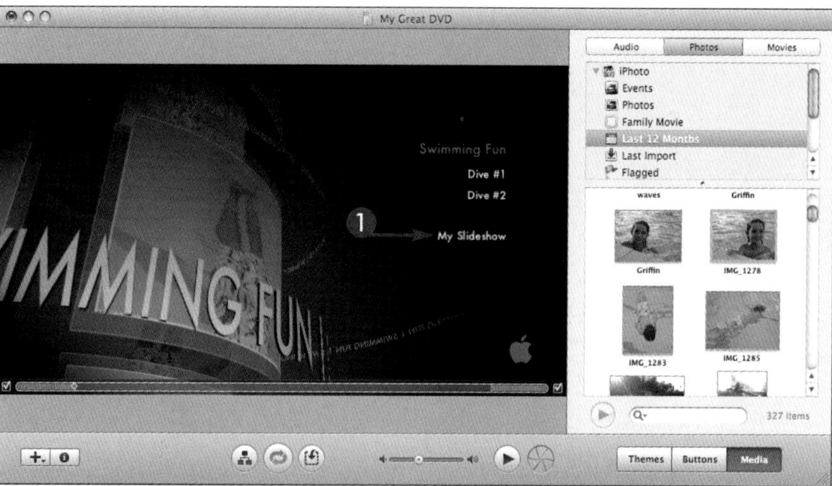

2. Click **Media**.
3. Click **Audio**.
4. Click a list item to display the available songs from GarageBand or iTunes.
5. Click and drag a song to the slideshow pane.

Note: *You can also click and drag an iTunes playlist, which is a collection of songs.*

- iDVD adds the song as background music.

6. Click the slider to adjust the music volume.

- You can select **Fit To Audio** to make the slideshow duration fit that of the song.

7. Click the **Preview** button (▶).

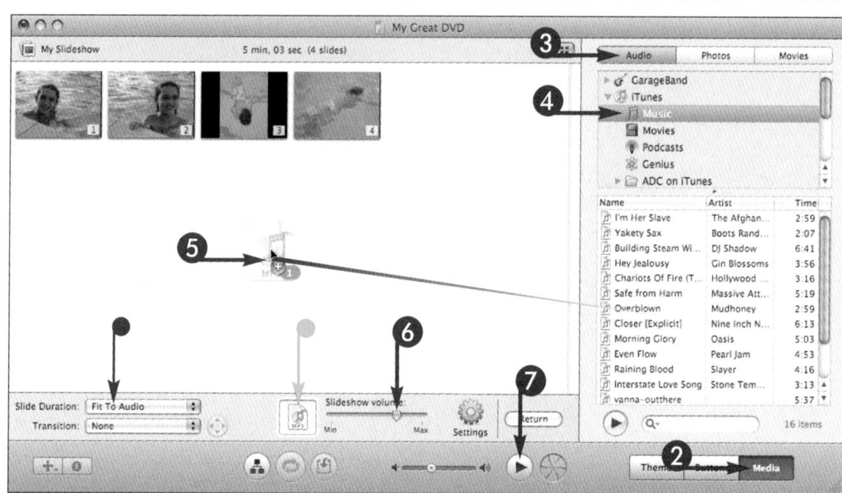

iDVD displays the slideshow and controller and plays the music.

- You can click and drag the slider to adjust the audio as it plays.

8 Click ▣ to stop the slideshow and return to the menu.

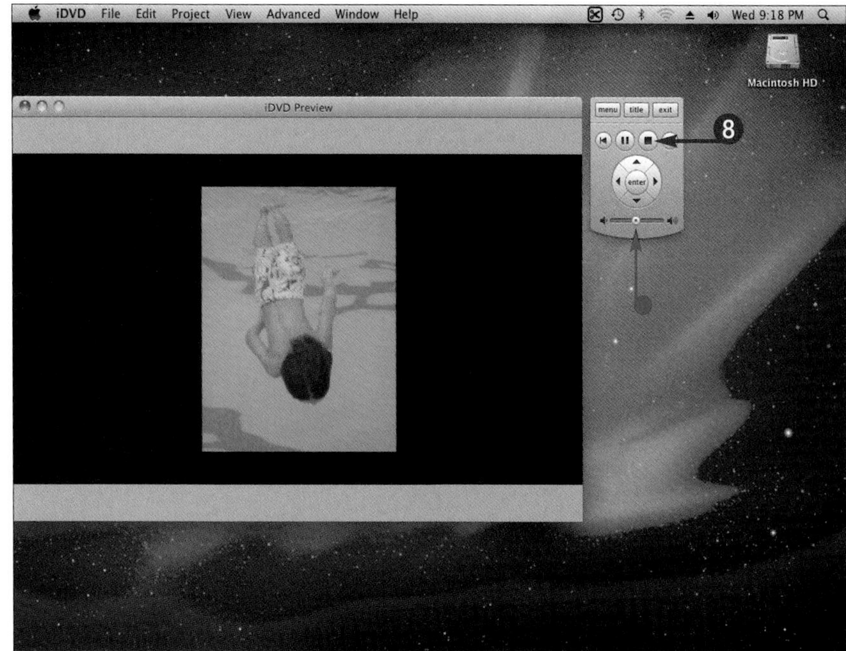

TIP

How do I add movies to a slideshow?

Follow these steps:

1 With the slideshow editor open, click **Media**.

2 Click **Movies**.

3 Click a list item to display the available movies on your computer.

4 Click and drag a movie to the slideshow.

iDVD adds the movie.

Note: *The slide duration setting does not apply to movies in a slideshow. The entire movie plays.*

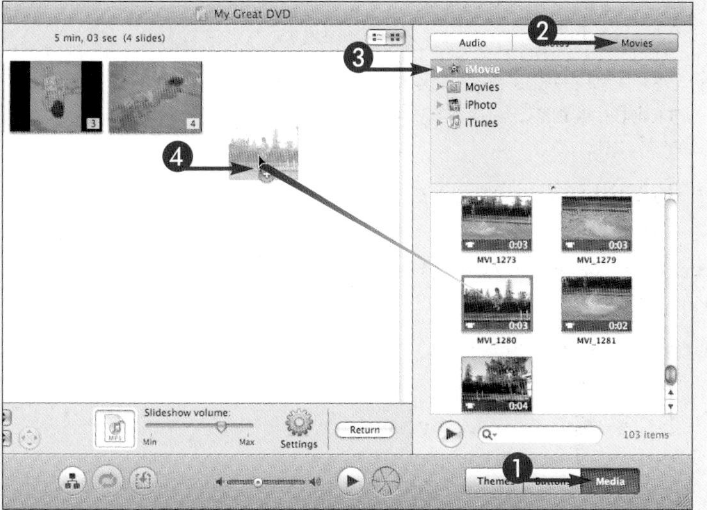

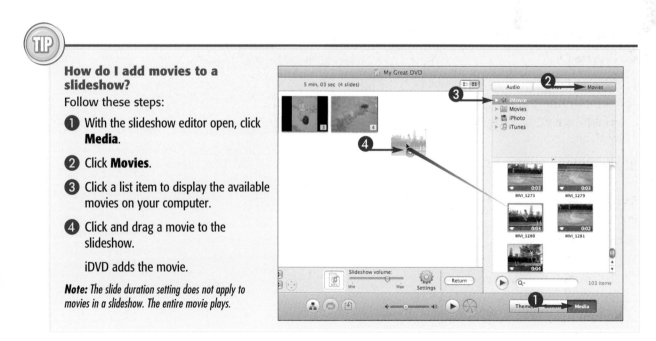

Add Media to a Drop Zone

You can add videos and still images to drop zones, which are sections in iDVD menus that can show previews of the content on a disc. The number and layout of drop zones in menus are determined by the theme you choose for the project.

Add Media to a Drop Zone

CLICK AND DRAG TO ADD

1. Display a menu in an iDVD project.

- Drop zones are labeled in the menu.

2. Click **Media**.
3. Click **Photos** or **Movies**.

   You can add movies, still images, and slideshows to a drop zone. You cannot add audio.

4. Click a list item to display the available content in the media pane.
5. Click and drag a media file to a drop zone.

- iDVD adds the media to the drop zone.

  To replace the media, click and drag another file to the drop zone.

  To remove media from a drop zone, Control-click a drop zone and click **Clear Drop Zone Contents**.

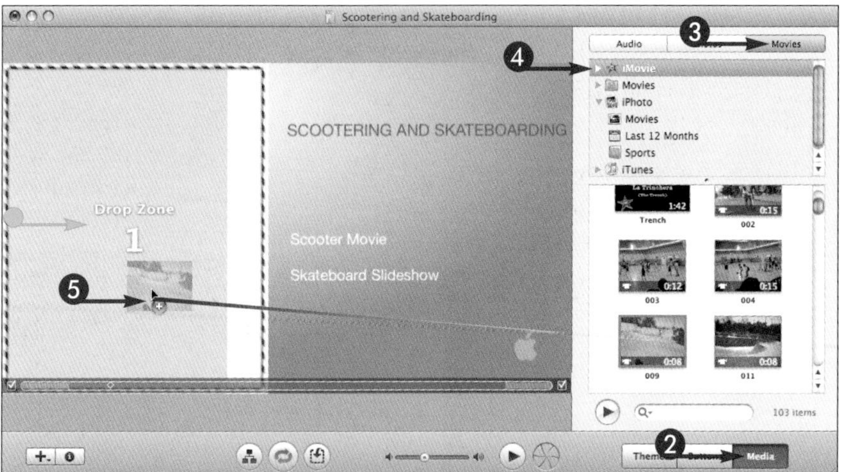

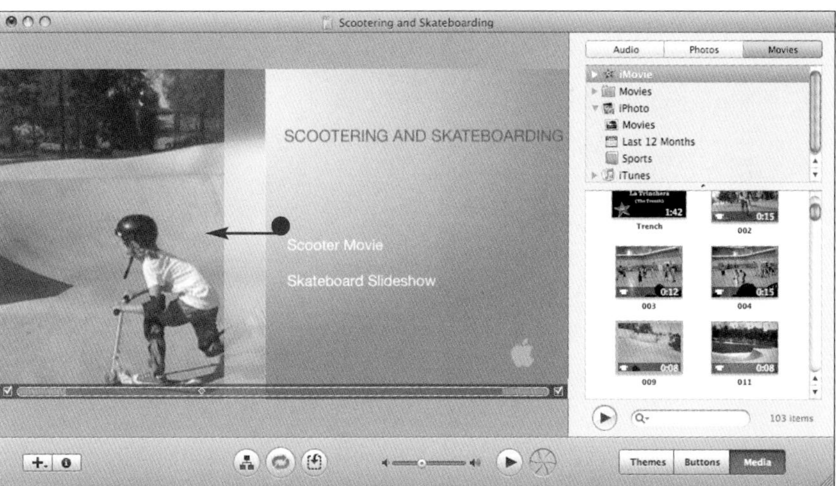

USE THE DROP ZONE EDITOR

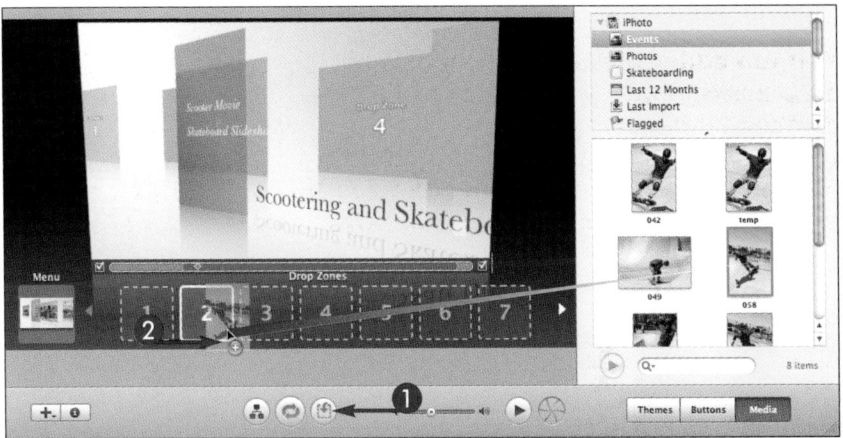

❶ Click **Edit Drop Zones** to open the drop zone editor.

iDVD displays icons for the drop zones in the menu.

❷ Click and drag a file from the media pane to a drop zone icon.

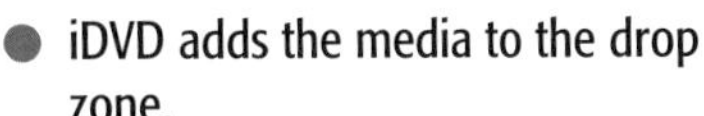

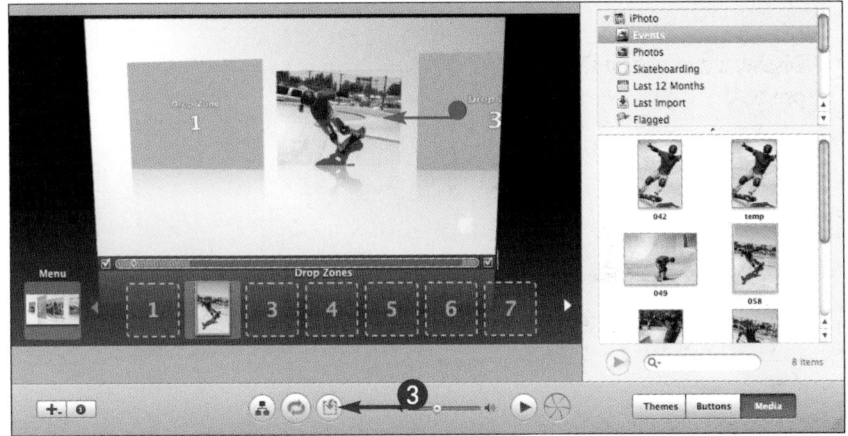

- iDVD adds the media to the drop zone.

To replace content, click and drag another file to a drop zone icon.

To remove media from a drop zone, click and drag the media from the drop zone icon to outside the drop zone editor.

❸ Click **Edit Drop Zones** to exit the drop zone editor.

TIP

How do I add background music to a menu?

Follow these steps:

❶ Click **Audio**.

❷ Click a list item to display the available music from GarageBand or iTunes in the media pane.

❸ Click and drag an audio file to the menu background.

iDVD adds the audio file as background music. To adjust the volume, see "Change Menu Settings."

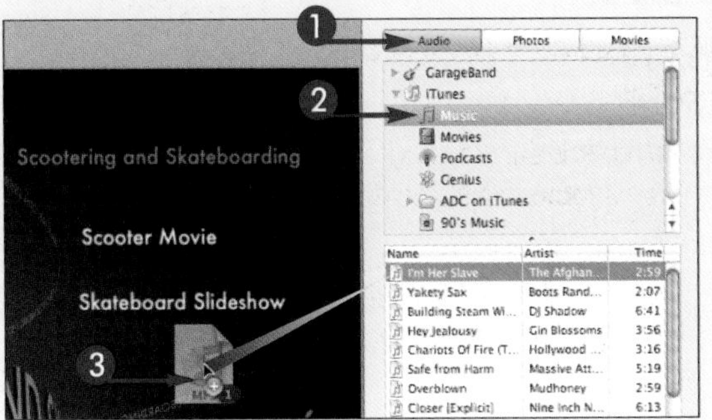

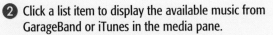

Autofill Drop Zones

iDVD can automatically fill the drop zones in your project with movie and photo content from your project. You can make changes to the autofilled content using the drop zone editor.

Autofill Drop Zones

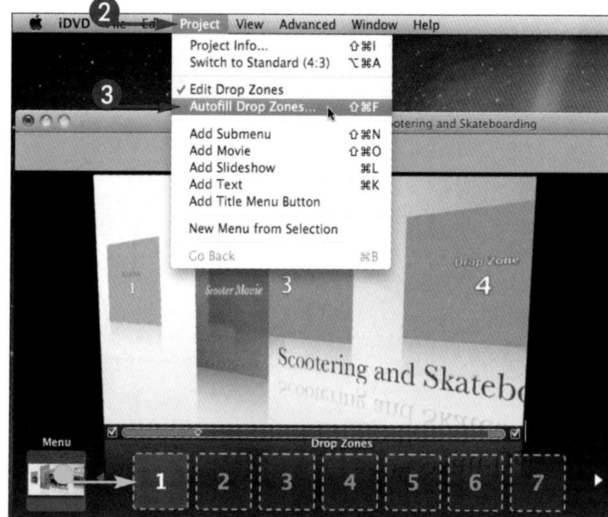

1. Display a menu in an iDVD project. The project should already have media associated with it.

Note: *To add media, see "Add a Movie" or "Add a Slideshow."*

- In this example, the drop zone editor is open. See "Add Media to a Drop Zone" for details.

2. Click **Project**.
3. Click **Autofill Drop Zones**.

- iDVD fills the drop zones in the menu with media from the project.
- You can edit the selections by clicking and dragging media files to the editor icons.

Edit Media in a Drop Zone

You can change how a movie is played or how a still photo is oriented in a drop zone. This helps you focus on specific actions or subjects in drop zones.

Edit Media in a Drop Zone

EDIT A MOVIE

1. Click a movie in a drop zone.
   - A line representing the movie appears.
2. Click and drag a slider to specify where the movie starts.
3. Click and drag a slider to specify where the movie ends.
4. Click away from the drop zone to save the movie edit.

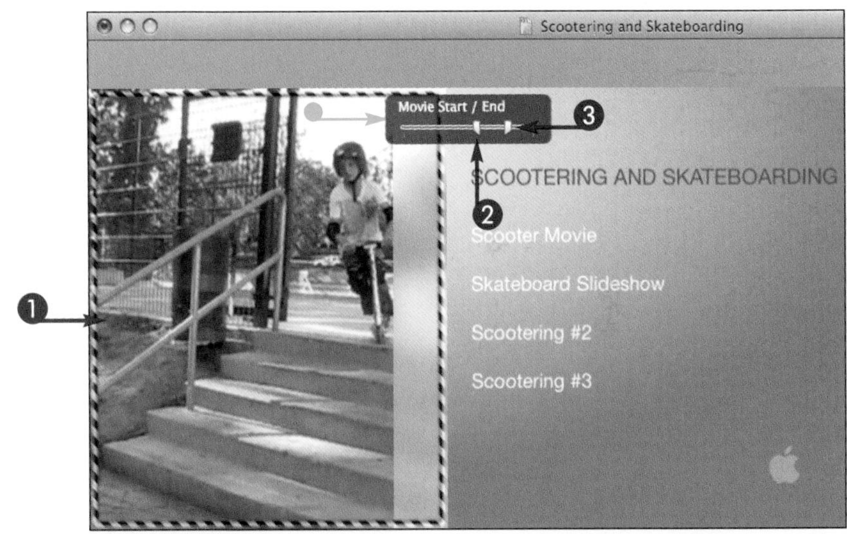

EDIT A STILL PHOTO

1. Click a still photo in a drop zone.

   iDVD selects the photo.
2. Press ⌘ and click and drag inside the photo to reposition it.
3. Click away from the drop zone to save the photo edit.

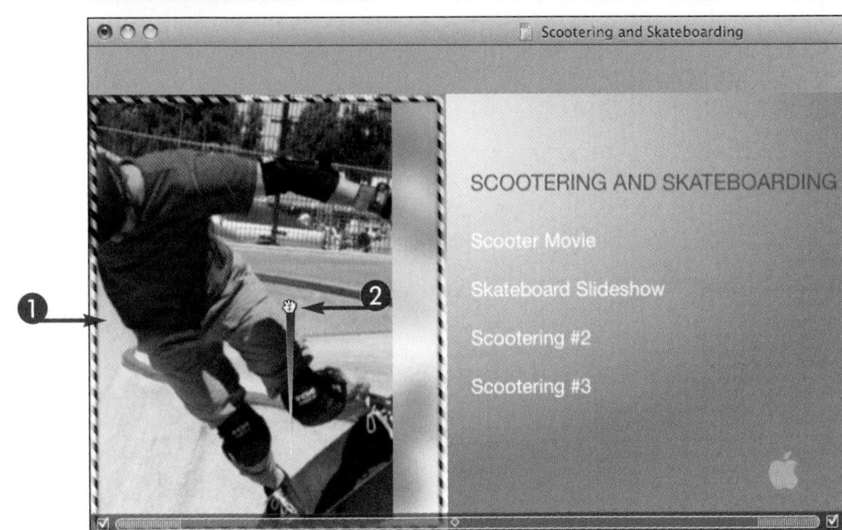

Customize a Button

You can customize the clickable buttons that allow you to play movies and slideshows or view submenus in your project. You can edit the text, change the font, or add graphics to suit the style of your project.

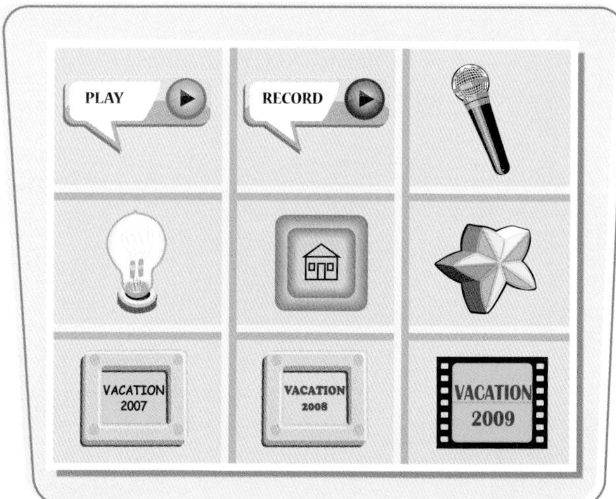

Customize a Button

EDIT THE TEXT

1. Click a button in a menu to select it.
2. Click the button again to make it editable.

Note: *Do not double-click the button, which opens the content.*

3. Type a label for the button.

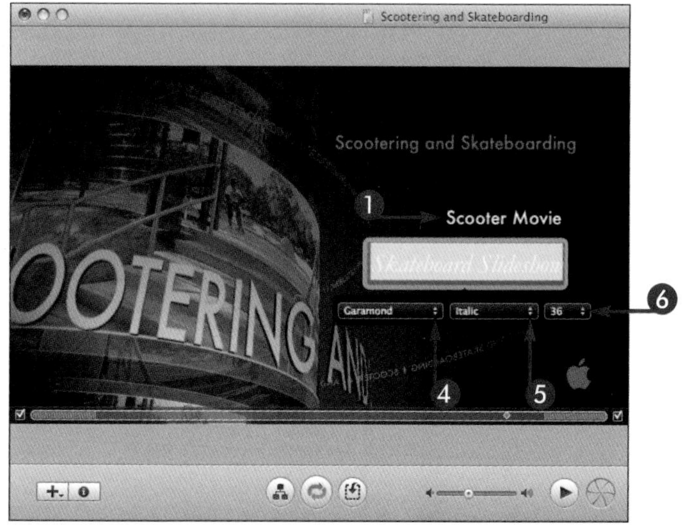

4. Select a font for the button.
5. Select a font style.
6. Select a font size.
7. Click away from the button to save the changes.

ADD A GRAPHIC

1. Click a menu button to select it.

❷ Click **Buttons**.

❸ Select a button category.

❹ Click a button style.

● iDVD customizes the button in the menu.

You can click and drag the button to reposition it.

How do I change the size of a button?

You can change the size of a button shape to make it fit in with the other buttons and graphics on the page.

❶ Control-click a button and select **Show Inspector Window** in the menu that appears.

The inspector appears. The inspector options vary depending on the button style.

❷ Click and drag the slider to adjust the size of the button shape.

❸ Click ⊠ to close the inspector and save the change.

Add a Submenu

When you create a new project from within iDVD, the program adds a single main menu to that project. You can add submenus to your project to organize your media content in a hierarchical fashion. You access a submenu by clicking a button on the main menu. Submenus can also have their own submenus.

Add a Submenu

1. Display the menu to which you want to add a submenu.
2. Click the add icon (+).
3. Click **Add Submenu** in the menu that appears.

iDVD adds a button for the new submenu.

Note: *To edit the text and style of the button, see "Customize a Button."*

4. Double-click the submenu button.

iDVD opens the new submenu.

5. Double-click the title to edit it.
6. Click and drag content from the media pane to add content to the submenu.

Note: *For details, see "Add a Movie," "Add a Slideshow," and "Add Media to a Drop Zone."*

Note: *To change the theme of a submenu, see Chapter 20.*

7. Double-click the back button ().

   The style of the back button varies depending on the theme of the menu.

   iDVD displays the parent menu from which the new submenu is linked.

- You can click **Show the DVD Map** to view your menu organization in map view.

Note: *For details, see "Use Map View."*

TIP

How do I create a submenu from existing buttons?

You can select one or more buttons in an existing menu and move them to a new submenu.

1. Shift-click to select the buttons you want to add.
2. Click **Project**.
3. Click **New Menu from Selection**.

   iDVD creates a new submenu and moves the selected buttons to it. You can double-click the new submenu button to access it.

Note: *To edit the button, see "Customize a Button."*

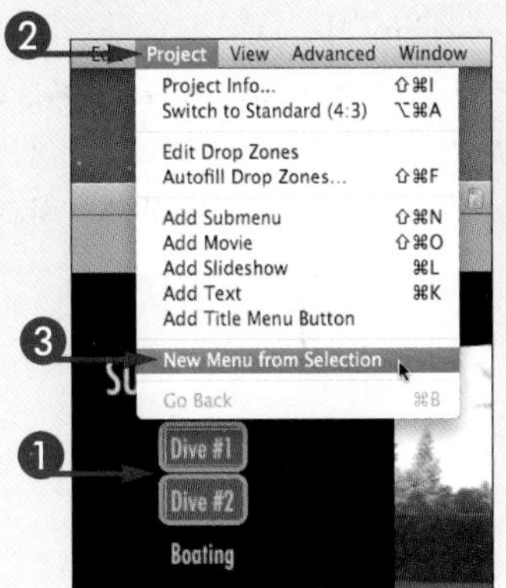

Change Menu Settings

You can open the Menu Info inspector to configure a menu. You can change the duration of a menu animation, control the volume of background music, and turn on a grid to help align menu buttons.

Menu Info Inspector
menu animation duration
background music volume
align menu buttons

Change Menu Settings

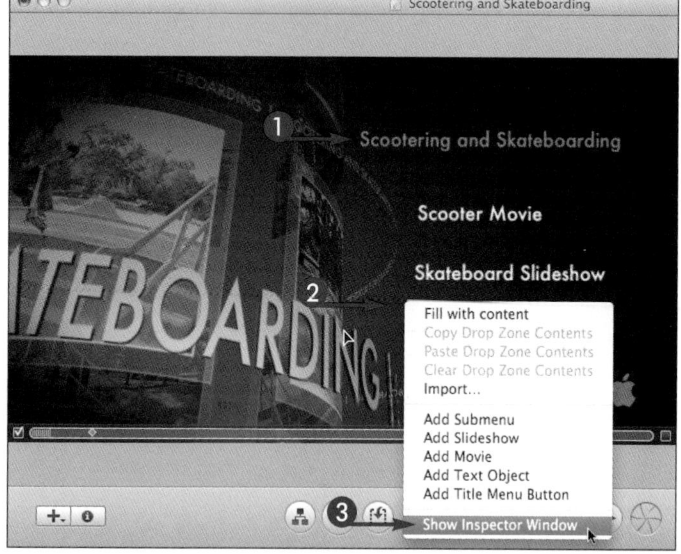

1. Display the menu whose settings you want to change.
2. Control-click the menu background.
3. Click **Show Inspector Window**.

Note: *You can also click the* ***Inspector*** *button ( ) in the toolbar.*

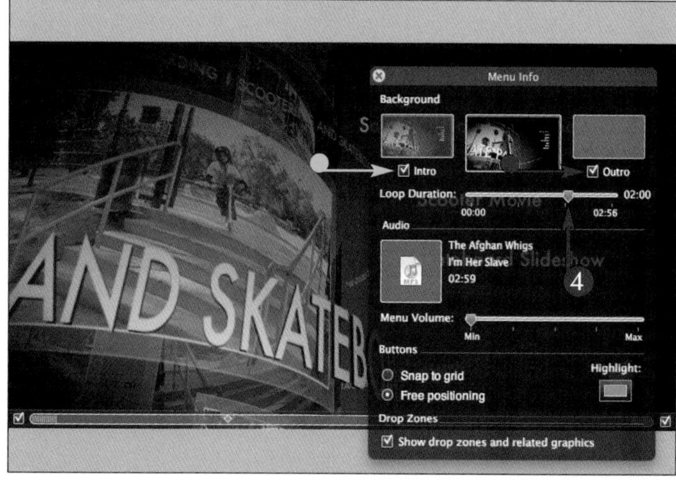

iDVD opens the Menu Info window.

4. Click and drag the slider to adjust the duration of the menu animation.

Some menus include an intro and an outro as part of the animation.

- You can click to disable the intro (☑ changes to ☐).
- You can click to disable the outro (☑ changes to ☐).

5. Click and drag the slider to adjust the volume of background music, if it exists.

   iDVD can use an invisible grid to align the buttons you add to a DVD menu.

6. Click to turn on the grid (○ changes to ◉).

7. Click ☒ to close the inspector and save the changes.

TIP

How do I change the highlight color for menu buttons?

iDVD uses color highlighting to show which button in a menu is active. You can change the color in the Menu Info window.

1. In the Menu Info window, click the highlight swatch.

   iDVD opens the Colors dialog.

2. Click a highlight color.

3. Click ◉ to close the dialog.

- The highlight color is updated.

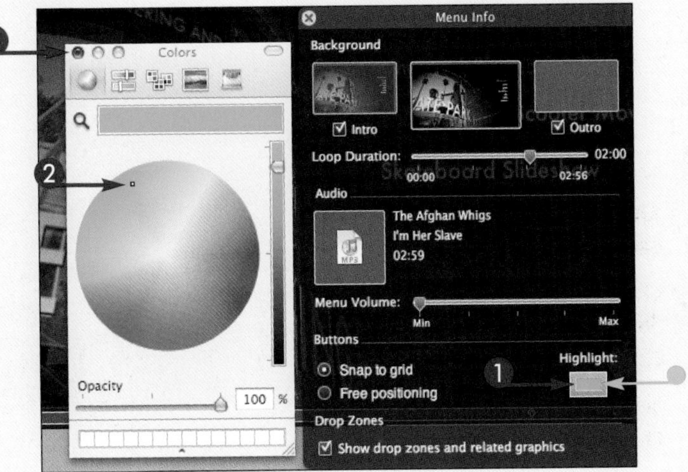

Use Map View

You can view your iDVD project as a chart by opening map view. In map view, boxes represent menus, movies, and slideshows. Lines represent the connections between the media items. You can add new content in map view as well as reorganize existing content.

Use Map View

ADD MEDIA

❶ Click **Show the DVD Map** to open your project in map view.

iDVD displays the menus, movies, slideshows, and other content hierarchically, as boxes connected by lines.

❷ Click and drag an item in the media pane to a menu box.

- iDVD adds the item to the map, connecting the item to the menu with a line.

A button for the item is added to the menu.

- You can double-click the menu to view it.

To delete content in map view, select the content and then press Delete.

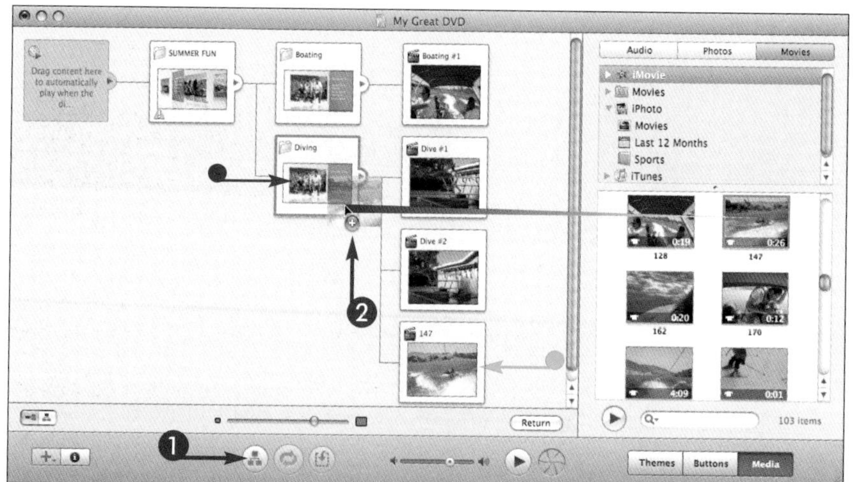

REARRANGE MEDIA

❶ Click and drag a media item in the map to a new menu.

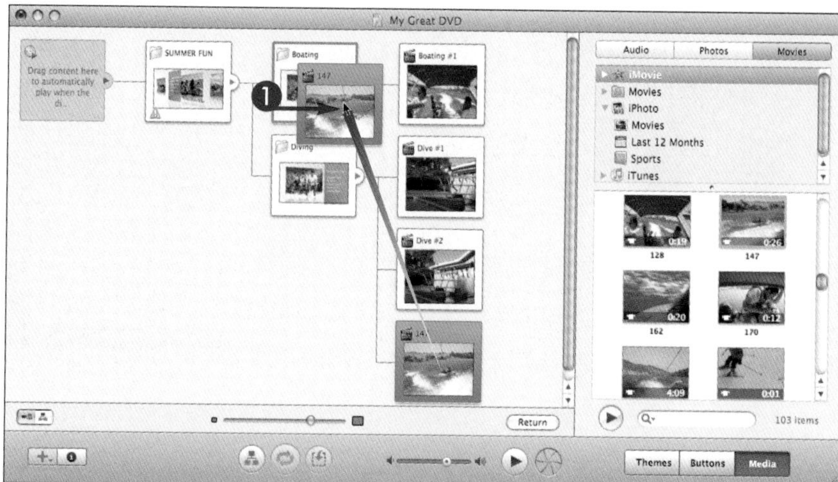

iDVD adds a button for the item to the new menu and deletes the button for the item in the old menu.

- The box for the item is connected to the new menu in map view.

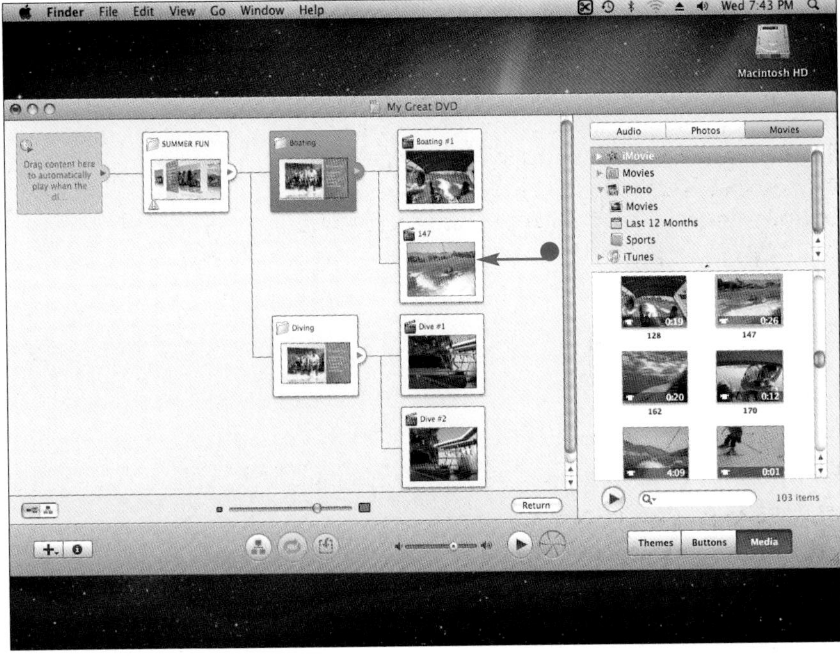

TIP

How do I change the map view layout?

You can change the size of the boxes in map view and also switch the layout from horizontal to vertical.

1. Click and drag the slider to change the size of the boxes.
2. Click to switch to a vertical layout.

- A vertical layout is displayed.
- You can click to switch back to a horizontal layout.

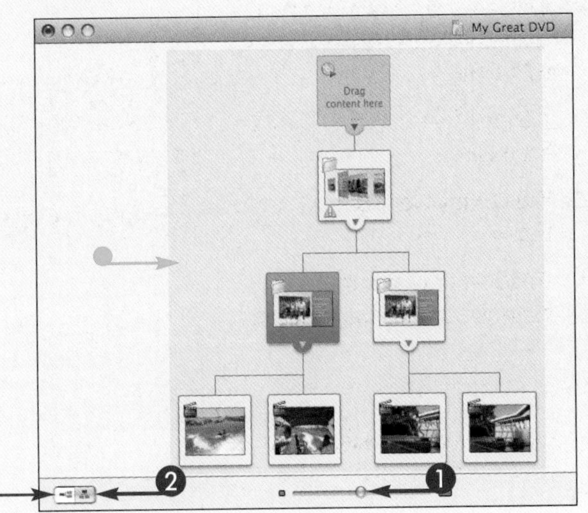

Preview a Project

You can preview an iDVD project to view how users will see the content when they play the disc in a DVD player. This lets you see how the graphics and animations display and how the menus and buttons work together. You navigate your project and play the movies and slideshows using an on-screen remote control.

Preview a Project

1. Open the project you want to preview.
2. Click the **Preview** button (▶).

- iDVD opens a preview window and a remote control.

3. Click the directional buttons on the remote control to select buttons in the DVD menu.
4. Click **Enter** to view the selected content.

   You can also click directly in the preview window to view content.

- In this example, a movie is selected.

iDVD plays the content.

5. Click here to pause and play a movie or slideshow.
6. Click ■ to stop a movie or slideshow and return to the previous menu.

- You can click ⏮ and ⏭ to move to previous or next slide in a slideshow.

7. Click **Menu** to return to the previous menu in the project.

- You can click **Title** to return to the main menu in the project.

8. Click **Exit** to quit the preview.

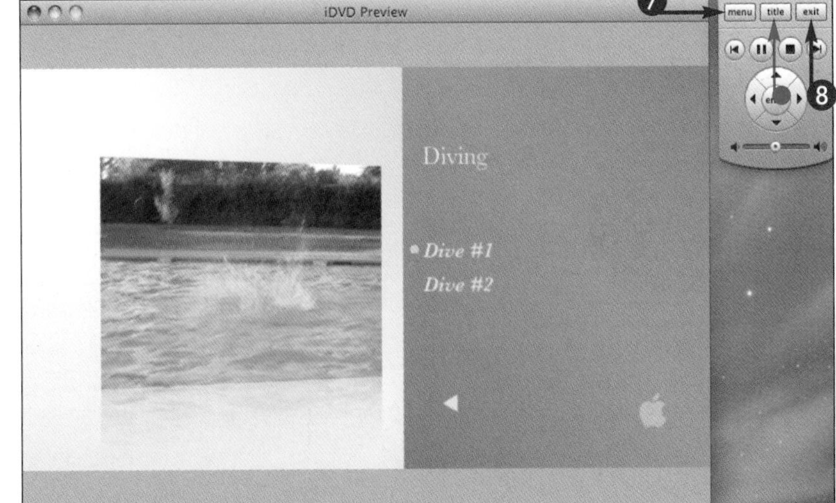

How can I check my project for missing content and other problems?

You can open map view and check for warning icons (⚠). Click **View** and then **Show Map** to display map view. Warnings appear when:

- A menu has empty drop zones, which are sections where you can add previews of the DVD content.
- A slideshow is empty.
- A movie button has not been assigned a movie.
- A menu contains no content buttons.
- A menu has too many buttons. The maximum number of buttons varies by theme, and is usually 6 or 12.
- A menu exceeds the maximum 15 minutes of playing time allowed.

Burn a Project to DVD

After you finish creating your project, you can burn it to disc using a DVD burner connected to your computer. Others can then view your project by playing the finished disc in a DVD player. It may take a long time to burn a disc, depending on the size of your project and speed of your computer, so plan accordingly.

Burn a Project to DVD

1. Open the project you want to burn.
2. Click the **Burn** button.

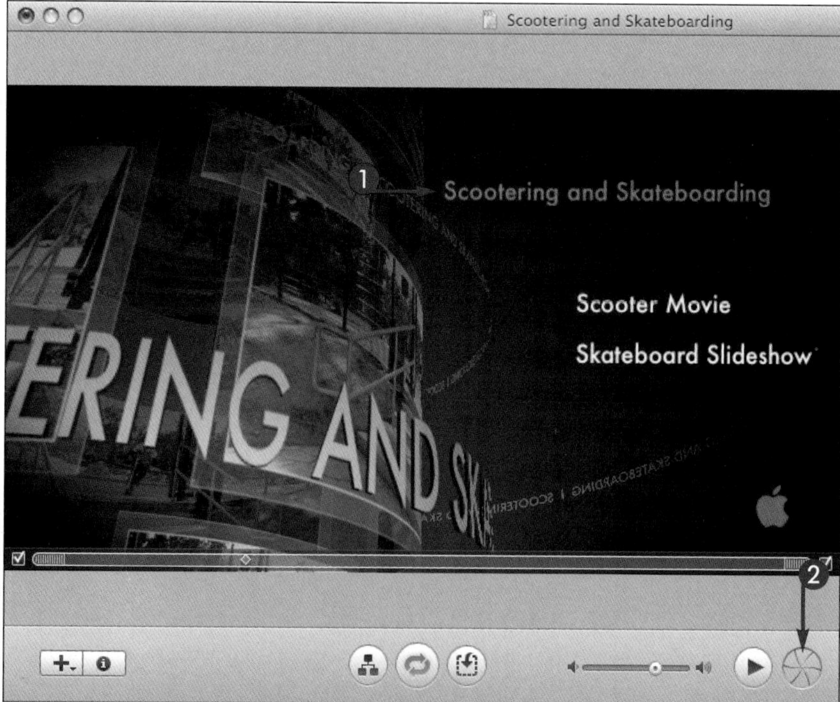

- If you do not have a blank DVD already in your DVD drive, a dialog appears prompting you to insert one.

3. Insert a blank DVD.

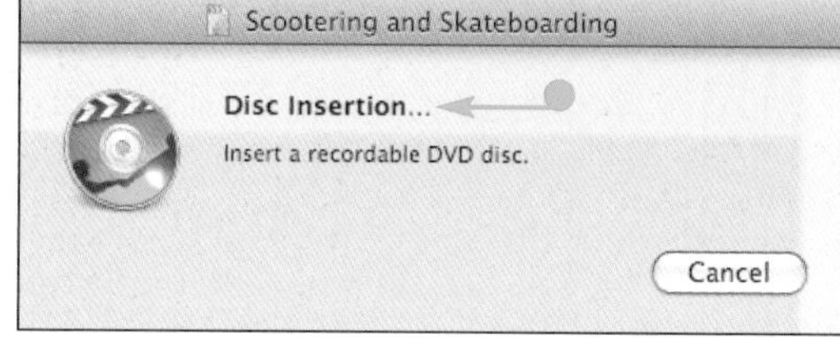

- iDVD encodes the content and burns the project to the disc, displaying the status as it works.
- You can click **Cancel** to stop the process.

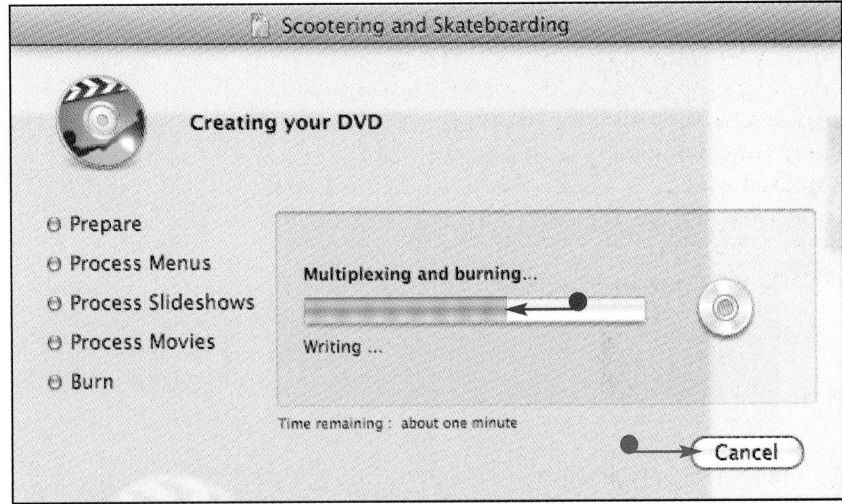

iDVD finishes burning the disc and displays a confirmation.

4 Click **Done**.

You can play the completed disc in a DVD player to view the project.

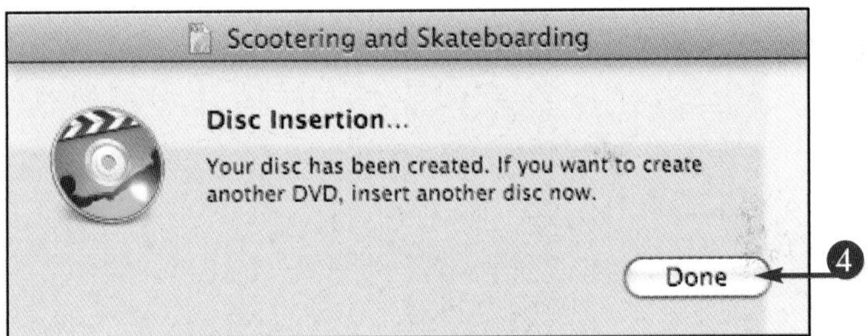

What types of DVDs can iDVD burn?

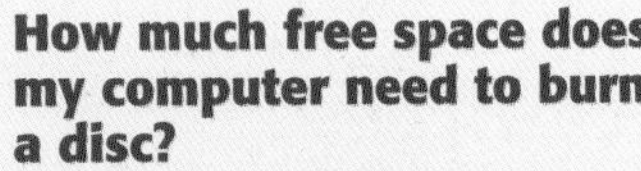

iDVD can burn any type of disc your DVD burner supports, including DVD-R, DVD-RW, DVD+R, and DVD+RW single-layer discs. It can also burn DVD+R DL double-layer discs. Single-layer discs can hold 4.7GB of data whereas double-layer discs can hold 8.5GB of data. For projects that can fit on a single-layer disc, DVD-R is the recommended disc format.

How much free space does my computer need to burn a disc?

Make sure you have at least twice as much free space available on your hard disk as your project uses. So if your project uses 3GB, make sure you have 6GB free space. You can check how much space your project uses by clicking **Project** and then **Project Info**. You can check how much space is available on your hard disk by Control-clicking the hard disk on your desktop and clicking **Get Info**.

Create a Disc Image

You can create a disc image of your iDVD project to make a file formatted just like a finished DVD. The file is saved to your hard drive and you can play it like you can a DVD. You can also burn DVDs from a disc image.

Create a Disc Image

1. Click **File**.
2. Click **Save as Disc Image**.

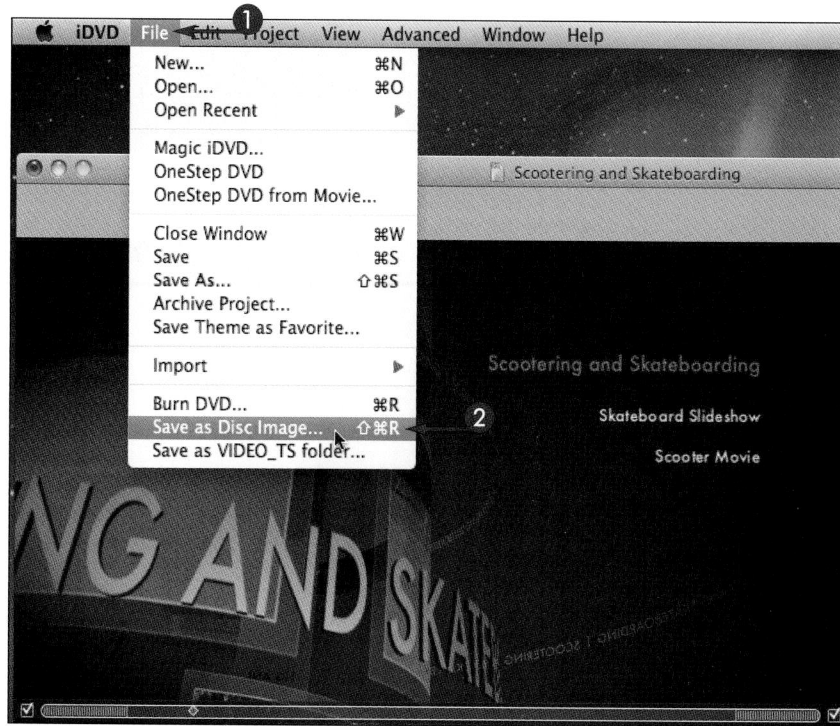

The Save Disc Image As dialog appears.

3. Type a file name.
4. Select where to save the disc image.
5. Click **Save**.

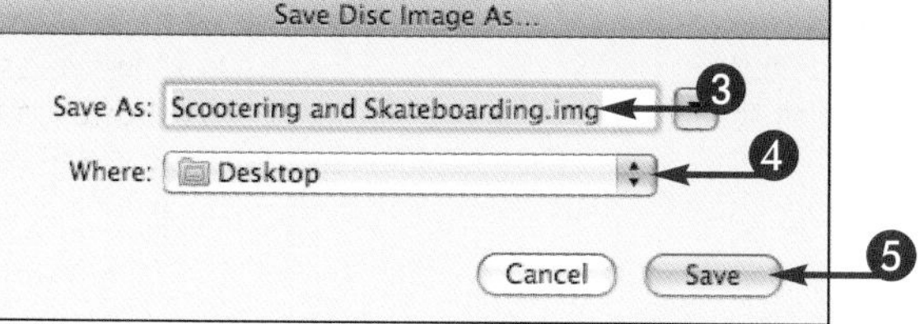

- iDVD encodes the content and saves the disc image, displaying the status as it works.
- You can click **Cancel** to stop the process.

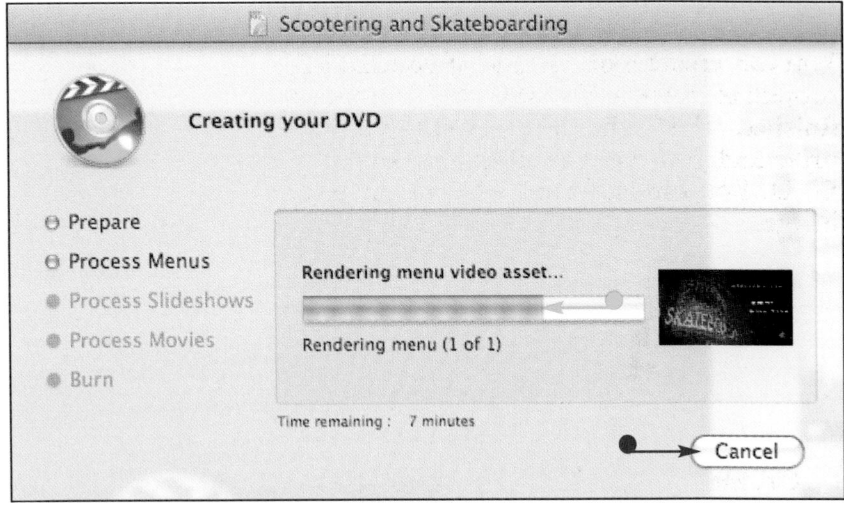

iDVD finishes and displays a confirmation dialog.

6 Click **OK**.

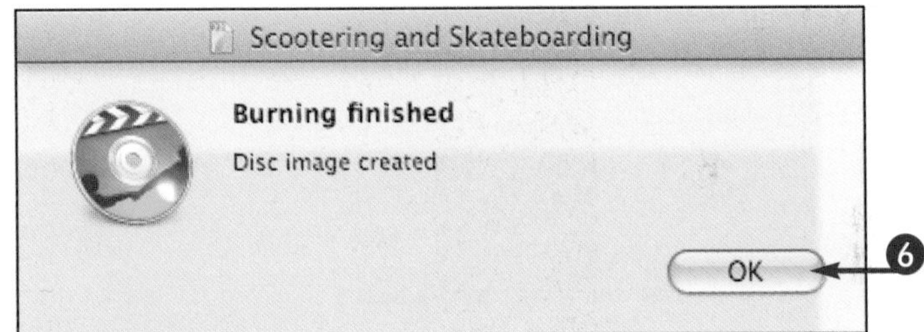

TIPS

How do I play a disc image like a DVD?

Disc images made in iDVD have an .img file extension. You can double-click the disc image file and the Mac operating system will *mount* the file. This allows the computer to treat the image as if it were a DVD. You can play a mounted disc image using the DVD Player program on your Mac.

How do I burn a disc image file to a DVD?

To burn a disc image in Mac OS X, open the Disk Utility program, select the disc image file, and then click the **Burn** button. You will be prompted to insert a blank DVD. Burning a DVD from a disc image is faster than burning one from a project in iDVD because the image content is already encoded.

Archive a Project

You can archive a project to create a copy that can be moved to other computers or backed up. All the movies, photos, themes, and other files associated with the project are included in the archived version.

Archive a Project

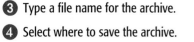

1. Click **File**.
2. Click **Archive Project**.

3. Type a file name for the archive.
4. Select where to save the archive.

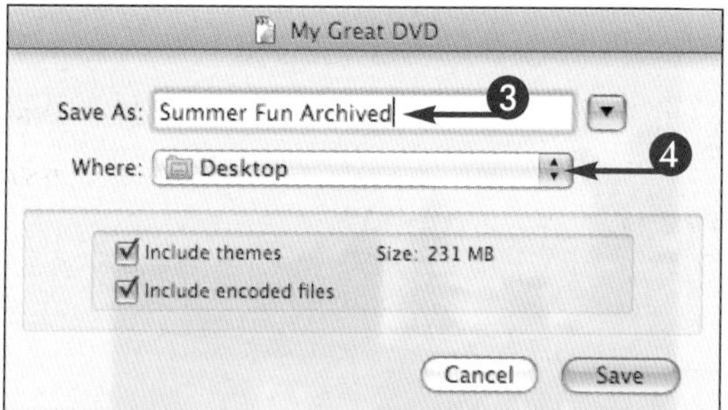

- You can click here if the people who will use the archive already have access to the themes used in the project (☑ changes to ☐).
- You can click to leave out any encoded files (☑ changes to ☐). iDVD will need to re-encode the archived project before burning it to a disc.

5 Click **Save**.

iDVD saves the project as a .dvdproj file, which you can open in iDVD on another computer.

- In this example, the archive is saved on the desktop.

TIP

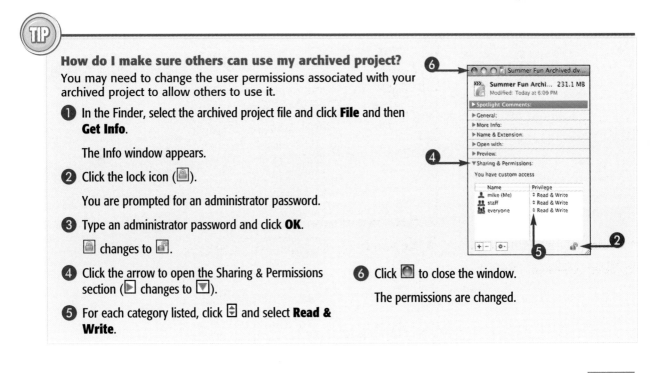

How do I make sure others can use my archived project?

You may need to change the user permissions associated with your archived project to allow others to use it.

1 In the Finder, select the archived project file and click **File** and then **Get Info**.

The Info window appears.

2 Click the lock icon (🔒).

You are prompted for an administrator password.

3 Type an administrator password and click **OK**.

🔒 changes to 🔓.

4 Click the arrow to open the Sharing & Permissions section (▶ changes to ▼).

5 For each category listed, click ⬍ and select **Read & Write**.

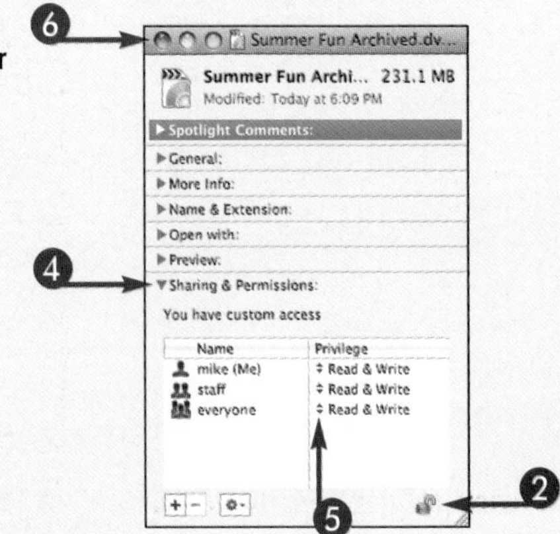

6 Click ● to close the window.

The permissions are changed.

Index

F

G

Index

Index

K

L

M

Index

Index